# THE FAMILY TREE OF
# REFORMED BIBLICAL THEOLOGY
Geerhardus Vos and John Owen –
Their Methods of and Contributions to the Articulation of
Redemptive History

Richard C. Barcellos, Ph.D.

Reformed Baptist Dissertation Series # 2

RBAP
Owensboro, KY

Requests for information should be sent to:

RBAP
1694 Wrights Landing Road
Owensboro, KY  42303
rb@rbap.net
www.rbap.net

Printed in the United States of America.

Cover design by Kalós Grafx Studios | www.kalosgrafx.com

Series:   Reformed Baptist Dissertation Series #2
          THE FAMILY TREE OF REFORMED BIBLICAL THEOLOGY:
          Geerhardus Vos and John Owen – Their Methods of and Contributions
          to the Articulation of Redemptive History,
          Richard C. Barcellos, Ph.D.

ISBN-13: 978-0-9802179-5-7
ISBN-10: 0-9802179-5-4

For those who love Reformed biblical theology and Reformed systematic theology, this is a satisfying, happy book, providing for us a family tree of continuity from the prince of the Puritans, John Owen, to the father of Reformed biblical theology, Geerhardus Vos. Now, who will add to the branches, and go back to the sixteenth century roots, adding to the fulsomeness and beauty of the Reformed family tree from Calvin and Bullinger to our own day?

Joel R. Beeke, Ph.D.
President of Puritan Reformed Theological Seminary, Grand Rapids, MI
Pastor of the Heritage Netherlands Reformed Congregation in Grand Rapids
Author of *The Quest for Full Assurance: The Legacy of Calvin and His Successors*


If a good doctoral dissertation fills a critically important gap or corrects a widely held error or changes the academic picture so that future students of an issue have a new and more accurate perspective on an important subject, Richard Barcellos' *The Family Tree of Reformed Biblical Theology* is a great dissertation for it does all of these, while encouraging greater confidence in the biblical character of the confessional standards of the Reformed Churches and stimulating further investigation and creative exposition of the sacred Scripture as the progressive self-revelation of our redeeming God.

First of all, Barcellos demonstrates a greatly underappreciated feature of the theology of John Owen (and other theologians of the era known misleadingly as the period of Protestant Scholasticism): that not only was his covenant or federal theology biblical (as opposed to a construct of Aristotelian logic), but that this biblical theology thoroughly incorporated the knowledge that God's revelation had been progressively given (as opposed to coming from a flat Bible). Secondly, he demonstrates that this hermeneutical development is also a natural progression and not a departure from the earlier biblical and Christocentric hermeneutic of Calvin. Third, he brings to the fore an important conviction of the great redemptive-historical theologian, Geerhardus Vos; namely, that his redemptive-historical, even eschatological, biblical theology supported the same confessional orthodoxy. Forth, all of these things are so thoroughly supported and interestingly presented that even those who already agree with him will find it a pleasurable and profitable read. Finally, --

By demonstrating the unity which is intrinsically there, Barcellos' book should promote a greater unity among Reformed biblical and systematic theologians, and, so doing, should bless the Church of Christ by encouraging a greater knowledge and deeper love for the Word of God. Here is a book no seminary library should be without and which no department of biblical studies, or historical theology can responsibly ignore. Whether one's great interest is in serious bible study, the history of hermeneutics, or Reformed theology or whether one has a preference for systematic theology or the redemptive-historical approach to biblical interpretation, Richard Barcellos' excellent treatment of the hermeneutics of two of history's greatest biblical scholars should be on your required reading shelf.

Richard W. Daniels
Ph.D., Westminster Theological Seminary
Author of *The Christology of John Owen*

Congratulations and gratitude are due to Dr. Richard Barcellos for giving us this wide-ranging, detailed study of the history of biblical theology. It serves well as an introduction to the rich biblico-theological heritage of Reformed theology. In addition, it provides a welcome corrective to the muddle-headed assumption that the work of earlier Reformed theologians was essentially system and proof-text driven.

Harvesting the best insights of recent scholarship, *The Family Tree of Reformed Biblical Theology* explores the strong line of continuity that runs from seventeenth century Oxford and the writings of John Owen to twentieth century Princeton and the work of Geerhardus Vos. It argues—surely rightly—that biblical theology in the tradition of Vos is not a novelty but was adumbrated in clear and powerful ways by earlier Reformed writers, and notably by Owen himself. Indeed, the author daringly asserts that Owen was a more Christocentric biblical theologian than Vos.

This is a work of bold and exciting scholarship that merits careful reading and reflection. In addition, however, it is also a work whose lessons working pastors should be encouraged to consider. For it points to resources that exemplify the spiritual power, and fruitful exposition that can arise from a thorough grasp of all the indicatives and imperatives of biblical theology.

With this substantial contribution Dr. Barcellos has put both the academy and the pulpit deeply in his debt.

Dr. Sinclair B. Ferguson
Senior Minister, First Presbyterian Church, Columbia, S.C.
Professor of Systematic Theology
Redeemer Theological Seminary, Dallas, Texas
Author of *John Owen on the Christian Life*

Geerhardus Vos has observed that Reformed theology "has from the beginning shown itself possessed of a true historic sense in the apprehension of the progressive character of the deliverance of truth. Its doctrine of the covenants on its historical side represents the first attempt at constructing a history of revelation and may be justly considered the precursor of what is at present called biblical theology." This is a clear indication of the substantive continuity and harmony he saw between his own biblical-theological work and earlier Reformed theology. In his view the orthodox Reformed confessions with the theological framework they entail, far from being hostile, are quite hospitable toward, in fact anticipate, giving greater, more methodologically self-conscious attention, as he did, to the redemptive-historical substance of Scripture.

Richard Barcellos, in a thoroughly researched, persuasively argued and clearly written manner, shows the soundness of Vos's self-perception. By means of a large-scale comparison of his work with that of the towering instance of 17th century Reformed orthodoxy, John Owen, Barcellos brings to light undeniable lines of affinity and the deeply rooted compatibility there is between the two. If Vos may be said to be the father of a Reformed biblical theology, then, in the author's words, Owen is "a grandfather (among many others) of a Reformed biblical theology." Those interested in Reformed theology, in particular issues of theological method, are indebted to Barcellos for this most welcome and helpful study.

Richard B. Gaffin, Jr., Ph.D.
Professor of Biblical and Systematic Theology, Emeritus
Westminster Theological Seminary


No serious contemporary student of Reformed theology can afford to work without benefit of the contributions of Geerhardus Vos. Likewise, no serious contemporary student of Reformed theology should attempt to work without reference to the insights of John Owen. They are among the giants of the tradition. Vos is well-known for his emphasis on eschatology; Owen for his Christ-centered perspectives. One might suspect that they have much in common--not just in terms of a general commitment to Reformed thinking, but specifically in their historically sensitive treatments of Scripture.

In this book, Richard Barcellos demonstrates that Vos and Owen ought to be read in concert, Owen setting out a foundation and Vos providing the superstructure of the building. John Owen's *Biblical Theology* is in many ways a precursor to Vos's book of the same title. Dr. Barcellos ably explains the significant commonalities shared by them, and in doing so evidences the depth and importance of such a well-formed historical approach to Scripture and theology. This book is of great importance.

James M. Renihan, Ph.D.
Dean, Professor of Historical Theology
Institute of Reformed Baptist Studies


Barcellos' thesis is clearly stated at the beginning of his abstract. "Geerhardus Vos' biblical theology should be viewed as a post-Enlightenment continuation of the pre-critical federal theology of seventeenth-century Reformed orthodoxy." By comparing Vos and John Owen, Barcellos makes his case. Vos' ideas are shown not to be as novel as many have thought. It is good to see a work of historical theology tying together various strands of Reformed and confessional Christianity. There is much more work to be done to tie together a continuous stream of theological reflection from seventeenth-century Reformed orthodoxy to the twentieth century. Barcellos uses the metaphor of a family tree to show Vos as the father of Reformed biblical theology and Owen as a more distant patriarch. The historical material sets a context for understanding the influences of enlightened thought on Christianity in general, and Vos in particular. He also demonstrates the influences of Reformed thinkers on Vos, with special reference to Princeton. Owen's learning was vast and immense. His legacy is without equal among English Reformed theologians. This comparative work adds to a growing corpus of important works as regards federal theology. This work will help to correct many misunderstandings. Barcellos is to be thanked for bringing some clarity in this area.

Mike Renihan
Pastor, Heritage Baptist Church, Worcester, MA
Adjunct Professor, Worcester State College
Ph.D., Wycliffe Hall, Oxford University and the University of Coventry

# TABLE OF CONTENTS

# LIST OF ABBREVIATIONS

*BTO*    John Owen, *Biblical Theology* (Pittsburgh, 1994, English translation of the Latin published in 1661).

*BTV*    Geerhardus Vos, *Biblical Theology: Old and New Testaments* (Grand Rapids, Reprinted, June 1988).

*CTJ*    Calvin Theological Journal

*DMBI*    Donald K. McKim, editor, *Dictionary of Major Biblical Interpreters* (Downers Grove, IL, 2007).

*ERF*    Donald K. McKim, editor, *Encyclopedia of the Reformed Faith* (Louisville, 1992).

*JETS*    Journal of the Evangelical Theological Society

*PRRD*    Richard A. Muller, *Post-Reformation Reformed Dogmatics, Four Volumes* (Grand Rapids, 2003).

*RBTR*    Reformed Baptist Theological Review

*RHBI*    Geerhardus Vos, *Redemptive History and Biblical Interpretation: The Shorter Writings of Geerhardus Vos*, ed. Richard B. Gaffin, Jr. (Phillipsburg, NJ, 1980).

*SJT*    Scottish Journal of Theology

*WCF*    *Westminster Confession of Faith*

*Works*    John Owen, *The Works of John Owen*, Twenty-Three Volumes (Edinburgh, various original and reprint dates).

*WTJ*    Westminster Theological Journal

# ACKNOWLEDGEMENTS

This project, though its topic was unconceived at the time, started in the mid 1990s when my fellow elders at the time (James P. Butler and C. Ron Martina) approved a proposal I brought to them for me to pursue a Ph.D. in Historical Theology. Subsequent to that time, Michael D. Crawford, Vince P. Nixon, and Matthew E. Troupe, also fellow elders of mine, supported my efforts in many, many ways. I am thankful to these brothers for their foresight and vision, though I am sure neither of them thought it would take this long. The dear people of Free Grace Church: A Reformed Baptist Congregation, Lancaster, CA, also supported my studies. And, of course, my wife Nan was very supportive and understanding along the way. She is my "good thing" from the Lord. My family has even endured a move from California to Kentucky to complete the dissertation, among other things. We have been the recipients of much kindness from the pastors and members of Heritage Baptist Church, Owensboro, KY. I want to give special thanks to my highly esteemed colleague, Dr. Sam Waldron, for kindly nudging me to "get that dissertation finished." Thanks also to Pastor David Charles and his dear wife who housed me, without complaint, during "crunch time." Special thanks also goes to Dr. Kenneth G. Talbot of Whitefield Theological Seminary for his patience with me as I completed post-graduate course work and struggled to finally hone in on a dissertation topic. I want to thank two dear men; Ronald D. Miller for reading my dissertation and offering suggestions which made for a much better presentation and Tim Hoak for the title. Most of all, I thank the Lord Jesus, the Messiah, the Son of God, the devil-conquering Seed of the woman, the last Adam, the First-born from the dead, my wrath-bearing Savior and only hope of righteousness before God, for saving me and preserving me for these many years as I seek to serve him and his glorious cause on the earth and for giving me the distinct privilege of sitting at the feet of giants. One day I shall see him just as he is!

Richard C. Barcellos
Owensboro, KY
September 2009

# ABSTRACT

The thesis of this study is that Geerhardus Vos' biblical-theological method should be viewed as a post-Enlightenment continuation of the pre-critical federal theology of seventeenth-century Reformed orthodoxy. Vos wrote in the context of the liberalism of the late nineteenth and early twentieth centuries. His biblical-theological methodology was largely a resuscitation of the federal theology of seventeenth-century Reformed orthodoxy adapted to the times in which it was written. It will be argued, therefore, that Vos should not be viewed as a novelty and/or radical paradigm shift within the Reformed theological tradition. John Owen will be used as a case test in comparing Vos' methodology with that of the seventeenth-century federal theology of Reformed orthodoxy. Two books will be the primary focus of the comparison and analysis of Vos and Owen – *Biblical Theology: Old and New Testaments* by Geerhardus Vos[1] and *Theologoumena pantodapa, sive, De natura, ortu, progressu et studio, verae theologiae* (*Theological Affirmations of All Sorts, Or, Of the Nature, Rise, Progress, and Study, of True Theology*[2]) by John Owen. The recently published English translation of Owen's work is entitled *Biblical Theology or The Nature, Origin, Development, and Study of Theological Truth in Six Books*.

The dissertation contains four major sections. The first section (PART I: PROLEGOMENA) provides an overall introduction to the dissertation and a brief and broad survey of the history of the discipline of biblical theology. The introduction poses several questions that will be answered in the course of the dissertation. In the survey of the history of biblical theology special focus will be placed upon Reformed theologians, especially when those of the pre-critical, post-Reformation seventeenth century (Owen's era) and the late nineteenth and early twentieth centuries (Vos' era) are discussed. This survey will be conducted to put federal theology and biblical theology in their respective historical contexts.

---

[1] Geerhardus Vos, *Biblical Theology: Old and New Testaments* (Grand Rapids: Wm. B. Eerdmans Publishing Company, 1948, reprinted, June 1988), referenced as *BTV* here on out.

[2] This is J. I. Packer's translation of the Latin title. Cf. John Owen, *Biblical Theology or The Nature, Origin, Development, and Study of Theological Truth in Six Books* (Pittsburgh, PA: Soli Deo Gloria Publications, 1994), xii, referenced as *BTO* here on out.

The second section (PART II: BIOGRAPHICAL, HISTORICAL, AND THEOLOGICAL) will discuss Geerhardus Vos and John Owen separately. It is comprised of a brief biography of Vos, and then a discussion of the historical-theological context in which Vos thought, taught, and to which he contributed. The section on Owen does basically the same thing – a brief biography and then a historical-theological discussion placing Owen in his seventeenth-century Reformed orthodox context. This will set the context for PART III, where the analysis of the two books mentioned above will be conducted.

The third section (PART III: ANALYSIS) forms the heart of the dissertation. It follows a linear, redemptive-historical approach, which can be found in both Vos and Owen. Both books mentioned above were studied section by section simultaneously. The outline is, roughly speaking, that of Vos. Each section considers Vos' then Owen's thoughts on the issue(s) at hand. An attempt was made to avoid anachronisms while studying Owen. Since Vos is a well-known commodity as a Reformed biblical theologian, his work forms the basis upon which Owen is compared. Attempt was made to identify elements of biblical theology first in Vos and then seek for similar elements and patterns in Owen. What will be amply observed is that Vos resurrected federal theology and adapted it to his post-Enlightenment context under the rubric of biblical theology.

The fourth section (PART IV: CONCLUSION) will be a discussion in light of our findings. It will compare and contrast, if and when necessary, Vos and Owen. It will offer some suggestions in terms of where and how Vos fits within the history of biblical theology and, especially, how he relates to Owen and the federal theology of the seventeenth-century Reformed orthodox.

The dissertation also contains two appendices: (1) an analytical outline of the dissertation and (2) a discussion on the Decalogue in the thought of key Reformed theologians with special reference to John Owen.

# CHAPTER ONE

# INTRODUCTION: JOHN OWEN *AND* GEERHARDUS VOS – REFORMED FEDERAL/BIBLICAL THEOLOGIANS?

## Introduction

In Reformed theological circles, the name Geerhardus Vos is immediately associated with the discipline of biblical theology, and rightly so. He has come to be known as "the father of a Reformed biblical theology."[1] J. I. Packer calls him "an all-time master in the field of Biblical Theology."[2] The importance of his writings cannot be disputed in Reformed circles, agree or disagree with his methodology and/or doctrinal formulations. Is it accurate, however, to assume that what has come to be called biblical theology in Reformed circles does not predate Vos in Reformed theology, at least in proleptic form?[3] Was Vos' method a novel and radical paradigm shift in the history and development of Reformed theological interpretation? Was he a pioneer among Reformed theologians to view the Bible as progressive, organic, redemptive revelation centered upon the concepts of covenant and Christ? Was he the first to place eschatology prior to soteriology in the revelational scheme of the Scriptures? In one sense, as far as the nomenclature, 'biblical theology', is concerned, Vos can rightly be understood as its father and founder among Reformed theologians. But . labels aside, is there a strand of Reformed biblical theology that predates Vos, labeled as it may be? And more specifically, can John Owen be included in the halls of such Reformed biblical theologians?

Though it is true that the title of the Soli Deo Gloria translation of Owen's *Theologoumena pantodapa, sive, De natura, ortu, progressu et studio, verae theologiae* (Theological Affirmations of All Sorts, Or, Of the Nature, Rise, Progress, and Study, of True Theology[4] [i.e., *Biblical Theology*] is technically and historically anachronistic, can it be substantiated that Owen, a seventeenth-century English Puritan and

---

[1] It appears that this label was first attached to Vos by Richard B. Gaffin, Jr. Cf. Geerhardus Vos, *Redemptive History and Biblical Interpretation: The Shorter Writings of Geerhardus Vos*, ed. Richard B. Gaffin, Jr. (Phillipsburg, NJ: P&R Publishing, 1980), xiv, referenced as *RHBI* here on out.

[2] Packer in Owen, *BTO*, xi.

[3] I am not claiming that Gaffin meant this by his statement referenced above.

[4] Owen, *BTO*, xii. This is Packer's translation of the Latin title.

Reformed orthodox theologian, stands within the bounds of a Reformed biblical-theological method, though predating the formal and historical inception of what we know as biblical theology in Protestant circles? Does Reformed theology have to wait until Vos to find adherents to a more redemptive-historical approach to Scripture?

### The Grandfather of Biblical Theology in the Reformed Tradition: The Federal Theology of the Reformed Orthodox

If Owen (and others) can be classified as something like protological Reformed biblical theologians,[5] this would not only demand a qualification when identifying Vos as the father of a Reformed biblical theology, but it would also give us insight into the theological methodology of Vos and Reformed orthodoxy, since Owen fits within that historical-theological school of thought and method. Though it certainly is not the intention of this dissertation to strip Vos of Gaffin's label, if we can prove that what Owen was doing has some essential parallels in what Vos did, that there is a large degree of continuity in their methodology (and theology), several issues will be brought to the table for reassessment and fresh consideration. First, we will be able to assert that Vos resuscitated federal theology[6] under the rubric of biblical theology as a self-conscious Reformed and confessional theologian. In other words, the grandfather of Reformed biblical theology is the federal theology of the seventeenth-century Reformed orthodox. This brings with it some further questions. Why did Vos have to resuscitate federal theology? Why the gap between Owen and the federal theology of Reformed orthodoxy and Vos and his articulation of biblical theology in the Reformed tradition? If there are links between Vos and the Reformed orthodox (and it will be argued that there are several), why the disconnect of time? What happened between Owen and Vos to retard the development of federalism among the Reformed?

Second, we will be able to call into (further) question the many negative claims terminating upon Reformed orthodox interpretive methodology which pit it against Calvin and the earlier Reformed theologians. This view paints Reformed orthodoxy as a rationalistic, neo-

---

[5] Cf. Owen, *BTO*, xiii, where Packer says, "Those with a taste for Owen, or for theology, or (best of all) both, will read this Puritan *proto-Biblical Theology* with joy, …" Emphases added.

[6] We will survey the federal theology of the seventeenth-century Reformed orthodox below.

Aristotelian, devolutionary movement away from Calvin, Christ, and the Scriptures.

Third, we will have to admit that Owenic federal theology and Vosian biblical theology are compatible with Reformed confessionalism. Neither Vos nor Owen repudiated their confessional commitments in light of their theological methodology and formulation. Neither viewed these issues in an either/or fashion – i.e., *either* federal/biblical theology *or* the Confession; *either* Moses, Christ, and Paul *or* Aristotle; *either* Calvin and the early Reformers *or* post-Reformation Reformed orthodoxy. Either (1) they consciously lived with the inconsistencies involved with the antithetical developmental theory of Reformation and post-Reformation Reformed theology or (2) they did not detect any or (3) there were none, at least not antithetically speaking.[7] For some time, it has been quite fashionable in academic halls to put a wedge between Calvin and the Calvinists, between federal/biblical theology and dogmatic/systematic theology, and between the Bible and the Confession. Some seek to force us to choose between two supposed enemies. Owen and Vos chose both and saw no contradiction in this. In fact, both believed that dogmatic/systematic theology is grounded in the text of Scripture, that federal/biblical theology precedes dogmatics, and that confessional theology (i.e., symbolics) assumes the previous work of exegesis, exegetical synthesis, and dogmatics.

### What is Biblical Theology and how does it relate to Federal Theology?

What is biblical theology? This question can be answered both historically and theologically. Historically speaking, it did not appear as an explicit theological discipline until the late eighteenth and early nineteenth centuries during the beginning decades of the critical era. It has undergone development and modification, depending on specific authors and their theological and philosophical presuppositions.[8]

Theologically speaking, biblical theology is a method of interpreting the Bible. For Reformed interpreters, it involves, roughly speaking, the study of the *historia salutis* (i.e., the historical unfolding of salvation as found in the Scriptures). One of the regulating questions of this dissertation is as follows: Does the study of the history of redemption and redemptive-historical formulation predate the historical inception of

---

[7] We will argue for this third position below.
[8] Cf. the section below on the history of biblical theology.

biblical theology as a distinct theological discipline in Reformed theology? Can the essential elements of biblical theology, understood as the study of the history of redemption, be traced back to at least the time of John Owen and Reformed orthodoxy? Our answer will be a resounding yes!

This dissertation seeks to display that Geerhardus Vos, in many senses, is "Owenic" in his approach to the history of redemption. In fact, several contemporaries of Owen displayed a keen respect for the history of salvation and its organic progress from creation, to fall, to redemption in Christ, to the consummation, as we shall see. This makes Owen a somewhat typical federal theologian and gives us further reason to believe that Vos resuscitated federalism under a new name and in a new and unique historical and theological context.

Some influential Evangelicals have claimed that the post-Reformation era did not view Scripture redemptive-historically, but statically. For instance, while tracing the history of New Testament theology, George Eldon Ladd says:

> The gains in the historical study of the Bible made by the reformers were soon lost in the post-Reformation period, and the Bible was once again used uncritically and unhistorically to support orthodox doctrine. The Bible was viewed not only as a book free from error and contradiction but also *without development or progress* [italics added]. The entire Bible was looked upon as possessing one level of theological value. History was completely lost in dogma, and philology became a branch of dogmatics.[9]

This dissertation takes issue with Ladd and many others. It does so on several fronts: (1) a favorable assessment of the Muller thesis (i.e., the post-Reformation era was not a betrayal of Calvin and the early reformers [cf. Chapter Six]); (2) evidence to the contrary from the seventeenth century itself; and (3) evidence from Geerhardus Vos which shows that he did not view himself as a novel paradigm shift among Reformed theologians and, in fact, was not. Vos viewed his own work in a broader historical context dating back at least to the post-Reformation era. Though Vos' contribution to Reformed theology came at a crucial point in the history of Christian thought and, more specifically, in the

---

[9] George Eldon Ladd, *A Theology of the New Testament* (Grand Rapids: William B. Eerdmans Publishing Company, 1993), 2. Cf. also, for example, Alister E. McGrath, *Reformation Thought: An Introduction* (Grand Rapids: Baker Book House, second edition, 1993).

early history of the biblical theology movement, his basic methodology can be found in Reformed orthodoxy – witness, John Owen and seventeenth-century Reformed orthodox federal theology. Though this can be shown to be true, it must also be admitted that this method did become somewhat dormant in Reformed theology until it was resuscitated and further developed by Vos. This is most likely due to the effects of the Enlightenment.

## The Methodological Approach of the Dissertation

A few words about the methodological approach of the dissertation may help at this juncture. We will examine the methodology and redemptive-historical formulations of Geerhardus Vos (late nineteenth century and early twentieth century) first then go back to examine Owen (seventeenth century). There is an obvious danger in this. We run the risk of anachronistic interpretation. In other words, we run the risk of interpreting Owen in light of Vos and imposing Vos' terminology, methodology, and theology upon Owen. Great care will be taken not to do this. This would turn things upside down and be an illustration of a historical-intepretive fallacy.

A justification for this approach is warranted. Why Vos first then Owen? Consider these well-known and agreed upon facts. First, it is generally agreed that Vos is *somewhat* of a paradigm shift among Reformed theologians in the field of biblical theology.

Second, Vos' methodology is universally accepted as biblical-theological/redemptive-historical. As mentioned above, he is known as the father of a Reformed biblical theology. So, why Vos first? Simply because his theological method is a somewhat well-known commodity in the Reformed tradition. No one doubts his credentials as a Reformed biblical theologian.

Third, surveying the histories of biblical theology (as we shall do) we will find that Owen is *not* mentioned as an adherent to the biblical-theological/redemptive-historical method and that seventeenth-century federalism is mentioned only in passing. However, upon examination of Owen's method in his *Biblical Theology* and elsewhere, we find Owen, and many of his contemporaries, fitting within the parameters of what constitutes biblical theology in the Reformed tradition as supremely exemplified by Vos, though of course not historically speaking.

Fourth, it is commonly held that Post-Reformation Reformed orthodoxy tended toward a rationalistic, neo-Aristotelian, hyper-dogmatic theology instead of exegesis and biblical theology. It is argued that the seventeenth century was a movement away from Calvin and, methodologically speaking, a movement away from the Bible as the foundation of theology, and philosophically speaking, a precursor to the devastating rationalism of the eighteenth century. But if what Vos did was, at the very least in seed form, already done by the Reformed orthodox, then accusations hurled at the Reformed orthodox must also be hurled at Vos. As we shall see, however, *in terms of methodology*, the accusations normally hurled at the Reformed orthodox do not stick. And if they do not stick on the seventeenth-century men, they cannot stick on Vos.

Fifth, John Owen is generally agreed upon as fitting within the era of Reformed orthodoxy. Granting this to be the case (which we will discuss below), one would assume that his method would have other contemporary adherents. If we can identify his method and show that it was contemporaneous with other Reformed orthodox theologians, we would have to admit that at least some within that school utilized what has come to be known as biblical theology, at least to a degree and obviously utilizing the theological nomenclature of that era.

Sixth, both Vos and Owen subscribed to very similar post-Reformation Reformed orthodox symbolic documents – the Savoy Declaration (Owen) and the Westminster Standards (Vos). If the links mentioned above can be established, we would have to conclude that, at least in the minds of Owen and Vos, federal/biblical theology is a handmaid and friend to symbolics and not its undoing.

In one sense, this dissertation attempts to go from the known (i.e., Vos as a Reformed, confessional, biblical theologian) to the relatively unknown (i.e., Owen as a Reformed, confessional, federal theologian). We will attempt to show that just as Vos was fundamentally anchored to the text of Scripture, so was Owen; just as Vos saw no contradiction with his biblical-theological/redemptive-historical methodology and his confessional commitment, neither did Owen. In fact, both saw a natural relationship between what we know as federal/biblical theology and dogmatics/systematic theology. Neither pitted one against the other in an antithetical manner. Both saw one as foundational to the other and the other dependent upon its foundation.

# CHAPTER TWO

# A BRIEF HISTORY OF BIBLICAL THEOLOGY

## Introduction

The primary focus of this chapter is upon biblical theology in two historical eras within the Reformed theological tradition. We want to know how and where John Owen and Geerhardus Vos fit in that tradition, what their contributions were, and how they compare to each other. A brief history of the discipline of biblical theology can assist us with understanding how it has been viewed since the time of the Reformation to the present.[1] This brief survey will be conducted with an eye toward identifying various phases in the discipline as a whole and the reasons why suggested by historians of biblical theology. We will identify such things as key persons, shifts in emphases, and various methodologies employed. Special concentration will be focused upon federal theology and the genesis of biblical theology (as a distinct, independent discipline) during the seventeenth and eighteenth centuries and biblical theology at the end of the nineteenth century and beginning of the twentieth. This will provide us with both a general survey of the discipline as a whole and a focus upon the historical eras surrounding Owen and, especially, Vos. We will look with keen interest when either Owen or Vos or their contemporaries are mentioned. As we work our way through this history, we will garner great appreciation and agreement with D. A. Carson, where he acknowledges that biblical theology has a "spotted history."[2]

---

[1] For a brief treatment of biblical theology prior to the Reformation, see Charles H. H. Scobie "History of biblical theology" in *New Dictionary of Biblical Theology*, eds. T. Desmond Alexander and Brian S. Rosner (Downers Grove, IL: InterVarsity, 2000, Reprinted 2003, 2006), 11-12 and J. Barton Payne, "Biblical Theology, OT, The Discipline of," in *Zondervan Pictorial Encyclopedia of the Bible, Volume One* (Grand Rapids: Zondervan Publishing House, 1975, 1976), 608. Scobie sees three periods in Church history in relation to biblical theology: (1) the period of an integrated biblical theology (prior to the end of the eighteenth century); (2) the period of an independent biblical theology (from the end of the eighteenth century until recently [He does not specify.]); and (3) the period of an intermediate biblical theology (recent trends). Scobie even says, "Yet it is surely nonsense to hold that the church had no biblical theology before the eighteenth century." Cf. Charles H. H. Scobie, "New Directions in Biblical Theology" in *Themelios* 17.2 (January/February 1992): 4.

[2] D. A. Carson, "Current Issues in Biblical Theology: A New Testament Perspective," Bulletin for Biblical Research 5 (1995): 18. Cf. also, Richard B. Gaffin, Jr.,

### Reformation and Post-Reformation Protestant Scholastic era

Gerhard F. Hasel, a Seventh-Day Adventist, says "The Reformers did not create the phrase 'Biblical theology' nor did they engage in Biblical theology as a discipline as subsequently understood."[3] Scobie, though, claims that Calvin "can be seen as the initiator of a truly biblical theology."[4] Elsewhere he says:

> When we come to the Protestant Reformation, the work of its leaders was clearly based on a form of biblical theology. Luther, Calvin and others sought to return to scriptural teaching and to judge later traditions and practices by norms derived from Scripture.[5]

George Eldon Ladd agrees, when he says, "The reformers insisted that the Bible should be interpreted literally and not allegorically, and this led to the beginnings of a truly biblical theology."[6] Book II of Calvin's *Institutes of the Christian Religion* contains a section which can be viewed at least as a proto-biblical theology.[7] What place did the Reformation have in the development of biblical theology? J. Barton Payne suggests:

> The Protestant Reformation in the 16th cent. reestablished two principles that were prerequisites to the development of Biblical theology: "the analogy of Scripture" recognized that the Bible is its own best interpreter, and "the literal sense" made possible a revival of interest in the truly historical development of revelation. ...but the conflict with Rom. sacerdotalism restricted the reformers into an understandable emphasis upon the final results of theology, rather than upon the unfolding of its earlier, OT stages.[8]

---

"Systematic Theology and Biblical Theology," *WTJ* 38 (1976): 282, "...biblical theology...has had a rather problematic history."

[3] Gerhard Hasel, *Old Testament Theology: Basic Issues in the Current Debate* (Grand Rapids: Wm. B. Eerdmans Publishing Co., 1991 [fourth] edition), 10.

[4] Scobie "History of biblical theology," 12. Cf. William D. Dennison, "Reason, History and Revelation: Biblical Theology and the Enlightenment," *Kerux*, 18.1 (May 2003): 19, where he acknowledges "kernels of Biblical Theology in Calvin and others during the Reformation..."

[5] Scobie, "New Directions in Biblical Theology," 4.

[6] Ladd, *A Theology of the New Testament*, 2.

[7] John Calvin, *Institutes of the Christian Religion*, ed. John T. McNeill and trans. Ford Lewis Battles, *Library of Christian Classics*, vols. 20-21 (Philadelphia: The Westminster Press, 1960), II.ix-xi.

[8] Payne, "Biblical Theology, OT, The Discipline of," I:608.

According to Hasel, some among the Radical Reformation offered "an approach resembling that of later Biblical theology"[9] as early as the 1530s. He claims that "the phrase 'biblical theology' actually appears for the first time in Wolfgang Jacob Christmann's *Teutsche Biblische Theologie* (Kempten, 1629)."[10] Christmann taught Hebrew and Logic at Heidelberg.[11] At this point, the phrase biblical theology referred to the use of proof texts "to support the traditional 'systems of doctrine' of early Protestant Orthodoxy."[12]

Protestant Orthodoxy produced, among other works, *Summa Doctrina de Foedere et Testamento Dei* [*Doctrine of the Covenant and Testament of God*] (1648) by Johannes Cocceius (1603-1669), which is viewed by some as a sort of proto-biblical theology. William Klempa claims that Cocceius' "writings include ...works on biblical theology."[13] Rowland S. Ward even says "He was thus in many ways the founder of Biblical theology."[14] Cocceius interpreted the Bible as an organic whole and gave special place to the concept of covenant in the unfolding of special revelation.[15] Payne comments:

> John Cocceius (1603-1669) organized his "federal theology" around God's successively revealed covenants–of works, with Adam in his innocency, and of grace, concerning God's redemptive activity with fallen man–and thus grasped Scripture's own key to the progress of divine revelation.[16]

---

[9] Hasel, *Old Testament Theology*, 11. Cf. also, Gerhard Hasel, *New Testament Theology: Basic Issues in the Current Debate* (Grand Rapids: Wm. B. Eerdmans Publishing Co., 1978, Re. 1993), 17.

[10] Hasel, *Old Testament Theology*, 11.

[11] http://translate.google.com/translate?hl=en&sl=de&u=http://www.ub.uniheidelber g.de/helios/fachinfo/www/math/homoheid/christmann.htm&sa=X&oi=translate&resnum =7&ct=result&prev=/search%3Fq%3DWolfgang%2BJacob%2BChristmann%26hl%3De n%26lr%3D%26rlz%3D1T4SUNA_en___US205. Accessed on January 15, 2007.

[12] Hasel, *Old Testament Theology*, 11. Cf. also, Hasel, *New Testament Theology*, 17.

[13] William Klempa, "Cocceius, Johannes (1603-1669)" in *Encyclopedia of the Reformed Faith*, ed. Donald K. McKim (Louisville: Westminster/John Knox Press, 1992), 73. We will discuss Cocceius below.

[14] Rowland S. Ward, *God & Adam: Reformed Theology and the Creation Covenant* (Wantirna, Australia, New Melbourne Press, 2003), 77.

[15] Scobie "History of biblical theology," 12; Payne, "Biblical Theology, OT, The Discipline of," I:608. Absent from most of the historical discussions consulted is the work of John Owen. J. I. Packer's introduction to Owen's *BTO*, cited above, is the only place where Owen is identified as doing the work of a proto-biblical theologian.

[16] Payne, "Biblical Theology, OT, The Discipline of," I:608.

Sadly, Ladd echoes the thought of others when it comes to the era of Protestant Orthodoxy, when he says:

> The gains in the historical study of the Bible made by the reformers were soon lost in the post-Reformation period, and the Bible was once again used uncritically and unhistorically to support orthodox doctrine. The Bible was viewed not only as a book free from error and contradiction but also without development or progress. The entire Bible was looked upon as possessing one level of theological     value. History was completely lost in dogma, and philology became a branch of dogmatics.[17]

Likewise, Nazarene scholar Willard H. Taylor says:

> Tragically, in the period following the Reformation, a Protestant scholasticism developed in which the maintenance of dogmas took precedence over the right of the Bible to stand as a judge of all doctrinal statement. Largely the Bible was used as a mine from which to glean supporting blocks for the various tenets of the church. The assumption prevailed that the Bible contains a single doctrinal system and upon investigation it can be demonstrated that it accords with the church's creed.[18]

### German Pietism

German Pietism brought a major shift to the function of biblical theology. Instead of supporting Protestant Orthodoxy, Philipp Jacob Spener (1635-1705), A. H. Franke (1663-1727), and other German pietists utilized biblical theology to *oppose* Protestant Orthodoxy.[19] Taylor says, "In the opinion of the pietists, notably P. J. Spener in his *Pia Desideria* in 1675, orthodox theology became "unscriptural" primarily in its form."[20] Writing in the pietist vein, C. Haymann (1708), according to Taylor, "was the first to produce a Biblical theology, and he has been credited with the first technical usage of this term."[21] This paved the way

---

[17] Ladd, *A Theology of the New Testament*, 2. We will discuss this unfortunate statement by Ladd in a subsequent section.

[18] Willard H. Taylor, "Biblical Theology" in *Zondervan Pictorial Encyclopedia of the Bible* (Grand Rapids: Zondervan Publishing House, 1975, 1976), I:593-94.

[19] Hasel, *Old Testament Theology*, 12.

[20] Taylor, "Biblical Theology," I:594.

[21] Taylor, "Biblical Theology," I:594.

for biblical theology as a separate discipline from dogmatics and in opposition to it. While discussing the influence of Pietism, Hasel says:

> This means that Biblical theology is emancipated from a role merely subsidiary to dogmatics. Inherent in this new development is the possibility that Biblical theology can become the rival of dogmatics and turn into a completely separate and independent discipline. These possibilities were realized under the influence of rationalism in the age of Enlightenment.[22]

## The Enlightenment

The Enlightenment brought in a new phase to biblical theology. With its anti-supernaturalism and rationalism came the denial of biblical inspiration. The Bible was then subject to the historical-critical method and became one of the ancient books of man's religious quest. Biblical theology became "a distinct disciple"[23] and a rival to dogmatic theology. It slowly but surely became a historical discipline antithetical to dogmatics.[24] The Enlightenment brought on a hermeneutical revolution. Hasel notes:

> A chief catalyst in the "revolution of hermeneutics" was the rationalist Johann Solomo Semler (1725-1791), whose four-volume *Treatise on the Free Investigation of the Canon* (1771-1775) claimed that the Word of God and Holy Scripture are not at all identical. This implied that not all parts of the Bible were inspired and that the Bible is a purely historical document which, as any other such document, is to be investigated with a purely historical and thus critical methodology. As a result Biblical theology can be nothing else but a historical discipline which stands in antithesis to traditional dogmatics.[25]

Gaffin offers this important historical observation concerning the genesis of Enlightenment biblical theology:

> More importantly, this development takes place, largely on German soil, in the context of the late Enlightenment with its rationalistic

---

[22] Hasel, *New Testament Theology*, 18.
[23] Gaffin, Jr., "Systematic Theology and Biblical Theology," 282.
[24] Hasel, *Old Testament Theology*, 13-14.
[25] Hasel, *New Testament Theology*, 20-21.

rejection of the inspiration and canonical unity of Scripture and its self-confessed, unambiguous point of departure in human autonomy.[26]

The German rationalist Johann Philipp Gabler (1753-1826) offered his famous inaugural lecture at the University of Altdorf in March of 1787. It was entitled *De justo discrimine theologiae biblicae et dogmaticae regundisque recte ultriusque finibus* or *An Oration on the Proper Distinction Between Biblical and Dogmatic Theology and the Specific Objectives of Each.*[27] Many scholars view this as "the beginning of Biblical theology's role as a purely historical discipline, completely independent from dogmatics."[28] It is of interest to note the comments of Sandys-Wunsch, where he says, "In most summaries of the history of biblical theology, Gabler's inaugural address is seen as an important turning-point, but rightly or wrongly it was not so seen by his contemporaries."[29]

Some claim that Gabler argued for a radical disjunction between biblical theology and dogmatic theology. It is probably more accurate to say that he argued that biblical theology, as he understood it, is the foundation from which "systematic theology may then properly be construed."[30] Indeed, Gabler's title suggests that he was not pitting biblical theology against dogmatics, *per se*. In his thinking, biblical theology was an inductive, historical, and descriptive discipline; dogmatic theology was deductive and philosophical. Gabler announces his thesis as follows:

> …it certainly seems to me that the one thing [i.e., biblical theology] must be more sharply distinguished from the other [i.e., dogmatics] than has been common practice up to now. And what I should like to

---

[26] Gaffin, "Systematic Theology and Biblical Theology," 282-83.

[27] The translation from the Latin is by John Sandys-Wunsch and Laurence Eldridge in John Sandys-Wunsch and Laurence Eldridge, "J. P. Gabler and the Distinction between Biblical and Dogmatic Theology: Translation Commentary, and Discussion of His Originality," *SJT* 33 (1980): 133-34. Cf. William D. Dennison, "Reason, History and Revelation: Biblical Theology and the Enlightenment," *Kerux*, 18.1 (May 2003) for a discussion of Gabler, the Enlightenment, and Reformed biblical theology from a Reformed-Vosian perspective.

[28] Hasel, *Old Testament Theology*, 16. Cf. Taylor, "Biblical Theology," I:594; Ladd, *New Testament Theology*, 2.

[29] Sandys-Wunsch and Eldridge, "J. P. Gabler and the Distinction between Biblical and Dogmatic Theology," 149.

[30] Carson, "Current Issues in Biblical Theology," 21.

establish here is the necessity of making this distinction and the method to be followed.[31]

Carson says of Gabler, "[A]s a descriptive enterprise biblical theology is less speculative, less difficult, more enduring, and more frankly biblical than the orthodox dogmatics *of the day*."[32]

We must not be too conciliatory to Gabler, however. His oration is fraught with Enlightenment philosophical pre-commitments and terminology. "...Gabler's call to get "back to the Bible" was filtered through modern rational-empirical and pietistic lenses."[33] He obviously denies plenary inspiration and inerrancy. For instance, he said, "...we must investigate what in the sayings of the Apostles is truly divine, and what perchance merely human."[34] He seems to hold to partial inspiration, though. Dennison agrees, when he says, "...the biblical authors are inspired only as they bear the divine message of salvation."[35] Gabler says:

> In this way it may finally be established whether all the opinions of the Apostles, of every type and sort altogether, are truly divine, or rather whether some of them, which have no bearing on salvation, were left to their own ingenuity.[36]

Gabler's method seeks to find the "universal ideas" of Scripture.[37] In effect, he is searching for a canon within the canon.

> Thus, as soon as all these things [i.e., what words of the Apostles are truly divine] have been properly observed and carefully arranged, at last a clear sacred scripture will be selected with scarcely any doubtful readings, made up of passages which are appropriate to the Christian religion of all times. These passages will show with unambiguous

---

[31] J. P. Gabler in Sandys-Wunsch and Eldridge, "J. P. Gabler and the Distinction between Biblical and Dogmatic Theology," 137.

[32] Carson, "Current Issues in Biblical Theology," 21. Emphases added.

[33] Dennison, "Reason, History and Revelation," 12.

[34] J. P. Gabler in Sandys-Wunsch and Eldridge, "J. P. Gabler and the Distinction between Biblical and Dogmatic Theology," 143.

[35] Dennison, "Reason, History and Revelation," 14.

[36] J. P. Gabler in Sandys-Wunsch and Eldridge, "J. P. Gabler and the Distinction between Biblical and Dogmatic Theology," 143.

[37] J. P. Gabler in Sandys-Wunsch and Eldridge, "J. P. Gabler and the Distinction between Biblical and Dogmatic Theology," 142.

words the form of faith that is truly divine; the *dicta classica*[38] properly so called, which can then be laid out as the fundamental basis for a more subtle dogmatic scrutiny. For only from these methods can those certain and undoubted universal ideas be singled out, those ideas which alone are useful in dogmatic theology.[39]

It is this method of biblical theology that would offer dogmatics the data from which it could then work.

Gabler and G. L. Bauer (1755-1806) have come to be known as "the founders of the independent discipline of Biblical and OT theology."[40] Scobie calls this "the period of independent biblical theology."[41] Slowly but surely biblical theology, among those utilizing the historical-critical method, became the rival of dogmatics and even sought to usurp it. Gaffin comments:

> The summary observation to be made at this point, then, is that as a distinct discipline biblical theology first emerges as part of the Enlightenment and in reaction to the alleged failure, especially in its dogmatics, of traditional (orthodox) Christianity to do justice to the historical character of the Bible.[42]

### Nineteenth-Century Germany (the salvation-historical school)

Payne suggests that since Gabler and others approached biblical theology with rationalism and distinguished it from dogmatics, "Bible-believing scholars were slow to recognize the possibilities that lay in the employment of progressive revelation to confirm rather than to explain away the supernatural."[43] This could explain why there was little biblical theology being written by supernaturalists at this time. This void of "Bible-believing scholars" doing biblical theology was soon filled by the salvation-historical school of nineteenth-century Germany.

---

[38] "This is a technical expression that refers to the standard collection of proof texts in the orthodox theology of the eighteenth century." Cf. Sandys-Wunsch and Eldridge, "J. P. Gabler and the Distinction between Biblical and Dogmatic Theology," 143, n. 2.

[39] Sandys-Wunsch and Eldridge, "J. P. Gabler and the Distinction between Biblical and Dogmatic Theology," 143.

[40] Hasel, *Old Testament Theology*, 17-18. Cf. also Hasel, *New Testament Theology*, 25; Payne, "Biblical Theology, OT, The Discipline of," I:608.

[41] Scobie, "New Directions in Biblical Theology," 4.

[42] Gaffin, "Systematic Theology and Biblical Theology," 283-84.

[43] Payne, "Biblical Theology, OT, The Discipline of," I:608.

According to Hasel, the German salvation-history school of the nineteenth century based its approach as follows:

> (1) the history of the people of God "as expressed in the Word"; (2) the idea of the inspiration of the Bible; and (3) the (preliminary) result of the history between God and man in Jesus Christ. Von Hofmann found in the Bible a record of linear saving history in which the active Lord of history is the triune God whose purpose and goal it is to redeem mankind. Since Jesus Christ is the primordial goal of the world to which salvation history aims and from which it receives its meaning, the OT contains salvation-historical proclamation. This an OT theology has to expound. Each book of the Bible is assigned its logical place in the scheme of salvation history. The Bible is not to be regarded primarily as a collection of proof-texts or a repository of doctrine but a witness to God's activity in history which will not be fully completed until the eschatological consummation.[44]

Taylor claims that J. C. K. von Hofmann can be called the father of the German salvation-historical school.

> von Hofmann's *Der Schriftbeweis*[45] (1826-55) ...sees the entire Bible as recording God's saving action in behalf of mankind. Both the OT and the NT are linked together in this "salvation history."[46]

Von Hofmann claimed that the Bible came about as a result of the activity of the Holy Spirit. Both the writings and their formation into the canon are results of the Spirit's activity. This has implications for hermeneutical methodology and canonical synthesis. Hasel explains:

> Since the Holy Spirit is responsible for the origin of the Biblical writings and the formation of the canon, a salvation-historical theology has the task to investigate the historical place of the products of the Holy Spirit. This is best achieved through an organic cross-section of the whole Bible along the salvation-historical lines and not through a proof-text method that is irresponsible to the context.[47]

---

[44] Hasel, *Old Testament Theology*, 22. Cf. also Hasel, *New Testament Theology*, 36-37. We will see some of these very same elements in both Owen (and federal theology) and Vos below.

[45] Loosely translated, "The Proof of Scripture."

[46] Taylor, "Biblical Theology," I:595.

[47] Hasel, *New Testament Theology*, 38. Hasel claims that Theodor Zahn was influenced by von Hafmann. Cf. Hasel, *New Testament Theology*, 38-39.

During the nineteenth century, E. W. Hengstenberg[48] and G. F. Oehler offered a more conservative approach to Old Testament theology. According to Payne, it was Hengstenberg, in his *Christology of the Old Testament*, "who first demonstrated the value of OT theology..."[49] According to Hasel, in his now famous *Theology of the Old Testament*, Oehler utilized what may be called the historico-genetic method[50] of biblical theology.

> Oehler's contribution was the most significant and lasting. He was the first since Gabler to publish a volume dealing extensively with the theory and method of a Biblical-theological understanding of OT theology. His massive *Theology of the OT* appeared in French and English. Oehler reacted both against the Marcionite strain introduced by F. Schleiermacher with the depreciation of the OT and the total uniformity of OT and NT as maintained by Hengstenberg. But he himself does not give up the unity of the Testaments. There is unity in diversity. Oehler accepts the division of OT and NT theology, but OT theology can function properly only within the larger canonical context. OT theology is a "historical science which is based upon grammatical-historical exegesis... The proper method for Biblical theology is "the historico-genetic" approach according to which grammatical-historical exegesis, not historical-critical exegesis, is to be combined with an "organic process of development" of OT religion. Oehler's OT theology is considered to be "the outstanding salvation-historical presentation of Biblical theology of the 19th century."[51]

Oehler's methodology is important for the purposes of this brief survey. Oehler's stated method is very similar to both Owen and Vos. For instance, while defining Old Testament theology, Oehler says:

---

[48] It is of interest to note here that, according to Marion Taylor, J. A. Alexander was dependent upon Hengstenberg's *Christology*. This is important because it shows that Old Princeton (at least J. A. Alexander) was reading salvation-history school works. Alexander gave way to William Henry Green who taught Geerhardus Vos. Cf. Marion Ann Taylor, *The Old Testament in the Old Princeton School (1812-1929)* (San Francisco: Mellen Research University Press, 1992), 121.

[49] Payne, "Biblical Theology, OT, The Discipline of," I:608.

[50] The phrase "historico-genetic" is Oehler's. Cf. Gustave Friedrich Oehler, *Theology of the Old Testament*, ed. George E. Day (Grand Rapids: Zondervan Publishing House, n.d.), 41-42.

[51] Hasel, *Old Testament Theology*, 21. The quotation marks in the Hasel quote are due to him quoting Oehler and/or others.

The theology of the Old Testament, the first main division of Biblical Theology, is *the historical exhibition of the development of the religion contained in the canonical books of the Old Testament.*

As a historical science, Biblical Theology is distinguished from the systematic statement of biblical doctrine by this, that while the latter investigates the unity of divine truth, as seen in the whole course of revelation, and the aggregate of its manifestations, the former has the task of exhibiting the religion of the Bible, according to its progressive development and the variety of the forms in which it appears. The theology of the Old Testament has therefore to follow the gradual progress by which the Old Testament revelation advanced to the completion of salvation in Christ; and to bring into view from all sides the forms in which, under the Old Covenant, the communion between God and man found expression.[52]

While listing various characteristics of the historico-genetic method, Oehler says:

According to the definition in § 2, the method of Biblical Theology is *historico-genetic.* As a historical science, it rests on the results of *grammatico-historical exegesis,* the business of which is to reproduce the contents of the biblical books according to the rules of language, with due regard to the historical circumstances under which the books originated, and the individual relations of the sacred writers. In the last respect the grammatico-historical exegesis passes over into psychological exposition, which goes back to the inner state of the writer's life—a species of exposition which, of course, is peculiarly indispensable in dealing with passages which, like the Psalms, the book of Job, and so forth, give immediate expression to inner experiences and frames of mind. But in this psychological exposition we reach a point where success is necessarily proportional to the measure in which the Spirit, which rules in the sacred writers, witnesses of Himself to the interpreter, enabling him to understand by personal experience the inner experiences of the writers.—If exegesis, however, goes no farther than the exposition of individual passages, it gives only an imperfect preparation for Biblical Theology, not the least important cause of the former defective condition of the latter was the fact that expositors limited themselves mainly to the explanation of isolated passages, which, thus isolated, might easily be made to favor any preconceived opinion. Exegesis, therefore, must proceed to grasp the sense of individual passages, first in its internal connection with the fundamental idea of the book in general, and with the system of thought

---

[52] Oehler, *Theology of the Old Testament*, 4.

characteristic of the author, and then in its wider connection with the circle of ideas proper to the special region of the dispensation of revelation to which the book belongs—a process which Schleiermacher in his *Hermeneutik* reckons as part of psychological exegesis. In this way, we reach the various forms in which revelation expresses its contents. But now *Biblical Theology,* which proposes to set forth revelation in its whole course and in the totality of its phenomena, must comprehend these forms as *members of an organic process of development.* And since every such process can be comprehended only from the points of its culmination, Biblical Theology must view the Old Testament in the light of the completed revelation of God in Christ for which it formed the preparation, —must show how God's saving purpose, fulfilled in Christ, moved through the preliminary stages of this history of revelation. While the external historical method deals with the contents of the Old Testament according to the presumed chronological order of the books, and then at most shows how new religious knowledge was added from time to time to what was already in existence–how the earlier knowledge was completed, deepened, corrected; while the dogmatist forces the doctrinal contents of the Old Testament into a framework brought to it from without; and while the method of philosophical construction deals in a similar manner with the Old Testament, by cutting it up critically until it can be fitted into a presupposed scheme of logical categories—the *genetic* method seeks to reproduce the living process of the growth of the thing itself. This method refuses, however, to find ripe fruit where only the bud exists; it aims to show how the fruit grew from the bud; it sketches the earlier stages in a way that makes it clear how the higher stages could, and necessarily did, spring from the former.[53]

## Nineteenth-Century Germany
## (the history of religions school)

The nineteenth century ended with the triumph of the "history of religions" approach to biblical theology (Old and New Testament). Ferdinand Christian Baur, "the founder and uncontested head of the

---

[53] Oehler, *Theology of the Old Testament*, 41-42. As will become apparent later, Oehler's methodological philosophy of biblical theology is similar to both Owen and Vos. Peter J. Wallace acknowledges that Oehler's work "bears some resemblance to Vos's later *Biblical Theology*…" Cf. Peter J. Wallace, "The Foundations of Reformed Biblical Theology: The Development of Old Testament Theology at Old Princeton, 1812-1932," *WTJ* 59:1 (1997): 52, n. 56.

Tubingen School,"[54] applied the Hegalian dialectic (i.e., thesis, antithesis, synthesis) to New Testament theology. Hasel comments:

> Baur's Hegelian dialectic lead him to view the history of Christianity as a struggle between the thesis of Jewish Christianity (Petrine materials, Matt., Rev.) and the antithesis of Gentile Christianity (Gal., 1-2 Cor., Rom., Luke) which resulted in the synthesis of early Catholicism (Mark, John, Acts) of the second century.[55]

Similarly, though with a variation of terms, Ladd describes Baur's method as follows:

> Under the influence of Hegel, F. C. Baur abandoned the rationalistic effort to find timeless truth in the New Testament, but in its stead found in the historical movements in the early church the unfolding of wisdom and spirit. The teaching of Jesus formed the point of departure. Jesus' teachings were not yet theology but the expression of his religious consciousness. Theological reflection began over the question of the Law. Paul, the first theologian, took the position that the Christian was freed from the Law (thesis). Jewish Christianity, represented particularly by James and Peter, took the opposite position, that the Law was permanently valid and must remain an essential element in the Christian church (antithesis). Baur interpreted the history of apostolic Christianity in terms of this conflict between Pauline and Judaistic Christianity. Out of the conflict emerged in the second century the Old Catholic Church, which effected a successful harmonization between these two positions (synthesis).[56]

One of the unique contributions of the Tubingen School was its effort to trace historical development in the Scriptures (primarily the New Testament). Though Baur and Tubingen were correct to approach the New Testament as "inseparably related to history,"[57] imposing the Hegalian dialectic forced many of its documents against themselves and produced a fractured, disorganized, antithetical theology.

This school of thought was fuelled, in part, by Julius Wellhausen and K. H. Graff and their pentateuchal criticism.[58] Hegelianism and Darwinism (evolutionary progress) were the philosophical bases upon

---

[54] Hasel, *New Testament Theology*, 31.
[55] Hasel, *New Testament Theology*, 31.
[56] Ladd, *A Theology of the New Testament*, 3.
[57] Ladd, *A Theology of the New Testament*, 3.
[58] Taylor, "Biblical Theology," I:595.

which their critical method was built. The Bible became, once again, *one* of man's religious books. It was subject to the evolutionary theory and was the object of historical scrutiny alone. It did not contain theology, properly understood as revelation from God. It merely contained what some ancient men thought about the Israelite and Christian religions. Pieter A. Verhoef describes the nineteenth century scheme of development in the Old Testament as follows:

> The principle of natural development in the sphere of nature and culture was applied to the religion of Israel. The theological approach to the Old Testament thus gave way to the description of the history of Israel's religion according to the evolutionistic scheme of a development from primitive beginnings to the ethical monotheism of the prophets. In this evolutionistic pattern the scholars of the nineteenth century had no use for a supernatural divine revelation.[59]

The New Testament was seen as containing competing versions of Christianity – Jesus, Paul, James, etc. – based on cultural and philosophical influences of the day.[60] The New Testament was reconstructed according to this method (i.e., Hegalianism) and much ink was spilled. Biblical theology was a purely historical science. Its task was to compare the biblical writings with the religious writings of that day. Inspiration was denied as was the Reformation principle of *analogia fide*. But this led to such diversity that many began to question the utility of such a method. Verhoef offers this concluding assessment:

> Reflecting upon these and other theories and attitudes with which scholars of the nineteenth century approached the Bible and especially the Old Testament, we can understand why a curious paralysis arrested the development of Biblical Theology and why these scholars have lost their aerial with regard to the divine revelation.[61]

## Twentieth Century
### (the "Biblical Theology Movement" and the conservative testimony)

The 1930s marked the beginnings of what many call "the Biblical theology movement." Hasel lists the various texts which were produced

---

[59] Pieter A. Verhoef, "Some Thoughts on the Present-Day Situation in Biblical Theology," *WTJ* 33, (1970): 6.

[60] Ladd, *A Theology of the New Testament*, 3.

[61] Verhoef, "Some Thoughts on the Present-Day Situation in Biblical Theology," 8.

from 1933-1972.[62] His list reflects a wide variety of theologians from various schools of thought. Most would be outside of the Reformed theological tradition. He does include, however, J. B. Payne and Geerhardus Vos.[63] This movement lasted for about twenty years and was comprised of works produced primarily by North American and European scholars "who shared liberal, critical assumptions and methods."[64] In large part, this movement was promoted by Neo-orthodox theologians who utilized historical-critical methods, yet viewed the Bible as witness to the divine Word.[65] Tired of the sterility and atomizing tendencies of Liberal criticism and the "fundamentalism" of the older Protestant orthodoxy, the Neo-orthodox biblical theologians sought a middle-ground. They utilized the historical-critical method and yet viewed the Bible as a witness to the Christ. Revelation was seen as God revealing himself in Christ and the Bible becoming a witness to this revelation (i.e., Barthianism[66]). "[W]hile the Bible *was not* the Word of God it could *become* the Word of God, namely, the medium for an existential encounter of the living God with a man."[67] Verbal, plenary inspiration was, obviously, denied.

Theologically conservative and historically orthodox theologians were not totally silent in the first half of the twentieth century. Princeton Seminary, for a time, continued to uphold a confessional theology that sought to interact with modern scholarship. Such luminaries as B. B. Warfield (dogmatics) and Geerhardus Vos (biblical theology) produced confessionally faithful expressions of Christian orthodoxy in the midst of wider theological confusion. Vos' own *Biblical Theology* stands as a monument among Reformed biblical theologies.[68]

After the Liberal reorganization of Princeton in 1929, Westminster Theological Seminary, Philadelphia, took up the old Princeton torch and became America's (and much of the world's) leading conservative, confessional seminary. O. T. Allis, E. J. Young, and John Murray all wrote, to varying degrees, within the biblical-theological vein of Vos.[69]

---

[62] Hasel, *Old Testament Theology*, 26-27.

[63] As does Taylor, "Biblical Theology," I:596.

[64] Gerhard F. Hasel, "Biblical Theology Movement" in *Evangelical Dictionary of Theology*, ed. Walter A. Elwell (Grand Rapids: Baker Book House, 1984, Fourth Printing, July 1986), 149.

[65] Hasel, "Biblical Theology Movement", 149.

[66] Payne, "Biblical Theology, OT, The Discipline of," I:609.

[67] Payne, "Biblical Theology, OT, The Discipline of," I:609.

[68] Payne, "Biblical Theology, OT, The Discipline of," I:609.

[69] Payne, "Biblical Theology, OT, The Discipline of," I:609-10.

**Late Twentieth Century to the Present**

Brevard S. Childs' book *Biblical Theology in Crisis* (1970) advocated an approach to biblical theology which was "based on the canonical form of the biblical texts."[70] This is called by some the "theological-historical" approach and is similar to G. F. Hasel's method. In the 1970s, George Eldon Ladd published his *A Theology of the New Testament*.[71] Graham Goldsworthy offered his popular *According to Plan: The Unfolding Revelation of God in the Bible* in 1991 which has enjoyed much success. According to Scobie, Childs' *Biblical Theology of the Old and New Testaments* (1992) is "[t]he most significant 20th-century biblical theology."[72]

Among both Reformed and non-Reformed evangelicals there seems to be no end to new treatments of biblical theology in one form or another. Reformed theologians are currently involved with biblical theology at various levels – G. K. Beale, O. Palmer Robertson, Richard B. Gaffin, Jr., and Michael Horton, to name a few.

**Conclusion**

As our brief history has shown us, biblical theology has a very uneven history. It is somewhat difficult to pin-point its historical inception. Most historians would acknowledge that some form of it was being conducted during the Reformation and post-Reformation eras. The federal theology of the seventeenth century is specifically acknowledged as at least a pre-curser to biblical theology. Johannes Cocceius is usually the name attached to federal theology. But the federal theology of the seventeenth-century Reformed orthodox has little to do with the biblical theology of the eighteenth century (This will become increasingly clear below.). And the biblical theology of Geerhardus Vos has little to do with that of the eighteenth century. Why is this? The answer we will explore is that Vos resuscitated much of the federal method that predates the critical era and applied it to his own day.

---

[70] Scobie "History of biblical theology," 18.
[71] Cited above.
[72] Scobie "History of biblical theology," 19.

# CHAPTER THREE

# THE LIFE, MINISTRY, AND IMPACT OF

# GEERHARDUS VOS

## The Life of Geerhardus Vos

Vos' somewhat mysterious life[1] began on March 14, 1862 in Heerenveen, Friesland, The Netherlands. His father, Rev. Jan Hendrick Vos, with German Old Reformed roots, was a pastor of six different congregations in the Netherlands before settling in Grand Rapids, Michigan, at the Christian Reformed Church. Here he served in his only long-term pastorate of nearly twenty years.[2] Geerhardus was educated in various schools and even tutored privately for a time in the Netherlands before moving to Grand Rapids with his family in the summer of 1881.

Vos entered the Theological School, which became Calvin Theological Seminary, in Grand Rapids in September of 1881. He quickly distinguished himself and was appointed as an instructional assistant on June 29, 1882, at the age of 20.[3] He spent two years at this school. In his second year, he "taught half-time and took courses half-time."[4] In the fall of 1883, Vos entered Princeton Theological Seminary "as a middler, i.e., a second-year theological student" as a result of his request to skip the first year in light of his previous academic accomplishments.[5] He was a student at Princeton for two years, sitting under such men as William Henry Green, A. A. Hodge, and C. W. Hodge.[6] He graduated in 1885 and earned the Hebrew fellowship award which was "a purse for future doctoral studies."[7]

In 1885, Vos enrolled at the University of Berlin. His intent was to pursue a Ph.D. in Old Testament. In 1886, Abraham Kuyper and Herman

---

[1] James T. Dennison, Jr., "Introduction: The Life of Geerhardus Vos" in *The Letters of Geerhardus Vos*, ed. James T. Dennison, Jr. (Phillipsburg, NJ: P&R Publishing, 2005), 14. This section is highly dependent upon Dennison's excellent and up-to-date biography of Vos, referenced as *Letters* from here on out.

[2] Dennison, *Letters*, 14-15, 18.

[3] Dennison, *Letters*, 18-19.

[4] Dennison, *Letters*, 19.

[5] Dennison, *Letters*, 19, n. 23.

[6] Dennison, *Letters*, 20.

[7] Dennison, *Letters*, 20.

Bavinck[8] desired Vos to become professor of Old Testament at the Free University of Amsterdam. Though Vos loved his motherland, he turned down the offer in light of parental disapproval.[9]

In the fall of 1886, Vos enrolled at the University of Strasbourg to complete his doctoral studies.[10] Due to health problems he was not able to pursue studies at the rate he expected. He majored in Semitic languages in the Department of Philosophy.[11] He was awarded a Ph.D. on April 26, 1888. His "dissertation was an exercise in Arabic textual criticism."[12]

Vos became professor of didactic and exegetical theology in September of 1888 at the Theological School in Grand Rapids. He was installed as professor at the Spring Street Christian Reformed Church. At one point, he was responsible for 23 hours of instruction.[13] In 1891 he was named rector of the school and delivered his now famous "The Doctrine of the Covenant in Reformed Theology" as his commemorating address.

In 1892, a formal call from Princeton came to "Vos to assume a newly created chair of biblical theology."[14] In the midst of theological turmoil at Princeton and an unstable academic environment in Grand Rapids, Vos finally accepted. He taught from September 1893 to May 1894, then delivered his famous inaugural address – "The Idea of Biblical Theology as a Science and as a Theological Discipline."[15] Vos' Princeton teaching career lasted 39 years.[16]

The year 1894 saw Vos ordained, being recognized by the Presbytery of New Brunswick, PCUSA, in New Jersey.[17] This year also saw Geerhardus take a wife – Catherine Frances Smith.[18] She bore four children, the eldest, Johannes Geerhardus, editor of some of his father's written works.

---

[8] According to Sinclair B. Ferguson in Geerhardus Vos, *Grace and Glory* (Edinburgh: The Banner of Truth Trust, 1994), vii.

[9] Dennison, *Letters*, 22-23. Cf. Vos, *RHBI*, x, n. 3.

[10] Dennison, *Letters*, 23.

[11] Dennison, *Letters*, 23.

[12] Dennison, *Letters*, 24.

[13] Dennison, *Letters*, 26. Cf. Vos, *RHBI*, x, where Gaffin claims 25 hours.

[14] Dennison, *Letters*, 30.

[15] Dennison, *Letters*, 36.

[16] Dennison, *Letters*, 49.

[17] Dennison, *Letters*, 41. He remained in the denomination for the rest of his life.

[18] Dennison, *Letters*, 41.

Vos lived in the same house in Princeton for 38 years. He spent most of those summers (26 consecutive from 1906-1932) in Roaring Branch, Pennsylvania, for rest, reading, reflection, and family time.[19] Roaring Branch is where Geerhardus and Catherine are buried.

Vos retired in 1932 and relocated to Santa Ana, California, where his son Jerry lived. Vos had spent a sabbatical in the southwest in 1923 and very much enjoyed the climate. He moved to California, in part, for health reasons.[20] Tragically, Catherine died in 1937 of pneumonia.

He moved to Grand Rapids again to live with his daughter, Marianne, in 1939. He lived his final 10 years there and died on August 13, 1949 in a convalescent hospital. Cornelius Van Til of Westminster Theological Seminary preached his funeral sermon with 45 people attending. He was buried next to Catherine near their home in Roaring Branch, while very few were present. Dennison comments, "No one from Princeton was present; no one from the PCUSA paid any attention; only two from the community were there. He was obscure in life, and obscure in death."[21]

## The Ministry of Geerhardus Vos

Vos taught at what became Calvin Theological Seminary and Princeton Theological Seminary for a combined 42 years. While at Calvin, he taught dogmatics, philosophy, non-Christian religions, and exegesis – including Greek.[22]

He was very familiar with the critical scholarship of his day. James T. Dennison, Jr. claims that he was

> thoroughly familiar with the German higher criticism, 18th and 19th century biblical theologies, and the exegetical scholarship on both sides of the Atlantic. ...Vos was fluent in German and Dutch and spent three postgraduate years in Germany under such notable critics as August Dillmann, Herman Strack and Bernhard Weiss. Yet his orthodoxy emerged unscathed. In fact, his firsthand acquaintance with the

---

[19] Dennison, *Letters*, 47.

[20] Dennison, *Letters*, 59.

[21] Dennison, *Letters*, 62-63. Dennison surmises that six people attended the burial, one of them being Bernardus Vos.

[22] Dennison, *Letters*, 26. Cf., Vos, *RHBI*, x.

historical-critical school reinforced his confidence in the Scriptures as an objective, supernatural self-disclosure of God.[23]

Princeton was the womb from which Vos gave birth to class lectures and his greatest literary achievements. Dennison surmises that he may have taught more than 4,000 students while at Princeton.[24] Between 1890 and 1919 Vos published 108[25] book reviews, most of these while at Princeton. His now influential books were penned during his Princeton days. His preaching was primarily confined to the chapel at Princeton Seminary between 1896 and 1913.[26] As we shall shortly see, though, his impact while alive was very minimal, especially compared to the resurgent interest in Vos in the last 40 years.

### The Impact of Geerhardus Vos

The impact of Geerhardus Vos has developed over the years since his death. He was relatively obscure in life[27] and theological impact.[28] Dennison says of Vos' obscurity at the time of his death, "...Vos continues in death as in life: obscure, ignored, and insignificant."[29] As to his lack of theological impact in his day, Dennison adds:

> A second curious enigma [the first being personal] to be explained is the neglect and dismissal of Vos's biblical-theological method and insights during his lifetime. While many lamented the neglect of Vos's writings and exegetical insights after his death, it seems clear that few assimilated and applied them while he was alive. If scholars manifested little or no interest in his writings,[30] this was all the more glaringly true of his students. ...Vos was largely forgotten as soon as his students completed his classes or earned their degrees. ...graduates did not base

---

[23] James T. Dennison, Jr., "What is Biblical Theology? Reflections on the Inaugural Address of Geerhardus Vos," *Kerux* 2.1 (May 1987): 34.

[24] Dennison, *Letters*, 81, n. 206.

[25] Danny E. Olinger, *A Geerhardus Vos Anthology: Biblical and Theological Insights Alphabetically Arranged* (Phillipsburg, NJ: P&R Publishing, 2005), 10.

[26] Vos, *Grace and Glory*, ix.

[27] Dennison calls him "a personal enigma." Dennison, *Letters*, 66.

[28] See Dennison, *Letters*, 67ff.

[29] Dennison, *Letters*, 68.

[30] Dennison notes, "A mere handful of reviews constitute the interaction, both before and after his death." Dennison, *Letters*, 67, n. 184.

their approach to Scripture, preaching, pastoral ministry, or the Christian life on the Vosian paradigm.[31]

He was esteemed as a Christian man, but his writings were not so fortunate. Even his colleagues made such a dichotomy. Danny E. Olinger notes:

> Upon Vos's death in 1949 the Trustee's Minutes in the *Princeton Student* (*sic?*) *Bulletin* noted that Vos was one of the most learned and devout in Princeton's long line of teachers, and yet the same Trustee's Minutes mention that his published writings were the despair of his contemporaries. All too often, liberals dismissed his writings while conservative brethren did not understand them.[32]

There were some who recognized his genius in his day (i.e., Kuyper, Bavinck, Warfield). Vos' student, J. Gresham Machen, writing home to his mother while attending Princeton, said of him:

> We had this morning one of the finest expository sermons I have ever heard. It was preached by Dr Vos…and rather surprised me. He is usually rather too severely theological for Sunday morning. Today he was nothing less than inspiring…Dr Vos differs from some theological professors in having a better-developed bump of reverence.[33]

According to H. Henry Meeter, Machen once said of Vos:

> If I knew half as much as Dr. Vos, I would be writing all the time….Take for example that work of Dr. Vos on the Kingdom of God. Every sentence might well be the topic sentence of a paragraph.[34]

Though Machen praised him in this instance, in a letter from Ned B. Stonehouse to Louis Berkhof, dated December 17, 1954, it appears that Stonehouse thought Machen never grasped Vos.[35]

---

[31] Dennison, *Letters*, 67.

[32] Olinger, *Anthology*, 1-2. There appears to be a typo here. In n. 5 on p. 1, Olinger references *Princeton Seminary Bulletin* 43.3 (Winter 1950): 42.

[33] N.B. Stonehouse, *J. Gresham Machen: A Biographical Memoir* (1954; reprint, Edinburgh: The Banner of Truth Trust, 1987), 72, as cited by Ferguson in Vos, *Grace and Glory*, viii.

[34] H. Henry Meeter, "Professor Geerhardus Vos: March 14, 1862-August 13, 1949," *The Banner* 84 (Sept. 2, 1949): 1046, as cited in Olinger, *Anthology*, 4.

[35] Dennison, *Letters*, 79.

John DeWaard studied under Vos at Princeton from 1922-1925. In 1936, in the *Presbyterian Guardian*, he wrote:

> I loved him when I studied there, I love him more now....As we
> listened to the lectures we forgot about the man speaking, while our
> minds were fixed on the wonders of the Word....Perhaps there is no
> one in our fellowship who can do what Dr. Vos succeeded so well in
> doing. But we can attempt to do the same thing in a small way.[36]

According to Olinger, Stonehouse taught "New Testament biblical theology at Westminster Seminary and always made known his indebtedness to his former mentor."[37]

Another of Vos' students, John Murray, said in 1974:

> Dr Vos is, in my judgment, the most penetrating exegete it has been my
> privilege to know, and I believe, the most incisive exegete that has
> appeared in the English-speaking world in this century.[38]

It is reported that Herman Ridderbos, during his 1975 tour of the United States, when meeting Vos' daughter, "seized her hand warmly when introduced and confessed a great deal of dependence upon her father in his own thinking."[39]

In the 1979 preface to Vos' *Redemptive History and Biblical Interpretation*, Richard B. Gaffin, Jr. comments, "Over a decade ago the theological genius and unparalleled biblical insight of Geerhardus Vos began to dawn on me."[40] In the introduction, Gaffin adds:

> Truly great biblical exposition does not become outdated. While
> originally addressed to contemporary issues and problems, it continues
> to lay hold of and shape the life and thought of subsequent generations
> of the church. Calvin's commentaries are a notable example. In some
> instances the real impact of exegetical labor may even fall beyond its

---

[36] Dennison, *Letters*, 81, n. 207.

[37] Olinger, *Anthology*, 2, n. 7.

[38] Quoted by Ferguson in Vos, *Grace and Glory*, ix. The quote comes from the 1974 Banner of Truth reprint of Vos' *Biblical Theology*.

[39] Dennison, *Letters*, 81, n. 208. Olinger notes that Stonehouse said of Ridderbos' *Coming of the Kingdom*, "It is refreshing...to receive a new reminder after fifty years [that] Vos's fundamental perspectives and conclusions are by no means outmoded." Cf. Olinger, *Anthology*, 2. The quote comes from Stonehouse's review of Ridderbos' book in *Westminster Theological Journal* (*WTJ*) 14 (1952): 160.

[40] Vos, *RHBI*, vii.

own time. Possessing rare and unprecedented insight into the meaning and right handling of Scripture, truly commensurate influence first begins to materialize in the interpretation and hermeneutical reflection of a later day, despite the warm appreciation and admiration of many contemporaries. This is the case with the work of Geerhardus Vos...[41]

In 1994 Sinclair B. Ferguson calls Vos "the theologian's theologian" and "a scholar *par excellence*."[42] Olinger lists J. Gresham Machen, H. Henry Meeter, Ned B. Stonehouse, John Murray, Cornelius Van Til, Anthony A. Hoekema, Edmund P. Clowney, Meredith G. Kline, Richard B. Gaffin, Jr., Sinclair B. Ferguson, and James T. Dennison, Jr. as a sampling of those who have recognized the value of Vos' writings and the impact in their own theological formulations.[43]

But praise for Vos on a larger scale did not come until about 40 years ago. Dennison claims that, though Vos was studied in seminaries prior to this time,

> [i]t was not until the early 1970s that students who read Vos began to rethink preaching and ministry on the basis of his exegesis of the semi-eschatological Pauline theology (or the eschatological perspective that he articulated so well in general). Vos was an assigned reading at many conservative, even Reformed, seminaries–but his system was not being "applied" to ministry. Academics used Vos to bolster their course bibliographies, but dismissed him as dense, impractical, and too hard.[44]

This resurgence came, in part, due to Edmond P. Clowney and Richard B. Gaffin, Jr. at Westminster Theological Seminary, Philadelphia, and Herman Ridderbos in The Netherlands.

Today Vos' legacy can be seen in the plethora of books being published in the biblical-theological vein within Reformed and Evangelical theological circles. Both scholarly and popular books have appeared on the publishing scene in the last several decades that bear the explicit, or at least implicit, marks of Vos' influence.[45] Probably the

---

[41] Vos, *RHBI*, ix.

[42] Vos, *Grace and Glory*, vii, viii.

[43] Cf. Olinger, *Anthology*, 2-6.

[44] Dennison, *Letters*, 67-68.

[45] Cf., for instance, among many others, Edmund P. Clowney, *Preaching and Biblical Theology* (Grand Rapids: William B. Eerdmans Publishing Company, 1961); Willem A. VanGemeren, *The Progress of Redemption: The Story of Salvation from Creation to the New Jerusalem* (Grand Rapids: Zondervan Publishing House, 1988), 15; Mark Strom, *The Symphony of Scripture: Making Sense of the Bible's Many Themes*

highest and most lasting compliment paid to him was coined by Gaffin, when he said, "...he is the father of a Reformed biblical theology..."[46]

Vos' impact has picked up steam as the years roll by. He was a great man with a great mind in his own day, though not recognized then as he is now. As Gaffin says, in his day "he was probably more respected than understood."[47] Though dead now, he speaks, and his voice has affected many and it appears that it will continue to for years to come.

---

(1990; Phillipsburg, NJ: P&R Publishing, 2001), 64, n. 5; Graeme Goldsworthy, *According to Plan: The Unfolding Revelation of God in the Bible–An Introductory Biblical Theology* (Downers Grove, IL: InterVarsity Press, 1991), 13; Simon Austen, *A Better Way: Jesus and Old Testament Fulfillment* (Geanies House, Fearn, Tain, Ross-shire, Great Britain: Christian Focus Publications, Ltd., 2003); Michael Horton, *God of Promise: Introducing Covenant Theology* (Grand Rapids: Baker Books, 2006), 8. Cf. also the published works of Richard B. Gaffin, Jr..

[46] Vos, *RHBI*, xiv.
[47] Vos, *RHBI*, xiii.

# CHAPTER FOUR

# GEERHARDUS VOS, OLD PRINCETON, AND THE

# DEVELOPMENT OF REFORMED BIBLICAL THEOLOGY

# IN HISTORICAL-THEOLOGICAL CONTEXT

## Introduction

To understand Vos' contribution to Reformed biblical theology in historical-theological balance, it is important to understand the context in which he thought and wrote and the possible influences upon his biblical-theological method. We have already discussed his education. Certainly those formative years of theological study impacted him. But what about the context at Princeton immediately antecedent to Vos' professorship and illustrious career? Was there a form of biblical theology taking place at Princeton prior to Vos? The very fact that a chair of biblical theology was created indicates that Princeton realized the need for such.

It is no secret that Old Princeton had some illustrious professors prior to Vos' acceptance of the chair of biblical theology in 1892. It has been claimed in the last several years that some of those professors displayed the fact that a form of biblical theology, a somewhat undeveloped form, was being conducted prior to Vos' professorship. This has been pointed out in at least two important recent sources: the first is a dissertation published in 1992 by Marion Ann Taylor entitled, *The Old Testament in the Old Princeton School (1812-1929)*[1] and the second is an article in the *Westminster Theological Journal* in 1997 by Peter J. Wallace entitled, "The Foundations of Reformed Biblical Theology: The Development of Old Testament Theology at Old Princeton, 1812-1932."[2] We will see that Richard B. Gaffin, Jr. was reluctant in 1976 to admit what Taylor hints at and what Wallace claims.[3] The first two sources mentioned above indicate clearly that biblical theology, though obviously not in its Vosian

---

[1] Marion Ann Taylor, *The Old Testament in the Old Princeton School (1812-1929)* (San Francisco: Mellen Research University Press, 1992).

[2] Peter J. Wallace, "The Foundations of Reformed Biblical Theology: The Development of Old Testament Theology at Old Princeton, 1812-1932," *WTJ* 59:1 (1997): 41-69.

[3] Richard B. Gaffin, Jr., "Systematic Theology and Biblical Theology," *WTJ* 38 (1976): 281-99.

form, predates Vos at Princeton. In fact, biblical theology was conducted by others outside of Princeton as well. We will look briefly at Old Princeton and biblical theology prior to Vos, possible influences upon Vos outside of Princeton or the sources Vos could have been relying on to help develop his own biblical-theological method early on in his ministry, and then suggest, tentatively, what exactly Vos' unique contribution was in light of the historical-theological context.

### Old Princeton and Biblical Theology prior to Vos

In Taylor's *Old Testament in the Old Princeton School*, while not approving of old Princeton's conservative, confessional Reformed theology, she analyzes various Princeton professors and their view of the Old Testament. Writing in one of the forewords, Mark Noll claims that Old Testament scholarship at "old Princeton seminary was fundamental to that institution's self-definition as a confessional defender of orthodox theology" and is "a surprisingly neglected theme."[4] Wallace says something similar about biblical theology, when he says, "The development of biblical theology at Princeton Theological Seminary prior to Geerhardus Vos (1862-1949) has been a neglected subject."[5] Noll goes on to say that old Princeton combined "confessional orthodoxy and distinguished learning."[6] Assuming Noll's claim that old Princeton was self-consciously confessional,[7] a claim which we affirm, one should assume that the theological methodologies utilized were viewed by their practitioners as consistent with their confessional, orthodox and Reformed tradition. We will now give brief attention to what sort of biblical-theological methodology emerged in these seminal days at Old Princeton.

### • Archibald Alexander

In the early days of Archibald Alexander's training (the early 1790s), his mentor William Graham had him "read a compendium of Turretin, the writings of John Owen and Jonathan Edwards and William Bates' The

---

[4] Taylor, *Old Testament in the Old Princeton School*, xi. Noll's comments come from the second foreword in Taylor's dissertation. The first foreword was written by Brevard S. Childs.

[5] Wallace, "Foundations," 41.

[6] Taylor, *Old Testament in the Old Princeton School*, xi.

[7] Cf. Wallace, "Foundations," 43.

Harmony of the Divine Attributes."[8] This shows that early on Alexander was exposed to some of the giants of the Reformed federal methodology. Taylor points out that "...[Alexander] understands the second part of the curse of the serpent in Genesis 3:15 as "the first intimation of the Messiah.""[9] We will see later the same interpretation in John Owen and others of his day.

- **Charles Hodge**

Unknown to some and of significance for our discussion, Hodge was Professor of Oriental and Biblical Literature at Princeton from 1822-1840.[10] He taught Old Testament prior to J. A. Alexander.[11] Commenting on Hodge's hermeneutic, Taylor says:

> The general hermeneutic which Hodge commends to his students is as follows: "The parts should be interpreted in coincidence with the drift and design of the whole, and that this general character and design may and must be learned before the details can be properly understood, is acknowledged in reference to all works w[h]en there is any continuity in reasoning or logical arrangement." Applying this hermeneutical principle to the book of Isaiah, Hodge suggests that Isaiah has to be interpreted in the light of the design of God's revelation which is salvation to mankind through a redeemer.[12]

This, as we shall see, has some clear echoes in the hermeneutical methodology of Vos, Owen, and seventeenth-century Reformed orthodoxy.

- **J. A. Alexander**

According to Taylor, J. A. Alexander read Calvin and Cocceius[13], believed that Genesis 3:15 contained Messianic prophecy,[14] and displays

---

[8] Taylor, *Old Testament in the Old Princeton School*, 4.

[9] Taylor, *Old Testament in the Old Princeton School*, 33.

[10] Taylor, *Old Testament in the Old Princeton School*, 47.

[11] Wallace, "Foundations," 43.

[12] Taylor, *Old Testament in the Old Princeton School*, 81.

[13] Taylor, *Old Testament in the Old Princeton School*, 115, 126. We will discuss Cocceius' contributions to Reformed orthodox federal theology below.

[14] Taylor, *Old Testament in the Old Princeton School*, 120.

dependence on Hengstenberg's *Christology*.[15] He saw development within the various periods of Messianic prophecy.[16] His hermeneutical "methodology ensures that a text is interpreted within its canonical context."[17] Charles Hodge said of him:

> His mind was analytical and comprehensive. He could unravel the most complicated mass of details and discover the principle by which they were reduced to order. This power he displayed to great advantage in the treatment of the Old Testament History, which he so taught as to make that economy appear as an organic whole, each part assuming its proper relation to every other part, and all culminating in the fuller revelation of the new economy.[18]

Taylor comments on J. A. Alexander's view of the organic development and growth of revelation:

> At the same time, he found development and growth within the scriptures as the scheme of salvation was gradually unfolded, an observation which was to become important to OT theology later in the century.[19]

Wallace echoes Taylor:

> Alexander's treatment of the flow of biblical history reads rather woodenly at times, compared to modern approaches, but in his day he was at the cutting edge of a more dynamic reading which saw individual texts in light of the whole, as well as the whole in light of individual texts.[20]

This hermeneutic, as we shall see, is a standard pre-critical principle, exemplified in *analogia fidei*.

---

[15] Taylor, *Old Testament in the Old Princeton School*, 121. Cf. Wallace, "Foundations," 43.

[16] Taylor, *Old Testament in the Old Princeton School*, 121.

[17] Taylor, *Old Testament in the Old Princeton School*, 122.

[18] Taylor, *Old Testament in the Old Princeton School*, 159. Taylor is quoting Hodge from H. C. Alexander, *Joseph Addison Alexander*, 2:506. This sounds like Vos in *BTV*, which we will discuss below.

[19] Taylor, *Old Testament in the Old Princeton School*, 159.

[20] Wallace, "Foundations," 47.

- **William Henry Green**

Vos sat under Green while a student at Princeton from 1883 to 1885. Taylor says of Green, "It was Green's belief that each book of scripture was 'a link in a chain...a member of an organism,' intentionally fashioned to occupy a specific place in the 'successive disclosures of divine truth.'"[21] He held to a "'comprehensive' hermeneutical approach" to interpreting Scripture.[22] "Green suggests that when seen within its larger canonical context, the book of Job contains much of the gospel."[23] Taylor continues:

> Green's work of examining the place of Job within the larger scheme of Holy Scripture is essentially that of a biblical theologian. His concerns in this area are timely in that the whole idea of biblical theology was being reshaped as a distinctive discipline during the nineteenth century. Almost two decades later, Princeton Seminary recognized Biblical Theology as a distinctive discipline and created the Charles Haley Chair of Biblical Theology.[24]

Commenting on Green's attempts to "refine an OT theology based on the concept of organic unity," Taylor says:

> During this period, Green was also continuing to refine an OT theology based on the concept of organic unity. In his 1865 article entitled "The Structure of the Old Testament," Green develops his thesis that there is "unity in multiplicity" and "singleness of aim with diversity of operations...under one superior and controlling influence" in the OT. "We are authorized to believe," states Green, "that there is a divine reason why each portion of divine revelation is what it is, and stands where it does; that nothing is superfluous and nothing lacking and that all is concatenated together in a masterly arrangement." Green then explores the two obvious ways of setting out the structure of the OT, that is, starting from the beginning or the end. He suggests that while the two methods lead to similar results the latter is to be preferred for three reasons: first, it demonstrates more clearly the interdependent relationship between the historical, poetical and prophetical books; second, it makes Christ the center of the OT so that "the meaning of

---

[21] Taylor, *Old Testament in the Old Princeton School*, 206.

[22] Taylor, *Old Testament in the Old Princeton School*, 207.

[23] Taylor, *Old Testament in the Old Princeton School*, 207.

[24] Taylor, *Old Testament in the Old Princeton School*, 207. As noted, Vos assumed that chair in 1892.

every part is to be estimated from its relation to him"; and third, it gives unity to the study of the Bible, for "everything in the Old Testament tends to Christ...[and] everything in the New Testament unfolds from Christ." In light of this Christocentric schema, Green then fleshes out the hermeneutical principles which enable the interpreter to see Christ in the OT. Specifically, Green points to the importance of typology and prophecy. In both instances, Green argues for a very broad interpretation of the terms: "Every bestowment of material good and every deliverance from temporal evil is a type of ultimate good and the ultimate salvation. Every prophecy of inferior good things is likewise indirectly a prophecy of Christ and of the benefits to be wrought [by] him."[25]

Wallace goes so far as to say that Green developed "the outlines of a distinctively Reformed biblical theology."[26] The Christocentricity of Green's hermeneutic is clear and has ample precedent in the federal theology of seventeenth-century Reformed orthodoxy, as will be shown below.

In 1976, Richard B. Gaffin said:

> This brief survey of representative writers permits the generalization that within the Reformed tradition Vos has *no predecessors* for *his conception* of biblical theology. In this respect his work can be called creative and injects a fresh impulse into Reformed theology.[27]

What Gaffin claimed in 1976 by way of generalization, Wallace challenged in 1997. Wallace claimed that "The development of biblical theology at Princeton Theological Seminary prior to Geerhardus Vos (1862-1949) has been a neglected subject."[28] In light of this, he took Gaffin to task with these words:

> Richard B. Gaffin, for instance, in a statement that ignores the theological work being done as early as the 1850s by Alexander (1809-1860) and Green (1825-1900), suggests that "Vos's work in biblical theology is largely without direct antecedents and indicates the originality with which he wrestled with the matter of biblical interpretation in the Reformed tradition."[29] Yet the pages of the *Biblical*

---

[25] Taylor, *Old Testament in the Old Princeton School*, 222-23.
[26] Wallace, "Foundations," 41.
[27] Gaffin, "Systematic Theology and Biblical Theology," 287. Emphases added.
[28] Wallace, "Foundations," 41.
[29] Wallace is referencing Gaffin, "Introduction" in Vos, *RHBI*, xii.

*Repertory and Princeton Review* from the 1840s throughout the 1870s reveal that Alexander and Green had been developing an understanding of salvation history that clearly foreshadows Vos' later work. Gaffin claims that Vos was the first to give "pointed, systematic attention to the *doctrinal* or *positive* theological significance of the fact that redemptive revelation comes as an organically unfolding historical process."[30] This states the case a bit too strongly.[31]

In light of the two studies mentioned above, it seems that Gaffin did overstate his case.

### Influences upon Vos outside of Princeton

- **Introduction**

Due to various unfortunate factors, it is difficult to determine Vos' early dependence on others with much certainty. Gaffin agrees, when he says:

In his inaugural address given in May 1894 Vos, conscious of occupying a new chair in the Seminary, undertakes a full treatment of biblical theology as a special discipline but does not give any real indication of how he is dependent upon others for the position he spells out.[32]

There are only two footnotes, which make passing reference to the work of T. D. Bernard (p. 19) and K. F. Nosgen (p. 35).[33]

Taylor acknowledges "...Vos' ...failure to cite indebtedness to others..."[34] She calls this one of Vos' foibles, along with his "ponderous writing style."

There are at least two influential sources, however, that are easy to identify: Thomas Dehany Bernard and the federal theology of seventeenth-century Reformed orthodoxy.

---

[30] Wallace is referencing Gaffin, "Introduction" in Vos, *RHBI*, xv.

[31] Wallace, "Foundations," 42.

[32] Gaffin, "Systematic Theology and Biblical Theology," 284.

[33] Gaffin, "Systematic Theology and Biblical Theology," 284, n. 6. The page numbers referred to by Gaffin are in Geerhardus Vos, *The Idea of Biblical Theology as a Science and as a Theological Discipline* (New York: Anson D.F. Randolph, 1894). These same footnotes occur in Vos, *RHBI*, 12 and 21.

[34] Taylor, *Old Testament in the Old Princeton School*, 356.

*   **Thomas Dehany Bernard**

Though Vos did not cite many authors, especially in his seminal
inaugural address, he did cite some who may shed light on what he was
reading and who was influencing him outside of Princeton in his early
days. For instance, Gaffin mentioned T. D. Bernard above, cited by Vos
in his inaugural address. *The Progress of Doctrine in the New Testament*
by Bernard is the only book footnoted in Geerhardus Vos' "The Idea of
Biblical Theology as a Science and as a Theological Discipline" in
support of his discussion on the elements of biblical theology. [35] It is
referenced in the context of Vos discussing the progressive, organic
character of Special Revelation. As one examines Bernard's book, it
becomes evident why Vos was inclined to reference it in his seminal
lecture. Obviously, he agreed with Bernard, at least at the point of the
quotation. Many statements by Bernard, however, have a 'Vosian' feel to
them. To some degree, Vos seems to have been influenced by Bernard or
at least had some degree of affinity with him, but to what degree is
beyond the scope of our focus. A few statements by Bernard from his last
lecture of the book will amply display the 'Vosian' feel of Bernard's
book.[36]

Bernard sees the Apocalypse as a book of restoration. After
referencing Revelation 21:1-2, he says:

> In taking these words for my text [i.e., referenced at the beginning of
> this lecture] I place myself at the point where the whole teaching of
> Scripture culminates. Here, at the last step, we have a definite and
> satisfactory completion of the former doctrine of the future. There is to
> be a perfect humanity; not only perfect individually, but perfect in
> society. There is to be a city of God. "The Holy City!"–there is the
> realization of the true tendencies of man. "New Jerusalem!"–there is
> the fulfillment of the ancient promises of God.[37]

---

[35] Vos, *RHBI*, 12, n. 1.

[36] For an extended overview and discussion of Bernard's book see Richard C.
Barcellos, "*The Progress of Doctrine in the New Testament*, by T. D. Bernard – A
Review Article (Part I)," *RBTR* IV:1 (January 2007): 7-26 and Richard C. Barcellos,
"*The Progress of Doctrine in the New Testament*, by T. D. Bernard – A Review Article
(Part II)," *RBTR* IV:2 (July 2007): 33-60.

[37] Thomas Dehany Bernard, *The Progress of Doctrine in the New Testament* (New
York: American Tract Society, n.d.), 206.

The Bible, for Bernard, is "one long account of the preparation of the city of God."[38] It is not merely concerned with personal salvation. Bernard acknowledges that "…it is, but it is more than this."[39] He comments:

> It places before us the restoration, not only of the personal, but of the social life; the creation, not only of the man of God, but of the city of God; and it presents the society or city, not as a mere name for the congregation of individuals, but as having a being and life of its own, in which the Lord finds his satisfaction and man his perfection. The "Jerusalem which is above" is, in relation to the Lord, "the Bride, the Lamb's Wife" (Rev. 21:9), and, in relation to man, it is "the Mother of us all" (Gal. 4:26). In its appearance the revealed course of redemption culminates, and the history of man is closed: and thus *the last chapters of the Bible declare the unity of the whole book, by completing the design which has been developed in its pages, and disclosing the result to which all preceding steps have tended.*[40]

Bernard understands the final vision of the Bible as "a conclusion by which all that went before is interpreted and justified."[41] He further says that "…a Bible that did not end by building for us a city of God would appear to leave much in man unprovided for, and much in itself unaccounted for."[42] Thankfully, as Bernard acknowledges, "neither of these deficiencies exist."[43] Bernard sees the consummation as something that "from the first, the desires of men and the preparations of God have been alike directed towards it."[44] In other words, the eschatology at the end of the Bible has been there from the beginning.[45] Indeed, Bernard gives this brief history of redemption to illustrate his point.

> At the beginning of the sacred story, the Father of the faithful comes forth into view, followed by those who are heirs with him of the same promise; and they separate themselves to the life of strangers, because they are "looking for a city which hath foundations, whose builder and

---

[38] Bernard, *Progress of Doctrine*, 208.
[39] Bernard, *Progress of Doctrine*, 208.
[40] Bernard, *Progress of Doctrine*, 208. Emphases added.
[41] Bernard, *Progress of Doctrine*, 209.
[42] Bernard, *Progress of Doctrine*, 209.
[43] Bernard, *Progress of Doctrine*, 209.
[44] Bernard, *Progress of Doctrine*, 209.
[45] We will discuss the primacy of eschatology in both Vos and the federal theology of seventeenth-century Reformed orthodoxy below.

maker is God." In due time solid pledges of the divine purpose follow. We behold a peculiar people, a divinely-framed polity, a holy city, a house of God. It is a wonderful spectacle–this system of earthly types, thus consecrated and glorified by miraculous interventions and inspired panegyrics. Do we look on the fulfilment of patriarchal hopes or on the types of their fulfilment? on the final form of human society or on the figures of the true? The answer was given by Prophets and Psalmists, and then by the word of the Gospel, finally by the hand of God, which swept that whole system from the earth. It was gone when the words of the text were written, and when the closing scene of the Bible presented the new Jerusalem, not as the restoration, but as the antitype of the old.[46]

The redemptive-historical types give way to their eschatological anti-types. Old Jerusalem was a type of the new Jerusalem, the city of God.

Bernard states very clearly that man is brought to this city and this eternal state of perfection by Jesus Christ, the Mediator.[47] But, as he says, now "is the day of preparation."[48] The members of that future society are being "sorted and collected out of the mass of mankind."[49] They are being trained and prepared for that great day.

And according to Bernard, that great day is not merely a restoration to Eden. Bernard does not view individual salvation as the goal of redemption. He reminds us that the final destination of redeemed humanity is a city.

If we think only of our individual portion, we miss the completeness of Scripture in its provision for the completeness of man. If individual blessedness were the highest thought of humanity, it might have been sufficient to have restored the lost garden of Eden, and to have left the inhabitants of the new earth to dwell safely in its wildernesses and sleep in its woods (Ezek. 34:25).[50]

Not so does the revelation of God inform the expectations of those who receive it. Other systems evade the demands of the highest tendencies of man: this provides that they shall be realized. It decrees not only the individual happiness, but the corporate perfection of man;

---

[46] Bernard, *Progress of Doctrine*, 209-10.
[47] Bernard, *Progress of Doctrine*, 210.
[48] Bernard, *Progress of Doctrine*, 210.
[49] Bernard, *Progress of Doctrine*, 210.
[50] Bernard, *Progress of Doctrine*, 212.

and closes the book of its prophecy by assuring the children of the living God that *"he hath prepared for them a city."*[51]

Bernard closes this final lecture with a recapitulation of his explanation of the progress of doctrine in the New Testament. He closes with these penetrating, encouraging, and doxological words:

> Only the written word of God, confidingly followed in the progressive steps of its advance, can lead the weakest or the wisest into the deep blessedness of the life that is in Christ, and into the final glory of the city of God.
>
> Perhaps in some minds this needful confidence may be strengthened by a review of the books of the New Testament in the light in which they have now been placed. When it is felt that these narratives, letters, and visions do in fact fulfil the several functions, and sustain the mutual relations, which would belong to the parts of one design, coalescing into a doctrinal scheme which is orderly, progressive, and complete, then is the mind of the reader in conscious contact with the mind of God; then the superficial diversity of the parts is lost in the essential unity of the whole: the many writings have become one Book; the many writers have become one Author. From the position of students, who address themselves with critical interest to the works of Matthew, of Paul, or of John, we have risen to the higher level of believers, who open with holy joy "the New Testament of our Lord and Saviour Jesus Christ," and, while we receive from his own hand the book of life eternal, we hear him saying still, "I have given unto them the words which thou gavest me."[52]

This brief sample of Bernard shows that he was working with some of the same hermeneutical and methodological tools that Vos later utilized, though in his own unique way. Bernard recognized in his own day "that the progressive character of revelation [wa]s thus coming more distinctly before the mind of the Church."[53] Vos took it one step further within the Reformed tradition.

Having said all of that, it is still difficult to know exactly how much and at what point Vos was dependant upon Bernard. The analysis above is only suggestive and is a subject worth exploring but beyond the purposes of this dissertation.

---

[51] Bernard, *Progress of Doctrine*, 213.
[52] Bernard, *Progress of Doctrine*, 213.
[53] Bernard, *Progress of Doctrine*, 21.

- **The Federal Theology of Reformed Orthodoxy**

Vos delivered his lecture entitled, "The Doctrine of the Covenant in Reformed Theology" in 1891 at the Theological School of the Christian Reformed Church in Grand Rapids, Michigan.[54] It is evident from the references he cites that he was very aware of the federal theology of the seventeenth century. Gaffin acknowledges that Vos saw himself in continuity with earlier Reformed theology.[55] Wallace claims a high degree of dependency of Vos on federal theology.[56] Vos' article shows clearly that he had read widely in seventeenth-century federal theology and was aware of several of the in-house discussions of that day–the Cocceian controversy;[57] issues involving the covenant of works;[58] the concepts of monopleurism (one-sided covenant) and dipleurism (two-sided) covenant;[59] a unique contribution of Owen in defending the formulation of the covenant of redemption;[60] and the differences of opinion on the function of the covenant of works in the Sinai covenant.[61]

We will see later that many of the issues that the seventeenth-century Reformed orthodox theologians grappled with are incorporated into Vos' discussion of redemptive history. This certainly proves some degree of dependence by Vos and substantiates Gaffin's claim that Vos was self-consciously working within the doctrinal parameters of earlier Reformed thought.

## Vos' Unique Contribution in Historical-Theological Perspective

There are at least four opinions as to Vos' unique contribution to the Reformed theological tradition.

---

[54] Vos, "The Doctrine of the Covenant in Reformed Thought" in *RHBI*, 234, n. *.
[55] Gaffin, "Biblical Theology and The Westminster Standards," 166.
[56] Wallace, "Foundations," 42. Cf. the discussion immediately below this section.
[57] Vos, "Doctrine of the Covenant," 234-35. We will discuss this below.
[58] Vos, "Doctrine of the Covenant," 242-45. We will discuss this below.
[59] Vos, "Doctrine of the Covenant," 245-46. We will discuss these concepts below.
[60] Vos, "Doctrine of the Covenant," 246. We will discuss this below.
[61] Vos, "Doctrine of the Covenant," 255. We will discuss this below.

- **The Methodological Unification of the Princeton Old Testament tradition with the Federal Theology of Reformed Orthodoxy**

Wallace claims:

> [W]hat is unique to Vos is the methodological unification of the Princeton Old Testament tradition with the federal theology of Reformed orthodoxy in the concept of the covenant. ... Vos brought his predecessors' work to new heights; he combined their insights with traditional federal theology to connect the redemptive plan of God with the flow of history in the person and work of Christ.[62]

In Wallace's thinking, Vos was similar to Oehler in that both attempt to show that the covenant is central and basic to Old Testament religion.[63] But Vos is unique in Reformed theology, according to Wallace, because he took the fruits of the Old Testament department at Princeton and "wove their conception of redemptive history together with traditional covenant theology."[64]

- **The Unprecedented Development of the Organic Nature of Revelation as an Unfolding, Historical Process**

Gaffin claims the following:

> But Vos is the first in the Reformed tradition, perhaps even the first orthodox theologian, to give pointed, systematic attention to the *doctrinal* or *positive* theological significance of the fact that redemptive revelation comes as an organically unfolding historical process and to begin working out the methodological consequences of this insight.[65]

We must be careful not to read too much into Gaffin's statement. He does not claim explicitly that Vos did what no one else had ever done, though he may, indeed, have left himself open to that interpretation. He claims that Vos is the first Reformed theologian *to give specific focus* to the concept of redemptive revelation as "an organically unfolding historical process and to begin working out the methodological consequences of this insight." Gaffin acknowledges that prior to Vos

---

[62] Wallace, "Foundations," 42.
[63] Wallace, "Foundations," 52, n. 56.
[64] Wallace, "Foundations," 61.
[65] Vos, *RHBI*, xv.

there was an awareness and appreciation for the historical character of revelation. He says, "Attention to the historical progress of revelation is given with the Reformed concentration on the idea of the covenant and is present in such dissimilar figures as Coccejus and Jonathan Edwards."[66]

- **The Primacy of Eschatology or Vos' Intersecting-Plane Hermeneutic: The Intersection of the Protological and the Eschatological[67]**

James T. Dennison, Jr., however, sees things a bit differently. He says:

> The progress of the history of revelation (*historia revelationis*) is, for Vos, the outworking of this protological/eschatological pattern ("eschatology becomes the mother of theology and that first of all theology in the form of a philosophy of redemptive history"[68]). Using his favorite analogy, Vos traces the unfolding history of redemption from the Garden of Eden to the New Jerusalem in terms of a flower blooming from bud to blossom. Inherent in the earlier stages of the flower are the later. Indeed, retrospectively and prospectively the flower, at every stage of growth, is organically related to history past, history present, and history future. This linear or horizontal dimension in the development of the history of redemption has been called the typological. But for Vos, typology is not enough. The dynamic of a theocentric (and Christocentric) revelation must recognize the vertical dimension. In other words, *Vos transforms biblical study by introducing an intersecting-plane hermeneutic*: the intrusion of the vertical into the horizontal, the penetration of the temporal by the eternal, the intersection of the protological and the eschatological.[69]

In an article discussing Vos' inaugural address at Princeton, Dennison says, "Vos has alerted us to the Copernican revolution in hermeneutics—eschatology is prior to soteriology; and all soteriology is eschatologically oriented."[70]

Danny E. Olinger sounds a similar note:

---

[66] Vos, *RHBI*, xv. Cf. also Gaffin, "Biblical Theology and The Westminster Standards,"166.

[67] Danny Olinger, "Vos's Verticalist Eschatology: A Response to Michael Williams," *Kerux* 7.2 (Sept. 1992): 30-38.

[68] Dennison is quoting Vos, "Hebrews, the Epistle of the Diatheke," in *RHBI*, 193.

[69] Dennison, *Letters*, 51-52. Emphases added.

[70] Dennison, "What is Biblical Theology? Reflections on the Inaugural Address of Geerhardus Vos," 40.

By placing the eschatological consideration first, something that Vos began to do with increasing consistency as he matured as a theologian, Vos blazed a comparatively new trail in Reformed theology.[71]

...Vos represented a theological revolution at Princeton Seminary.[72]

Vos, then, while working within the confines of the old system, continually pushed Princeton in a new direction theologically. Vos saw the Bible as leading with eschatology, he saw Jesus Christ leading with eschatology, and he believed that the Christian should lead with eschatology.[73]

Failure to grasp the primacy of eschatology to Vos leads to a failure to understand Vos fully. Foundational to Vos's hermeneutic is seeing Paul as arguing that Adam irrespective of sin had an eschatology, the hope of a higher future and communion with God. Before man needed to be saved from his sin, he had an eschatology in that he possessed a future hope. As Vos argued in *Biblical Theology*, man was created perfectly good in a moral sense, yet he could rise to a still higher estate. The eschatological state is the goal of man irrespective of the fall into sin.[74]

- **The Consistent Outworking of the Reformed Hermeneutical Principle that Scripture interprets Scripture**

William D. Dennison claims:

In Reformed theology...the covenant and Christocentric typology provided a fundamental link in understanding and stressing the unity of Scripture; they are at the core of the meaning of Scripture. This same understanding is found at the heart of Vos's Biblical Theology.

Furthermore, one cannot overlook the hermeneutical principle of the Reformation, i.e., "that Scripture interprets Scripture." The Reformed view of the historical continuity of Scripture testifies specifically to the hermeneutical principle of the Reformers; this hermeneutical principle

---

[71] Olinger, *Anthology*, 14. Olinger does say "a *comparatively* new trail." Emphasis added.

[72] Olinger, *Anthology*, 15.

[73] Olinger, *Anthology*, 15.

[74] Olinger, *Anthology*, 15-16. As we shall see, the concept of an Edenic eschatology predates Vos and can be found in the federal theology of seventeenth-century Reformed orthodoxy.

is nonsense without the unfolding history of revelation. For this reason, Richard B. Gaffin, Jr. has stressed that the analogy of Scripture is implicitly Biblical-theological; this hermeneutical principle depicts the essence of the discipline of Biblical Theology. In light of Gaffin's observation, it is easy to conclude that *Vos's work was a consistent outworking of the Reformed principle of hermeneutics.*[75]

## Conclusion

It is premature at this point to interact with these views. We will do so in the conclusion of the dissertation. However, this much can be said: Vos does represent a milestone in Reformed theology in terms of the outworking of biblical theology. He was not the first within the Reformed tradition to do federal/biblical theology, but he is, nonetheless, a monument in the Reformed tradition and due consideration and respect must be given him.

---

[75] Dennison, "Reason, History and Revelation: Biblical Theology and the Enlightenment," 22-23. Emphases added. Though I do not want to make too much of Dennison's statement, I think it is worth standing on its own at this point in light of the implications of *analogia fide*, which we will discuss below.

# CHAPTER FIVE

# THE LIFE, MINISTRY, AND LEGACY OF JOHN OWEN

## The Life and Ministry of John Owen

John Owen was born in 1616,[1] the same year William Shakespeare died.[2] His father, Henry Owen, was a 'Puritan' nonconformist of Welsh descent.[3] Relatively nothing is known of his mother. Andrew Thomson says:

> Little is known regarding the childhood of Owen; and no records whatever have descended to tell us of the mother to whom was committed the training of his most susceptible years, and who was to be the Monica to this future Augustine.[4]

After receiving the rudiments of an education at home, Owen entered a private academy at Oxford, being "initiated into the principles of classical learning, by Edward Sylvester..."[5] At age 12, Owen entered Queen's College, which, according to Peter Toon, "was not exceptional

---

[1] Andrew Thomson, *John Owen: Prince of Puritans* (Ross-shire, Great Britain: Christian Focus Publications, 1996, re. 2004), 14. Thomson's biography was written in the nineteenth century and is also contained in the Banner of Truth edition of Owen's Works, Vol. I:XXI-CXXII. Cf. also William Orme, *The Life of John Owen* (Choteau, MT: Gospel Mission Press, re. 1981), 7 (Orme's biography was first published in 1826); Peter Toon, *God's Statesman: The Life and Work of John Owen* (Grand Rapids: Zondervan Publishing House, 1973), 1-2; Robert W. Oliver, "John Owen – his life and times" in Robert W. Oliver, ed., *John Owen: The Man and his Theology* (Darlington, England: Evangelical Press, 2002), 11-39; Sinclair B. Ferguson, *John Owen on the Christian Life* (Edinburgh: The Banner of Truth Trust, 1987), 1-19; Sebastian Rehnman, *Divine Discourse: The Theological Methodology of John Owen* (Grand Rapids: Baker Academic, 2002) 18-20; Kelly M. Kapic, *Communion with God: The Divine and the Human in the Theology of John Owen* (Grand Rapids: Baker Academic, 2007), 21-28; Kapic, "Owen, John (*1616-1683*)" in Donald K. McKim, editor, *Dictionary of Major Biblical Interpreters* (Downers Grove, IL: IVP Academic, 2007), 795-99; Carl R. Trueman, *John Owen: Reformed Catholic, Renaissance Man* (Aldershot, Hampshire, UK: Ashgate Publishing, 2007), 1-5; and Barry H. Howson, "The Puritan Hermeneutics of John Owen: A Recommendation" in *WTJ* 63 (2001): 351-54.

[2] Toon, *God's Statesman*, 1.

[3] Orme, *Owen*, 7; Oliver, *Owen*, 12.

[4] Thomson, *Owen*, 14.

[5] Thomson, Owen, 14; Orme, *Owen*, 7; Toon, *God's Statesman*, 3.

at that time."[6] Owen's older brother, William, was a student there as well. "Both Owens graduated BA in 1632 and proceeded to their Master's degrees in 1635."[7] During much of his early student life, Owen devoted himself to study so hard that he gave only four hours per day for sleep. Though he gave recourse to his body through physical exercise, years later he would bear the pain of those early years.[8] Owen received his M.A. in 1635 at 19 years of age.[9] He then began studying for his B.D. (a seven year course[10]), but soon left Oxford in 1637 due to his "conscientious dislike of a new body of statutes, drawn up for its government by Archbishop Laud."[11]

Though Owen had embraced Puritan doctrine, his soul was not at peace with God. In his 21st year, he went to hear the well-known Presbyterian Edmund Calamy preach, only to see an unknown preacher mount the pulpit.[12] It was through this unknown preacher's sermon on Matthew 8:26 that Owen received assurance of peace with God.[13]

Owen's first published work came in 1642 – *A Display of Arminianism*.[14] He was 26 years old. In 1643, he became pastor of a church in Fordham, Essex. In that same year his *The Duty of Pastors and People Distinguished* was published.

He was married in 1643 to Mary Rooke.[15] She bore him their first child, John, in 1644. She bore him 11 children, all of whom died prior to Owen's death.[16] In 1655 two of their children died in the plague.[17] In

---

[6] Toon, *God's Statesman*, 5. Cf. Thomson, *Owen*, 15, where he claims that entrance to Queen's at the age of 12 "...in the case of most youths would have been most injudiciously premature."

[7] Oliver, *Owen*, 13.

[8] Thomson, *Owen*, 15-16. Thomson adds, "Owen when he began to feel his iron frame required to pay the penalty of his youthful enthusiasm, was accustomed to declare that he would willingly part with all the learning he had accumulated by such means, if he might but recover the health which he had lost in the gaining of it." Cf. Thomson, *Owen*, 16. Trueman adds that Owen had "a growing reputation as a flautist, a long jumper, and a javelin thrower." Cf. Trueman, *John Owen*, 2.

[9] Oliver, *Owen*, 13 and Toon, *God's Statesman*, 6.

[10] Toon, *God's Statesman*, 6.

[11] Orme, *Owen*, 11.

[12] Oliver, *Owen*, 14. Cf. Orme, *Owen*, 19ff; Trueman, *John Owen*, 3.

[13] Toon, *God's Statesman*, 12, 13.

[14] Oliver, *Owen*, 14; Orme, *Owen*, 22; Trueman, *John Owen*, 3. For a chronological list of Owen's published works see Thomson, *Owen*, 163-6 and Toon, *God's Statesman*, 179-81. Toon has 1643 as the date of publication. Owen, *Works*, X:4 has 1642.

[15] Toon, *God's Statesman*, 17.

[16] Trueman, *John Owen*, 3.

[17] Toon, *God's Statesman*, 63.

January of 1676 she died and Owen remarried 18 months later. His second wife, Michel, "brought Dr. Owen a considerable fortune; which…made his condition easy, and even affluent, so that he was able to keep a carriage during his remaining years."[18]

On April 29, 1646, at the age of 30, John Owen "preached before the House of Commons in St Margaret's Church, Westminster…"[19] His sermon was from Acts 16:9 and titled *A Vision of Unchangeable Free Mercy.* He dealt with the Parliament's stewardship of the gospel. In this same year, Owen became "minister of the Gospel at Coggeshall."[20] Obadiah Sedgwick was Owen's immediate predecessor.[21] Sedgwick was member of the Westminster Assembly and moved to London in 1646. Toon reports that "as many as 2,000 people crowded into the church each Lord's Day to hear the young divine expound the Bible."[22] It was while here that Owen studied John Cotton's *Keyes of the Kingdom of Heaven* (1644) and embraced the Congregational way.[23] Soon after, Owen met Oliver Cromwell and was asked to serve as his chaplain in Ireland.[24]

In 1650, Cromwell became Chancellor of Oxford. Soon after that, Owen became Dean of Christ Church (1651)[25] and then Vice-Chancellor (1652).[26] He had bestowed upon him the D. D. on December 22, 1653.[27] Owen preferred not to use the title "Dr." and instead preferred to be known simply as John Owen.[28] During his service as Dean and Vice-Chancellor, Owen attempted many changes at Oxford, some of which were aimed at the lax morals among its students. Some of these attempted changes were instituted; others were not, such as academic dress.[29] He was a strong disciplinarian and a principled leader. His term as Vice-Chancellor ended in 1657 and his service as Dean ended in 1659.

In September of 1658, "representatives of Congregational churches throughout England and Wales began to arrive for a synod scheduled to begin on the 29th September at the Savoy Palace."[30] Owen served on the

---

[18] Thomson, *Owen*, 113.
[19] Toon, *God's Statesman*, 1, 19ff.
[20] Toon, *God's Statesman*, 25.
[21] Toon, *God's Statesman*, 25.
[22] Toon, *God's Statesman*, 26.
[23] Toon, *God's Statesman*, 27ff.; Trueman, *John Owen*, 3-4.
[24] Toon, *God's Statesman*, 36ff.; Trueman, *John Owen*, 4.
[25] Toon, *God's Statesman*, 47ff., esp. 53-63; Trueman, *John Owen*, 4.
[26] Toon, *God's Statesman*, 63ff.; Trueman, *John Owen*, 4.
[27] Toon, *God's Statesman*, 73.
[28] Toon, *God's Statesman*, 73.
[29] Toon, *God's Statesman*, 73, 74, 79.
[30] Toon, *God's Statesman*, 103; Trueman, *John Owen*, 4.

six-man committee which prepared a draft of a declaration of faith and church order. Serving with Owen were Thomas Goodwin, Philip Nye, William Bridge, William Greenhill, and Joseph Caryl.[31] Owen wrote the preface. Toon says that *The Savoy Declaration* was thoroughly Calvinistic, as its parent document *The Westminster Confession of Faith*, but "with perhaps a stronger emphasis on federal theology…"[32] Its major departure from the WCF was its views on the civil magistrate and ecclesiology. Its Congregational ecclesiology was highly influenced by John Cotton's *The Keyes of The Kingdom of Heaven* (1644).[33]

In 1661, Owen's *Theologoumena Pantodapa* (i.e., *BTO*) was published. According to Toon:

> …[Owen] outlined the nature, rise and progress of "true" theology from the time of Adam to the fully developed and revealed theology of the New Testament. He argued that the true statement of Biblical theology was to be found in Calvinistic orthodoxy. This work, …was highly valued in Dissenting Academies in the eighteenth century…[34]

Carl Trueman calls this "a major Latin work of covenant theology…"[35]

Owen's *Exposition of the Epistle to the Hebrews* was published in four volumes. The first was published in 1668 and the last posthumously in 1684. According to Chalmers, he who masters this work will be "very little short…of being an erudite and accomplished theologian."[36] It was, without doubt, his greatest exegetical work. According to Trueman, "As Henry Knapp has demonstrated in impressive detail, …Owen's commentary on Hebrews is a masterpiece of linguistics, textual exegesis, interaction with exegetical traditions, and theological synthesis."[37]

In 1773, Joseph Caryl died and his church merged with John Owen's smaller Congregational church at Leadenhall Street.[38] During Owen's latter years he had three assistants, the last being David Clarkson who also became pastor of the church upon Owen's death in 1683.[39]

---

[31] Toon, *God's Statesman*, 103-04.
[32] Toon, *God's Statesman*, 104.
[33] Toon, *God's Statesman*, 105; Trueman, *John Owen*, 3.
[34] Toon, *God's Statesman*, 56. We will analyze this work in subsequent sections of this dissertation.
[35] Trueman, *John Owen*, 5.
[36] As quoted in Thomson, *Owen*, 102. Cf. Owen, *Works*, XVII:XI.
[37] Trueman, *John Owen*, 10.
[38] Toon, *God's Statesman*, 151.
[39] Toon, *God's Statesman*, 155-56.

## The Legacy of John Owen

John Owen is known as the 'Prince of the Puritans.' J. I. Packer goes so far as to say that Owen is by common consent

> the greatest among Puritan theologians. For solidity, profundity, massiveness and majesty in exhibiting from Scripture God's ways with sinful mankind there is no one to touch him. ...In his own day he was seen as England's foremost bastion and champion of Reformed evangelical orthodoxy...[40]

Thomson pays this tribute, saying, "...when the fame of Owen's learning and intellectual power had spread far and wide, ...even foreign divines are said to have studied our language in order that they might read his works..."[41] Orme says:

> OWEN, GOODWIN, BAXTER and HOWE, were the four leading men among the non-conformist worthies. But however each of the others might excel the subject of this memoir, in some one or more particulars; yet there is little danger of mistake in assigning the foremost place to Dr. Owen. As a theologian, in learning, and in profound, discriminating, and accurate views of the system of revealed truth, he was superior to them all; and we do not know that any theologian has since arisen in the Christian Church who ought to bear away the palm from JOHN OWEN.[42]

Thomson agrees, saying:

> Who among all the Puritans was the most remarkable for his intimate and profound acquaintance with the truths of revelation? Who could shed the greatest amount of light upon a selected portion of the Word of God, discovering its hidden riches, unfolding its connections and harmonies, and bringing the most abstruse doctrines of revelation to bear upon the conduct and the life? Who was the 'interpreter, one amongst a thousand?' Or let other excellencies that we are about to specify be chosen as the standard, and will not the name of John Owen, in this case, obtain, an unhesitating and unanimous suffrage?[43]

---

[40] J. I. Packer, *A Quest for Godliness: The Puritan Vision of the Christian Life* (Wheaton, IL: Crossway Books, 1990), 81.

[41] Thomson, *Owen*, 26.

[42] Orme, *Owen*, 226.

[43] Thomson, *Owen*, 130-31.

Packer adds:

> [Owen] was one of the greatest of English theologians. In an age of
> giants, he overtopped them all. C.H. Spurgeon called him the prince of
> divines. He is hardly known today, and we are the poorer for our
> ignorance.[44]

Since Packer made the statement above there has been a surge of
discussion concerning Owen's theology.[45] He is no longer the obscure
figure he once was – known and loved by precious few. Esteem for him
is growing in various circles through reprints of his works, publications
of some of his writings in modern English, articles, dissertations, and
monographs. The man whom Spurgeon called the prince of divines is
becoming better and more widely known – and rightly so. Carl Trueman
gives Owen this tribute, "...no one should dispute his right to be taken
seriously as one of early modern England's most articulate and
thoughtful theological voices."[46] He is known not only as a great
theologian (one of the greatest of all-time), but as a Trinitarian, Christ-
centered theologian.[47]

Can Owen also be labeled a federal theologian? And if so, was he
unique in his day or did he have Reformed orthodox comrades who were
doing similar work? In order to properly answer these crucial questions
we must investigate theological methodology in Owen's day and then
investigate Owen himself. To these questions we now turn our attention.

---

[44] Packer, *Quest for Godliness*, 191.

[45] See the bibliography at the end of this dissertation.

[46] Trueman, *John Owen*, 128.

[47] Cf. the discussions in Richard Daniels, *The Christology of John Owen* (Grand
Rapids: Reformation Heritage Books, 2004), 5; Kapic, *Communion with God*, 31; and
Carl R. Trueman, *The Claims of Truth: John Owen's Trinitarian Theology* (Carlisle,
Cumbria, UK: Paternoster Press, 1998) and Trueman, *John Owen* in their entirety.
Daniels says, "He is thoroughly Trinitarian in his thinking, convinced that the Triune God
has chosen to deal with man by way of a mediator. Whether the action is directed from
God to us or from us to God, Christ is the focus. True Trinitarian thinking, it would seem,
must be Christocentric, and Christocentric thinking, Trinitarian. Owen's emphasis upon
the Holy Spirit, as great as that was, was primarily for what the Spirit accomplishes: the
restoration and transformation of fallen man through the knowledge of God in Christ.
This is the "hinge" of Owenian thought, as Owen believed it was the sum and substance
of all biblical religion." Daniels, *Christology*, 5-6. Cf. also Toon, *God's Statesman*, 166,
where Toon claims that Owen grew over the years in his conviction that Christ was "[t]he
sum, substance and centre of the Old and New Testaments..."

# CHAPTER SIX

# JOHN OWEN IN HISTORICAL-THEOLOGICAL
# CONTEXT: SEVENTEENTH-CENTURY REFORMED
# ORTHODOXY, JOHN OWEN, AND FEDERAL
# THEOLOGY

## Introduction

Much has been written in the last few decades concerning the reassessment or reappraisal of seventeenth-century Reformed orthodoxy.[1] Older scholarship viewed the seventeenth century as a downward movement, increasingly tending toward rationalism and proof-texting, driven by a central-dogma (i.e., the decree of predestination), highly Aristotelian in the worst sense, and away from the supposedly more biblical, Christocentric methodology of the sixteenth-century Reformers.[2] For instance, while tracing the history of New Testament theology, George Eldon Ladd says:

> The gains in the historical study of the Bible made by the reformers were soon lost in the post-Reformation period, and the Bible was once again used uncritically and unhistorically to support orthodox doctrine. The Bible was viewed not only as a book free from error and contradiction but also without development or progress. The entire Bible was looked upon as possessing one level of theological value.

---

[1] Cf., for example, Carl R. Trueman and R. Scott Clark, editors, *Protestant Scholasticism: Essays in Reassessment* (Carlisle, Cumbria, UK: Paternoster Press, 1999); Willem J. van Asselt and Eef Dekker, editors., *Reformation and Scholasticism: An Ecumental Enterprise* (Grand Rapids: Baker Academic, 2001); Richard A. Muller, *Post-Reformation Reformed Dogmatics*, 4 volumes (Grand Rapids: Baker Academic, 2003), which will be referenced as *PRRD* from here on out; Richard A. Muller, "The Myth of "Decretal Theology"," *CTJ*, 30 (1995): 159-67; Richard A. Muller, "Calvin and the "Calvinists": Assessing Continuities and Discontinuities Between the Reformation and Orthodoxy," *CTJ* 30 (1995): 345-75 [Part One] and 31 (1996): 125-60 [Part Two].

[2] Cf. Rehnman, *Divine Discourse*; Kapic, *Communion with God*; Trueman, *John Owen*; and Trueman, *Claims of Truth* for discussions concerning these claims as they relate to Owen.

History was completely lost in dogma, and philology became a branch of dogmatics.[3]

A contemporary historical theologian who adheres to this older position is Alister E. McGrath. In a chapter entitled, 'Protestant Orthodoxy,' McGrath paints this dismal picture for us:

It seems to be a general feature of the history of Christian thought, that a period of genuine creativity is immediately followed by a petrification and scholasticism, as the insights of a pioneering thinker or group of thinkers are embodied in formulae or confessions. (The term *Confession* is particularly applied to Protestant professions of faith of the sixteenth and seventeenth centuries, such as the Augsburg Confession (1530)). For many critics of Orthodoxy, particularly within Pietistic circles, Orthodoxy merely guarded the ashes of the Reformation, rather than tending its flame. The period of Orthodoxy between the first phase of the Reformation and the Enlightenment is characterized by its *confessionalism*, which effectively replaced the dynamism of the first phase of the Reformation with a static understanding of the nature of theology. It was this tendency which Alexander Schweizer (1808-88) criticized in his famous remark: 'Once the fathers confessed their faith–today most Christians just believe their confessions'.[4]

---

[3] Ladd, *A Theology of the New Testament*, 2. Cf. also, for example, Alister E. McGrath, *A Life of John Calvin* (Grand Rapids: Baker Book House, 1990), 202-18 (esp. 212, n. 46 where he acknowledges dependence upon Brian Armstrong) and *Reformation Thought*, 130ff. Older advocates of this view from the twentieth century include Brian H. Armstrong, *Calvinism and the Amyraut Heresy: Protestant Scholasticism and Humanism in Seventeenth Century France* (Madison: University of Wisconsin Press, 1969) and R. T. Kendall, *Calvin and English Calvinism*. Influential nineteenth- and early twentieth-century advocates include Alexander Schweizer, Heinrich Heppe, Paul Althaus, and Hans Emil Weber (Cf. Muller, "Calvin and the "Calvinists"," I:345-46, notes 1-4 for bibliographic information and Muller, "Calvin and the "Calvinists"", II:147-48 for discussion about their "tendentious and anachronistic readings of the thought of the Reformers and the Protestant orthodox...").

[4] Alister E. McGrath, "Protestant Orthodoxy" in Gillian R. Evans, Alister E. McGrath, and Allan D. Galloway, editors, *The Science of Theology* (Grand Rapids: Eerdmans Publishing Co., 1986), 151. Absent from McGrath's discussion of Protestant orthodoxy is a meaningful level of discussion of and interaction with primary sources. Even when he refers to a primary source, it is not properly referenced; it's merely quoted

An older scholar who adheres to this view of scholasticism is Charles S. McCoy. For instance, McCoy says of the Reformed scholastics, "Starting with the Eternal Decree of predestination, the Reformed scholastics deduced their theological systems."[5]

This view has been vigorously and critically reassessed. The conclusions stemming from this reassessment (which we will note below), in the mind of this researcher, are cogent and compelling because much better-researched. They rely on primary source documents, not anachronistic revisionism. We agree with Richard A. Muller, where he says, "...we are dealing here with a 'modern aversion to scholasticism' rather than with a balanced historical assessment."[6] The more recent research takes into consideration the broader issues of the various levels of context which must be understood before interpreting historical documents. These levels of context include the educational background of each author, the educational curriculum of the schools and universities, and the impact of the Renaissance and Reformation upon the scholastic method.[7] For these reasons, we agree with the validity of these conclusions and will work within their historical-interpretive model. But what does this reassessment involve and what are its conclusions? To this we turn our attention.

---

as proof with no bibliographic information. The "For Further Reading" list at the end of the chapter, interestingly enough, contains the titles of mostly secondary sources. The one apparent exception is Heppe's *Reformed Dogmatics*, but even that is merely a collection of various writings of sixteenth- and seventeenth-century authors and tainted with Heppe's faulty view of Beza (cf. van Asselt and Dekker, "Introduction" in van Asselt and Eef Dekker, editors, *Reformation and Scholasticism*, 17-18). McGrath gives the appearance of rehashing the pronouncements of secondary sources and using primary sources in a simplistic, proof-texting fashion. Commenting on McGrath's essay, Muller, *PRRD*, I:45, n. 24, says, "...it appears to rest entirely on secondary sources." The same view of Protestant Scholasticism can be seen in McGrath's *Reformation Thought*, 129-31.

   [5] Charles S. McCoy, "Johannes Cocceius: Federal Theologian" in *SJT* 16 (1963): 366. Cf. Willem J. van Asselt, "The Fundamental Meaning of Theology: Archetypal and Ectypal Theology in Seventeenth-Century Reformed Thought" in *WTJ* 64 (2002): 319-20.

   [6] Muller, "Calvin and the "Calvinists"," II:149.

   [7] Muller, "Calvin and the "Calvinists"," II:159.

## The Reassessment[8] of Protestant Scholasticism:
## The "Muller"[9] Thesis

- **Introduction: "Old" and "New" School Views of Protestant Scholasticism**

This reassessment claims that older scholarship was simply wrong on several counts (see below) and that not only was there a large degree of theological continuity between the sixteenth- and seventeen-century Reformed (and Lutheran) theologians, there was a degree of methodological discontinuity[10] and, though complex,[11] healthy development as well. Following Richard A. Muller, a new breed of scholars have emerged, seeking to correct decades and decades of bad press hurled at Protestant scholasticism from various fronts. Whereas the older scholarship accused Protestant scholasticism as being blindly committed to Aristotelianism, a presupposed central-dogma (i.e., the decree of predestination), and to careless proof-texting, the newer scholarship has gone *ad fontes* and has viewed them in light of their historical, theological, philosophical, and cultural contexts.[12] The more recent scholarship has come away with a very different, positive reading. Martin I. Klauber reduces Muller's thesis to the following:

> He argues that although the theologians of the post-Reformation period used a scholastic methodology to clarify Reformed theological system they remain in essential agreement with the first generation of Reformed thought in content.[13]

The connection with the past, according to Muller and his comrades, actually goes farther back than the Reformers. Just as the Reformers

---

[8] For a brief justification for reassessment, see Carl R. Trueman and R. Scott Clark, "Introduction" in Trueman and Clark, editors, *Protestant Scholasticism*, xi-iii.

[9] Muller is in quotes because he would be the first to say that he did not invent or discover this thesis. Cf. Trueman and Clark, "Introduction" in Trueman and Clark, editors, *Protestant Scholasticism*, xiii-xiv. For a brief presentation of the "Muller" thesis see Richard A. Muller, "Orthodoxy, Reformed" in *ERF*, 265-69.

[10] Muller, *PRRD*, I:46; Muller, "Calvin and the "Calvinists"," I:366.

[11] Muller, *PRRD*, I:51; Muller, "Calvin and the "Calvinists"," I:366 and "Calvin and the "Calvinists"," II:136.

[12] Cf. especially Trueman and Clark, editors, *Protestant Scholasticism*, van Asselt and Eef Dekker, editors, *Reformation and Scholasticism*, and Muller, *PRRD*.

[13] Martin I. Klauber, "Continuity and Discontinuity in Post-Reformation Reformed Theology: An Evaluation of the Muller Thesis," *JETS* 33/4 (December 1990): 467.

were connected methodologically and theologically with what preceded them, though not monolithically, so with the post-Reformation scholastics. In fact, Muller's thesis is actually the fruit of the previous studies of contemporary Reformation scholars applied to the post-Reformation scholastic era. Trueman and Clark acknowledge this, when they say:

> [Muller] ...has extended and applied to the field of Reformed orthodoxy the insights scholars such as [David C.] Steinmetz and [Heiko A.] Oberman have brought to Reformation studies. He has thus refused to judge orthodoxy by anachronistic criteria or by the theology of one or two randomly selected individuals, and has emphasized the importance of understanding Reformed theology as part of an ongoing Western tradition which extends back through the Middle Ages to the early church. The theologies of the Reformation and the post-Reformation era are neither wholly continuous nor wholly discontinuous with the past – they are, rather, changes in direction within the wider Augustinian, anti-Pelagian tradition of Western theology. As such the era of orthodoxy must not be set over against its past but must be studied in the context of its medieval and Reformation roots.[14]

One branch of the older position is labeled the discontinuity theory by van Asselt and Dekker in their introduction to *Reformation and Scholasticism*.[15] This theory claims that "scholastic orthodoxy [is] a fatal deviation from the Reformation."[16] Muller describes this theory as advocating that Reformed orthodoxy was "an undifferentiated, doctrinaire, Aristotelian, metaphysical monolith at odds with the heritage of the Reformation."[17] A slavish dependency upon Aristotelianism, among other things, is a hallmark of this older theory. W. G. T. Shedd, for instance, claims, "In Baxter and Owen, both of whom were also very diligent students of the Schoolmen, we perceive more of the influence of

---

[14] Trueman and Clark, "Introduction" in *Protestant Scholasticism*, xiv.

[15] van Asselt and Dekker, "Introduction" in *Reformation and Scholasticism*, 29. There are actually several older theories (cf. Muller, "Calvin and the "Calvinists"," *CTJ* 30 (1995): I:346ff. for such theories and their late nineteenth- and early twentieth-century origins and subsequent adaptations by more modern historians and theologians.).

[16] van Asselt and Dekker, "Introduction" in *Reformation and Scholasticism*, 29. Cf. the words of Ladd and McGrath above.

[17] Muller, "The Problem of Protestant Scholasticism – A Review and Definition" in van Asselt and Dekker, editors, *Reformation and Scholasticism*, 45.

the Aristotelian system."[18] Shedd adds, "This body of divinity [i.e., English theology of the seventeenth century], which without question is the most profound that the English mind has originated, owes its systematic form and structure to the Grecian intellectual methods."[19]

Alister McGrath, as stated above, represents the assessment of the older scholarship. Muller quotes him:

> The starting point of theology thus came to be general principles, not a specific historic event. The contrast with Calvin will be clear... Calvin focused on the specific historical phenomenon of Jesus Christ and moved out to explore its implications... By contrast, Beza began from general principles and proceeded to deduce their consequences for Christian theology.[20]

Muller then points his readers to several recent studies of Beza which have proven McGrath's claims as unfounded.[21] Carl Trueman adds:

> It is perhaps ironic that one of the principle pieces of evidence used by advocates of the 'Calvin against the Calvinist' thesis are Beza's *Tabula Praedestinationis* and Perkin's [*sic*] adaptation of this in *A Golden Chaine*. These are cited as examples of how predestination comes to dominate Reformed theology and reflect its nature as a predestinarian deductive system. However, as Barth so clearly understood, the tables were intended to be read from the bottom up rather than the top down, and so they are anything but deductive; further, and more important for this section, Perkins's [*sic*] addition of a central column to Beza's much sparser original, a column which outlines the work of Christ and connecting the history of Christ to the order of salvation, clearly

---

[18] William G. T. Shedd, *History of Christian Doctrine*, I (Minneapolis: Klock & Klock, 1889, re. 1978), 92. In note 2 on pages 92-93, Shedd quotes Baxter's comments about his dependence upon Aquinas, Scotus, Durandus, Occam, and their disciples. There is no such reference for Owen. Just what *the Aristotelian system* is Shedd does not tell us.

[19] Shedd, *History of Christian Doctrine*, I:92-93.

[20] Muller, "The Problem of Protestant Scholasticism – A Review and Definition" in *Reformation and Scholasticism*, 46. Muller is quoting McGrath from *Reformation Thought*, 129-30. Muller claims that "the definition derives, without citation but with clear verbal reliance, from Brian G. Armstrong, *Calvinism and the Amyraut Heresy: Protestant Scholasticism and Humanism in Seventeenth Century France* (Madison: University of Wisconsin Press, 1969), 32." In Muller, "The Problem of Protestant Scholasticism – A Review and Definition" in *Reformation and Scholasticism*, 46, n. 3, he says of McGrath, "The form taken in Alister McGrath's *Reformation Thought* is illustrative of his immersion ...in twenty-five year old secondary sources..."

[21] Muller, "The Problem of Protestant Scholasticism – A Review and Definition" in *Reformation and Scholasticism*, 47, n. 5.

indicates the concern of the Reformed Orthodox to do justice to Christology and historical narrative flow in their formulation of salvation. What they refuse to do is to abandon either ontology or economy for the sake of the other.[22]

A form of the discontinuity theory is seen in what may be called the "decretal theology" theory, or as Muller puts it, "abstract decretalism."[23] It asserts that Reformed theology went from Calvin (and Christ) through Beza to predestination and the decree of God as the starting point of theology from which all else is deduced. In other words, Reformed theology went from a Christocentric (viewed positively) to a theocentric (viewed negatively) starting point. Or as McGrath puts it:

> Calvin's approach appears to be analytic and inductive – i.e., proceeding from the concrete event of redemption in Christ to an exploration of its implications (such as predestination and election) – and is thus able to remain profoundly Christocentric: Orthodoxy, by contrast, took its starting point in the intratrinitarian decision to redeem or damn – and thus assumed a strongly theocentric cast.
>
> The fact that predestination is the central dogma of Reformed Orthodoxy thus reflects the theological method employed by the theologians of that school...[24]

Muller confronts the decretal theology theory, among other places,[25] in his "The Myth of "Decretal Theology"" referenced above.[26] In section two of that article, "Peeling the Historical Onion," Muller peels the layers of the historical onion of decretal theology and denies the validity of each. His assertions are as follows: "*Predestination is not the starting*

---

[22] Trueman, *John Owen*, 87, n. 76. At the end of the footnote Trueman adds, "For Barth's views, see *CD* 2.2, 78; contrast this with the misreading of the Perkins' table offered by James B Torrance, 'Strengths and Weaknesses of the Westminster Theology' in Alasdair I C Heron, *The Westminster Confession in the Church Today* (Edinburgh: St Andrew Press, 1982), 40—54."

[23] Muller, "The Myth of "Decretal Theology"," 159-67.

[24] McGrath, "Protestant Orthodoxy" in *The Science of Theology*, 158.

[25] Cf. especially Richard A. Muller, "The Use and Abuse of a Document: Beza's *Tabula praedestinationis*, the Bolsec Controvesy, and the Origins of Reformed Orthodoxy" in Trueman and Clark, editors, *Protestant Scholasticism*, 33-61.

[26] This article is not a technical defense of Muller's thesis. It occurs in the "*Scholia*: Notes and Comments for the Minister" section of *CTJ* and, therefore, does not intend to be a thoroughly argued and documented defense of the thesis. The article, however, does reflect the conclusions of the thesis and assumes its historical-theological research and analysis.

*point of the system.*"[27] "*The Reformed system is biblical and historical, not purely deductive.*"[28] "*Later Reformed theology did not distort the heritage of the Reformation.*"[29] "*Christ is not reduced to a mere means to God's end.*"[30] "*The assertion of salvation by grace alone ought not to be seen as a problem.*"[31] The use of the Aristotelian causality model (i.e., efficient cause, formal cause, material cause, and final cause) "is a purely heuristic device, a form of explanation intended not to indicate any sort of determinism …"[32] "*The eternal decree does not, therefore, abolish history – it makes history possible.*"[33] "*The older Reformed theology did not ignore the work of God in history.*"[34] "*The distinction between the eternal decree and its execution is just that: a distinction, not a disjunction or a separation.*"[35] "*The decree does not remove free choice, responsibility, and incentive. It makes them possible.*"[36]

What many scholars are concluding is that "…Protestant scholasticism was an institutional theology, confessionally in continuity with the insights of the Reformers and doctrinally in continuity with the Christian tradition as a whole."[37] In the words of Muller himself:

> The contribution of the orthodox or scholastic theologians to the history of Protestantism, then, was the creation of an institutional theology, confessionally in continuity with the Reformation and

---

[27] Muller, "The Myth of "Decretal Theology"," 162. For an example of one who views scholasticism as a theology deduced from predestination, cf. McCoy, "Johannes Cocceius: Federal Theologian" in *SJT* 16 (1963): 360, where he says, "Whereas the scholastic system is based upon deduction from the doctrine of predestination, however, the teaching which Cocceius sets forth is given structure by the concept of the covenant between God and man and is developed by exegesis."

[28] Muller, "The Myth of "Decretal Theology"," 162.

[29] Muller, "The Myth of "Decretal Theology"," 163.

[30] Muller, "The Myth of "Decretal Theology"," 163.

[31] Muller, "The Myth of "Decretal Theology"," 164.

[32] Muller, "The Myth of "Decretal Theology"," 164.

[33] Muller, "The Myth of "Decretal Theology"," 165.

[34] Muller, "The Myth of "Decretal Theology"," 165. As we will see, the federal theology of the seventeenth century clearly did not ignore God's work in history. This will be especially clear in Owen's *BTO*.

[35] Muller, "The Myth of "Decretal Theology"," 166.

[36] Muller, "The Myth of "Decretal Theology"," 166.

[37] Willem J. van Asselt, "Cocceius Anti-Scholasticus?" in van Asselt and Eef Dekker, editors, *Reformation and Scholasticism*, 231.

doctrinally, in the sense of the larger system of doctrine, in continuity with the great tradition of the church.[38]

After examining the sources of Reformed orthodox theology, Muller concludes elsewhere:

> An examination of the sources of Reformed orthodoxy (and, we might add, of Protestant orthodoxy in general) easily and clearly sets aside the stereotypes of this theology. At the very least, the standard claims about central dogmas, legalism, rationalism and proof-texting biblicism fail because they are simplistic. How simple and, indeed, simple- minded it would be to deduce a theology from one principle, and by contrast, how complex it in fact is to construct that theology out of exegetical arguments nuanced by extensive knowledge of the biblical and cognate languages, attention to the exegetical tradition and acknowledgment of the significance of creeds, confessions and the wealth of the tradition. How equally simple it would be to give one's theology over to an "ism"–whether legalism, rationalism or Aristotelianism; and by contrast how complex it is in fact to balance out a wide variety of issues, sub-themes and ancillary sources, to develop a critical perspective on the philosophical tradition that modifies it at crucial points, and to retain the rationality of exposition without ever allowing reason to have principal status. Would that the modern theologies that criticize this older orthodoxy were able to match its expertise in the many theological disciplines! Would that they were able to understand (and master) as clearly and well the hierarchy of sources, with Scripture as ultimate norm, followed by ecumenical creeds, churchly confessions, the wealth of the tradition, and the various ancillary disciplines in a descending order of authority![39]

Van Asselt and Dekker offer 10 characteristics of the newer type of research on Protestant scholasticism:

---

[38] Muller, *PRRD*, I:28; cf. Richard A. Muller, "Sources of Reformed Orthodoxy: The Symmetrical Unity of Exegesis and Synthesis" in Michael S. Horton, editor, *A Confessing Theology for Postmodern Times* (Wheaton, IL: Crossway Books, 2000), 52, where he says, "…in the tradition of the Reformers, these successor theologians took the catholicity of Protestantism seriously, claimed for themselves and their churches the best of the Christian tradition, and appropriated it critically, for the clarification and for the defense of the faith."

[39] Muller, "Sources of Reformed Orthodoxy," 57.

1.  Scholasticism is a scientific method of research and teaching, and does as such not have a doctrinal content, neither does it have reason as its foundation.
2.  There is a continuity between the Medieval, Reformation and Post-reformation Era (which is of course, not to deny that there are many differences).
3.  "Aristotelianism" is exceedingly problematic when applied with a broad brush, and should rather be avoided if used unspecified.
4.  Syllogisms are used by any person in a reasoning process (but not always consciously and explicitly), and are therefore, in themselves, not a sign of anything beyond that reasoning process, let alone of Aristotelianism.
5.  The scornful way in which Luther and Calvin treated scholasticism is not to be taken as an overall hermeneutical principle to read scholasticism.
6.  Let the scholastics themselves define scholasticism.
7.  Protestant scholasticism does not proceed by abstracting proof texts out of Scripture, nor does Medieval scholasticism avoid or neglect Scripture and scriptural language.
8.  Christian faith, and therefore, Christian theology, has its own view of life, its own frame of thought and is not to be identified with any philosophical system.
9.  Parts of that unique Christian frame of thought are the contents of will and contingency.
10. The relative placement of a *locus* in a system of doctrine does not as such change its content.[40]

*   **Scholasticism Defined**

Scholasticism refers to an academic style and method of discourse[41] or even "a form of scientific practice"[42] and not a theology or a particular philosophical school. Muller, while describing Protestant scholasticism, says:

> Scholasticism is a methodological approach to theological system which achieves precision of definition through analysis of doctrinal *loci*

---

[40] van Asselt and Dekker, "Introduction," 39.
[41] Muller, *PRRD*, I:30; van Asselt and Dekker, "Introduction," 13-14; and Trueman and Clark, "Introduction," xiv-xv.
[42] van Asselt and Dekker, "Introduction," 13.

in terms of scripture, previous definition (the tradition), and contemporary debate.[43]

The work of these theologians is well described by the two terms "scholastic" and "orthodox." The former term refers primarily to method, the latter, primarily to dogmatic or doctrinal intention. In the late sixteenth and the seventeenth centuries, both Reformed and Lutheran theologians adopted a highly technical and logical approach to theological system, according to which each theological topic or *locus* was divided into its component parts, the parts analyzed and then defined in careful propositional form. In addition, this highly technical approach sought to achieve precise definition by debate with adversaries and by use of the Christian tradition as a whole in arguing its doctrines. The form of theological system was adapted to a didactical and polemical model that could move from biblical definition to traditional development of doctrine, to debate with doctrinal adversaries past and present, to theological resolution of the problem. This method is rightly called scholastic both in view of its roots in medieval scholasticism and in view of its intention to provide an adequate technical theology for schools—seminaries and universities. The goal of this method, the dogmatic or doctrinal intention of this theology, was to provide the church with "right teaching," literally, "orthodoxy."[44]

"[Scholastic] well describes the technical and academic side of this process of the institutionalization and professionalization of Protestant doctrine in the universities of the late sixteenth and seventeenth centuries."[45] It is important to remember that the scholasticism utilized by the Protestants was "influenced by both the Renaissance and the Reformation" and was practiced in "a context not at all identical with that of medieval scholasticism."[46] Scholasticism is not a philosophy or a theology; it is a method of discourse utilized by theologians and philosophers for several centuries.

---

[43] Richard A. Muller, *Christ and the Decree: Christology and Predestination in Reformed Theology from Calvin to Perkins* (Grand Rapids: Baker Book House, 1986, Second printing, November 1988), 11.

[44] Richard A. Muller, *Dictionary of Latin and Greek Theological Terms* (Grand Rapids: Baker Book House, 1985, Second printing, September 1986), 8; Muller, "Calvin and the "Calvinists"," I:367-73.

[45] Muller, *PRRD*, I:34.

[46] Muller, *PRRD*, I:30, 35.

- **Orthodoxy Defined**

Orthodox refers to those Protestant theologians who stood

> within the confessional framework of the Reformed churches and
> which [are] understood as conveying the "right teaching" of those
> churches, whether scholastic, catechetical, exegetical, or homiletical, as
> determined by the standards of the era. "Orthodox," in other words,
> functions as a historical denominator – and reference to the era of
> orthodoxy indicates the time of the institutionalization of the
> Reformation according to its confessional norms, namely the era
> extending roughly from the latter part of the sixteenth through the early
> eighteenth centuries.[47]

Trueman defines Reformed orthodoxy as:

> the tradition of Protestant thought which found its creedal expression
> on the continent in such documents as, among others, the *Belgic
> Confession*, the *Heidelberg Catechism* and the *Canons of Dordt*, and in
> Britain in the Westminster Assembly's *Confession of Faith and Larger
> and Shorter Catechisms*.[48]

Reformed orthodoxy is, then, one link in the chain "of the wider ongoing
Western tradition of theological and philosophical thought…"[49]

- **Conclusion**

The validity of this reassessment is gaining ground as more monographs,
dissertations, and journal articles are published which examine
seventeenth-century Reformed orthodoxy in its various contexts from
primary sources. Scholars are concluding (and I think correctly) that
Reformed orthodoxy was not a defection from the theology of the
sixteenth-century Reformers. Reformed scholasticism was the
continuance of a heuristic method (i.e., the scholastic method) utilized
for centuries (Muller argues from the twelfth through the seventeenth,
though not monolithically)[50] with its own nuances, yet in harmony and

---

[47] Muller, *PRRD*, I:30, 33-34; cf. also Muller, *Dictionary*, 8; Muller, *Christ and the Decree*, 12; and van Asselt and Dekker, "Introduction," 13.

[48] Trueman, *John Owen*, 6.

[49] Trueman, *John Owen*, 6.

[50] Muller, *PRRD*, I:35, 37.

general continuity with the wider, Western Christian theological tradition.[51]

## The Era of High Orthodoxy (ca. 1640-1685-1725)[52]

This era of Reformed orthodoxy, according to Muller,

> rests upon a confessional summation of the faith, has a somewhat sharper and more codified polemic against its doctrinal adversaries, and possesses a broader and more explicit grasp of the tradition, particularly of the contribution of the Middle Ages. Characteristic of the initial phase of this era are internal or intraconfessional controversies, such as the broader Amyraldian controversy and the debate over Cocceian federal theology as well as the vast expansion of debate with the Socinians over the doctrine of the Trinity. In this phase of the high orthodox period are found such authors as Johannes Cocceius, Samuel Maresius, Andreas Essenius, Gisbertus Voetius, Friedrich Spanheim the elder, Marcus Friedrich Wendelin, Franz Burman, Francis Turretin, Edward Leigh, Matthew Poole, John Owen, and Stephen Charnock.[53]

John Owen, as indicated by Muller, fits within this era of Reformed orthodoxy. The literature on Owen shows that he fits not simply chronologically, but methodologically and theologically.[54]

The era of high orthodoxy witnessed "changes in the style of dogmatics."[55] Muller says:

> The creativity of the high orthodox era was more in the way of nuance and elaboration – well illustrated in the development of covenant theology in the hands of Cocceius and his followers and in the detailed exposition of other trajectories in orthodoxy by such writers as Voetius, Turretin, and Mastricht.[56]

Muller continues:

> High orthodoxy, then, is the era of the full and final development of Protestant system prior to the great changes in philosophical and

---

[51] Trueman and R. Scott Clark, "Introduction," xiv.

[52] Muller, *PRRD*, I:31.

[53] Muller, *PRRD*, I:31-32.

[54] See the section below entitled "John Owen: Reformed Orthodox Theologian."

[55] Muller, *PRRD*, I:73; Muller, *Christ and the Decree*, 13.

[56] Muller, *PRRD*, I:75; Muller, *Christ and the Decree*, 13.

scientific perspective that would, in the eighteenth and nineteenth centuries, utterly recast theological system into new forms.[57]

This era was characterized by polemical works aimed at Roman Catholicism, Arminianism, and Socinianism, and was the high point of the systematic elaboration of Reformed theology prior to the onslaught of the Enlightenment and post-Enlightenment critical era.[58] According to Trueman, John Owen played a unique role in the high orthodox development of the doctrine of the covenant of redemption[59] and, as will be argued in the main section of this dissertation, he also played a key role in the development of federal theology (specifically in casting it in a more redemptive historical/linear/*historia salutis* model).

## The Theological Methodology of Reformed Orthodoxy

### • Introduction

We have noted that the method of the Reformed orthodox was scholastic. However, as also noted, it was not one and the same with medieval scholasticism, nor was it a form of post-Reformation Aristotelian rationalism. It was a "method of presentation"[60] which utilized *various weapons* and was *commonplace* in the theological schools of the day.[61] Muller comments on the Reformed scholastic method as follows:

> The fundamental characteristic of the approach to theology found in the system of a Reformed scholastic like Francis Turretin is a movement from a basic doctrinal question to a statement of the "state" of the controversy, to a resolution of the debate using the authorities and tools at hand, with Scripture standing as the foremost authority, followed by tradition (principally the fathers of the first five centuries), classical, and philosophical sources, and supported by rational argumentation concerning the right understanding of the various authorities. Thus, the Reformed scholastics — beginning in the time of the Reformation itself in the scholastic aspects of the theologies of Vermigli, Musculus, and Hyperius — certainly sought to formulate a logically or rationally defensible body of doctrine, but they sought also to formulate a body of

---

[57] Muller, *PRRD*, I:80.
[58] Cf. Trueman, *John Owen*, 7.
[59] Cf. Trueman, *John Owen*, 80-92 for a discussion of this.
[60] Klauber, "An Evaluation of the Muller Thesis," 471.
[61] Muller, "Calvin and the "Calvinists"," I:370.

doctrine defensible in the light of the best exegetical results of the time and in the light of the catholic tradition to which they laid claim. Rational argumentation never displaced exegetical interest — indeed, the most scholastic of seventeenth-century Protestant theologians would assume that the defensibility of their theology was grounded in its intimate relationship with exegesis.[62]

This assessment of Muller is fast becoming the assessment of many. The theological methodology of the Reformed orthodox was, in the first place, exegetical. In order to get a firmer grip on their methodology, we will examine it from the vantage point of *what it is not*–a hyper-syllogistic method; an Aristotelian, rationalistic method; a universal method–and *what it is*–a pre-critical method; an exegetically-based method; a redemptive-historically sensitive method; and a multi-sourced method. The last four mentioned methodological characteristics are especially visible in Owen's writings.

- **Not a Hyper-Syllogistic Method**

Their method was not reduced to syllogistic argumentation *ad nauseam*. In fact, Muller claims that "[f]ew of the orthodox or scholastic Protestants lapsed into constant or exclusive recourse to syllogism as a method of exposition."[63] Syllogistic argumentation was utilized, but mostly in polemic contexts and not as an exegetical tool. Logic–the science of necessary inference–was utilized by the Reformed orthodox in the drawing out of good and necessary conclusions from the text of Scripture,[64] but it was a servant and not lord of the interpreter. Muller says that "the drawing of logical conclusions appears as one of the final hermeneutical steps in the [Reformed orthodox exegetical] method..."[65]

- **Not an Aristotelian, Rationalistic Method**

The Protestant scholasticism of the post-Reformation era must be distinguished from rationalism. The Reformed orthodox did not place human reason above, or even equal to, divine revelation.[66] The place and

---

[62] Muller, "Calvin and the "Calvinists"," I:368.
[63] Muller, "Calvin and the "Calvinists"," I:369.
[64] Cf. Muller, *PRRD*, II:497-500 for a discussion of the use of logic in interpretation.
[65] Muller, *PRRD*, II:501.
[66] Cf. *WCF* 1:10 for confessional embodiment to this conviction.

function of reason was subordinate to the authority of Scripture. Reason was an instrument not an axiomatic principle.[67] The Protestant scholastics utilized a modified (or Christian) Aristotelianism "that had its beginnings in the thirteenth century."[68] Muller explains:

> It is important to recognize what this use entailed and what it did not. The Christian Aristotelianism of the Protestant orthodox drew on rules of logic and devices such as the fourfold causality in order to explain and develop their doctrinal formulae—and only seldom, if ever, to import a full-scale rational metaphysics or physics into their theology. Contrary to what is sometimes claimed, the fourfold causality (i.e., first, formal, material, and final causes) does not imply a particular metaphysic. Specifically, it is not by nature "deterministic." One can use the model to delineate the soteriological patterns of the eternal decree of God and its execution in time; one can also use the model to describe the sources and effects of human sinfulness and human moral conduct; or one can use the model to explain how a carpenter makes a table. The large-scale result of Christian Aristotelianism was not, in other words, a fundamentally Aristotelian Christianity: Aristotle would have disowned this hybrid philosophy with its infinite God who created the world out of nothing! There was, certainly, less imposition of rational metaphysics on theology in the seventeenth-century orthodox affirmations of divine eternity, omniscience, and immutability than there is in the twentieth-century claims of a changing God whose very being is in flux and who lacks foreknowledge of future contingency![69]

Van Asselt says, "[the] facile equation of Scholasticism and Aristotelianism is no longer tenable."[70]

- **Not a Universal Method**

As well, simply because an author utilized the scholastic method in some of his writings did not mean he used it in all of them. For instance, Muller offers Beza as an example.[71] Elsewhere, Muller says, "In the cases of Perkins, Ames, Voetius, and Baxter, works of piety and works

---

[67] Muller, "Calvin and the "Calvinists"," I:374.

[68] Muller, "Sources of Reformed Orthodoxy," 55. Cf. van Asselt, "The Fundamental Meaning of Theology," 322, where he says that the Reformed theology of the late sixteenth century (*i.e.*, Franciscus Junius) critically received the Christian tradition.

[69] Muller, "Sources of Reformed Orthodoxy," 55.

[70] van Asselt, "The Fundamental Meaning of Theology," 329, n. 42.

[71] Muller, "Calvin and the "Calvinists"," I:370.

of scholastic theology emanated from the same pens."[72] Muller goes on to say:

> ...there is no clear division between Protestant scholasticism and federal theology. Theologians who wrote works of piety that followed a "positive" or "catechetical" method also wrote more technical and academic works using the scholastic method – and many of the scholastic, as well as "positive" works were covenantal in their theology.[73]

This observation applies to Johannes Cocceius and John Owen. As we shall see, Owen utilized the scholastic method in some treaties and a more practical, pastoral approach in others. Both Cocceius and Owen utilized the federal model as well as the *loci* model. Also, within the body of Owen's *BTO*, we see him use the scholastic method but also ridicule it.[74] This obviously shows that Owen could use a method he fully realized was abused by others and that the scholastic method was just that–a method and not a theology.

- **A Pre-Critical Method**

The Reformed orthodox obviously predate the Enlightenment and the critical assault on the Holy Scriptures. The Enlightenment gave birth to, among other things, a rationalistic approach to the interpretation of Scripture. This can be seen, for instance, in the early developments of Biblical Theology, as noted above. Typical Enlightenment rationalism and anti-supernaturalism is evidenced in the following statements made by Benjamin Jowett, a Greek professor at Oxford in the mid-nineteenth century. David C. Steinmetz quotes Jowett and comments:

> Jowett argued that "Scripture has one meaning–the meaning which it had in the mind of the Prophet or Evangelist who first uttered or wrote, to the hearers or readers who first received it."[75] Scripture should be

---

[72] Muller, "Calvin and the "Calvinists"," II:145.

[73] Muller, "Calvin and the "Calvinists"," II:146.

[74] Cf. Rehnman, *Divine Discourse*, Chapter 4, "Faith and Reason," especially the sections "The Abuse of Reason in Theology" and "A Contextual Line of Explanation," 119-28 and the "Conclusion" to this dissertation.

[75] Benjamin Jowett, "On the Interpretation of Scripture," *Essays and Reviews*, 7th ed. (London: Longman, Green, Longman and Roberts, 1861), 378, quoted in David C. Steinmetz, "The Superiority of Pre-Critical Exegesis," *Theology Today* (April 1980): 27.

interpreted like any other book and the later accretions and venerated traditions surrounding its interpretation should, for the most part, either be brushed aside or severely discounted. "The true use of interpretation is to get rid of interpretation, and leave us alone in company with the author."[76]

Jowett obviously reduces meaning to the intent of the human author alone. In critical hermeneutical theory, there was no room whatsoever for the medieval concept of "double literal sense"[77] or for the Reformation and post-Reformation concepts of *sensus literalis* (literal sense), *analogia Scripturae* (analogy of Scripture), *analogia fidei* (analogy of faith), and *scopus Scripturae* (scope of Scripture).[78] In post-modern thought, man, the reader, is king of interpretation; in the modern/Enlightenment theory man, the author, was. In the Middle Ages, however, and in the Reformation and post-Reformation eras, though through differing hermeneutical principles, the meaning of Scripture was not determined by the human author's intent alone or the reader. Ultimately, the meaning of Scripture was determined by God, the author of Scripture.[79]

- **An Exegetically-Based Method**[80]

Though the Reformed orthodox were confessionally one in a historical sense (i.e., the *Belgic Confession*, the *Heidelberg Catechism*, the *Canons of Dordt*, and in Britain in the Westminster Assembly's *Confession of Faith and Larger and Shorter Catechisms*), this did not mean they viewed the exegetical task as complete and, therefore, unnecessary, nor that there was no room for disagreement over the exegesis of individual texts. Muller comments:

the biblicism of the seventeenth-century orthodox must not be read as an era of dogmatizing exegesis devoid of careful textual analysis and

---

[76] Steinmetz is quoting Jowett, "On the Interpretation of Scripture," 384. Cf. Steinmetz, "The Superiority of Pre-Critical Exegesis," 27.

[77] Steinmetz, "The Superiority of Pre-Critical Exegesis," 31.

[78] We will discuss these below.

[79] This, of course, does not imply that pre-critical exegesis always arrived at God's meaning of the text. We will tease this out below. Cf. Packer, *Quest for Godliness*, 98, for a brief discussion of the Puritans as pre-modern exegetes.

[80] Cf. Muller, "Sources of Reformed Orthodoxy," 46-48; Muller, *PRRD*, II:482ff; Packer, *Quest for Godliness*, 98; and Thomas D. Lea, "The Hermeneutics of the Puritans," *JETS* 39/2 (June 1996): 273.

devoid of any variety in interpretation among those of an orthodox confessional persuasion. Instead, the age ought to be viewed as the great age of Protestant linguistic study and Judaica, of the textual analysis that led to such monumental productions as the London Polyglot Bible. ...the Protestant orthodoxy must be recognized as producing highly varied and diverse exegetical works and commentaries, ranging from text-critical essays, to textual annotations, theological annotations, linguistic commentaries based on the study of cognate languages and Judaica, doctrinal and homiletical commentaries, and, indeed, all manner of permutations and combinations of these several types of effort.[81]

Biblical exegesis, in fact, experienced a revival of sorts within the Reformed orthodox of the seventeenth century. Muller says:

Contrary to much of the "received wisdom" concerning the seventeenth century, the era of orthodoxy was a time of great exegetical, textual, and linguistic development in Protestantism–and, indeed, it was the orthodox exegetes who were responsible for the major monuments to biblical scholarship.[82]

Carl R. Trueman says, "...the seventeenth century witnessed a remarkable flourishing of linguistic and exegetical studies, driven by both the positive and the polemical exigencies of Protestantism's commitment to scripture, in the original languages, as being the very Word – and words – of God."[83] Trueman continues elsewhere:

A high view of the authority and integrity of the biblical text as God's word written was [a] major factor in fuelling the development of careful attention both to the biblical languages and other cognate tongues, and to issues of textual history and criticism. The idea that the seventeenth-century Reformed were interested neither in careful exegesis nor in the literary and linguistic contexts of the Bible is simply untrue. Indeed, the linguistic and exegetical work of this century was far more elaborate than that which had marked the earlier Reformation. ...the exegesis of the Reformed Orthodox is far from the dogmatically-driven Procusteanism [*sic*] of popular mythology.[84]

---

[81] Muller, "Calvin and the "Calvinists"," II:132-33.
[82] Muller, "Sources of Reformed Orthodoxy," 46.
[83] Trueman, *John Owen*, 8-9.
[84] Trueman, *John Owen*, 37; Cf. Muller, *PRRD*, II:482ff. for a fascinating discussion of the practice of exegesis among the Reformed orthodox.

- **A Redemptive-Historically Sensitive Method**

Not only were the Reformed orthodox exegetically driven, their hermeneutic was a whole-Bible hermeneutic, evidenced in such concepts as their highly nuanced view of *sensus literalis* (literal sense), *analogia Scripturae* (analogy of Scripture), *analogia fidei* (analogy of faith), and *scopus Scripturae* (scope of Scripture).[85] It is of vital importance to understand the nuances involved with these concepts in order to properly understand the Reformed orthodox and John Owen, in particular.

**1. *Sensus literalis*.** *Sensus literalis* (literal sense) was a complex idea for the Reformed orthodox. It is defined by Muller as follows:

> The fundamental literal or grammatical sense of the text of Scripture, distinguished into (1) *sensus literalis simplex*, the simple literal sense, which lies immediately in the grammar and the meaning of the individual words, and (2) *sensus literalis compositus*, the constructed or compound literal sense, which is inferred from the Scripture as a whole or from individual clear, and therefore normative, passages of Scripture when the simple literal sense of the text in question seems to violate either the *articuli fidei* [articles of faith or Christian doctrine]... or the *praecepta caritatis* [precepts of love or Christian ethics]...[86]

This definition is important historically for at least two reasons: (1) it was an implicit denial of the medieval quadriga (i.e., fourfold pattern of meaning: literal or historical, tropological or moral, allegorical or doctrinal, and anagogical or ultimate/eschatological[87]); and (2) it was a safeguard against the rationalistic hyper-literalism of Socinianism, which was used to deny crucial elements of the historic, Western Christian doctrine of God. The quadriga was a hermeneutical paradigm utilized

---

[85] Packer lists six governing principles of interpretation for the English Puritans: 1. Interpret Scripture *literally and grammatically*. 2. Interpret Scripture *consistently and harmonistically*. 3. Interpret Scripture *doctrinally and theocentrically*. 4. Interpret Scripture *christologically and evangelically*. 5. Interpret Scripture *experimentally and practically*. 6. Interpret Scripture *with a faithful and realistic application*. Cf. Packer, *Quest for Godliness*, 101-05. Cf. Barry Howson, "The Puritan Hermeneutics of John Owen: A Recommendation," *WTJ* 63 (2001): 354-57.

[86] Muller, *Dictionary*, 279. Muller discusses the literal sense in depth in *PRRD*, II:469-82.

[87] Cf. Muller, *Dictionary*, 254-55; Muller, *PRRD*, II:469ff.; and Steinmetz, "The Superiority of Pre-Critical Exegesis," 30ff.

since the time of John Cassian[88] that was replaced by the Reformers, and especially the post-Reformation Reformed orthodox, with a simpler approach, though still complex. Though they argued that each text had one, literal sense, they also saw "several levels of meaning"[89] or "diverse senses"[90] which belonged "to the single intention of the Spirit."[91] If the words of the text cannot stand on their own without contradicting some clear teaching of Scripture, then the intent of the author (ultimately God) was to go beyond the words themselves either by a figure of speech, typology, or prophecy. Either way, the sense is one–that is, the true meaning is that intended by the author, who is God. Each text has but one meaning, the meaning intended by God, and that one meaning is conveyed either through the words of the text properly or in themselves (i.e., grammatically) or through the words of the text improperly or in what they signify (i.e., spiritually, figuratively, typologically).[92] Divine authorial intent never changes. What God revealed, for instance, in Hosea 11:1, always had a near-historical and a far-eschatological/Christological meaning (Matthew 2:15), though not necessarily understood as such by Hosea or his audience.[93] Muller quotes Aquinas at this point favorably, where he says, "the literal sense is that which the author intends, and the author of Scripture is God."[94]

**2. *Analogia Scripturae*.** *Analogia Scripturae* (analogy of Scripture), as defined by Muller, involves "the interpretation of unclear, difficult, or ambiguous passages of Scripture by comparison with clear and unambiguous passages that refer to the same teaching or event."[95]

**3. *Analogia fidei*.** *Analogia fidei*, however, is broader than *analogia Scripturae*. It refers to

> the use of a general sense of the meaning of Scripture, constructed from the clear or unambiguous *loci*..., as the basis for interpreting unclear or

---

[88] Steinmetz, "The Superiority of Pre-Critical Exegesis," 30.

[89] Muller, *PRRD*, II:474.

[90] Muller, *PRRD*, II:475.

[91] Muller, *PRRD*, II:474.

[92] Muller, *PRRD*, II:474.

[93] Cf. for example, William Ames, *The Marrow of Theology* (Durham, NC: The Labyrinth Press, 1983), 204 (XXXVIII:30).

[94] Muller, *PRRD*, II:476; Muller is quoting Aquinas, *Summa theologiae*, Ia, q. 1, a. 10.

[95] Muller, *Dictionary*, 33; cf. Muller, *PRRD*, II:490-91, and 493-97.

ambiguous texts. As distinct from the more basic *analogia Scripturae*..., the *analogia fidei* presupposes a sense of the theological meaning of Scripture.[96]

Both of these interpretive tools (and the *senses literalis*) presuppose "the canonical character of the whole of Scripture and the assumption that the canon, as such, was inspired and the infallible rule of faith."[97]

**4. *Scopus Scripturae*.** This "whole-Bible" hermeneutic was also manifested in their understanding of the *scopus* of Scripture.[98] Though *scopus* could refer to the immediate pericope, it also had a wider, redemptive-historical focus. *Scopus*, in this latter sense, referred to the center or target of the entirety of canonical revelation; it is that to which the entire Bible points. For the Reformers and for the seventeenth-century Reformed orthodox, Christ was the *scopus* of Scripture.

The *First Helvetic Confession* of 1536 gave early Reformed expression to this concept in Article V, entitled the Scope of Scripture.[99] The first sentence of that article reads as follows:

> The position of this entire canonical scripture [or of the entire actual canonical scripture] is this, that God is kindhearted [or shows kindness] to the race of men, and that he has proclaimed [or demonstrated] this kindness [or goodwill] through Christ his Son.[100]

William Ames, for instance, says, "The Old and New Testaments are reducible to these two primary heads. The Old promises Christ to come and the New testifies that he has come."[101]

Kelly M. Kapic says of John Owen:

---

[96] Muller, *Dictionary*, 33; cf. Muller, *PRRD*, II:491-92 and 493-97.

[97] Muller, *PRRD*, II:474, 492.

[98] For a helpful historically and theologically aware introduction to this concept see Muller, *PRRD*, II:206-23. Cf. also Martin I. Klauber, "Hermeneutics and the Doctrine of Scripture in Post-Reformation Reformed Thought," *Premise*, Volume II, Number 9 (October 19, 1995): 8ff. and James M. Renihan, "Theology on Target: The Scope of the Whole," *RBTR*, II:2 (July 2005): 36-53.

[99] Cf. Philip Schaff, *The Creeds of Christendom, Volume III: The Evangelical Protestant Creeds* (Grand Rapids: Baker Books, Reprinted 1996), 212.

[100] This English translation of the original Latin was provided by Amy Chifici, M.A. Cf. Schaff, *Creeds, III*, 212-13, for the German and Latin originals.

[101] Ames, *Marrow of Theology*, 202 (XXXVIII:5).

For Owen, all Scripture points to Christ, for "the revelation of the person of Christ and his office, is the foundation whereon all other instructions of the prophets and apostles for the edification of the church are built and whereinto they are resolved" (Works, 1:314-15). Owen attempts to avoid allowing the original context and meaning of any Old Testament passage to be lost; yet, he also maintains that a Christian exegete must ultimately find the passage's Christological meaning.[102]

Isaac Ambrose gives eloquent expression to the concept of Christ as *scopus* of Scripture in later Reformed thought:

Keep still Jesus Christ in your eye, in the perusal of the Scriptures, as the end, scope and substance thereof: what are the whole Scriptures, but as it were the spiritual swaddling clothes of the holy child Jesus? 1. Christ is the truth and substance of all the types and shadows. 2. Christ is the substance and matter of the Covenant of Grace, and all administrations thereof; under the Old Testament Christ is veiled, under the New Covenant revealed. 3. Christ is the centre and meeting place of all the promises; for in him the promises of God are yea and Amen. 4. Christ is the thing signified, sealed and exhibited in the Sacraments of the Old and New Testament. 5. Scripture genealogies use to lead us on to the true line of Christ. 6. Scripture chronologies are to discover to us the times and seasons of Christ. 7. Scripture-laws are our schoolmasters to bring us to Christ, the moral by correcting, the ceremonial by directing. 8. Scripture-gospel is Christ's light, whereby we hear and follow him; Christ's cords of love, whereby we are drawn into sweet union and communion with him; yea it is the very power of God unto salvation unto all them that believe in Christ Jesus; and therefore think of Christ as the very substance, marrow, soul and scope of the whole Scriptures.[103]

Muller, commenting on *scopus* in seventeenth-century Reformed thought, says:

Christ...is the *fundamentum* and *scopus* of Scripture inasmuch as he is the redemptive center on which the entire *principium cognoscendi* or cognitive foundation rests and in whom it find [*sic*] its unity.[104]

---

[102] Kelly M. Kapic, "Owen, John (*1616-1683*)" in Donald K. McKim, editor, *Dictionary of Major Biblical Interpreters*, 797-98.

[103] Isaac Ambrose, *Works* (1701), 201, as quoted in Packer, *A Quest for Godliness*, 103.

[104] Muller, "Calvin and the "Calvinists"," II:156.

...the theologies of the Reformers and of their orthodox successors consistently place Christ at the center of their discussions of redemption, consistently understand Christ as the center and fulfillment of divine revelation, and equally consistently understand the causality of salvation as grounded in the divine purpose. Christ, as Mediator, must be subordinate to the divine purpose, even as Christ, considered as God, is the one who with the Father and the Spirit decrees salvation before the foundation of the world: Causal theocentricity guarantees redemptive Christocentricity. Neither the doctrine of God nor the doctrine of Christ, however, serves as the basis of a neatly deduced system: The *loci* themselves arise out of the interpretation of Scripture.[105]

James M. Renihan, commenting on the confessional theology of the Reformed orthodox, says:

It is necessary to insist that there is a further step to identify in this process, which is to say that in agreement with Athanasius, the English Reformed confessors understood their statement to imply that Christ is the scope of all Scripture. This is evident in at least two ways. First, the Reformed authors, following the text of Holy Writ, argue that Christ is the incarnation of the glory of God. If the scope of Scripture is to give all glory to God, and all glory comes to God through Him, then by definition this statement must have reference to the person of Jesus Christ. Secondly, they recognized the intimate relationship present between the two testaments and their constituent books. The Old, whether considered as a whole or in its parts, is an anticipation of the work of God in Christ. From the *protevangelium* through the historical revelation of the Covenant of Grace in the history of Israel, everything looked forward to his coming. Likewise, the New is the full revelation of the promises progressively revealed in the Old. This unity finds it fullness in Jesus Christ and his work. In every place, the Bible points to Christ—he is the target—the scope of Scripture.[106]

According to Reformed orthodoxy, then, Christ is the *scopus* (target) toward which the whole of Scripture tends. This view of the *scopus* of Scripture was closely related to their view of the relation between the testaments. The relationship between the testaments was seen in terms of

---

[105] Muller, "Calvin and the "Calvinists"," II:155.

[106] Renihan, "Theology on Target: The Scope of the Whole," 43-44. Renihan makes these comments after quoting John Owen, who, according to Renihan, was, in effect, exegeting "the scope of the whole" terminology as found in the *Westminster Confession, Savoy Declaration,* and *Second London Confession.*

a promise/fulfillment, figure/reality, type/anti-type motif.[107] Hence, "the New Testament may be understood as the interpreter of the Old."[108] Revelation was progressive, self-interpreting, and consummated in the coming of Christ.

Here we must be careful not to infuse later, neo-orthodox concepts of Christocentricity into the historical data. The Christocentricity of the Reformed and Reformed orthodox was redemptive-historical and not principial, as Muller points out.[109] In other words, it came as a result of Scripture functioning as the *principium cognoscendi* (principle of knowing) or cognitive foundation of our knowledge of God. Scripture, and not Christ the Mediator, is a fundamental principle or foundation of theology in Reformed orthodoxy.[110] They started with Scripture and concluded Christocentricity in terms of the *historia salutis*. Their Christocentricity is revelational and connected to redemption. As Muller says, such "Christocentrism consistently places Christ at the historical and at the soteriological center of the work of redemption."[111] But we must still be careful with the term Christocentricity. Christology must not be viewed as the central dogma of the Reformed orthodox. As Muller says:

> Such doctrines as God, predestination, Christ, and covenant provide not alternative but coordinate *foci* – and the presence of each and every one of these topics in theology rests not on a rational, deductive process but on their presence as *loci* in the exegetical or interpretive tradition of the church.[112]

The method of Reformed orthodoxy, then, started with the text of Scripture and its exegesis, went to the synthesizing of Scripture in terms of interpreting difficult passages in light of clearer ones and identifying its (i.e., Scripture's) unifying theme or themes based on its various levels of meaning[113], and then (and only then) categorizing the exegetical and

---

[107] Muller, *PRRD*, II:492.

[108] Muller, *PRRD*, II:492.

[109] Muller, "Calvin and the "Calvinists"," II:157.

[110] Muller, *Dictionary*, 245-46.

[111] Muller, "Calvin and the "Calvinists"," II:157.

[112] Muller, "Calvin and the "Calvinists"," II:157.

[113] Steinmetz, "The Superiority of Pre-Critical Exegesis," 27-38, for a discussion of levels of meaning and also Muller, *PRRD*, II:469-82.

canonical-theological findings in the long-practiced *loci* method of dogmatics.

- **A Multi-Sourced Method[114]**

As stated above, the Reformed orthodox method was foundationally exegetical and based on the Scriptures. But the Reformed orthodox wanted to place their findings within the long tradition of Western theology. They did this by utilizing various sources in the process of their theological formulation. Muller identifies the sources of Reformed orthodoxy, in terms of their over-all theological enterprise, as follows:

> 1) Scripture, exegesis, and ancillary disciplines; 2) the ancient creeds and the confessions of the Reformed churches; 3) the church fathers; 4) the theological tradition generally, including the medieval doctors and the Reformers; and 5) the philosophical tradition and reason, specified as logic, rhetoric, and their methodological applications.[115]

### John Owen: Reformed Orthodox Theologian

How does all of this relate to John Owen and our purposes? John Owen fits into the era of high orthodoxy chronologically, methodologically, and theologically. Hence, we should assume that he will utilize the methodological tools of the day. This has been shown to be the case in several more recent studies.[116] There are at least five reasons why Owen must be considered a Reformed orthodox theologian: his education; his sources; his intellectual context; his writings; and the utilization of key hermeneutical principles and trajectories. These reasons are standard among the secondary literature.

- **Owen's Education**

As discussed in the biographical section on Owen, he received a rudimentary education at home, entered a private, classical academy at

---

[114] Muller, "Sources of Reformed Orthodoxy," 45-55.

[115] Muller, "Sources of Reformed Orthodoxy," 45-46.

[116] For thorough and up-to-date research substantiating this see Rehnman, *Divine Discourse*, 15-46, Rehnman, "John Owen: A Reformed Scholastic at Oxford" in van Asselt and Dekker, editors, *Reformation and Scholasticism*, 181-203, and Trueman *John Owen*, 1-33.

Oxford[117], and then entered Queens College, Oxford, at the age of 12.[118] The curriculum at Oxford, though affected by both the Renaissance and Reformation, was basically medieval.[119] The most influential professor at Oxford for Owen was his Reformed tutor, Thomas Barlow.[120] Barlow lectured in metaphysics and was the university's chief authority in polemics.[121] Barlow created a bibliography for theological students. Trueman's discussion on it is fascinating and relevant and, thus, will be quoted in full. He says:

> Some idea of the kind of bibliographical emphases to which an Oxford theology student of Owen's day would have been exposed is provided in the fascinating, and posthumously published, basic theological reading list of Thomas Barlow, Owen's tutor. Barlow allows his convictions about the nature of theology and of human knowledge of God to shape the catalogue: there is a light of nature and a light of scripture which are the foundations for natural theology and revealed theology respectively. Of these, Barlow stresses Aquinas, and commentators on Aquinas, as of particular use, indicating his own strong Thomist instincts, many of which parallel concerns in Owen. Barlow immediately proceeds, however, to list over six pages of editions of the Hebrew and Greek texts of the Old and New Testaments, of the Septuagint and the Vulgate, and various lexical and linguistic aids. He then follows with sections devoted to biblical commentaries (from ancient to modern, and reflecting many theological perspectives, from orthodox to heretical), works on ancient Jewish society, a variety of books on the canon, basic outlines of early church history, and books on the apocrypha and non-canonical early writings. Thus, the first 21 of the book's 70 pages are devoted specifically to books of direct relevance to understanding the text and the context of scripture. Then, a little later in the treatise, Barlow spends time listing useful books on biblical chronology and geography, including maps, with which the Bible student should be familiar. The biblical emphasis, even in this book list provided by the most philosophical of seventeenth-century Oxford's theologians, is clear and exemplary.[122]

---

[117] Thomson, *Owen*, 14; Orme, *Owen*, 7; Toon, *God's Statesman*, 3.

[118] Toon, *God's Statesman*, 5. Cf. Thomson, *Owen*, 15, where he claims that entrance to Queen's at the age of 12 "...in the case of most youths would have been most injudiciously premature."

[119] Rehnman, "John Owen: A Reformed Scholastic at Oxford," 182.

[120] Rehnman, "John Owen: A Reformed Scholastic at Oxford," 182.

[121] Rehnman, *Divine Discourse*, 20.

[122] Trueman *John Owen*, 9-10.

Owen's university education exposed him to a scholastic method of study via its curriculum and professors, primarily Barlow and John Prideaux.[123] His education forced him to study various sources and become familiar with the intellectual currents (movements and persons) of the past and present, as will be seen below. This type of education would surely prepare a young man to apply a theological methodology which, as we have seen, was the method of the Reformed orthodox.

- **Owen's Sources**

In good Reformed orthodox fashion, John Owen utilized various sources in his theological method. This can be seen in at least two ways: his library and quotations and references in his writings.

**1. Owen's sources in his library.** Concerning Owen's library, Barry Howson says, "In 1684 his extensive library was sold by public auction. It contained 1,418 Latin treatises, 32 bound volumes of Greek and Latin manuscripts, and 1,454 English books."[124] Owen's library "included the major authors of patristic, mediaeval, and contemporary theology"[125] and "collections on philosophy, history, geography and travel."[126]

**2. Owen's sources in his writings.** Owen's sources referenced in his writings included Christian as well as non-Christian authors. Rehnman lists Euripides, Hesiod, Homer, Horace, Aelian, Plutarch, Aristotle, Plautus, Suetonius, Pliny and Virgil as non-Christian authors referenced in various works by Owen.[127] Owen also frequently referenced patristic literature. Rehnman lists the following names and number of references: Ambrose 36, Augustine 206, Chrysostom 57, Clement of Alexandra 50, Clement of Rome 33, Epiphanius 36, Eusebius 94, Gregory of Nazianus 16, Gregory of Nyssa 2, Hilary 12, Ignatius 25, Irenaeus 30, Jerome 92, Justin Martyr 44, Lactantius 32, Origen 55, and Tertullian 122.[128] Owen quoted (both positively and negatively) various medieval scholastics, among whom are Anslem, Aberlard, Peter Lombard, John of Damascus,

---

[123] Rehnman, "John Owen: A Reformed Scholastic at Oxford," 191.

[124] Howson, "Hermeneutics of John Owen," 353. Howson gets these figures from Toon, *God's Statesman*, 174, n. 1.

[125] Rehnman, "John Owen: A Reformed Scholastic at Oxford," 184, n. 13.

[126] Rehnman, "John Owen: A Reformed Scholastic at Oxford," 184, n. 13.

[127] Rehnman, *Divine Discourse*, 28. Cf. n. 37 for the references in Owen where these authors are cited.

[128] Rehnman, *Divine Discourse*, 29, n. 44.

Bernard of Clairvaux, Scotus, Bonaventure, and especially Thomas Aquinas.[129]

Owen's education was obviously instrumental in the formation of his personal library and the subsequent utilization of sources referenced in his writings.

- **Owen's Intellectual Context**

John Owen was a post-Reformation, pre-Enlightenment theologian. Recent studies have concluded that his intellectual context was eclectic. Various influences played their unique roll in shaping his thinking and method. Rehnman lists five such influences: the Reformed tradition, humanism, a renovated and revitalized form of scholasticism, philosophical eclecticism, and Augustinianism.[130]

- **Owen's Writings**

Various attributes of Owen's writings witness to the fact of his Reformed orthodox methodology and theology. He utilized various methods for the articulation of theology. The Banner of Truth edition of Owen's *Works* breaks down the 23 volumes under four divisions: Doctrinal (I-V), Practical (VI-IX), Controversial (X-XVI), and Expository (XVII-XXIII [Owen's commentary on Hebrews]). This displays the variety of approaches Owen took while articulating his theology. He utilized the scholastic method,[131] an exegetical/expository method,[132] a more federal or linear/redemptive-historical method,[133] a catechetical method,[134] and at other times a more churchly method–sermons.[135] While articulating his theology, he was in constant discussion with the Christian tradition. Trueman says, "...Owen also articulates his theology in terms both of

---

[129] Rehnman, "John Owen: A Reformed Scholastic at Oxford." 190-94.

[130] Rehnman, "John Owen: A Reformed Scholastic at Oxford," 183-201. Cf. also, Kapic, *Communion with God*, 28ff., Trueman, *Claims of Truth*, 1-46.

[131] Cf. *A Display of Arminianism, The Death of Death in the Death of Christ* and *A Dissertation on Divine Justice*, all contained in Owen, *Works*, X and *Vindiciae Evangelicae: or, the Mystery of the Gospel Vindicated and Socinianism Examined* in Owen, *Works*, XII.

[132] Cf. Exposition of *Psalm 130* in Owen, *Works*, VI and especially his monumental commentary on Hebrews, *Works*, XVII-XXIII.

[133] Cf. *BTO*.

[134] *Two Short Catechisms* in Owen, *Works*, I

[135] Cf. Owen, *Works*, VIII, IX, and *Posthumus Sermons* in *Works*, XVI.

careful exegesis and of constructive dialogue with the exegetical and theological traditions of the church."[136] According to Trueman elsewhere, Owen's exposition of Hebrews displays some of the characteristics of Reformed orthodoxy noted above. He says, "As Henry Knapp has demonstrated in impressive detail, ...Owen's commentary on Hebrews is a masterpiece of linguistics, textual exegesis, interaction with exegetical traditions, and theological synthesis."[137]

- **Owen's Utilization of Key Hermeneutical Principles and Trajectories**

**1. The Holy Spirit is the only infallible interpreter of the Bible.** In classic, pre-critical and Reformed orthodox fashion, Owen briefly articulates his view of special hermeneutics and the Scripture:

> ...for although the Scripture hath many things in *common* with other writings wherein *secular arts* and *sciences* are declared, yet to suppose that we may attain the sense and mind of God in them by the mere use of such *ways and means* as we apply in the investigation of truths of other natures is to exclude all consideration of God, of Jesus Christ, of the Holy Spirit, of the end of the Scriptures themselves, of the nature and use of the things delivered in them; and, by consequent, to overthrow all religion.[138]

Owen obviously and firmly believed that the Bible should not be interpreted like any other book. How can it be, it–and it alone–is the word of God. In Owen's *BTO*, he says:

> The only unique, public, authentic, and infallible interpreter of Scripture is none other than the Author of Scripture Himself, by whose inspiration they are the truth, and by whom they possess their perspicuity and authority, that is, God the Holy Spirit.[139]

---

[136] Trueman *John Owen*, 7.

[137] Trueman, *John Owen*, 10.

[138] Owen, *Works*, IV:208.

[139] Owen, *BTO*, 797. Cf. Ferguson, *John Owen*, 196-99; Howson, "Hermeneutics of John Owen," 351-76; Lea, "The Hermeneutics of the Puritans," 271-84; Packer, "The Puritans as Interpreters of Scripture" in *Quest for Godliness*, 97-105; and Leland Ryken, "The Bible" in *Worldly Saints: The Puritans as they Really Were* (Grand Rapids: Zondervan Publishing House, 1986), 137-54.

**2. The scope of Scripture is God in Christ as Redeemer.** Christ as *scopus Scripturae* can be seen in Owen's writings in many ways. In his work on the Person of Christ, Owen says, "The *end* of the Word itself, is to instruct us in the knowledge of God in Christ."[140] A few pages later he goes on to say:

> Christ is the image of the invisible God, the express image of the person of the Father; and *the principal end* of the whole Scripture, especially of the Gospel, is to declare him so to be, and how he is so.[141]

In these two instances he uses the term 'end' in a technical sense. In other words, Christ is *scopus Scripturae*.

Christ as *scopus Scripturae* can be seen from an exegetical standpoint in Owen as well. Commenting on Genesis 3:15 as the first promise of the only means of delivery from the effects of sin–Christ, he says:

> This is the very foundation of the faith of the church; and if it be denied, nothing of the economy or dispensation of God towards it from the beginning can be understood. The whole doctrine and story of the Old Testament must be rejected as useless, and no foundation be left in the truth of God for the introduction of the New.[142]

Without a soteriological/Messianic interpretation of Genesis 3:15, in the mind of Owen, subsequent Scripture makes no sense. A Christocentric hermeneutic is the foundation of proper biblical interpretation.

In Owen, *Works*, XVII, writing on the "Oneness of the Church" throughout redemptive history, Owen argues that the object of saving faith throughout redemptive history is "the *Seed* that was in the promise..."[143] In this brief exercitation, Owen argues that God first gave the promise of salvation to Adam based on Genesis 3:15. In fact, God's Church is founded "in the promise of the Messiah given to Adam."[144] Owen argues that all subsequent revelation serves to unfold the first promise of the gospel to Adam. This promise is the first revelation of the covenant of grace.[145] Subsequent revelation unfolds the promise of the

---

[140] Owen, *Works*, I:65. Emphasis added.

[141] Owen, *Works*, I:74. Emphasis added.

[142] Owen, *Works*, I:120. Cf. Daniels, *Christology of John Owen*, 230-61.

[143] Owen, *Works*, XVII:121, 142.

[144] Owen, *Works*, XVII:120.

[145] Owen, *Works*, XVII:120.

Redeemer and, in fact depends upon it. In his treatise on the Person of Christ, Owen says:

> This principle is always to be retained in our minds in reading of the Scripture,–namely, that the revelation and doctrine of the person of Christ and his office, is the foundation whereon all other instructions of the prophets and apostles for the edification of the church are built, and whereinto they are resolved; as is declared, Eph. ii. 20—22. So our Lord Jesus Christ himself at large makes it manifest, Luke xxiv. 26, 27, 45, 46. Lay aside the consideration hereof, and the Scriptures are no such thing as they pretend unto,—namely, a revelation of the glory of God in the salvation of the church; nor are those of the Old Testament so at this day unto the Jews, who own not this principle, 2 Cor. iii. 13— 16. There are, therefore, such revelations of the person and glory of Christ treasured up in the Scripture, from the beginning unto the end of it, as may exercise the faith and contemplation of believers in this world, and shall never, during this life, be fully discovered or understood; and in divine meditations of these revelations doth much of the life of faith consist.[146]

For Owen, "the revelation and doctrine of the person of Christ and his office" is the hermeneutical key providing interpretive cohesiveness for all of Scripture.

Owen's Christocentricity has been identified by several recent studies. In an article on John Owen dealing with Owen's *Dissertation on Divine Justice* and subtitled "An Exercise in Christocentric Scholasticism," Carl Trueman says, "…his theology is, at heart, thoroughly christocentric."[147] Trueman entitles his conclusion "Owen's Christocentrism" and says:

> In asserting the necessity of Christ's sacrifice, Owen is presenting a Reformed theology that cannot displace the historical person of the mediator from the center of the drama of redemption. There can be no eternal justification based purely on the decree: Salvation is as surely linked to history as it is to eternity. It is those who predicate the necessity of incarnation and atonement solely on the decretive will of God who run the risk of marginalizing the historical person of Christ and undermining the importance of salvation history. In this context, Owen's scholasticism serves not to eclipse Christ but to place him at

---

[146] Owen, *Works*, I:314-15.
[147] Carl R. Trueman, "John Owen's *Dissertation on Divine Justice*: An Exercise in Christocentric Scholasticism," *CTJ* 33 (1998): 97.

the center. Indeed, as is clear from his argument, if it was not for his Thomist understanding of God's causal relationship to creation and his acceptance of the validity of the analogy of being, Owen would have no way of attacking his opponents' position. While it is true that his use of such arguments depends on assumptions that he does not justify, it is also true that any rejection of their validity renders his christocentrism epistemologically unsustainable. In the context of this dispute, at least, it is the rejection of natural theology, not its acceptance, that is the enemy of Christ-centered theology.[148]

In fact, Trueman goes so far as to say that on the issue of divine justice and the incarnation, Owen "is arguably not less christocentric than [his] opponents, including Calvin himself, but actually more so."[149]

Kelly Kapic argues that Owen's anthropology is formulated "in a christocentric pattern, pointing to Jesus Christ as the incarnate and true image of God."[150] Even the Sabbath is Christologically transformed by Christ, thus further displaying the Christocentricity of Owen's thought.[151]

Sebastian Rehnman acknowledges this of Owen, "His theology has, for all its adherence to scholasticism and contrary to the argument of much modern scholarship on Reformed orthodoxy, a Christocentric and practical character."[152]

Richard W. Daniels shows that not only redemption, but creation and providence are christocentric for Owen.[153] Commenting on the doctrines of creation and providence in Owen's thought, Daniels says, "It is difficult to conceive of a more Christocentric view of the purpose of God in creation than this, which subjects the creation and history of the universe to the manifestation of the glory of God in its renovation by the Son."[154] After acknowledging that Owen's Christocentricity was not unique among the English Puritans, he then says:

In the development of this Christocentric theological system, however, Owen was unsurpassed. The lines which he traces from the doctrine of the person of Christ are bold,

---

[148] Trueman, "John Owen's *Dissertation on Divine Justice*," 103.

[149] Trueman, "John Owen's *Dissertation on Divine Justice*," 103.

[150] Kapic, *Communion with God*, 65.

[151] Kapic, *Communion with God*, 212-14. Cf. Owen, *Works*, XVIII:263-460 for Owen's masterful treatment of a day of sacred rest.

[152] Rehnman, *Divine Discourse*, 181.

[153] Daniels, *Christology of Owen*, 178-93.

[154] Daniels, *Christology of Owen*, 180.

and long enough to reach every subject of doctrinal inquiry, showing that "by him, all things" [including all doctrinal truths] consist" (Col. 1:17).[155]

In Daniels' concluding words to his study on Owen's Christology, he gives this tribute to him:

> it is one thing to say Christian theology ought to be Christocentric, it is quite another to actually understand the entire spectrum of theological *loci* Christocentrically, or to articulate one's theology in a way that manifests this Christocentricity. Owen does this, as we have observed with regard to the knowledge of God, creation, providence, the redemption of man, the mediatorial kingdom, the church, and the Christian life.[156]

### Federal Theology among the Reformed Orthodox and Beyond

It is no secret that various Reformed orthodox theologians articulated theology utilizing a federal or covenantal model. There are many sources (primary and secondary) available for the contemporary reader which amply display and discuss this model.[157] We will briefly examine a few

---

[155] Daniels, *Christology of Owen*, 517.

[156] Daniels, *Christology of Owen*, 519.

[157] For instance, for primary sources see Herman Witsius, *The Economy of the Covenants Between God and Man: Comprehending A Complete Body of Divinity, Two Volumes* (Escondido, CA: The den Dulk Christian Foundation, Reprinted 1990); Nehemiah Coxe and John Owen, *Covenant Theology From Adam to Christ* (Owensboro, KY: RBAP, 2005); Samuel Bolton, *The True Bounds of Christian Freedom* (Edinburgh: The Banner of Truth Trust, Reprint edition of 1978); Edward Fisher, *The Marrow of Modern Divinity: In Two Parts – Part I. the Covenant of Works and the Covenant of Grace; Part II. An Exposition of the Ten Commandments* (Edmonton, AB, Canada: Still Water Revival Books, Reprint edition of 1991); Francis Turretin, *Institutes of Elenctic Theology, Volume Two* (Phillipsburg, NJ: P&R Publishing, 1994); and for secondary works see A. T. B. McGowan, *The Federal Theology of Thomas Boston* (Edinburgh: Rutherford House, 1997); John Von Rohr, *The Covenant of Grace in Puritan Thought* (Atlanta: Scholars Press, 1986); John L. Girardeau, *The Federal Theology: Its Import and Its Regulative Influence* (Greenville, SC: Reformed Academic Press, 1994); Charles S. McCoy and J. Wayne Baker, *Fountainhead of Federalism: Heinrich Bullinger and the Covenantal Tradition* (Louisville: Westminster/John Know Press, 1991); Mark W. Karlberg, *Covenant Theology in Reformed Perspective: Collected Essays and Book Reviews in Historical, Biblical, and Systematic Theology* (Eugene, OR: Wipf and Stock Publishers, 2000); Lyle D. Bierma, *German Calvinism in the Confessional Age: The Covenant Theology of Caspar Olevianus* (Grand Rapids: Baker Book House, 1996); Rowland S. Ward, *God & Adam: Reformed Theology and The Creation Covenant – An*

of the more important federal theologians of the seventeenth century to further set the context in which Owen wrote his *BTO*. This brief survey understands federal theology as a method and not as a distinct school.[158]

Federal or covenant theology did not begin in the seventeenth century. The seventeenth-century Reformed orthodox built upon the labors of their Reformed predecessors, who built upon the labors of others before them. Such theologians as Zwingli, Bullinger, Calvin, Ursinus, Olevianus, Rollock, Perkins, Ames, and Ball all played key roles in the early development of federal theology.[159] We will look briefly at some of the key contributors to the development of federalism in the early and late seventeenth century, and even into the eighteenth century, to further set the wider context of John Owen.

- **William Perkins**

William Perkins, a late sixteenth-century English theologian, was a theology professor at Christ College, Cambridge.[160] He is known by some as the father or chief architect of English Puritanism. He had several works of note, especially his *The Art of Prophesying* and *A*

---

*Introduction to the Biblical Covenants – A Close Examination of the Covenant of Works* (Wantirna, Australia: New Melbourne Press, 2003); Peter Golding, *Covenant Theology: The Key of Theology in Reformed Thought and Tradition* (Ross-shire, Scotland: Christian Focus Publications, 2004); Peter Lillback, *The Binding of God: Calvin's Role in the Development of Covenant Theology* (Grand Rapids: Baker Academic, 2001); Willem J. van Asselt, *The Federal Theology of Johannes Cocceius (1603-1669)* (Leiden, Boston, Koln: Brill, 2001); John Murray, "Covenant Theology" in *Collected Writings, Volume Four* (Edinburgh: The Banner of Truth Trust, 1982), 216-40; Geerhardus Vos, "The Doctrine of the Covenant in Reformed Theology" in *RHBI*, 234-67.

[158] Cf. van Asselt, "The Fundamental Meaning of Theology," 323, where he notes, "This should warn us against any facile juxtaposition of federal-biblical theology with scholastic-dogmatic theology..." 'This' in context refers to the fact that many late sixteenth- and seventeenth-century Reformed theologians utilized Junius' classification of archetypal and ectypal knowledge. Van Asselt claims that this is true of continental Reformed theologians as well as some English Puritans. John Owen makes such distinctions in his *BTO* (Cf. Chapter Eight of this dissertation, Owen, *BTO*, Chapter 3 Book I, and Rehnman, *Divine Discourse*, 57-71 for an extended discussion as it relates to Owen.). Once again, this is further evidence that Reformed scholasticism was a complex method and not a static system of theology. Reformed orthodox theologians could be and were often both scholastic and federal.

[159] For a well-referenced treatment of the history of federal theology in the post-Reformation era see Ward, *God & Adam*. Cf. also Golding, *Covenant Theology*, 13-66.

[160] Donald K. McKim, "Perkins, William (1558-1602)" in McKim, editor, *ERF*, 274-75.

*Golden Chaine. The Art of Prophesying* was a hermeneutical and homiletical handbook which influenced English and American Puritanism.[161] Those who influenced Perkins' theology most were men like John Calvin, Peter Martyr Vermigli, Theodore Beza, Jerome Zanchi, Casper Olevianus, and Franciscus Junius.[162] Perkins utilized Ramist logic while articulating his theology. Peter Ramus was a sixteenth-century French logician and philosopher who simplified Aristotelianism and developed a system of analysis that was utilized by the Cambridge Puritans and passed on to their heirs. Ramism analyzed discourse by defining and dividing. Axioms were divided into two parts or dichotomies. Divisions could be subdivided down to their smallest units. As an affect of humanism in Ramist logic, there was an emphasis on practicality. This contribution of Ramism in Puritanism created the tendency in Puritan exegesis of Scripture to create sermons under two main considerations–exposition/doctrine and use. [163]

- **William Ames**

William Ames, student of William Perkins at Christ College, Cambridge, became professor of theology at the University of Franeker, the Netherlans in 1622. Ames' major work was his *The Marrow of Theology*.[164] This work was very influential among various groups of Protestants in the seventeenth century. It follows Perkins' utilization of Ramist logic in the articulation of theology. Ames has been called the "chief architect of the federal theology."[165]

Ames was Johannes Cocceius' (see below) theology professor and could have been the source behind two of his contributions to federalism–(1) a mediating position on the relation between the *ordo salutis* and the *historia salutis* and (2) the concept of a progressive

---

[161] McKim, "Perkins, Williams (1558-1602)" in McKim, editor, *DMBI,* 815.

[162] McKim, "Perkins, Williams (1558-1602)" in McKim, editor, *DMBI,* 815.

[163] Cf. McKim, "Perkins" in *DMBI,* 816 and McKim, "Ramus, Peter (1515-1572)" in *ERF,* 314.

[164] William Ames, *The Marrow of Theology* (Durham, NC: The Labyrinth Press, 1983).

[165] Jan van Vliet, "Decretal Theology and the Development of Covenant Thought: An Assessment of Cornelis Graafland's Thesis with a Particular View to Federal Architects William Ames and Johannes Cocceius," *WTJ* 63 (2001): 405 and 414. Van Vliet is quoting Perry Miller.

abrogation of the covenant of works.[166] Commenting on Ames' teaching on the relation between the *ordo* and *historia salutis*, van Vliet says, "The horizontal movement and the vertical "strikes" are continually in a state of intersection; predestination and covenant meet in unity."[167] In his discussion "The Administration of the Covenant of Grace before the Coming of Christ" Ames combines aspects of the *ordo salutis* with aspects of the *historia salutis*. He does this in the three major Old Testament redemptive-historical epochs: from Adam to Abraham,[168] from Abraham to Moses,[169] and from Moses to Christ.[170] In each redemptive-historical epoch, Ames shows how the stages of the *ordo salutis* were exemplified or as Ames says, "adumbrated."[171]

Ames held to what van Vliet calls "a form of [the progressive] abrogation of the covenant of works."[172] Commenting on the New Covenant, Ames says:

> 4. The testament is new in relation to what existed from the time of Moses and in relation to the promise made to the fathers. But it is new not in essence but in form. In the former circumstances the form of administration gave *some evidence of the covenant of works*, from which this testament is essentially different.[173]

While discussing Christian freedom under the New Covenant, Ames continues, "9. Freedom comes, first, in doing away with government by law, or *the intermixture of the covenant of works*, which held the ancient people in a certain bondage."[174] Ames viewed the Old or Mosaic Covenant as containing elements of the covenant of works which are not included in the New Covenant. This could well be where Cocceius first heard of the progressive abrogation of the covenant of works, though in seed form. Cocceius' theory of progressive abrogation will be discussed below.

---

[166] Cf. van Vliet, "Decretal Theology and the Development of Covenant Thought," 416 for a fascinating discussion suggesting this very thing.

[167] van Vliet, "Decretal Theology and the Development of Covenant Thought," 415.

[168] Ames, *The Marrow of Theology*, 203 (XXXVIII:14-19).

[169] Ames, *The Marrow of Theology*, 204 (XXXVIII:20-28).

[170] Ames, *The Marrow of Theology*, 204-5 (XXXVIII:30-5).

[171] Ames, *The Marrow of Theology*, 203 (XXXVIII:29).

[172] van Vliet, "Decretal Theology and the Development of Covenant Thought," 418.

[173] Ames, *The Marrow of Theology*, 206 (XXXVIII:4). Emphasis added.

[174] Ames, *The Marrow of Theology*, 206 (XXXVIII:9). Emphasis added.

Finally, Ames' method of articulating the covenant of grace was chronological or along redemptive-historical lines.[175] He also saw the promise of the redeemer in Genesis 3:15.[176]

- **Johannes Cocceius**

One of the most important and controversial Reformed orthodox federal theologians of the seventeenth century was Johannes Cocceius (1603-1669), a student of Ames.[177] Though German born, Cocceius lived most of his life in The Netherlands. He attended the University of Franeker from 1626-1629. He ended his teaching career as professor of theology at Leiden from 1650-1669. He wrote commentaries, works on philology, dogmatics, ethics, and his famous *Summa doctrinae de foedere et testament Dei* (*Doctrine of the Covenant and Testament of God*) in 1648.[178] This was the classic continental federal theology. "By means of the concept of *foedus* he sought to do justice, also in systematic theology, to the historical nature of the biblical narrative."[179] Some of his followers (i.e., Cocceians) sought to integrate elements of Cartesian philosophy into his federalism, "in spite of Cocceius's rejection of such a union."[180] Integrating covenant and kingdom he "developed a theology of history, or in his own words, "a prophetic theology.""[181] Cocceius held a

---

[175] Cf. Ames, *The Marrow of Theology*, 202-10 (XXXVIII and XXXIX) and van Vliet, "Decretal Theology and the Development of Covenant Thought," 416.

[176] Ames, *The Marrow of Theology*, 203 (XXXVIII:14).

[177] Cf. William Klempa, "Cocceius, Johannes (1603-1669)" in Donald K. McKim, editor, *ERF*, 73-74; Willem J. van Asselt, "Cocceius, Johannes" in McKim, editor, *DMBI*, 315-20; Willem J. van Asselt, "Cocceius Anti-Scholasticus?" in van Asselt and Dekker, editors, *Reformation and Scholasticism*, 227-51; Willem J. van Asselt, *The Federal Theology of Johannes Cocceius (1603-1669)* (Leiden, Boston, Koln: Brill, 2001), 23-33; Willem J. van Asselt, "Structural Elements in the Eschatology of Johannes Cocceius," *CTJ* 35 (2000): 76-104; Willem J. van Asselt, "The Doctrine of the Abrogations in the Federal Theology of Johannes Cocceius (1603-1669)," *CTJ* 29 (1994): 101-16; Charles S. McCoy and J. Wayne Baker, *Fountainhead of Federalism* (Louisville: Westminster/John Knox Press, 1991), 63-79; Jan van Vliet, "Decretal Theology and the Development of Covenant Thought: An Assessment of Cornelis Graafland's Thesis with a Particular View to Federal Architects William Ames and Johannes Cocceius," *WTJ* 63 (2001): 393-420.

[178] It is of interest to note that the most famous "Biblical Theologian" of the seventeenth-century Reformed orthodox also wrote a work on Dogmatics.

[179] van Asselt, "Cocceius, Johannes" in McKim, editor, *DMBI*, 315.

[180] van Asselt, "Cocceius, Johannes" in McKim, editor, *DMBI*, 315.

[181] van Asselt, "Cocceius, Johannes" in McKim, editor, *DMBI*, 318; cf. van Asselt, "Structural Elements in the Eschatology of Johannes Cocceius," 85ff. for a discussion on

controversial view of the Sabbath, which was confronted by Voetius and his followers, as well as issues of continuity and discontinuity between the Old and New Testaments.[182]

Cocceius' view of the covenant of works infused eschatology into his theology from the Garden of Eden.[183] "The covenant of works opened up the possibility of a history with an eschatological prospect." [184] Paradise "was a symbol and pledge of a 'better habitation.'"[185] He was not the only Reformed orthodox to argue in this manner. If fact, as we shall see, the intersection of protology and eschatology through the doctrine of the covenant of works was quite common. Cocceius viewed the covenant of works not as a contract, "but rather *amicitia*, friendship—a concept that has medieval roots and which extends back into classical antiquity."[186] He viewed God's covenant as "essentially monopleuric" (one-sided) and yet assuming a dipleuric (two-sided) character once man engaged himself and concurred with God's "covenantal initiative."[187]

He held a very unique view of progressive revelation in that he saw the covenant of works progressively abrogated as salvation history unfolded and advanced.[188] Van Asselt comments:

> One of the most peculiar constructions in the theological system of Johannes Cocceius certainly is the doctrine of the so-called abrogations. This doctrine, which is closely connected with the doctrine of the covenant of works and the covenant of grace, occurs in both systematic main works of Cocceius: *in the Summa Doctrinae de Foedere et Testamento Dei* of 1648 (§58) and in the *Summa Theologiae ex Scripturis repetita* of 1662 (cap. 31 §1). Briefly formulated, this doctrine describes some five degrees (*gradus*) by which God leads man

---

Cocceuis' doctrine of the epochs of the church as he found them in the book of Revelation and his fascination with the number seven in Scripture.

[182] van Asselt, "Cocceius, Johannes" in McKim, editor, *DMBI*, 316-17.

[183] van Asselt, *The Federal Theology of Johannes Cocceius,* 264.

[184] van Asselt, "Structural Elements in the Eschatology of Johannes Cocceius," 82.

[185] van Asselt, *The Federal Theology of Johannes Cocceius,* 264.

[186] van Asselt, *The Federal Theology of Johannes Cocceius,* 24, n. 3.

[187] van Asselt, *The Federal Theology of Johannes Cocceius,* 39.

[188] Cf. van Asselt, *The Federal Theology of Johannes Cocceius,* 271-87 for an extensive discussion.

into eternal life and by which the consequences of the violation of the covenant of works through the Fall are gradually abrogated.[189]

Cocceuis' five degrees of abrogation were: (1) by the fall, (2) by the covenant of grace revealed through the first promise of salvation (Genesis 3:15)[190] and its subsequent unfolding in both testaments, (3) by the incarnation, (4) by the intermediate state, and (5) by the eternal state.[191] These degrees or stages of abrogation combine the *historia salutis* with the *ordo salutis*. Indeed, van Asselt says, "...the historical and the existential moments are combined."[192] Each epoch of the *historia salutis* has a corresponding state of condition in the *ordo salutis*.[193] Cocceius saw movement and development along salvation-historical lines and sought to give expression to that via the slow but certain abrogation of the covenant of works and the slow but certain increasingly fulfilled covenant of grace. His views gave the appearance of driving a wedge between issues of forgiveness and justification in the Old and New Testaments and, thus, his theory was rejected firmly by Voetius and his followers. Van Asselt argues that the Cocceians themselves failed to develop their teacher in a manner that accurately reflected his thought and, thus, "the doctrine of abrogations as a means of coordination of salvation history and *ordo salutis* broke down, it became obsolete and so disappeared in Cocceian theology."[194]

Despite his oddities, Cocceius' major contribution was the further development of the utilization of the concept of covenant throughout redemptive history (and even predating it via the *pactum salutis*) and articulating his theology in a more historical-linear fashion, though

---

[189] van Asselt, "The Doctrine of the Abrogations in the Federal Theology of Johannes Cocceius (1603-1669)," 101; cf. also van Asselt, "Structural Elements in the Eschatology of Johannes Cocceius," 83.

[190] van Asselt, *The Federal Theology of Johannes Cocceius*, 58.

[191] van Asselt, "The Doctrine of the Abrogations in the Federal Theology of Johannes Cocceius (1603-1669)," 107-08; van Asselt, "Structural Elements in the Eschatology of Johannes Cocceius," 83; van Asselt, *The Federal Theology of Johannes Cocceius*, 271-72.

[192] van Asselt, "The Doctrine of the Abrogations in the Federal Theology of Johannes Cocceius (1603-1669)," 110.

[193] van Asselt, "The Doctrine of the Abrogations in the Federal Theology of Johannes Cocceius (1603-1669)," 110 and van Asselt, *The Federal Theology of Johannes Cocceius*, 278-82. Cf. the discussion in van Vliet, "Decretal Theology and the Development of Covenant Thought," 412ff.

[194] van Asselt, "The Doctrine of the Abrogations in the Federal Theology of Johannes Cocceius (1603-1669)," 116.

certainly not exclusively. He moved from the *pactum salutis* to the covenants of works and grace. "One of the most important features of Cocceius' theology is what we shall refer to as his *historical method.*"[195] Cocceius viewed redemptive history as covenantal history and progressive. He utilized the *analogia Scripturae* and *analogia fidei*, as well as analogy, typology,[196] and "his so-called prophetic exegesis"[197] method of interpreting and applying prophecy. Through his view of the abrogations, "Cocceuis brought about a powerful dynamism in his view of the covenant, which simultaneously lent it a strong eschatological orientation."[198] Cocceius saw revelation as redemptive, progressive, and eschatological from its inception.[199]

- **Nehemiah Coxe**

Nehemiah Coxe was a Particular Baptist.[200] He is important in our brief survey for at least three reasons: (1) Coxe was the co-editor (and most likely the "senior" editor) of the Particular Baptist *Second London*

---

[195] van Asselt, *The Federal Theology of Johannes Cocceius*, 291.

[196] van Asselt, *The Federal Theology of Johannes Cocceius*, 56.

[197] van Asselt, "Structural Elements in the Eschatology of Johannes Cocceius," 78.

[198] van Asselt, "Structural Elements in the Eschatology of Johannes Cocceius," 83, cf. *Ibid.*, 102, where van Asselt says of Cocceuis, "…historical dynamics are of central importance to him."

[199] McCoy called Cocceius "the most eminent theologian of the federal school" (cf. McCoy, "Johannes Cocceius: Federal Theologian" in *SJT* 16 (1963): 352) and (we think wrongly) "*not* scholastic " (cf. McCoy, "Johannes Cocceius: Federal Theologian," 353). McCoy's analysis of Cocceius is fraught with Barthian presuppositions. For instance, he says, "God's Word, which is primarily Jesus Christ, is revealed through Scripture, not in the words alone, but from faith to faith under the illumination of the Holy Spirit." Cf. McCoy, "Johannes Cocceius: Federal Theologian," 355. "The language of Scripture places before us in its words only metonymy, metaphor and the like; God gives the message." Cf. McCoy, "Johannes Cocceius: Federal Theologian," 358. In the article just referenced, McCoy devotes a whole section to trying to prove that Cocceius was anti-scholastic. However, cf. van Asselt, "Cocceius Anti-Scholasticus?" in van Asselt and Eef Dekker, editors, *Reformation and Scholasticism*, 231-51 where he challenges and puts to rest McCoy's anti-scholastic interpretation of Cocceius.

[200] For a brief biography cf. James M. Renihan, "An Excellent and Judicious Divine: Nehemiah Coxe" in Nehemiah Coxe and John Owen, edited by Ronald D. Miller, James M. Renihan, and Francisco Orozco, *Covenant Theology From Adam to Christ* (Owensboro, KY: Reformed Baptist Academic Press, 2005), 7-24; James M. Renihan, "Confessing the Faith in 1644 and 1689" in *RBTR* III:1 (July 2006): 33ff.; and Michael A. G. Haykin, *Kiffin, Knollys and Keach* (Leeds, England: Reformation Today Trust, 1996) for an introduction to three key Particular Baptists of the seventeenth century.

*Confession of Faith (2$^{nd}$ LCF)*;[201] (2) Coxe agreed with John Owen and other seventeenth-century Reformed orthodox theologians on the function of the covenant of works as it related to the Mosaic covenant in redemptive history;[202] and (3) Coxe authored *A Discourse of the Covenants that God made with men before the Law...*, which is structured after the federal model, utilizes Reformed orthodox theological nomenclature, concepts, and sources, and is semantically Reformed orthodox, except portions of his exposition of the Abrahamic covenant(s).[203]

Coxe's treatise discusses God's covenant with Adam, God's covenant with Noah, and God's covenant(s) with Abraham.[204] It is constructed in a linear-historical trajectory from creation, to fall, to redemption in typical federal fashion.

Coxe holds a robust federal view of the covenant of works. He called it the covenant of creation,[205] covenant of works,[206] covenant of friendship,[207] and a covenant of rich bounty and goodness.[208] Coxe held that God created Adam in his image with the law written in his heart. It was the sum of this law that was promulgated on Mount Sinai and delivered more briefly by our Lord "who reduced it to two great commandments respecting our duty both to God and our neighbor..."[209] Added to this moral law was "a positive precept in which he charged man not to eat of the fruit of one tree in the midst of the garden of Eden.[210] The covenant of works or creation was not co-extensive with creation but an addition to it. Coxe says:

---

[201] Cf. Renihan, "An Excellent and Judicious Divine: Nehemiah Coxe," 19-21 and Renihan, "Confessing the Faith in 1644 and 1689," 33ff.

[202] Cf. Richard C. Barcellos, "John Owen and New Covenant Theology..." in Coxe and Owen, *Covenant Theology*, 353-54. Coxe himself defers to Owen in Coxe and Owen, *Covenant Theology*, 30.

[203] Cf. Coxe and Owen, *Covenant Theology*, 71-140.

[204] For an outline of Coxe's treatise where this can be observed easily see Richard C. Barcellos, "Appendix One: Outline of Coxe" in Coxe and Owen, *Covenant Theology*, 313-15.

[205] Coxe and Owen, *Covenant Theology*, 39, 46, 49, 53, 58.

[206] Coxe and Owen, *Covenant Theology*, 45, 49, 53.

[207] Coxe and Owen, *Covenant Theology*, 49, 51. This seems to be dependent upon Cocceius.

[208] Coxe and Owen, *Covenant Theology*, 49.

[209] Coxe and Owen, *Covenant Theology*, 43. For a brief survey of the highly nuanced view of the functions of the Decalogue in redemptive history in Reformed orthodoxy see Appendix Two of this dissertation.

[210] Coxe and Owen, *Covenant Theology*, 43.

In this lies the mystery of the first transaction of God with man and of his relationship to God founded on it. This did not result immediately from the law of his creation but from the disposition of a covenant according to the free, sovereign, and wise counsel of God's will. Therefore, although the law of creation is easily understood by men (and there is little controversy about it among those that are not degenerate from all principles of reason and humanity), yet the covenant of creation, the interest of Adam's posterity with him in it, and the guilt of original sin returning on them by it, are not owned by the majority of mankind. Nor can they be understood except by the light of divine revelation.[211]

It is not from any necessity of nature that God enters into covenant with men but of his own good pleasure. Such a privilege and nearness to God as is included in covenant interest cannot immediately result from the relationship which they have to God as reasonable creatures, though upright and in a perfect state.[212]

Adam had "the promise of an eternal reward on condition of his perfect obedience to these laws."[213] The tree of life functioned sacramentally as "a sign and pledge of that eternal life which Adam would have obtained by his own personal and perfect obedience to the law of God if he had continued in it."[214] Adam's violation of the positive precept of Genesis 2:17 was also a violation of "that eternal law that is written in his heart."[215]

Coxe sees the covenant of grace introduced via the promise of the gospel first revealed in Genesis 3:15. The *2nd LCF* (1677), 7:3 says, "This Covenant [the covenant of grace in context; cf. 7:2] is revealed in

---

[211] Coxe and Owen, *Covenant Theology*, 49.

[212] Coxe and Owen, *Covenant Theology*, 36.

[213] Coxe and Owen, *Covenant Theology*, 44, 51. Coxe gives three proofs with discussion for the promise of an eternal reward on pages 45-46.

[214] Coxe and Owen, *Covenant Theology*, 45. Coxe justifies this function of the tree of life as follows: "The allusion that Christ makes to it in the New Testament (Revelation 2:7). ...The method of God's dealing with Adam in reference to this tree after he had sinned against him and the reason assigned for it by God himself [i.e., Genesis 3:22ff.]. ...This also must not be forgotten: that as Moses' law in some way included the covenant of creation and served for a memorial of it (on which account all mankind was involved in its curse), it had not only the sanction of a curse awfully denounced against the disobedient, but also a promise of the reward of life to the obedient. Now as the law of Moses was the same in moral precept with the law of creation, so the reward in this respect was not a new reward, but the same that by compact had been due to Adam, in the case of his perfect obedience." Here Coxe is articulating Owen's (and others') view of the function of the covenant of works under the Mosaic covenant.

[215] Coxe and Owen, *Covenant Theology*, 43, 51.

the Gospel; first of all to Adam in the promise of Salvation by the seed of the woman...”[216] In his *Discourse of the Covenants*, he says:

> 11. It was from this design of love and mercy that when the Lord God came to fallen man in the garden in the cool of the day, and found him filled with horror and shame in the consciousness of his own guilt, he did not execute the rigor of the law on him. Instead he held a treaty with him which issued in a discovery of grace. By this a door of hope was opened to him in the laying of a new foundation for his acceptance with God and walking well pleasing before him.
>
> 1. For in the sentence passed on the serpent (which principally involved the Devil whose instrument he had been in tempting man, and who probably was made to abide in his possession of the serpent until he had received this doom, Genesis 3:15) there was couched a blessed promise of redemption and salvation to man. This was to be worked out by the Son of God made of a woman, and so her seed, and man was to receive the promised salvation by faith and to hope in it. In this implied promise was laid the first foundation of the church after the fall of man which was to be raised up out of the ruins of the Devil's kingdom by the destruction of his work by Jesus Christ (1 John 3:8).[217]

Later Coxe adds:

> From the first dawning of the blessed light of God's grace to poor sinners faintly displayed in the promise intimated in Genesis 3:15, the redeemed of the Lord were brought into a new relation to God, in and by Christ the promised seed, through faith in him as revealed in that promise.[218]

This understanding of Genesis 3:15 gives Coxe's work a Christocentric flavor from the beginning. In the first paragraph, he says:

> The great interest of man's present peace and eternal happiness is most closely concerned in religion. And all true religion since the fall of man must be taught by divine revelation which God by diverse parts

---

[216] Cf. *A Confession of Faith Put Forth by the Elders and Brethren of many Congregations of Christians (baptized upon Profession of their Faith) in London and the Country, Printed in the Year, 1677* (Auburn, MA: B&R Press, Facsimile edition, 2000), 27.

[217] Coxe and Owen, *Covenant Theology*, 55.

[218] Coxe and Owen, *Covenant Theology*, 59.

and after a diverse manner[219] has given out to his church. He caused this light gradually to increase until the whole mystery of his grace was perfectly revealed in and by Jesus Christ in whom are hid all the treasures of wisdom and knowledge. God, whose works were all known by him from the beginning, has in all ages disposed and ordered the revelation of his will to men, his transactions with them, and all the works of his holy providence toward them, with reference to the fullness of time and the gathering of all things to a head in Christ Jesus. So in all our search after the mind of God in the Holy Scriptures we are to manage out inquiries with reference to Christ. Therefore the best interpreter of the Old Testament is the Holy Spirit speaking to us in the new. There we have the clearest light of the knowledge of the glory of God shining on us in the face of Jesus Christ, by unveiling those counsels of love and grace that were hidden from former ages and generations.[220]

Not only is this statement programmatic for a Christocentric understanding of Scripture, it also reflects the fact that Coxe viewed special revelation as progressive. The *2^nd LCF*, 7:2 says, "This covenant is revealed in the Gospel; first of all to Adam in the promise of Salvation by the seed of the woman, and afterwards by farther steps, until the full discovery thereof was completed in the new Testament." Coxe saw Christ as the hermeneutical center and focal-point of the whole Bible (i.e, *scopus*).

Coxe utilized Reformed orthodox theological nomenclature and concepts. For instance, in the preface of his work, Coxe says:

The usefulness of all divine truth revealed in the Holy Scriptures and the great importance of what particularly concerns those *federal* transactions which are the subject of the following treatise are my defense for an essay to discover the mind of God in them.[221]

Coxe clearly held to a covenant of redemption between the Persons of the Trinity before the world began.[222] In the first chapter of his work, he briefly discusses the monopleuric (i.e., God's sovereign initiation or

---

[219] Here he is dependent upon Beza. Cf. Coxe and Owen, *Covenant Theology*, 33, n. 1.

[220] Coxe and Owen, *Covenant Theology*, 33.

[221] Coxe and Owen, *Covenant Theology*, 29. Emphasis added.

[222] Cf. Coxe and Owen, *Covenant Theology*, 54 and *2^nd LCF* 7:3 and 8:1.

proposal[223]) and dipleuric (i.e., man's restipulation[224]) nature of covenantal engagements between God and men. Coxe defines the "general notion of any covenant of God with men" as follows: "A declaration of his sovereign pleasure concerning the benefits he will bestow on them, the communion they will have with him, and the way and means by which this will be enjoyed by them."[225] Covenantal engagements spring from God's "condescending love and goodness."[226] Covenant is not co-extensive with creation.[227] God sovereignly proposes covenants with men in order to bring them to an advanced or better state than they are currently in and ultimately "to bring them into a blessed state in the eternal enjoyment of himself."[228] Adam "was capable of and made for a greater degree of happiness than he immediately enjoyed [which] was set before him as the reward of his obedience by that covenant in which he was to walk with God."[229] Coxe even held the view that "Moses' law in some way included the covenant of creation and served for a memorial of it..."[230] This was the view of both Ames and Cocceius above, as well as John Owen.[231] Finally, Coxe utilized typology in a manner similar to others in his day.[232]

Coxe utilized Reformed orthodox sources. In Coxe's "Preface to the Reader" he acknowledges John Owen's commentary on Hebrews 8.

---

[223] Cf. Coxe and Owen, *Covenant Theology*, 35 and Muller, *Dictionary*, 122, where he says, "**foedus monopleuron...:** *one-sided or one-way covenant*; the covenant as bestowed by God and exhibiting his will toward man."

[224] Cf. Coxe and Owen, *Covenant Theology*, 35 and Muller, *Dictionary*, 120, where he says, "**foedus dipleuron...:** *two-sided or two-way covenant*; *Foedus dipleuron*, therefore, indicates, not the covenant in itself or in its underlying requirements, but rather the further relationship of God and man together in covenant, and particularly the free acceptance on the part of man of the promise of God and of the obedience required by the covenant."

[225] Coxe and Owen, *Covenant Theology*, 36. Coxe is quoting or paraphrasing Cocceuis' *Doctrine of the Covenant and Testament of God* (cf. Coxe and Owen, *Covenant Theology*, 36, n. 7).

[226] Coxe and Owen, *Covenant Theology*, 36.

[227] Cf. Coxe and Owen, *Covenant Theology*, 36, and 49 both quoted above.

[228] Coxe and Owen, *Covenant Theology*, 36.

[229] Coxe and Owen, *Covenant Theology*, 47.

[230] Coxe and Owen, *Covenant Theology*, 46.

[231] Cf. Owen, *Works*, XXII: 78, 80, 81, 142 and Richard C. Barcellos, "John Owen and New Covenant Theology: Owen on the Old and New Covenants and the Functions of the Decalogue in Redemptive History in Historical and Contemporary Perspective" in *RBTR* I:2 (July 2004): 12-46, which includes discussion and proof of Owen's view.

[232] Cf. Coxe and Owen, *Covenant Theology*, 45 (the tree of life as a type of the eschatological state), 47-48 (Adam as a type of Christ), 57 (the garments or coats of skin as a type of imputed righteousness), and 62-64 (the Ark as a type of Christ or the church).

Coxe had thought about continuing his treatment of God's federal transactions with man by dealing with the Mosaic covenant, however, Owen's treatment of these issues satisfied him.[233] Coxe quotes or references many Reformed orthodox theologians throughout his work: for instance, Beza,[234] Cocceius,[235] Rivet,[236] Ainsworth,[237] Strong,[238] Pareus,[239] Owen,[240] Whiston,[241] and Junius.[242]

Coxe articulated Reformed orthodox views of the covenants of works and grace, though with his Particular Baptist view of the function of the covenant of circumcision made with Abraham. He understood revelation to be progressive and Christo-climactic. Christ, for Coxe, was the *scopus* of Scripture. Coxe also articulated a view of the Garden of Eden that we have seen before: God offered an eternal reward of unbroken communion and future blessedness with him to Adam. In other words, Adam had an eschatology; protology is eschatological in Coxe's federal scheme.

## • Herman Witsius

The Dutch theologian Herman Witsius (1636-1708) served several congregations as pastor then became professor of theology, serving "at Franeker (1675-1680), then at Utrecht (1680-1698), and finally at Leiden

---

[233] Coxe and Owen, *Covenant Theology*, 30. Coxe said, "That notion (which is often supposed in this discourse) that the old covenant and the new differ in substance and not only in the manner of their administration, certainly requires a larger and more particular handling to free it from those prejudices and difficulties that have been cast on it by many worthy persons who are otherwise minded. Accordingly, I designed to give a further account of it in a discourse of the covenant made with Israel in the wilderness and the state of the church under the law. But when I had finished this and provided some materials also for what was to follow, I found my labor for the clearing and asserting of that point happily prevented by the coming out of Dr. Owen's third volume on Hebrews. There it is discussed at length and the objections that seem to lie against it are fully answered, especially in the exposition of the eighth chapter. I now refer my reader there for satisfaction about it which he will find commensurate to what might be expected from so great and learned a person."

[234] Coxe and Owen, *Covenant Theology*, 33.
[235] Coxe and Owen, *Covenant Theology*, 34, 36.
[236] Coxe and Owen, *Covenant Theology*, 33, 84, 86.
[237] Coxe and Owen, *Covenant Theology*, 61, 86.
[238] Coxe and Owen, *Covenant Theology*, 77.
[239] Coxe and Owen, *Covenant Theology*, 77.
[240] Coxe and Owen, *Covenant Theology*, 108.
[241] Coxe and Owen, *Covenant Theology*, 111.
[242] Coxe and Owen, *Covenant Theology*, 126.

(1698-1707)."[243] He published his famous *The Economy of the Covenants Between God and Man Comprehending A Complete Body of Divinity*[244] in 1677. It was offered as somewhat of a peace effort between the Voetians and Cocceians.[245] According to Ramsey and Beeke, "In governing his systematic theology by the concept of covenant, Witsius uses Cocceian methods while maintaining essentially Voetian theology."[246] "Witsus wrote his *magnum opus* on the covenants to promote peace among Dutch theologians who were divided on covenant theology."[247] His *Economy of the Covenants* contains four books: Book I – The Covenant of Works; Book II – The Covenant of Redemption; Book III – The Covenant of Grace (*ordo salutis*); and Book IV – The Covenant of Grace (*historia salutis*).[248]

Witsius starts his *magnum opus* by discussing divine covenants in general.[249] He offers a brief study of the etymology of the Hebrew and

---

[243]Herman Witsius, *The Economy of the Covenants Between God and Man Comprehending A Complete Body of Divinity*, Two Volumes (Escondido, CA: The den Dulk Christian Foundation, Reprinted 1990). For a brief biographical sketch see D. Patrick Ramsey and Joel R. Beeke "Introduction: The Life and Theology of Herman Witsius (1636-1706)" in *An Analysis of Herman Witsius's The Economy of the Covenants* (Grand Rapids: Reformation Heritage Books and Fearn, Ross-shire, Scotland: Christian Focus Publications, 2002), vi.

[244] Ramsey and Beeke "Introduction: The Life and Theology of Herman Witsius (1636-1706)" in *An Analysis of Herman Witsius's The Economy of the Covenants*, iii-xxiv.

[245] See the discussion above for the issues at stake and Ramsey and Beeke "Introduction: The Life and Theology of Herman Witsius (1636-1706)," vi.

[246] Ramsey and Beeke "Introduction: The Life and Theology of Herman Witsius (1636-1706)," vii.

[247] Ramsey and Beeke "Introduction: The Life and Theology of Herman Witsius (1636-1706)," x.

[248] Cf. Ramsey and Beeke "Introduction: The Life and Theology of Herman Witsius (1636-1706)," xi for a slightly different, though essentially the same breakdown.

[249] Cf. Richard A. Muller, "The Covenant of Works and the Stability of Divine Law in Seventeenth-Century Reformed Theology: A Study in the Theology of Herman Witsius and Wilhelmus A` Brakel," in *CTJ* 29 (1994): 80, where he says, "The Reformed orthodox understanding of covenant rested on a complex of exegetical, etymological, theological, and legal considerations that evidence concern for the text of scripture, the culture of the Jews and other ancient Near Eastern peoples, the linguistic and cultural transition from Hebrew into Greek and Latin, the Christian exegetical tradition, and the doctrinal appropriation of ancient covenant language in the light of other fundamental theological questions – notably the relationship of Adam and Christ, the *imago Dei*, the problem of original righteousness and original sin, the history of salvation recorded in Scripture, and the distinction of law and gospel."

Greek words for covenant.[250] He then states "the nature of the covenant of God with man" in these words:

> A covenant of God with man, is an agreement between God and man, about the way of obtaining consummate happiness; including a combination of eternal destruction, with which the contemner of the happiness, offered in that way, is to be punished.[251]

He argues that covenants are comprised of a promise, a condition, and a sanction.[252] The covenant of works, or nature, or of the law[253] is "an agreement between God and Adam...by which God promised eternal life and happiness..., if he [i.e., Adam] yielded obedience...; threatening him with death if he failed but in the least point: and Adam accepted this condition."[254] Here we see Witsius utilizing the concepts of monopleurism[255] and dipleurism as did Coxe. Muller comments:

> In their understanding of both covenants, moreover, both Witsius and a` Brakel bear witness to a resolution of the seeming problem of monopleuric and dipleuric definitions of covenant — and, in so doing, evidence yet another aspect of continuity with the intentions of the Reformers. Over against the view which has tended to set monopleuric against dipleuric definitions, as if the former indicated a reliance on the doctrine of election and the latter an almost synergistic emphasis on human responsibility, the lengthy etymological and exegetical discussion offered by Witsius indicates that all covenants between God and human beings are founded on divine initiative and are, in that sense, monopleuric. At the same time, these covenants, once made,

---

[250] Witsius, *Economy of the Covenants*, I:42-44. Cf. Muller, "The Covenant of Works and the Stability of Divine Law in Seventeenth-Century Reformed Theology," in *CTJ* 29 (1994): 81.

[251] Witsius, *Economy of the Covenants*, I:45.

[252] Witsius, *Economy of the Covenants*, I:46. Cf. Muller, "The Covenant of Works and the Stability of Divine Law in Seventeenth-Century Reformed Theology," in *CTJ* 29 (1994): 84.

[253] Witsius, *Economy of the Covenants*, I:50.

[254] Witsius, *Economy of the Covenants*, I:50. Cf. Muller, "The Covenant of Works and the Stability of Divine Law in Seventeenth-Century Reformed Theology," in *CTJ* 29 (1994): 75-101.

[255] Cf. Muller, "The Covenant of Works and the Stability of Divine Law in Seventeenth-Century Reformed Theology," in *CTJ* 29 (1994): 85.

bespeak a mutuality: The human partner must in some way consent to the covenant and exercise responsibility within it.[256]

Also, a hint of Edenic eschatology can be seen here as well. Adam was to keep the law of nature, which is comprised of the Decalogue in substance[257] and was "implanted ...at his creation,"[258] as well as keep the positive precept forbidding him from eating of the tree of the knowledge of good and evil (Genesis 2:16-17).[259] Witsius sees Adam in a probationary state and capable of arriving at a higher, more blessed state of existence. He says:

> That man was not yet arrived at the utmost pitch of happiness, but [was] to expect a still greater good, after his course of obedience was over. This was hinted by the prohibition of the most delightful tree, whose fruit was, of any other, greatly to be desired; and this argued some degree of imperfection in that state, in which man was forbid the enjoyment of some good.[260]

The more blessed state of existence was "eternal life, that is the most perfect fruition of himself [i.e., God], and that forever, after finishing his course of obedience..."[261] This promise of life flowed out of God's goodness and bounty and not out of any strict necessity.[262] The Garden of Eden, according to Witsius, was a pledge, a type, a symbol, both temporary and anticipatory of a better state yet to be enjoyed.[263] In other words, protology is, as we have seen in other Reformed orthodox theologians, eschatological.

Witsius cites Hosea 6:7 as proof that Adam broke covenant with God in the Garden when he sinned.[264] Adam's sin brought him and the entire human race to spiritual ruin.[265]

The covenant of redemption is the pre-temporal foundation for the temporal covenant of grace.[266] The covenant of grace is made between

---

[256] Muller, "The Covenant of Works and the Stability of Divine Law in Seventeenth-Century Reformed Theology," in *CTJ* 29 (1994): 86.
[257] Witsius, *Economy of the Covenants*, I:62.
[258] Witsius, *Economy of the Covenants*, I:60.
[259] Witsius, *Economy of the Covenants*, I:60, I:68ff.
[260] Witsius, *Economy of the Covenants*, I:69; cf. also I:123-24.
[261] Witsius, *Economy of the Covenants*, I:73.
[262] Witsius, *Economy of the Covenants*, I:76ff.
[263] Witsius, *Economy of the Covenants*, I:106ff., esp. I:109.
[264] Witsius, *Economy of the Covenants*, I:135.
[265] Witsius, *Economy of the Covenants*, I:146ff.

God and the elect.[267] It is first revealed in Genesis 3:15[268] and then progressively unfolded in five redemptive-historical epochs: Adam to Noah; Noah to Abraham; Abraham to Moses; Moses to Christ; and the New Testament.[269]

Book IV is where Witsius follows a more *historia salutis* model. Genesis 3:15 is the first promise of the gospel and the first revelation of the covenant of grace. This crucial text is programmatic for Witsius. His exposition of Genesis 3:15 covers twenty pages.[270] He then traces the covenant of grace through Noah, Abraham, Moses, and the prophets. Of interest to our survey is the fact that Witsius holds that the Mosaic covenant cannot be viewed simply as a covenant of grace or works. It is a national covenant, subservient to both the covenants of works and grace. Witsius says, "It was a *national covenant* between God and Israel...[It] supposed a covenant of grace...and the doctrine of the covenant of works..."[271]

Witsius, as others we have surveyed, is somewhat typical in his articulation of federalism. He starts with the covenant of works. Adam sins and brings ruin upon himself and the entire human race. Because of God's pre-temporal purpose to save the elect through a Mediator, he reveals his purposes of grace through the first gospel promise in Genesis 3:15. This gospel promise is progressively expanded through various historical types[272] and through explicit Old Testament prophecies and culminates in our Lord Jesus Christ, the *scopus* of Scripture.

- **Jonathan Edwards**

Though Edwards was neither European nor seventeenth-century Reformed orthodox, he certainly wrote within that theological tradition and was very aware of the intellectual currents of his day.[273] Probably America's greatest theologian to date, Edwards was a prolific student and writer. He was somewhat unique in that he utilized a pre-critical

---

[266] Witsius, *Economy of the Covenants*, I:165.
[267] Witsius, *Economy of the Covenants*, I:281ff.
[268] Witsius, *Economy of the Covenants*, II:108ff.
[269] Witsius, *Economy of the Covenants*, I:313-16.
[270] Witsius, *Economy of the Covenants*, II:108-28.
[271] Witsius, *Economy of the Covenants*, II:186.
[272] Witsius, *Economy of the Covenants*, II:188-231.
[273] D. A. Sweeney, "Edwards, Jonathan (*1703-1758)*" in McKim, editor, *DMBI*, 397.

hermeneutic, though living during the early days of the emerging critical era.[274]

In 1739 Edwards preached a series of sermons that ended up being slightly revised and published in 1774 as *A History of the Work of Redemption, containing the outlines of a Body of Divinity, including a view of Church History, in a method entirely new.*[275] In this work, Edwards sought, first, to discuss the redemptive story-line of the Bible in its scriptural order and then to give a history of the church as the implications of redemption accomplished applied throughout history. In his Preface, he says this body of divinity is unique in that it is written in the form of a history in order to show the most remarkable events "from the fall to the present time" and even to the end of the world which are "adapted to promote the work of redemption…"[276]

Edwards' *History of Redemption* is divided into three periods: I. From the Fall to the Incarnation; II. From Christ's Incarnation to His Resurrection; and III. From Christ's Resurrection to the End of the World. Each period is further subdivided. The first period contains these subheadings: from the fall to the flood, from the flood to Abraham, from Abraham to Moses, from Moses to David, from David to the Babylonian Captivity, and from the Babylonian Captivity to the incarnation of Christ. The biblical section is approached in a linear fashion, tracing the biblical history of redemption chronologically.

From the outset of the first period in Edwards' scheme, his Christocentricity is clear and ample. He says, "As soon as man fell, Christ entered on his mediatorial work."[277] Christ's mediatorial work is founded in the covenant of redemption where "He stood engaged with the Father to appear as man's mediator, and to take on that office when there should be occasion, from all eternity."[278]

His Christocentricity is further displayed, when he says that "the gospel was first revealed on earth, in these words, Gen. iii. 15."[279] "This was the first revelation of the covenant of grace; the first drawing of the light of the gospel on earth."[280] Edwards views redemptive history as

---

[274] Sweeney, "Edwards, Jonathan (*1703-1758*)" in McKim, editor, *DMBI*, 399.

[275] Cf. Jonathan Edwards, *The Works of Jonathan Edwards*, Volume One (Edinburgh: The Banner of Truth Trust, reprinted 1990), 532-619.

[276] Edwards, *Works*, I:532. We will focus on the sections dealing with biblical history alone.

[277] Edwards, *Works*, I:536.

[278] Edwards, *Works*, I:536.

[279] Edwards, *Works*, I:537.

[280] Edwards, *Works*, I:537.

Christocentric and progressive. "Thus you see how that gospel-light which dawned immediately after the fall of man, gradually increases."[281] He utilizes typology to see Christ progressively revealed in the Old Testament until the fullness of time had come.

The incarnation and subsequent life, death, and resurrection of Christ were climactic events in Edwards' thought. The second period, from the incarnation to the resurrection, is

> the most remarkable article of time that ever was or ever will be. Though it was but between thirty and forty years, yet more was done in it than had been done from the beginning of the world to that time.[282]

Edwards even has traces of doctrinal formulations seen as far back as Ames. He intersects *historia salutis* with *ordo salutis*, though he extends what he calls "the work of redemption" to the end of the world. He says:

> And here, by the way, I would observe, that the increase of gospel-light, and the progress of the work of redemption, as it respects the church in general, from its erection to the end of the world, is very similar to the progress of the same world and the same light, in a particular soul, from the time of its conversion, till it is perfected and crowned in glory. Sometimes the light shines brighter, and at other times more obscurely; sometimes grace prevails, at other times it seems to languish for a great while together; now corruption prevails, and then grace revives again. But in general grace is growing: from its first infusion, till it is perfected in glory, the kingdom of Christ is building up in the soul. So it is with respect to the great affair in general, as it relates to the universal subject of it, and as it is carried on from its first beginning, till it is perfected at the end of the world.[283]

He also sees a two-fold utility of the Decalogue as given by God to Moses: (1) as "a new exhibition of the covenant of works"[284] and (2) as a rule of life.[285] Commenting on "God's giving the moral law in so awful a manner at mount Sinai,"[286] he says:

---

[281] Edwards, *Works*, I:546.
[282] Edwards, *Works*, I:572.
[283] Edwards, *Works*, I:539-40.
[284] Edwards, *Works*, I:547.
[285] Edwards, *Works*, I:548.
[286] Edwards, *Works*, I:547.

And it was a great thing, whether we consider it as a new exhibition of the covenant of works, or given as a rule of life.

The covenant of works was here exhibited as a schoolmaster to lead to Christ, not only for the use of that nation, under the Old Testament, but for the use of God's church throughout all ages of the world...

If we regard the law given at mount Sinai–not as a covenant of works, but–as a rule of life, it is employed by the Redeemer, from that time to the end of the world, as a directory to his people, to show them the way in which they must walk, as they would go to heaven: for a way of sincere and universal obedience to this law is the narrow way that leads to life.[287]

Though Edwards' title includes the words *in a method entirely new*, some elements contained in this work have precedent in seventeenth-century Reformed orthodoxy. Edwards articulated redemptive history in a Federal model. He held to the covenants of redemption, works, and grace. He saw the gospel first revealed in Genesis 3:15 and then progressively amplified in the Old Testament until the climactic event of the incarnation occurred along with its necessary redemptive accompaniments.

### John Owen: Reformed Orthodox Federal Theologian?

With this as the background for our analysis of John Owen's *BTO*, we now know some of the terms, concepts, and doctrinal formulations (and their meanings) to look for in his treatment of the history of redemption. How does Owen structure his work? Does he view protology as infused with eschatology via the covenant of works? Is the covenant of works co-extensive with creation? Is there a theology of Edenic probation in Owen? Is the covenant of works based on God's goodness and benevolence or justice? How does the concept of law–moral and positive–function in Owen's theology of the Garden? What happened at the fall to Adam and his posterity? How does Genesis 3:15 function in Owen's overall discussion? When was the first gospel promise given and

---

[287] Edwards, *Works*, I:547-48. Edwards presents a two-fold utility of the moral law given at Sinai. The way in which he presents the material may lead some to think he is presenting two mutually exclusive positions; either "a new exhibition of the covenant of works" or "a rule of life." I think it better to take it as both/and. For a discussion on the highly nuanced views of the Reformed orthodox on the functions of the Decalogue in redemptive history see Richard C. Barcellos, "John Owen and New Covenant Theology," 12-46.

how does this relate to the covenant of grace and subsequent revelation? How does the Mosaic covenant function in the broad spectrum of redemptive history according to Owen? What place does the Mediator, our Lord Jesus Christ, play in Owen's system? Answers to these and other pertinent questions will be pursued in our survey of Owen's *BTO*.

# CHAPTER SEVEN

# ANALYSIS OF GEERHARDUS VOS' NATURE AND

# METHOD OF BIBLICAL THEOLOGY

## Introduction

This chapter will examine one of Vos' earliest lectures on biblical theology (1894), a magazine article from 1902, and his last published book (while living) in 1948. Material will be gathered from these three primary sources to give us a working knowledge of what Vos viewed as biblical theology. These three sources give us a prolegomena of Vos' biblical-theological methodology from his own pen. *Redemptive History and Biblical Interpretation* contains his 1894 lecture entitled, "The Idea of Biblical Theology as a Science and as a Theological Discipline."[1] His 1902 magazine article, "The Nature and Aims of Biblical Theology," was reprinted in *Kerux* in 1999.[2] And finally, Vos' famous *Biblical Theology: Old and New Testaments* contains an ample discussion of what Vos intended by biblical theology in 1948, a year before his death. These will give us samples from his early years at Princeton and his final days on the earth. We will examine each in historical order and then draw some concluding observations.

## "The Idea of Biblical Theology as a Science and as a Theological Discipline"

This lecture was delivered on May 8, 1894 as Vos' "[i]naugural address as Professor of Biblical Theology in Princeton Theological Seminary..."[3] He was 32 years old and just embarking upon his teaching ministry at Princeton. Vos spoke as a representative of Reformed orthodox theology on an issue that had been the nearly exclusive property "of the liberal/critical biblical-theological enterprise"[4] for over 100 years.

---

[1] Vos, *RHBI*, 3-24.

[2] Geerhardus Vos, "The Nature and Aims of Biblical Theology," *Kerux* 14.1 (May 1999): 3-8. This article is reprinted from *The Union Seminary Magazine* 13/3 (February – March 1902): 194-99. It will be referenced as "Nature and Aims" from here on out.

[3] Vos, *RHBI*, 3.

[4] Dennison, "What is Biblical Theology? Reflections on the Inaugural Address of Geerhardus Vos," 34.

- **Introduction**

**1. Reasons for lecture.** In the introductory section of this lecture, Vos lays out his reasons for approaching this subject. The primary reason was because biblical theology was "a new chair"[5] at Princeton, Vos being the first to occupy it. He thought it his duty to present this material. Vos says, "I consider it my duty to introduce to you this branch of theological science, and to describe, in general terms at least, its nature and the manner in which I hope to teach it."[6] But there is a second reason.

> This is all the more necessary because of the wide divergence of opinion in various quarters concerning the standing of the newest accession to the circle of sacred studies. Some have lauded her to the skies as the ideal of scientific theology, in such extravagant terms as to reflect seriously upon the character of her sisters of greater age and longer standing. Others look upon the new-comer with suspicion, or even openly dispute her right to a place in the theological family. We certainly owe it to her and to ourselves to form a well-grounded and intelligent judgment on the question. I hope that what I shall say will in some degree shed light on the points at issue, and enable you to judge impartially and in accordance with the facts of the case.[7]

Vos sets out, then, to introduce to his Princeton colleagues his method of biblical theology in the acknowledged context of the abuse of some and suspicion of others concerning it as a legitimate theological discipline.

**2. Definition of theology.** Before Vos defines what he means by biblical theology, he offers a definition "of what Theology is in general."[8] He defines theology in general as "knowledge concerning God."[9] He then argues that theology is a science all its own – it is unique and to be distinguished from all other sciences. This is so, says Vos, not only due to the object of theology – God – but also due to its "altogether unique

---

[5] Vos, *RHBI*, 3.
[6] Vos, *RHBI*, 3-4.
[7] Vos, *RHBI*, 4.
[8] Vos, *RHBI*, 4. Vos follows a similar pattern over 40 years later in his *BTV*, as will be seen below.
[9] Vos, *RHBI*, 4.

relation to this object, for which no strict analogy can be found elsewhere."[10] He says:

> In all the other sciences man is the one who of himself takes the first step in approaching the objective world, in subjecting it to his scrutiny, in compelling it to submit to his experiments–in a word, man is the one who proceeds actively to make nature reveal her facts and her laws. In Theology this relation between the subject and object is reversed. Here it is God who takes the first step to approach man for the purpose of disclosing His nature, nay, who creates man in order that He may have a finite mind able to receive the knowledge of His infinite perfections. In Theology the object, far from being passive, by the act of creation first posits the subject over against itself, and then as the living God proceeds to impart to this subject that to which of itself it would have no access. For "the things of God none knoweth, save the Spirit of God." Strictly speaking, therefore, we should say that not God in and of Himself, but God in so far as He has revealed Himself, is the object of theology.[11]

Vos is quick to ground theology in revelation. God is the revealer. Man is the passive recipient of this revelation. God is the object of theology's quest, but only in so far as he has revealed himself. "…[T]heology presupposes an active self-disclosure of God."[12]

**3. Supernatural revelation in light of the presence of sin in man.** Vos then discusses how man's sinful condition and God's desire to be known brings about "that new self-disclosure of God which we call supernatural revelation."[13] Though man in sin retains some knowledge of God, in order to possess "all pure and adequate information in divine things"[14] "…the objective self-manifestation of God as the Redeemer"[15] is necessary and brings into being "a new order of things."[16] Redemptive revelation comes as the objective, self-disclosure of God as Redeemer and is subsequently deposited in the Holy Scriptures so that "the human

---

[10] Vos, *RHBI*, 4.

[11] Vos, *RHBI*, 4-5.

[12] Dennison, "What is Biblical Theology? Reflections on the Inaugural Address of Geerhardus Vos," 35.

[13] Vos, *RHBI*, 5.

[14] Vos, *RHBI*, 5.

[15] Vos, *RHBI*, 5.

[16] Vos, *RHBI*, 5.

mind is enabled to obtain that new knowledge"[17] by the new birth and illumination of the Holy Spirit. Assuming other sub-branches of exegetical theology – the origin of Scripture, its canonization, the Hebrew and Greek languages of the Old and New Testaments, and the exegesis of its content – brings Vos to his definition of biblical theology.

- **Definition of Biblical Theology**

**1. Its basic elements.** The first evidence of a definition of biblical theology occurs relatively early in the lecture:

> In general, then, *Biblical Theology is that part of Exegetical Theology which deals with the revelation of God.* It makes use of all the results that have been obtained by all the preceding studies in this department. Still, we must endeavor to determine more precisely in what sense this general definition is to be understood. For it might be said of Systematic Theology, nay of the whole of Theology, with equal truth, that it deals with supernatural revelation. *The specific character of Biblical Theology lies in this, that it discusses both the form and contents of revelation from the point of view of the revealing activity of God Himself.* In other words, *it deals with revelation in the active sense, as an act of God, and tries to understand and trace and describe this act,* so far as this is possible to man and does not elude our finite observation. *In Biblical Theology both the form and contents of revelation are considered as parts and products of a divine work.*[18]

This seminal definition has several features. First, biblical theology is a branch of exegetical theology. It is not an island, nor is it the end of all theological formulation. Second, biblical theology deals with the revelation of God. Vos was quick to point this out. It is not a history of religion. It is not subjective. It deals with God's objective revelation of himself in the Holy Scriptures alone. Third, biblical theology builds off of the results of the other preceding aspects of exegetical theology. It is the culmination of exegetical theology, though, as stated above, not the end of all theology. Fourth, and most instructively for our purposes, biblical theology deals with both the *form* and *contents* of the Word of God.[19]

---

[17] Vos, *RHBI*, 5.

[18] Vos, *RHBI*, 7. Emphases added.

[19] As seen above, some among the seventeenth-century Reformed orthodox understood federal theology in a similar fashion.

Prior to transitioning into a discussion of the history of biblical theology and its current state, Vos adds this definition, "Biblical Theology, rightly defined, is nothing else than *the exhibition of the organic progress of supernatural revelation in its historic continuity and multiformity.*"[20] Just how he came to that definition can be seen as we examine the characteristic features of supernatural revelation discussed by Vos.

**2. Its detailed elaboration: The Characteristic Features of Supernatural Revelation.** Vos comments upon his initial definition as he proceeds and adds "feature[s] characteristic of supernatural revelation."[21] As Vos says, this approach is based on "what the study of Biblical Theology itself has taught us."[22] The characteristic features of supernatural revelation, as we shall see, will form the regulating principles for Vos' methodology. These features will become evident especially in Vos' exposition of the history of special revelation in his classic work *Biblical Theology*, which we will analyze below. Vos saw them as biblically derived principles for the proper exhibition of the historical unfolding of redemption in both the Old and New Testaments. Commenting on this, he says:

> Here, as in other cases, the organism of a science can be conceived and described only by anticipating its results. The following statements [i.e., features characteristic of supernatural revelation], accordingly, are not to be considered in the light of an *a priori* construction, but simply formulate what the study of Biblical Theology itself has taught us.[23]

The features delineated below become programmatic for Vos and his biblical-theological methodology.

Vos' subsequent outline is sometimes difficult to follow. In fact, at this point of his lecture, a distinct outline is difficult to trace. It appears that after the introductory comments discussed above, Vos presents "the features of God's revealing work."[24] He does so under the following headings with a degree of over-lap: (1) its historical progress, (2) organic development, (3) covenantal-expansiveness, (4) Christ-centeredness, and (5) multiformity of teaching. Some of these features seem to grow out of

---

[20] Vos, *RHBI*, 15.
[21] Vos, *RHBI*, 7.
[22] Vos, *RHBI*, 7.
[23] Vos, *RHBI*, 7.
[24] Vos, *RHBI*, 7.

the previous ones. Assuming this developmental structure, Vos' lecture takes on one of the characteristics of his subject matter – i.e., organic development. Each feature prepares for that which follows and each subsequent feature further develops its antecedents.

### (1) Historical Progress

The first feature he offers is the *historical progress* of supernatural revelation.[25] Vos says, "The self-revelation of God is a work covering ages, proceeding in a sequence of revealing words and acts, appearing in a long perspective of time. The truth comes in the form of growing truth, not truth at rest."[26] He states two reasons for the historical progress of revelation: (1) because of its nature and (2) because of its practical intent.

Concerning the former, Vos means by this the fact that revelation is connected to God's wider work of redeeming the entire universe. He says, "It constitutes a part of that great process of the new creation…"[27] He then concludes:

> As soon as we realize that revelation is at almost every point interwoven with and conditioned by the redeeming activity of God in its wider sense, and together with the latter connected with the natural development of the present world, its historic character becomes perfectly intelligible and ceases to cause surprise.[28]

Vos then distinguishes between what he calls the "two stages" of God's redeeming process – the objective, redemptive acts of God in history (i.e., *historia salutis*[29]) and the subjective application of redemption to individual sinners (i.e., *ordo salutis*[30]).

Concerning the practical intent of revelation, he argues that God intended the knowledge of redemptive revelation "to enter the actual life of man, to be worked out by him in all its practical bearings."[31]

---

[25] Vos, *RHBI*, 7. Cf. Dennison, "What is Biblical Theology? Reflections on the Inaugural Address of Geerhardus Vos," 37-38 for a brief discussion of this.

[26] Vos, *RHBI*, 7.

[27] Vos, *RHBI*, 8.

[28] Vos, *RHBI*, 8.

[29] Latin for the history of salvation (i.e., salvation history/redemptive history/redemption accomplished). This is objective and outside of man's personal experience.

[30] Latin for the order of the application of salvation (i.e., redemption applied). This is subjective and becomes the experience of all the elect in space and time.

[31] Vos, *RHBI*, 10.

## (2) Organic Development

Adding a slightly advanced and more nuanced element of his definition of biblical theology, Vos now says "that it is that part of Exegetical Theology which deals with the revelation of God in its historic continuity."[32] This provides us with a second characteristic feature of revelation – its *organic development*. Describing what he means by this, Vos says:

> When, nevertheless, Biblical Theology also undertakes to show how the truth has been gradually set forth in greater fullness and clearness, these two facts can be reconciled in no other way than by assuming that the advance in revelation resembles the organic process, through which out of the perfect germ the perfect plant and flower and fruit are successively produced.[33]

He further describes the material increase of revelation as "an internal expansion, an organic unfolding from within."[34] This organic concept displays itself as the elements of truth grow out of each other and each preceding epoch prepares the way for a future one. Each epoch "was prepared for by what preceded, and being in turn preparatory for what follows."[35] "So dispensation grows out of dispensation, and the newest is but the fully expanded flower of the oldest."[36] Semel comments:

> Redemptive history moves through stages. Each one is not merely a return to a former state of affairs, but rather, incorporating what has

---

[32] Vos, *RHBI*, 10. Dennison, "What is Biblical Theology? Reflections on the Inaugural Address of Geerhardus Vos," 37-38 for a brief discussion of this.

[33] Vos, *RHBI*, 11.

[34] Vos, *RHBI*, 11.

[35] Vos, *RHBI*, 11. Cf. Bernard, *Progress of Doctrine*, 44, for strikingly similar words. Since this is the only book referenced in Vos' lecture to this point, we may safely assume Vos has relied, at least in part, upon Bernard for some of his thoughts. Vos references another book late in his discussion but for a different purpose than his reference to Bernard. As mentioned above, further investigation needs to be conducted in order to determine just how dependent Vos was on Bernard. For a detailed analysis of Bernard's book see Barcellos, "*The Progress of Doctrine in the New Testament*, by T. D. Bernard – A Review Article (Part I)," 7-26, "*The Progress of Doctrine in the New Testament*, by T. D. Bernard – A Review Article (Part II)," 33-60 and chapter four above.

[36] Vos, *RHBI*, 11.

preceeded [*sic*], each stage moves on to a higher stage, one never seen or realized before, until the final stage is attained.[37]

This leads Vos to state that, since the basic needs of man are fundamentally the same,

> it follows that the heart of divine truth, that by which men live, must have been present from the outset, and that each subsequent increase consisted in the unfolding of what was germinally contained in the beginning of revelation. The Gospel of Paradise is such a germ in which the Gospel of Paul is potentially present; and the Gospel of Abraham, of Moses, of David, of Isaiah and Jeremiah, are all expansions of this original message of salvation, each pointing forward to the next stage of growth, and bringing the Gospel idea one step nearer to its full realization.[38]

Though Vos does not here identify "the Gospel of Paradise" with Genesis 3:15, it is no stretch of the imagination to conclude that this is what he intended.[39]

## (3) Covenantal-Expansiveness[40]

A third characteristic feature of revelation emerges, when Vos says:

> In this Gospel of Paradise we already discern the essential features of a covenant-relation, though the formal notion of covenant does not attach to it. And in the covenant-promises given to Abraham these very features reappear, assume greater distinctiveness, and are seen to grow together, to crystallize, as it were, into a formal covenant. From this time onward the expansive character of the covenant-idea shows itself.[41]

---

[37] Lawrence Semel, "Geerhardus Vos and Eschatology," *Kerux*, 10.2 (Sept. 1995): 34.

[38] Vos, *RHBI*, 11.

[39] Cf. Vos, *BTV*, 41-44, esp. 43-44, for an explicit reference to Genesis 3:15 in a similar context of discussion. We will discuss Vos' utilization of Genesis 3:15 below.

[40] Cf. Semel, "Geerhardus Vos and Eschatology," 28-30 for a brief discussion of the centrality of covenant in Vos and Vos' discussion of *diatheke* in Geerhardus Vos, *The Teaching of the Epistle to the Hebrews* (Eugene, OR: Wipf and Stock Publishers, 1956, reprinted 2001), 27-45.

[41] Vos, *RHBI*, 11.

Redemptive revelation, therefore, is *covenantally-expansive*, according to Vos.

Three years prior to the delivery of this lecture, Vos gave his now famous lecture "The Doctrine of the Covenant in Reformed Theology."[42] In it he not only acknowledged the centrality of the covenant concept in historic Reformed theology, but he agreed with it and expounded upon it. Much of that lecture (pp. 242-67) is aimed at proving that and how the doctrine of the covenant answers all the exigencies involved with man's relationship to God. For instance, Vos says:

> God does not exist because of man, but man because of God. This is what is written at the entrance of the temple of Reformed theology. When this principle is applied to man and his relationship to God, it immediately divides into three parts: 1. All of man's work has to rest on an antecedent work of God; 2. In all of his works man has to show forth God's image and be a means for the revelation of God's virtues; 3. The latter should not occur unconsciously or passively, but the revelation of God's virtues must proceed by way of understanding and will and by way of the conscious life, and actively come to external expression. We hope to show how this threefold demand has been reckoned with precisely in the doctrine of the covenant. Let us now in succession take a look at (1) the covenant of works, (2) the covenant of redemption, and (3) the covenant of grace.[43]

While beginning his discussion of the covenant of grace, Vos says:

> If the work of salvation has a covenantal form at its roots, then the rest of its unfolding is bound to correspond to it and proceed in a covenantal way. The covenant of redemption does not stand by itself, but is the basis of the economy of salvation[44]

We will see in subsequent discussions just how important the concept of covenant is in Vos' theology. But we must not miss the fact that it was present in his seminal lecture on biblical theology. What appears to be a passing comment is actually pregnant with implications for Vos'

---

[42] Vos, *RHBI*, 234-67. This was delivered in 1891 in Grand Rapids as the "rectoral address at the Theological School of the Christian Reformed Church" (Vos, *RHBI*, 234, note *).

[43] Vos, *RHBI*, 242.

[44] Vos, *RHBI*, 252. We will explore one of Vos' contributions to the Reformed tradition later. That contribution involves incorporating the Federal model into his biblical-theological model. This is no small matter, as we shall see below.

biblical-theological methodology. This is a warranted deduction due to at least two factors: (1) because of the statements referenced above from Vos' lecture on the covenant in Reformed theology and the fact that these predate the lecture on biblical theology presently under discussion and (2) because of what Vos says in the lecture on biblical theology. When Vos says, "In this Gospel of Paradise we already discern the essential features of a covenant-relation" and "in the covenant-promises given to Abraham *these* very features reappear, assume greater distinctiveness, and are seen to grow together, to crystallize, as it were, into a formal covenant," we must remember to interpret this in light of "From this time onward the expansive character of the covenant-idea shows itself."[45]

### (4) Christ-Centeredness

Though Christ-centeredness does not appear in Vos' lecture as a separate heading, the language he uses warrants its inclusion in a list of the features of supernatural revelation. While discussing the organic character of revelation, Vos says:

> Hence from the beginning all redeeming acts of God aim at the creation and introduction of this new organic principle, which is none other than Christ. All Old Testament redemption is but the saving activity of God working toward the realization of this goal, the great supernatural prelude to the Incarnation and the Atonement. And Christ having appeared as the head of the new humanity and having accomplished His atoning work, the further renewal of the kosmos is effected through an organic extension of His power in ever widening circles.[46]

He then discusses how Messianic revelation picks up steam as redemptive history unfolds. The human nature of Christ, for instance, "is successively designated as the seed of the woman, the seed of Abraham, the seed of Judah, the seed of David..."[47] He calls this "[t]he various stages in the gradual concentration of Messianic prophecy..."[48] He sees all of the various lines of revelation finding their terminus in Christ as he is revealed in the New Testament. He says most eloquently:

---

[45] Vos, *RHBI*, 11.
[46] Vos, *RHBI*, 12.
[47] Vos, *RHBI*, 12.
[48] Vos, *RHBI*, 12.

All the separate lines along which through the ages revelation was carried, have converged and met at a single point. The seed of the woman and the Angel of Jehovah are become one in the Incarnate Word. And as Christ is glorified once for all, so from the crowning glory and perfection of His revelation in the New Testament nothing can be taken away; nor can anything be added thereunto.[49]

Dennison agrees with the Christocentric thrust of Vos' methodology:

Word and deed coalesce in the display of the new order advanced by God for sinful man. The heart of this new order is Christ. From beginning to end, from creation to new creation, the principle by which God makes all things new is the person and work of his Son. Christ Jesus is the central meaning of all revelation—word and deed. He is the one of whom the law and the prophets bear witness. The Christological meaning and structure of revelation is the goal toward which every interpreter of the Word of God must direct his efforts. Christ Jesus in his fullness—by way of anticipation (Old Testament), by way of accomplishment (New Testament), by way of consummation (parousia). Vos heartily endorsed the dictum of Augustine:

The New Testament is in the Old concealed;
The Old Testament is by the New revealed.[50]

Commenting on the claim that "Vos's method guarantees that our preaching will be theocentric and Christocentric,"[51] Dennison adds:

...our preaching must be Christocentric for we live on the nether side of the fall, east of Eden. Christ Jesus is our Daysman–our sole redeemer. Our only way to the Father is by him. All Scripture bears witness to him (cpr. Lk. 24:44). Ever since Genesis 3:15, there has been a Christological dimension to the Word of God because ever since Genesis 3:15 God has graciously inaugurated a new order for fallen man–the order of redemption through his Son.[52]

---

[49] Vos, *RHBI*, 13.

[50] Dennison, "What is Biblical Theology? Reflections on the Inaugural Address of Geerhardus Vos," 38.

[51] Dennison, "What is Biblical Theology? Reflections on the Inaugural Address of Geerhardus Vos," 36.

[52] Dennison, "What is Biblical Theology? Reflections on the Inaugural Address of Geerhardus Vos," 37. Cf. James T. Dennison, Jr., "Vos on the Sabbath: A Close Reading" in *Kerux* 16.1 (May 2001): 66, where Dennison says, "We are reminded once more of the central agenda in Vos's writings–Jesus Christ."

### (5) Multiformity of Teaching

In noting the element of multiformity of teaching found in Scripture, Vos is getting at the various genres employed by God, and those who employed them, to communicate to man. He says:

> ... we witness a striking multiformity of teaching employed... All along the historic stem of revelation, branches are seen to shoot forth, frequently more than one at a time, each of which helps to realize the complete idea of the truth for its own part and after its own peculiar manner. The legal, the prophetic, the poetic elements in the Old Testament are clearly-distinct types of revelation, and in the New Testament we have something corresponding to these in the Gospels, the Epistles, the Apocalypse. Further, within the limits of these great divisions there are numerous minor variations, closely associated with the peculiarities of individual character. Isaiah and Jeremiah are distinct, and so are John and Paul. And this differentiation rather increases than decreases with the progress of sacred history. It is greater in the New Testament than in the Old. The laying of the historic basis for Israel's covenant-life has been recorded by one author, Moses; the historic basis of the New Testament dispensation we know from the fourfold version of the Gospels. The remainder of the New Testament writings are in the form of letters, in which naturally the personal element predominates. The more fully the light shone upon the realization of the whole counsel of God and discloses its wide extent, the more necessary it became to expound it in all its bearings, to view it at different angles, thus to bring out what Paul calls the *much-variegated*, the manifold, wisdom of God.[53]

This element of Scripture highlights its humanness. However, even though there is a human element to Scripture seen in its variety of genres and individual human authors, it was God himself who shaped the individuals for his purposes of revealing himself as Redeemer.

---

[53] Vos, *RHBI*, 13-14. Cf. Dennison, "What is Biblical Theology? Reflections on the Inaugural Address of Geerhardus Vos," 39.

## "The Nature and Aims of Biblical Theology"

- **Introduction**

In the opening paragraph of this article, Vos acknowledges the relative novelty of biblical theology. He mentions two extremes:

> Many look upon the new-comer with suspicion, while others run into the opposite extreme of paying her such exclusive honor and attention as to treat her older sisters with unmerited coldness and neglect.[54]

Vos then seeks to justify the entrance of biblical theology into the theological arena. His claim is that "the great subject of supernatural revelation in its historic aspect"[55] has received "scant notice."[56] Vos argues that anyone who believes in supernatural revelation will surely see the need for "what Biblical theology sets out to do."[57] What does biblical theology, according to Vos, set out to do? Biblical theology sets out

> ...to ascertain its [i.e., the supernatural self-disclosure of God] laws, to observe its methods, to trace the mutual adjustment of its various stages, to watch the ripening of its purposes–in a word, to investigate its philosophy, so far as this is possible to the human mind.[58]

The task of biblical theology, then, is to identify the laws, methods, adjustments, purposes, or the philosophy of God's self-disclosure as presented to us in Holy Scripture.

---

[54] Vos, "Nature and Aims," 3. This 1902 statement by Vos reveals his early and keen awareness of excess in two directions – suspicion and neglect of biblical theology due to its relative novelty and "excessive honor and attention" to the point of "coldness and neglect" of other theological disciplines. This balanced perspective was maintained by Vos throughout his career and still serves as a warning. It will be furthered displayed that Owen, though with some apparently contradictory statements, on the whole, would agree with Vos on this point. The various disciplines of the theological encyclopedia must never be viewed in competition with each other. Each plays its unique part in the grand symphony of theology.

[55] Vos, "Nature and Aims," 3.
[56] Vos, "Nature and Aims," 3.
[57] Vos, "Nature and Aims," 4.
[58] Vos, "Nature and Aims," 4.

Systematic theology, according to Vos, deals with God's "revelation as a finished product, to be logically apprehended and systematized."[59] Biblical theology deals with revelation "as a process of divine activity in history."[60]

> Sacred history deals with the redemptive realities created by the supernatural activity of God. Biblical theology deals with the redemptive knowledge communicated in order to interpret these realities.[61]

What biblical theology seeks to uncover is the redemptive knowledge communicated to us in sacred history that interprets the great redemptive acts and words of God. Sacred history records "the redemptive realities created by the supernatural activity of God."[62] Biblical theology seeks to interpret those redemptive realities with revealed redemptive knowledge.

- **The General Features of God's Revealing Work**

**1. Historic progress.** Vos sets out "the general features of God's revealing work"[63] in an attempt "to obtain a more definite conception of Biblical theology..."[64] The first feature is the *historic progress* of God's revealing work. "The self-revelation of God is a work covering ages."[65] Though it is conceivable that God could have communicated all that he desired at once, in fact, he did not. This may be due in part to man's finitude. But Vos argues that it is due more to the fact that "[r]evelation is not an isolated act of God."[66] Revelation exists because redemption exists. Redemption involves "the formation of the new world... and this new world does not come into being suddenly and all at once, but is realized in a long historical process."[67] Revelation interprets the redemptive acts of God and that activity spans many centuries

---

[59] Vos, "Nature and Aims," 4.
[60] Vos, "Nature and Aims," 4.
[61] Vos, "Nature and Aims," 4.
[62] Vos, "Nature and Aims," 4.
[63] Vos, "Nature and Aims," 4.
[64] Vos, "Nature and Aims," 4.
[65] Vos, "Nature and Aims," 4.
[66] Vos, "Nature and Aims," 5.
[67] Vos, "Nature and Aims," 5.

culminating in the incarnation, atonement, and resurrection of Christ. When objective, redemptive activity is complete, then and only then is supernatural revelation complete. Revelation does not follow the subjective application of redemption. "Revelation is designed to prepare, to accompany, and to interpret the great objective acts of God, such as the incarnation, the atonement, the resurrection."[68] When God's objective-redemptive acts in history ceased, then revelation ceased.

But Vos argues as well that God's self-revelation as historical progress has a practical aspect as well. Revelation is interwoven "with the historic life of the chosen race... to secure for it a practical form in all its parts."[69] Vos sees this principle of practicality finding...

> its clearest expression in the idea of covenant as the form of God's self-revelation to Israel. The covenant is an all-comprehensive communion of life, in which every self-disclosure is made subservient to a practical end.[70]

**2. Organic development.** While further discussing historic progress, Vos gives a second feature of God's revealing work: *organic development*. He acknowledges material increase in knowledge throughout the ages of redemptive history, but is careful to qualify. He says that

> this increase nowhere shows the features of external accretion, but appears throughout as an organic unfolding from within. The elements of truth are seen to grow out of each other. The gospel of paradise is a germ in which the gospel of Paul is potentially present. Dispensation grows out of dispensation, and the newest is but the fully expanded flower of the oldest.[71]

**3. Ever-increasing multiformity.** As a result of this organic character, Vos sees a third feature of God's revealing work: *ever-increasing multiformity*. He sees both the various genres within Scripture and their individual authors as elements of this multiformity.[72]

---

[68] Vos, "Nature and Aims," 5.
[69] Vos, "Nature and Aims," 5.
[70] Vos, "Nature and Aims," 5.
[71] Vos, "Nature and Aims," 5-6.
[72] Vos, "Nature and Aims," 6.

• **Conclusion**

**1. Definition of Biblical Theology.** At this point in the article, Vos pauses and gives this definition of biblical theology: "Biblical theology, rightly defined, is nothing else than the exhibition of the organic progress of supernatural revelation in its historic continuity and multiformity."[73]

**2. Suspicion surrounding Biblical Theology.** One of the reasons for suspicion cast upon biblical theology in Vos' day was due to the application of the evolutionary theory to the Bible. This bore its ugly fruit in the history of religions school primarily in Germany. Vos now briefly deals with this issue and quite forcefully. He acknowledges that evolutionary philosophy "has affected the treatment of Biblical theology more than that of any other discipline."[74] This is so due to the principle of historic progress, which both evolution and Vos' understanding of the task of biblical theology share. However, he is quick to say state that the analogy between the two is only formal and he quickly gives the reason why. Vos says:

> ...the development sketched in the Bible is totally different from the naturalistic evolution, by the help of which present-day philosophy seeks to explain the history of the universe. Nevertheless, the formal similarity has not unnaturally aroused suspicion against Biblical theology as such, all the more so since, as a matter of fact, many modern theologians have applied this naturalistic principle to the explanation of the growth of Biblical truth. ...our modern Biblical theologians professedly deal, not with the progress of supernatural revelation, in which they do no longer believe, but with the development of subjective religion in Biblical times, and devote their labors to the discovery and reproduction of a number of diminutive doctrinal systems, often contradictory among themselves, which they profess to find in the Bible. ...All this, however, while deeply deplorable, and imposing upon every student of Biblical theology as increased responsibility, lest by his own attitude he should give countenance to this fatal tendency, has nothing to do with the nature of the science itself. It represents a perversion and corruption of it, which should not be allowed to prejudice us against its cultivation in a proper Biblical spirit. If the objective character of revelation, its infallibility, the plenary inspiration of the Scriptures as containing its record be

---

[73] Vos, "Nature and Aims," 6.
[74] Vos, "Nature and Aims," 6.

firmly upheld, there is no danger that anti-Christian principles will creep in to exercise their destructive influence upon the minds of our students.[75]

This extensive quote reveals several important issues for our purposes. Vos was very well acquainted with the abuse that biblical theology was enduring in his day and he was quick to confront it. He was clear and strong in his opposition to the history of religions school and its evolutionary presuppositions. Vos was quick to affirm the objective character of revelation, and the infallibility and plenary inspiration of Scripture as presuppositional safeguards for biblical theology.

**3. Practical value of Biblical Theology.** Vos continues the article with the practical results of the cultivation of biblical theology. *First*, it reveals to its students "the organic structure of revealed truth."[76] This has the benefit of displaying the "relative importance of the single aspects and elements of truth."[77] This keeps students of Scripture from "that one-sidedness in the appreciation of truth, which is the source of all heresy…"[78] Biblical theology helps us understand the various doctrines of the Bible in their proper proportion and relation to the vital, organic unfolding of the whole. *Second*, biblical theology, by placing the old truths in their original historical settings, "imparts new life and freshness"[79] to them. This will guard against "a too abstract presentation"[80] of truth. *Third*, biblical theology reminds us of the vital importance of correct knowledge for spiritual growth. *Fourth*, "Biblical theology meets the charge that the fundamental doctrines of our faith rest on an arbitrary exposition of isolated proof-texts."[81] He argues that the system whose "doctrines grow organically on the stem of revelation, and are interwoven with its whole structure" will stand. It is of interest to note that Vos' doctrinal system was that of the Westminster Standards. *Fifth*, "the highest practical aim of Biblical theology is that it grants us a new vision of the glory of God."[82] He closes this section with these soul-stirring words:

---

[75] Vos, "Nature and Aims," 6-7.
[76] Vos, "Nature and Aims," 7.
[77] Vos, "Nature and Aims," 7.
[78] Vos, "Nature and Aims," 7.
[79] Vos, "Nature and Aims," 7.
[80] Vos, "Nature and Aims," 7.
[81] Vos, "Nature and Aims," 7-8.
[82] Vos, "Nature and Aims," 8.

As eternal, he lives above the sphere of history. He is the Being, and not the becoming one. But, since for our salvation he has condescended to work and speak in the form of time, and thus to make his work and his speech partake of the peculiar glory that belongs to all organic growth, we must also seek to know him as the One that is, that was, and that is to come, in order that our theology may adequately perform its function of glorifying God in every mode of his self-revelation to us.[83]

**4. Biblical Theology as the History of Special Revelation.** Vos closes this article with a brief excursus on the use of the phrase biblical theology. He acknowledges that it is open to serious objection because it gives the appearance that it posits itself against the other theological disciplines by the use of the adjective "biblical." He suggests that the use of the name History of Special Revelation can obviate any supposed difficulties.

## "The Nature and Method of Biblical Theology"

- **Introduction**

Vos' *Biblical Theology* was published in 1948. In the preface, he credits his son, Johannes G. Vos, for editing the material for publication.[84] The material had "previously been issued at various theological institutions in mimeographed form."[85]

- **Working Definition of Biblical Theology and Its Implications**

In the Preface and Introduction, Vos provides us with something of a working definition of biblical theology. In the Preface, he says:

> ...Biblical Theology deals with the material [of the Bible] from the historical standpoint, seeking to exhibit the organic growth or development of the truths of Special Revelation from the primitive pre-redemptive Special Revelation given in Eden to the close of the New Testament canon.[86]

---

[83] Vos, "Nature and Aims," 8.
[84] Vos, *BTV*, vi.
[85] Vos, *BTV*, vi.
[86] Vos, *BTV*, vi.

There are several aspects to this defenition of biblical theology worth noting for our purposes.

**1. Biblical Theology deals with the Bible from the historical standpoint.** It both takes the Bible as history and deals with it according to its own redemptive-historical timeline.

**2. Biblical Theology seeks to exhibit the organic growth and development of the truths of Special Revelation.** This, of course, assumes that the Bible is one book, fully interrelated in its various revelational epochs.

**3. Biblical Theology begins in the Garden of Eden and ends with the closed canon of the New Testament.** Biblical theology, then, seeks to disclose the progressive, organic revelation contained in the Old and New Testaments.

• **The Use of the Phrase Biblical Theology**

Vos also discusses the use of the phrase biblical theology. He says:

> The term 'Biblical Theology' is really unsatisfactory because of its liability to misconstruction. All truly Christian Theology must be Biblical Theology – for apart from General Revelation the Scriptures constitute the sole material with which the science of Theology can deal. A more suitable name would be 'History of Special Revelation', which precisely describes the subject matter of this discipline. Names, however, become fixed by long usage, and the term 'Biblical Theology', in spite of its ambiguity, can hardly be abandoned now.[87]

What is biblical theology according to Vos? In brief, it is the 'History of Special Revelation.' It is the unfolding drama of God's self-disclosure to man from Genesis to Revelation. Though it begins with pre-redemptive, Special Revelation in Eden, it ends with the redemptive, Special Revelation of the closing words of the New Testament.

---

[87] Vos, *BTV*, v.

- **Theology and the Necessity of Revelation**

In the Introduction, a more ample definition and discussion is provided. He begins the discussion with a definition of theology. He defines theology simply as "the science concerning God."[88]

Vos then argues for the necessity of revelation. He makes a distinction between impersonal objects and personal, spiritual beings. Vos says, "…Only in so far as such a being chooses to open up itself can we come to know it. …Such a life we can know only through revelation."[89] He asserts, therefore, that God must reveal himself if we are to know him. "The inward hidden content of God's mind can become the possession of man only through a voluntary disclosure on God's part. God must come to us before we can go to Him."[90] He also argues that God must create in order for him to be known outside of himself.

> In all scientific study we exist alongside of the objects which we investigate. But in Theology the relation is reversed. Originally God alone existed. He was known to Himself alone, and had first to call into being a creature before any extraneous knowledge with regard to Him became possible. Creation therefore was the first step in the production of extra-divine knowledge.[91]

Finally, he argues from the fall into sin to the necessity of Special Revelation.

> Still a further reason for the necessity of revelation preceding all satisfactory acquaintance with God is drawn from the abnormal state in which man exists through sin. Sin has deranged the original relation between God and man. It has produced a separation where previously perfect communion prevailed. From the nature of the case every step towards rectifying this abnormality must spring from God's sovereign initiative. This particular aspect, therefore, of the indispensableness of revelation stands or falls with the recognition of the fact of sin.[92]

Vos assumes the historicity of Adam and the fall into sin in this statement. The fall destroys man's created ability to commune with God.

---

[88] Vos, *BTV*, 3.
[89] Vos, *BTV*, 3.
[90] Vos, *BTV*, 3-4.
[91] Vos, *BTV*, 4.
[92] Vos, *BTV*, 4.

He sees the presence of sin in man and its noetic affects as a further reason for the need of revelation.

## • Main Features of the Divine Activity of Revelation

After a brief discussion of the division of theology, Vos defines biblical theology in the following succinct words. "Biblical Theology is that branch of Exegetical Theology which deals with the process of the self-revelation of God in the Bible."[93] What follows is a four-page explanation, but not of the definition itself. Vos sets out the main features of the divine activity of revelation. We will list Vos' headings and give brief comment under each. It is of interest to note that these features are in basic agreement with "the features of God's revealing work"[94] previously discussed as contained in his Princeton lecture of 1894.

**1. The historic progressiveness of the revelation-process.** Here Vos observes that revelation "unfolded itself in a long series of successive acts."[95] Though revelation could have been completed "in one exhaustive act,"[96] it was not and Vos points out why.

> ...because revelation does not stand alone by itself, but is (so far as Special Revelation is concerned) inseparably attached to another activity of God, which we call *Redemption*. Now redemption could not be otherwise than historically successive, because it addresses itself to the generations of mankind coming into existence in the course of history. Revelation is the interpretation of redemption: it must, therefore, unfold itself in installments as redemption does. And yet it is also obvious that the two processes are not entirely co-extensive, for revelation comes to a close at a point where redemption still continues.[97]

In the final sentence above, Vos is, of course, speaking about the necessary distinction between redemption *accomplished*, or the objective acts of God done outside of the human person, and redemption *applied*, or the subjective acts of God which enter into the human subject. The former acts are revealed in the Bible alone; the latter enter the human

---

[93] Vos, *BTV*, 5.
[94] Vos, *RHBI*, 7.
[95] Vos, *BTV*, 5.
[96] Vos, *BTV*, 5.
[97] Vos, *BTV*, 5-6.

subject by the ministry of the Holy Spirit. The former include "the incarnation, the atonement, [and] the resurrection of Christ."[98] The latter include "regeneration, justification, conversion, sanctification, [and] glorification."[99] The former take center stage in the *historia salutis*; the latter take center-stage in the souls of men and are what constitute the elements of the *ordo salutis*. When objective redemption was accomplished, revelation soon came to a close. However, subjective redemption will continue until the last day and throughout the eternal state (i.e., glorification).

**2. The embodiment of divine revelation in history.** Here Vos says that "...revelation...becomes incarnate in history."[100] He is speaking especially of the death and resurrection of Christ. He makes a crucial distinction between what he calls 'act-revelation' and 'word-revelation.' 'Act-revelation' refers to "the great outstanding acts of redemption."[101] 'Word-revelation' refers to the subsequent divine interpretation of 'act-revelation.' Vos explains:

> In such cases redemption and revelation coincide. Two points, however, should be remembered in this connection: first, that these two-sided acts did not take place primarily for the purpose of revelation; their revelatory character is secondary; primarily they possess a purpose that transcends revelation, having a God-ward reference in their effect, and only in dependence on this a man-ward reference for instruction. In the second place, such act-revelations are never entirely left to speak for themselves; they are preceded and followed by word-revelation. The usual order is: first word, then the fact, then again the interpretive word. The Old Testament brings the predictive preparatory word, the Gospels record the redemptive-revelatory fact, the Epistles supply the subsequent final interpretation.[102]

**3. The organic nature of the historic process of divine revelation.** Vos says that "[t]he organic nature of the progression of revelation explains several things."[103] It explains how revelation, though diverse, can yet be

---

[98] Vos, *BTV*, 6.
[99] Vos, *BTV*, 6.
[100] Vos, *BTV*, 6.
[101] Vos, *BTV*, 7.
[102] Vos, *BTV*, 7.
[103] Vos, *BTV*, 7.

perfect. It is organic. It is a growing organism. It is interconnected. What may be but in seed-form at the beginning becomes mature as redemptive history unfolds and develops. Vos says, "The organic progress is from seed-form to the attainment of full growth; yet we do not say that in the qualitative sense the seed is less perfect than the tree."[104]

The organic nature of the historic process also argues that, even in the earliest days of redemptive history, the knowledge necessary to salvation was present. Vos again says:

> The feature in question explains further how the soteric sufficiency of the truth could belong to it in its first state of emergence: in the seed-form the minimum of indispensable knowledge was already present.[105]

The organic nature of the historic process "explains how revelation could be so closely determined in its onward movement by the onward movement of redemption."[106] Since redemption is organically progressive, revelation is as well. And they proceed together, accordingly. This can be seen by the fact that, since redemption "does not proceed with uniform motion,"[107] neither does revelation. As redemption "is 'epochal' in its onward stride,"[108] so is revelation. Vos says, "We can observe that where great epoch-making redemptive acts accumulate, there the movement of revelation is correspondingly accelerated and its volume increased."[109] This can be seen in no better place than the coming, ministry, death, and resurrection of Christ. The incarnation, death, and resurrection of Christ are the apex of all of God's redemptive acts. Corresponding to that, the Gospels, the book of Acts, the Epistles, and the book of Revelation were all written within several decades of each other. As noted above, word-revelation closely follows act-revelation. Divine, revelatory interpretation comes after divine, revelatory actions.

The organic nature of the historic process, finally, explains the "increasing multiformity"[110] of revelation. Because revelation is organic and because it unfolds over time and in various historical contexts, it takes on the character of multiformity. Various literary genres are used in

---

[104] Vos, *BTV*, 7.
[105] Vos, *BTV*, 7.
[106] Vos, *BTV*, 7.
[107] Vos, *BTV*, 7.
[108] Vos, *BTV*, 7.
[109] Vos, *BTV*, 7.
[110] Vos, *BTV*, 7.

this process to fit various historical situations. Vos says, "There is more of this multiformity observable in the New Testament than in the Old, more in the period of the prophets than in the time of Moses."[111] Various authors are used in this process as well. What keeps this revelation from taking on the character of its organs – i.e., fallible and weak men? God! He is active in the world he made. He fashions men beforehand to be his instruments of revelation and he preserves the integrity of their writings by his Spirit.

**4. The practical adaptability of divine revelation.** The final main feature of divine revelation "consists in its practical adaptability."[112] Vos says it was given that it might be "practically interwoven with the inner experience of life."[113]

- **Guiding Principles in Opposition to Critical/Rationalistic Biblical Theology**

Vos also discusses what he calls "Guiding Principles." He offers these in opposition to what he calls the "perverse influences" of the critical methods of the "rationalistic brand of Biblical Theology," first advocated by J. P. Gabler in the eighteenth century.

**1. "[T]he recognition of the infallible character of revelation as essential to every legitimate theological use made of this term."[114]** He bases the infallibility of revelation upon the personality of God.

> If God be personal and conscious, then the inference is inevitable that in every mode of self-disclosure He will make a faultless expression of His nature and purpose. He will communicate His thought to the world with the stamp of divinity on it. If this were otherwise, then the reason would have to be sought in His being in some way tied up in the limitations and relativities of the world, the medium of expression obstructing His intercourse with the world. Obviously the background of such a view is not Theism but pantheism.[115]

---

[111] Vos, *BTV*, 7.
[112] Vos, *BTV*, 8.
[113] Vos, *BTV*, 8.
[114] Vos, *BTV*, 11.
[115] Vos, *BTV*, 11-12.

**2. "Biblical Theology must likewise recognize the objectivity of the groundwork of revelation."**[116] Here Vos is arguing for the fact that revelation (i.e, "real communication from God to man"[117]) comes from outside of man. Either it was spoken by God (i.e., "dictation") or the Holy Spirit worked inwardly "upon the depths of human sub-consciousness causing certain God-intended thoughts to well up therefrom."[118] This is a unique work of the Spirit upon and within the human authors of Scripture and not to be understood in an existential sense.

**3. "Biblical Theology is deeply concerned with the question of inspiration."**[119] Here Vos is quick to poke at the history of religions school of biblical theology. He argues that if the object of study is none other than the beliefs and practices of men in the past and there is no concern for the factuality of their beliefs and practices on a higher level than merely "a reliable record," then "[a] Biblical theology thus conceived ought to classify itself with Historical Theology, not with Exegetical Theology."[120] Instead of this critical approach to biblical theology, Vos asserts:

> Our conception of the discipline, on the other hand, considers its subject matter from the point of view of revelation from God. Hence the factor of inspiration needs to be reckoned with as one of the elements rendering the things studied 'truth' guaranteed to us as such by the authority of God.[121]

Vos is quick to add that what he means by inspiration involves plenary inspiration. He forcefully denies partial inspiration. He says, "The conception of partial inspiration is a modern figment having no support in what the Bible teaches about its own make-up."[122] He argues that either inspiration is absolute, comprehensive, and plenary or

---

[116] Vos, *BTV*, 12.
[117] Vos, *BTV*, 12.
[118] Vos, *BTV*, 12.
[119] Vos, *BTV*, 12.
[120] Vos, *BTV*, 13.
[121] Vos, *BTV*, 13.
[122] Vos, *BTV*, 13.

"nothing at all."[123] Inspiration is not to be confined to "verbal disclosure, but embraces facts."[124]

- **Methodological Approach**

In the Introduction to *Biblical Theology*, Vos has a brief discussion on the method of biblical theology. What he means by method is how we should "divide the course of revelation..."[125] He argues that it should be divided into time periods because God used the principle of periodicity in the unfolding of revelation. He then adds:

> From this it follows that the periods should not be determined at random, or according to subjective preference, but in strict agreement with the lines of cleavage drawn by revelation itself. The Bible is, as it were, conscious of its own organism; it feels, what we cannot always say of ourselves, its own anatomy. *The principle of successive Berith-makings (Covenant-makings), as marking the introduction of new periods, plays a large role in this, and should be carefully heeded.*[126]

Vos says, "Our dogmatic constructions of truth based on the finished product of revelation, must not be imported into the minds of the original recipients of revelation."[127] He adds that we should seek to "enter into their outlook and get the perspective of the elements of the truth as presented to them."[128]

Vos argues against discussing each book separately due to the fact that "this leads to unnecessary repetition, because there is so much that all have in common."[129] Instead, he advocates we "apply the collective treatment in the earlier stages of revelation, where the truth is not as yet much differentiated, and then to individualize in the later periods where greater diversity is reached."[130]

---

[123] Vos, *BTV*, 13.

[124] Vos, *BTV*, 13.

[125] Vos, *BTV*, 16.

[126] Vos, *BTV*, 16. Emphases added. Cf. Semel, "Geerhardus Vos and Eschatology," 28-30 for a brief discussion of the centrality of covenant in Vos and Vos' discussion of *diatheke* in Geerhardus Vos, *The Teaching of the Epistle to the Hebrews*, 27-45.

[127] Vos, *BTV*, 16.

[128] Vos, *BTV*, 16.

[129] Vos, *BTV*, 16.

[130] Vos, *BTV*, 16. Vos closes this section with the practical uses of biblical theology.

## Conclusion

The three Vos sources above are in basic harmony with each other. Vos views the task of biblical theology as describing the history of Special Revelation according to the laws of revelation. He views revelation as redemptive, historical, organic, progressive, Christocentric, epical-covenantal, and multiform. As we have seen in chapter six, these are some of the same elements utilized by the federal theology of seventeenth-century Reformed orthodoxy. We will see Vos expand upon these elements below and see John Owen identify and expand upon some of the same elements in his discussions on methodology and formulation. This observation adds credence to our contention that Vos resuscitated federal theology under the rubric of biblical theology and applied it to the historical-theological issues of his day.

# CHAPTER EIGHT

# JOHN OWEN'S *BIBLICAL THEOLOGY*:
# PURPOSE AND DEFINITION OF THEOLOGY

## Purpose of Owen's *Biblical Theology*

John Owen's *Theologoumena/Biblical Theology* was most likely "his introductory lectures to students of theology at the University of Oxford..."[1] "[I]t consists of dissertations on the origin, nature, and progress of the knowledge of God..."[2] He describes his intentions in the epistle to the reader in these words, "Clearly it attempts to set out the nature of true Theology, and maps out the course and method by which others may follow in a God-honoring fashion."[3] Toward the end of this epistle, he says:

> I do not think it necessary here to review at any length the whole order and arrangement of the work point by point. I will simply sum it all up. I decided, after a preliminary statement concerning the name and nature of theology, to record the *advances* made in various ways *by divine revelation*, paying particular attention to the *historical order* of events, splitting it into its *important phases* since the first appearance of true theology and, also, recording the defections of many from the truth and the errors resulting therefrom, the various corruptions in the worship of the Church, judged by the standard set by revelation, the many falls of the ancient church, and its restorations by grace. This would conclude with the last and final rejecting of Judaism.
>
> After I had embarked on this plan, many points requiring consideration emerged, particularly the famous reformation of the Jewish Church by Ezra after the Captivity. This led to a full discussion of the antiquities and rites of that ancient Church.
>
> In the final section, I attempt an exposition of *gospel theology itself*. I have explained from the Scriptures what gospel theology is, wherein its nature lies, who alone are fitted for the study of it, how and by what method they might achieve it, what are their most likely stumbling blocks, and all this together with a consideration of the nature,

---

[1] Rehnman, *Divine Discourse*, 18.
[2] Rehnman, *Divine Discourse*, 18.
[3] Owen, *BTO*, xxiii-xxiv.

establishment, and progress of true churches founded upon true theology.[4]

Toward the end of this massive work, Owen says, "It has been my professed intent and stated purpose–almost my one and only purpose in this work–to set forth the theology of Christ."[5]

Book One covers Natural Theology in nine chapters. Owen first sets out to remind his readers of the importance of defining terms. "In sacred things, names have been determined by the Holy Spirit, and so must be treated reverently and with care."[6] He realizes, however, that there is accepted nomenclature in theology and that it is necessary to use such, though with caution.[7]

>...in any subject of study, the material being considered must have an agreed nomenclature; so we will rest content with the terminology accepted by common consent so long as we exercise necessary caution. It is our business to teach with accuracy those truths which our terminology is intended to represent.[8]

### Owen's Definition of Theology

What is theology?[9] Owen answers this question by first exploring how the ancient Jews and Greeks defined it. He notes that in Greek usage, and according to Augustine[10], theology refers to "teaching or discourse *about* God."[11] This is almost the same definition utilized by Vos.[12] Owen

---

[4] Owen, *BTO*, xlix-l. Emphases added. Cf. Owen, *BTO*, 591, where he says, "It has been my professed intent and stated purpose–almost my one and only purpose in this work–*to set forward the theology of Christ*." Emphases added. On page 605, he says concerning Christ, "...He is theology's main and great subject."

[5] Owen, *BTO*, 591.

[6] Owen, *BTO*, 1.

[7] For a brief discussion on this cf. Rehnman, *Divine Discourse*, 50.

[8] Owen, *BTO*, 3. This reveals Owen's tenacious adherence to the authority of Scriptures and his conciliatory attitude toward conventional/historical theological nomenclature. This is a sure sign of the Reformed orthodox way. The Reformed orthodox, as we have seen, were ultimately committed to the authority of Scripture, but they also realized that God had illuminated many teachers of his word throughout history.

[9] Owen is following a well-established pattern for presenting theological prolegomena. Cf. van Asselt, "The Fundamental Meaning of Theology," 324-25 and Rehnman, *Divine Discourse*, 50ff.. In Vos' prolegomenous discussion, he also defined theology.

[10] Cf. Rehnman, *Divine Discourse*, 54.

[11] Owen, *BTO*, 4.

argues that theology cannot be numbered among the sciences. Vos does a similar thing, as we have seen.[13] Owen says:

> ...if you will consider the origin, the subject matter, the purpose, the methods of learning and teaching, in short, the whole concept and purpose of theology, it will be at once evident that it simply cannot be numbered in any manner among the sciences, be they practical or speculative; nor can it suffer itself to be bound by their methodology and rules. Indeed, the very terms "method" or "technique," etc., which are quite proper in the sciences, can have no validity here, where we are to deal with God's will as revealed in the Scriptures.[14]

Theology deals "with God's will as revealed in the Scriptures."[15] According to Owen, this sets it apart from all other intellectual endeavors. The method of constructing a body of doctrine based on the same principles used by other sciences is loathed by Owen. He says:

> Such a body of doctrine, being arrived at totally apart from the principles inherent in the Holy Scriptures, lacks all credibility for itself and cannot reach any of the ends of either theoretical or practical theology, and so never can be theology—properly so called. By the study of systems of this nature, habits of mind are formed in harmony with the system. This may be scholastic, but it is not founded in faith![16]

In Chapter 3 of Book I, Owen gives this definition of theology.

> "The doctrine of God with regard to Himself, His works, His will, His worship, as well as our required obedience, our future rewards and punishments, all as revealed by God Himself to the glory of His name." This is the Word of God–this is theology.[17]

---

[12] Cf. Vos, *RHBI*, 4 and the discussion in the previous chapter.

[13] Vos, *RHBI*, 4. We have also seen where Owen argues for special hermeneutics when it comes to Scripture, in opposition to general hermeneutics in arts and science, cf. Owen, *Works*, IV:208. This is typical pre-critical hermeneutical theory. Cf. note 9 below.

[14] Owen, *BTO*, 9. Cf. van Asselt, "The Fundamental Meaning of Theology," 326, where van Asselt shows that Junius denied the identification of theology with science.

[15] Owen, *BTO*, 9. He later adds that theology considers "the truths of Almighty God and the worship and obedience which is His due..." *BTO*, 14.

[16] Owen, *BTO*, 12. Cf. Rehnman, *Divine Discourse*, 93 for discussion and proof that Turretin held a similar view, as did others in Owen's day.

[17] Owen, *BTO*, 16-17.

Theology, for Owen, starts with God's knowledge of himself. Owen makes a distinction between this kind of knowledge and the creature's. God "alone may know Himself perfectly (Psalm 147:5)."[18] Owens posits the typical scholastic distinction between archetypal and ectypal theology discussed briefly in Chapter Six above. "Archetypal theology is thus the original, first, or principal divine self-knowledge, which is coterminous with the essence and omniscience of God."[19] Ectypal theology is, for Owen, revealed theology.[20] It is dependent upon divine revelation and, with reference to men[21], primarily found in the authoritative, pure, clear Word of God in all its parts.

> ...Scripture is our theology, to such an extent that we assign complete authority to every part of it, and to each and every truth contained in it.[22]

> ...we can see that theology, considered objectively or in the abstract, that is, in its own true nature, is nothing but the pure, clear Word of God, and our part is the apprehension of it with our rational faculties as they are illuminated by God.[23]

The apprehension of ectypal theology by all humans (except the God-man and believers who have died[24]) is considered under two headings by Owen: (1) Adam's theology prior to the fall and (2) all theology after the fall. "Adam's theology was simple, pure, and

---

[18] Owen, *BTO*, 15.

[19] Rehnman, *Divine Discourse*, 60. Rehnman has an excellent discussion on these issues among the Reformed orthodox on pages 57-71. Cf. also, Trueman, *John Owen*, 36-37 and Willem J. van Asselt, "The Fundamental Meaning of Theology: Archetypal and Ectypal Theology in Seventeenth-Century Reformed Thought" in *WTJ* 64 (2002): 319-35.

[20] Cf. Rehnman *Divine Discourse*, 61ff. for discussion.

[21] The Reformed orthodox included angels as recipients of ectypal theology since they have rational faculties.

[22] Owen, *BTO*, 17. Owen believed, as did Vos and the seventeenth-century Reformed orthodox, in the verbal, plenary inspiration of the Scriptures.

[23] Owen, *BTO*, 17.

[24] Owen, *BTO*, 16. Owen draws a distinction between theology as understood by Christ and all other humans. Cf. van Asselt, "The Fundamental Meaning of Theology," 330 for a brief discussion on Junius' discussion of a three-fold division (i.e., Christ, glorified souls [i.e., the theology of the blessed], men on the earth [i.e., the theology of pilgrims]) of the communication of ectypal theology. Cf. Rehnman, *Divine Discourse*, 57, where he says, "A similar concise rehearsal is found in Mastricht, Turretin, Coccejus, Baxter, and Braunius."

undivided until his fall."[25] All theology since then is "varied and complex ...and many other distinctions and complications must be advanced for examination."[26] There is pre-lapsarian theology and post-lapsarian theology. This forms a basis for Owen's method, a method that sees growth and development in theology, yet never goes far from its initial basis and essence, as we shall see.

---

[25] Owen, *BTO*, 17.
[26] Owen, *BTO*, 17.

# CHAPTER NINE
# GENERAL AND SPECIAL REVELATION

**Geerhardus Vos**

- **Introduction**

Vos states that the main distinction to be made in the mapping out of the field of revelation is between General and Special Revelation. General Revelation (or Natural Revelation) comes to all because it "comes through nature."[1] Special Revelation (or Supernatural Revelation[2]) comes to a limited circle because "it springs from the sphere of the supernatural through a specific self-disclosure of God."[3]

Vos discusses the relationship between General and Special Revelation under two considerations: (1) their relationship prior to and apart from sin and (2) their relationship "as it exists in a modified form under the regime of sin."[4]

- **The Relationship between General and Special Revelation prior to and apart from Sin**

Natural revelation consists of two sources – "nature within and nature without."[5] Vos sees nature without dependant upon nature within to "lead to an adequate conception of God."[6] Because God reveals himself through man's religious consciousness (i.e., nature within), nature without could lead to an adequate knowledge of God. Man's created status as *imago Dei* makes knowledge of God possible. Nature without fills out the knowledge man possesses from nature within. It is for this reason that Vos says that the Bible "never assumes, even in regard to the heathen, that man must be taught the existence of God or a god."[7] Vos views this kind of knowledge as antecedent knowledge – i.e., it is

---

[1] Vos, *BTV*, 19.

[2] Vos uses the phrases General Revelation and Natural Revelation and Special Revelation and Supernatural Revelation interchangeably. We will do the same.

[3] Vos, *BTV*, 19.

[4] Vos, *BTV*, 19.

[5] Vos, *BTV*, 19.

[6] Vos, *BTV*, 19.

[7] Vos, *BTV*, 19.

antecedent to nature without because man was created *imago Dei* after the heavens and the earth.

But Vos does not stop there. He says that we must add to General Revelation another category of revelation, even prior to the fall into sin – Supernatural Revelation. He acknowledges that "we usually associate [this] with redemption, but this is not exclusively so."[8] We will comment on this below.

- **The Relationship between General and Special Revelation under the Regime of Sin**

While considering the relationship between General and Special Revelation under sin, Vos is quick to point out, "It is a mistake to think that the sole result of the fall was the introduction of a supernatural revelation."[9] He discusses this further in a later section. Here he affirms that sin caused the structure of General Revelation to be disturbed and in need of correction. The knowledge of God possible from both nature within and nature without has been made subject to error and distortion due to the fall. He argues that "The innate sense of God as lying closer to the inner being of man is more seriously affected by this than his outward observation of the writing of God in nature."[10]

Man's natural knowledge of the nature of God is distorted due to sin and must be corrected. This correction, however, "cannot come from within nature itself..."[11] This correction must come from that which is "supplied by the supernaturalism of redemption."[12]

Vos then discusses the most important function of Special Revelation under sin. It "does not lie in the correction and renewal of the faculty of perception of natural verities."[13] Instead, the most important function of Special Revelation after the fall into sin is "the introduction of an altogether new world of truth, that relating to the redemption of man."[14] This new world of truth differs from "the supernatural revelation in the state of rectitude..."[15] Its *form* and *content* differ and the *manner* in which man receives it differs.

---

[8] Vos, *BTV*, 19.
[9] Vos, *BTV*, 20.
[10] Vos, *BTV*, 20.
[11] Vos, *BTV*, 20.
[12] Vos, *BTV*, 20.
[13] Vos, *BTV*, 20.
[14] Vos, *BTV*, 20.
[15] Vos, *BTV*, 20.

**1. The *form* of Special Revelation is changed under the regime of sin.**
"Under the rule of redemption an external embodiment is created to
which the divine intercourse with man attaches itself."[16] Before the fall
such divine intercourse was direct and there was no need for 'external
embodiment.' As well, prior to the fall into sin "there existed no need of
providing for the future remembrance of past intercourse."[17] There was
an ever-flowing stream of revelation accessible. But the present
enjoyment of redemption, with its "looser, more easily interrupted, only
in principle restored, fellowship..."[18] necessitates a more permanent
form of revelation.

**2. The *content* of revelation is changed.** Revelation now focuses upon
redemption. This "new redemptive revelation is given a permanent form,
first through tradition, then through its inscripturation in sacred, inspired
writings."[19] Vos comments on the new content of revelation due to the
fall:

> As to the newness in the content, this is the direct result of the new
> reaction of the divine attitude upon the new factor of sin. A different
> aspect of the divine nature is turned towards man. Many new things
> belong to this, but they can all be subsumed under the categories of
> justice and grace as the two poles around which henceforth the
> redeeming self-disclosure of God revolves. All the new processes and
> experiences which the redeemed man undergoes can be brought back to
> the one or the other of these two.[20]

Redemptive, Special Revelation is new revelation. "It is inaccessible
to the natural mind as such."[21] Though God does not start over and
though he still regards the world of nature, the world of redemption is not
entered as "a natural transition from the state of nature. Nature cannot
unlock the door of redemption."[22]

---

[16] Vos, *BTV*, 21.

[17] Vos, *BTV*, 21.

[18] Vos, *BTV*, 21.

[19] Vos, *BTV*, 21.

[20] Vos, *BTV*, 21. Vos elaborates on "the categories of justice and grace as the two
poles around which henceforth the redeeming self-disclosure of God revolves" on page
41 of *BTV*. In the seventeenth century, these two poles were called law and gospel.

[21] Vos, *BTV*, 21.

[22] Vos, *BTV*, 21.

**3. The "*mood* of man in which he receives the supernatural approach of God"[23] has fundamentally changed as well.** In the prelapsarian state the approach was one of trustful friendship. But sin has greatly altered God's approach to man. "[I]n the state of sin the approach of the supernatural causes dread."[24]

## John Owen

- **Introduction**

Owen has two categories of revelation (i.e., "God's words"[25]) – "the natural word of His creation or the written and transmitted word which has been granted to succeed the obliteration of the natural word by the infection of sin."[26] Commenting on Psalm 19:1-7, he says, "This psalm praises the two-fold manner of our knowledge of God, that is, His works and His Word. In comparing and contrasting the two, the Psalmist seeks to illustrate the glory of God from the whole circle of creation."[27]

- **General Revelation/Natural Theology[28]**

The revelation of the works of God (i.e., General Revelation) "…is quite catholic" and "[n]o translation is needed for this."[29] The works of God include creation and providence. General/Natural Revelation – creation and providence – is not sufficient, however, for proper knowledge and worship of God, though it still "affirms most eloquently the power, the glory, the being of God."[30]

> …creation and providence, viewed through the medium of the innate awareness of God, and with the indwelling conscience of every man,

---

[23] Vos, *BTV*, 21. Emphasis added.

[24] Vos, *BTV*, 21.

[25] Owen, *BTO*, 20. In Owen's words, the first word is "the natural word of His creation." The second word is "a supernatural or a revealed word."

[26] Owen, *BTO*, 20. Notice that Owen identifies revelation in the original state of man as 'the natural word.'

[27] Owen, *BTO*, 38-39.

[28] Cf. Rehnman, *Divine Discourse*, 73-83 for discussion.

[29] Owen, *BTO*, 39.

[30] Owen, *BTO*, 39. Along with the mention of Psalm 19, Owen references Romans 1:18-20; 2:14-5; Acts 14:15-7 and 17:24-9 in the broader context of this discussion.

certainly prove that God exists, that He is all-powerful, and that He is all-just.[31]

Creation and providence reveal some things about God's attributes but not what is necessary for proper worship and salvation. The knowledge of proper worship and redemption cannot be found in creation, nor are they discernable in providence. Owen clearly states that "...salvation cannot come from Natural Theology."[32] "[N]atural theology can never teach Christ!"[33] Natural Theology for Owen and Reformed orthodoxy was revealed theology (via creation and providence) and did not refer to a separate and independent source of knowledge.[34] It was "that knowledge of God and divine things which is accessible to the mind through the light of nature, and a knowledge which is properly called natural since it derives its origin from necessity or the principles of nature."[35]Natural Revelation for Owen and the Reformed orthodox, according to Sebastian Rehnman, was not a preparation for Christianity because natural theology is both distorted and inaccurate due to the fall.[36]

- **Special Revelation/Supernatural Theology**[37]

The Scriptures were given to reveal God as Redeemer in Christ. "Other great and wonderful traits in the Godhead, such as His grace and mercy to sinners are matters which are not revealed in creation but in

---

[31] Owen, *BTO*, 40.

[32] Owen, *BTO*, 45. Owen's "Digression on Universal Grace" in Book 1, Chapter 6, is an argument against the Pelagian doctrine "that sinners themselves are endowed with the ability to use God's revelation in nature in conjunction with the 'universal grace' and so be saved." Owen, *BTO*, 47.

[33] Owen, *BTO*, 54. In his "Digression on Universal Grace," 58-59, Owen says, "What, do such great scholars really profess to believe, that everything needed to know God, to find Him propitious, to flee to Him in total confidence, is all contained within His works of providence alone? Do not these same learned ones also admit that providence alone cannot reveal Christ? And will they not agree that belief in Christ is necessary for a true, living faith, and the attainment of salvation? If this was not true, what use would there be of the written word? Or in what sense could we confess that only through Christ was the gospel revealed, and life and immortality brought to light?"

[34] Cf. van Asselt, "The Fundamental Meaning of Theology," 333 for a brief discussion.

[35] Rehnman, *Divine Discourse*, 74.

[36] Rehnman, *Divine Discourse*, 77.

[37] We will discuss Adam's pre-fall theology or pre-redemptive supernatural theology in Chapter Ten.

Christ…"[38] Redemptive revelation was given after the fall and terminates upon Christ.[39]

> …the revelation of God's mercy in the promise and in the sending of His Son could only be given after the fall, and as all saving knowledge can only come through the preaching of Christ, then it follows with certainty that salvation cannot come from natural theology.[40]

No one can be saved apart from knowledge not available via nature. "[A]ll saving knowledge depends absolutely upon an awareness of the covenant of grace."[41] In order to be saved one must have the knowledge of redemption, which is only revealed in the Bible. Owen says, "…unless we know Jesus Christ and God's way of reconciling the world to Himself through Christ, then we are not in the way of salvation."[42] He goes on to add:

> The sum total of that knowledge which a sinner might glean from study of the works of creation and providence is, after all, but a knowledge of God as Creator and Governor of His creation. About redemption, there remains a profound silence, except in the Word.[43]

The Bible, and the Bible alone, reveals God as Redeemer in Christ. The reason why we have Holy Scripture is because God had purposed redemption prior to creation ("His intention, purpose, or decree"[44] "concerning the salvation of His elect"[45]) and has ordained the means "to bring this purpose about which might be termed His revealed will or precept."[46] The purpose of the Bible is rooted in the revelation of the eternal, redemptive will of God. The Bible is because redemption is. If men are to be saved, they must believe the type of revelation that is not

---

[38] Owen, *BTO*, 40.

[39] In the "Digression on Universal Grace," 63, Owen affirms that "…the Word itself (…magnifies Christ's name above all things)…"

[40] Owen, *BTO*, 45.

[41] Owen, *BTO*, 53.

[42] Owen, *BTO*, 53.

[43] Owen, *BTO*, 53.

[44] Owen, *BTO*, 50.

[45] Owen, *BTO*, 50. This is a veiled reference to the covenant of redemption.

[46] Owen, *BTO*, 50.

available via nature – they must believe in the Christ who is revealed through the preaching of the gospel. Owen says, "The revealing of Christ the Mediator through the preaching of the gospel is absolutely necessary for the winning of souls to salvation."[47] "Salvation is only in Christ."[48]

---

[47] Owen, *BTO*, 57.
[48] Owen, *BTO*, 74.

# CHAPTER TEN
# PRE-REDEMPTIVE, SPECIAL REVELATION

## Geerhardus Vos

- **Introduction**

Pre-redemptive Special Revelation for Vos involves the disclosure of the covenant of works.[1] Concerning the content of pre-redemptive Special Revelation, Vos says:

> We understand by this, as already explained, the disclosure of the principles of a process of *probation* by which man was to be raised to a state of religion and goodness, *higher*, by reason of its unchangeableness, than what he already possessed.[2]

He is quick to acknowledge that "this disclosure is exceedingly primitive...[and] largely symbolic."[3] This symbolism is not so much expressed in words as in tokens.

> ...these tokens partake of the general character of Biblical symbolism in that, besides being means of instruction, they are also typical, that is sacramental, prefigurations conveying assurance concerning the future realization of the things symbolized. The symbolism does not lie in the account as a literary form, which would involve denial of the historical reality of the transactions. It is a real symbolism embodied in the actual things.[4]

---

[1] This is similar to the formulation of the federal theologians examined in Chapter Six and that of John Owen, as we shall observe briefly.

[2] Vos, *BTV*, 27. Emphases added. Here Vos clearly articulates concepts (i.e., probation and Edenic eschatology) already noted in the doctrine of the covenant of works in various federal theologians of seventeenth-century Reformed orthodoxy. Cf. Lawrence Semel, "Geerhardus Vos and Eschatology," 28-30 for a brief discussion of the content of pre-redemptive Special Revelation in Vos.

[3] Vos, *BTV*, 27.

[4] Vos, *BTV*, 27.

As Semel says, "Genesis reveals to us that Adam was first to have an earthly/natural existence and then after his earthly task was completed, he would enter"[5] a higher state of existence.

Vos then discusses "[f]our great principles [which] are contained in this primeval revelation, each of them expressed by its own appropriate symbol."[6]

- **The Principle of Life and what is Taught concerning it by the Tree of Life**

The Garden of Eden, according to Vos, was "specifically a place of reception of man into fellowship with God in God's own dwelling-place."[7] It was not merely an abode for man. Vos notes that subsequent revelation picks up on the theme of the Garden in various places and for various purposes. For instance, it is picked up "in eschatological form at the end of history, where there can be no doubt concerning the principle of paradise being the habitation of God, where He dwells in order to make man dwell with Himself."[8] It is picked up by "the Prophets and the Psalter, viz., connected with the streams so significantly mentioned in Genesis as belonging to the garden of God, here also in part with eschatological reference."[9] He comments further:

> The prophets predict that in the future age waters will flow from Jehovah's holy mountain. These are further described as waters of life, just as the tree is a tree of life. But here also the waters flow from near the dwelling-place of Jehovah (His mountain), even as the tree stood in the midst of the garden. Still in the Apocalypse we read of the streams of the water of life proceeding from the throne of God in the new Jerusalem, with trees of life on either side. It will be observed that here the two symbolisms of the tree of life and the waters of life are interwoven. For the Psalter, cp. Psa. 65.9; 46.4, 5. The truth is thus clearly set forth that life comes from God, that for man it consists in nearness to God, that it is the central concern of God's fellowship with man to impart this.[10]

---

[5] Semel, "Geerhardus Vos and Eschatology," 31.

[6] Vos, *BTV*, 27. Symbolism and typology were hermeneutical principles utilized by the seventeenth-century Reformed orthodox, as noted in Chapter Six above.

[7] Vos, *BTV*, 27.

[8] Vos, *BTV*, 28.

[9] Vos, *BTV*, 28. Here Vos is playing a familiar tune – protology is inherently eschatological.

[10] Vos, *BTV*, 28.

Vos points out that eschatological significance is attributed to the Garden and the tree of life by subsequent revelation. This divine commentary is highly instructive. It not only gives us a window into Vos' whole-Bible hermeneutic,[11] but it attributes what has come to be known as last things (i.e., eschatology) to the first part of the Bible. This makes pre-redemptive, Special Revelation eschatological. Protology is eschatological and, hence, eschatology precedes soteriology. In fact, "...eschatology shapes the whole biblical message."[12]

What was the specific function of the tree of life? Vos states that it "was associated with the higher, the unchangeable, the eternal life to be secured by obedience throughout his [i.e., man's] probation."[13]

> In the garden, Adam is created in a changeable condition. He is created righteous but he can sin. He is created with life but he can die. A *higher state* is set before him as a goal to attain. This *higher state* is represented in the tree of life. In association with it the confirmed state of eternal life would be given.[14]

Since no prohibition is contained concerning the tree of life and since man had not eaten of it prior to his fall (Genesis 3:22), Vos argues that this "seems to point to the understanding that the use of the tree was reserved for the future, quite in agreement with the eschatological significance attributed to it later."[15] If man would have passed his probation under the covenant of works, he would have had title to the tree. But he failed. Man in sin is not entitled to eat of the tree of life, nor was man as created. Vos says:

> After the fall God attributes to man the inclination of snatching the fruit against the divine purpose. But this very desire implies the understanding that it somehow was the specific life-sacrament for the time after the probation.[16]

---

[11] This hermeneutic was noted in Chapter six, where we examined various seventeenth-century Reformed orthodox theologians.

[12] Semel, "Geerhardus Vos and Eschatology," 31.

[13] Vos, *BTV*, 28. This, once again, is very familiar language.

[14] Semel, "Geerhardus Vos and Eschatology," 32. Emphases added. Semel is parroting Vos who parrots seventeenth-century Reformed orthodoxy.

[15] Vos, *BTV*, 28. Vos means by 'later' later Special Revelation. Again, Vos allows subsequent revelation to shed light on antecedent revelation. This is commonplace among the Reformed orthodox (i.e., *analogia fidei*) and stems from their view of the divine authorship of the Scriptures. Cf. the discussion in Chapter Six above.

[16] Vos, *BTV*, 28.

## • Probation and what is Taught concerning it in the Symbolism of the Tree of Knowledge of Good and Evil

Concerning the function of the tree of knowledge of good and evil, Vos holds what he calls the view most commonly held in the past. He says:

> The tree is called the tree of 'knowledge of good and evil', because it is the God-appointed instrument to lead man through *probation* to that state of religious and moral maturity wherewith his *highest blessedness* is connected.[17]

But why did God forbid the eating of the fruit of *this* tree? He did not forbid it because he was jealous that man might become like him. If God were jealous that man might become like him by eating of this tree, why would he have planted the tree in the garden in the first place?[18] Obtaining the "knowledge of good and evil is not necessarily an undesirable and culpable thing."[19] The knowledge of good and evil was not forbidden; eating of the tree was. The prohibition applied to man under probation. The prohibition was positive law added to the natural law for a distinct purpose and goal. The purpose of the prohibition was probationary. The choice of this tree by God was arbitrary.[20] The arbitrariness highlights the fact that God was placing an unexplained, unmotivated demand upon Adam for the sake of God and God alone. Vos says:

> To do the good and reject the evil from a reasoned insight into their respective natures is a noble thing, but it is a still nobler thing to do so out of regard for the nature of God, and the noblest thing of all is the ethical strength, which, when required, will act from personal attachment to God, without for the moment enquiring into these more abstruse reasons. The pure delight in obedience adds to the ethical value of the choice. In the present case it was made the sole determinant factor, and in order to do this an arbitrary prohibition was

---

[17] Vos, *BTV*, 31. Emphases added. Once again, this language echoes that of the Reformed orthodox doctrine of the covenant of works. Cf. Vos, *RHBI*, 243, where Vos affirms that the means whereby Adam was to attain to "the highest freedom" was the covenant of works.

[18] Vos, *BTV*, 29.

[19] Vos, *BTV*, 31.

[20] Vos, *BTV*, 32.

issued, such as from the very fact of its arbitrariness excluded every force of instinct from shaping the outcome.[21]

The tree was the means ordained by God "to lead man through probation to …[a] state of religious and moral maturity" he had not yet attained, and which was not co-equal with creation.[22] For Vos, to know good and evil is reflective of "maturity in the ethical sphere…"[23] It involves a state of existence, of being acquainted with the antithesis between good and evil. And this could be attained "by taking either fork of the probation-choice."[24] Man was to attain this ethical maturity (a state of existence) once probation was passed, and not prior to it. He could attain to it either during the probation or upon its completion.

> Had he stood, then the contrast between good and evil would have been vividly present to his mind: the good and evil he would have known from the new illumination his mind would have received through the crisis of temptation in which the two collided.[25]

However, he attained this knowledge prior to passing probation, which was to attain to it "in an evil way."[26] It was not eating of the tree, as if the fruit in itself had power to confer knowledge, that would give man the knowledge of good and evil. It was the choice man made either to obey and refrain from eating or disobey and eat that would give him the experiential knowledge of good and evil or the ability to make a clear distinction between the two.

- **The Principle of Temptation and Sin Symbolized in the Serpent**

What God instituted as a means of probation, the serpent uses as a means of temptation. Vos holds what he calls "the old, traditional view according to which there were present both a real serpent and a demonic

---

[21] Vos, *BTV*, 32.

[22] Vos, *BTV*, 31. Cf. Olinger, "Vos's Verticalist Eschatology: A Response to Michael Williams," 36-37 and Dennison, Jr., "Vos on the Sabbath: A Close Reading," 65. Cf. also the discussion of "Federal Theology among the Reformed Orthodox and Beyond" in Chapter Six.

[23] Vos, *BTV*, 30.

[24] Vos, *BTV*, 32.

[25] Vos, *BTV*, 32.

[26] Vos, *BTV*, 31.

power, who made use of the former to carry out his plan."[27] The serpent was used by Satan to tempt the woman. Vos obviously holds that Genesis 3 is a narrative not to be allegorized.

The woman was tempted probably because she "had not personally received the prohibition from God as Adam had; cp. 2.16, 17."[28] The temptation has two stages, both with the purpose of injecting doubt into Eve's mind. The first stage occurs when the serpent asks, "Has God indeed said?" (Genesis 3:1). This is designed to doubt a fact. The second stage of temptation seeks to get the woman to distrust God's wisdom. "Has God indeed said, 'You shall not eat of every tree of the garden?'" (Genesis 3:1). Vos says:

> In this phrasing the Serpent hints at the possibility that, should such a prohibition have been actually issued, God has made it far too sweeping through excluding man from the use of the fruit of every tree.[29]

Eve responds to both stages of temptation. She acknowledges that "God has said" (Genesis 3:3) and she states that "We may eat the fruit of the trees of the garden..." (Genesis 3:2). However, in verse 3 she quotes the words of God in an inexact form – "...nor shall you touch it..." Vos adds, "In this unwarranted introduction of the denial of the privilege of 'touching' the woman betrays a feeling, as though after all God's measures may have been too harsh."[30]

Satan follows this with a categorical denial, not of the fact of the spoken words of God, nor merely of the threat contained in his words – "You will not surely die" (Genesis 3:4), but of the veracity of the statement. In other words, according to Vos, Satan is calling God a liar and attributing a reason for such lying – "For God knows that in the day you eat of it your eyes will be opened, and you will be like God, knowing good and evil" (Genesis 3:5). As Vos states, "God is one whose motives make His word unreliable. He lies from selfishness..."[31]

---

[27] Vos, *BTV*, 34.
[28] Vos, *BTV*, 35.
[29] Vos, *BTV*, 35.
[30] Vos, *BTV*, 35.
[31] Vos, *BTV*, 36.

- **The Principle of Death Symbolized by the Dissolution of the Body**

Based on Genesis 2:17, Vos holds "that death is the penalty of sin, that the race became first subject to death through the commission of the primordial sin."[32] "The words 'dust thou art, and unto dust thou shalt return' occur in a curse."[33] Death is not natural to man; it is not coextensive with creation. "Death is adjusted in its form to the natural, material constitution of man, but it does not spring as a necessity from this natural, material constitution."[34]

Vos continues by discussing immortality. In one sense, philosophically considered, man was created immortal. "[E]ven when the body is dissolved, [the soul] retains its identity of individual being."[35] This is true of man before and after the fall. Theologically, man was created immortal in that he had "nothing in him which would cause death."[36] Vos continues:

> In this second sense it can be appropriately said that man as created was 'immortal', but not that after the fall he was so, for through the act of sinning the principle of death entered into him; whereas before he was only liable to die under certain circumstances, he now inevitably had to die. His immortality in the first sense had been lost.[37]

There is a third sense of immortality. Vos labels this kind of immortality eschatological. "Again, 'immortality' can designate, in eschatological language, that state of man in which he has been made immune to death, because immune to sin."[38] Man did not possess this kind of immortality at creation. The highest sense of immortality is now a result of redemption. Vos sees man in three stages or states of existence: created, fallen, and redeemed.

Vos next discusses mortality in the "various stages or states in the history of man..."[39] Man is not, philosophically speaking, mortal. He cannot cease to exist in all senses. His being cannot go into non-

---

[32] Vos, *BTV*, 36.
[33] Vos, *BTV*, 37.
[34] Vos, *BTV*, 38.
[35] Vos, *BTV*, 38.
[36] Vos, *BTV*, 38.
[37] Vos, *BTV*, 38-39.
[38] Vos, *BTV*, 39.
[39] Vos, *BTV*, 39.

existence. Yet man as created was both immortal and mortal: "mortal as not yet lifted above the contingency of death, but non-mortal as not carrying death as a disease within himself."[40] But the fall into sin brought mortality with it. Because of sin, man "must die; death works in him."[41] He is yet immortal, only in the philosophical sense, though mortal. In redemption, however, Vos sees man as mortal in a qualified sense.

> ...during his earthly state death still exists and works in his body, whilst from the centre of his renewed spirit it has been in principle excluded, and supplanted by an immortal life, which is bound in the end to overcome and extrude death. In this case the coexistence of mortality and immortality is based on the bipartite nature of man.[42]

- **EXCURSUS: The Covenant of Works and the Embodiment of the Sabbath Principle**

Vos does not discuss the Sabbath at this early juncture of his *Biblical Theology*. However, his discussion of revelation in the period of Moses mentions the Sabbath and in words which imply that the Sabbath should be considered as part of pre-redemptive, Special (symbolic and typological) Revelation. Vos argues that the Sabbath principle symbolizes and typifies "the eschatological structure of history" and "was true before, and apart from, redemption."[43] Then comes one of the most important and far-reaching statements made by Vos in all of his writings: "The eschatological is an older strand in revelation than the soteric."[44] He goes on to say "[t]hat the... 'Covenant of Works' was nothing but an embodiment of the Sabbatical principle."[45] If the probation of the Covenant of Works had "been successful, then the sacramental Sabbath would have passed over into the reality it

---

[40] Vos, *BTV*, 39.

[41] Vos, *BTV*, 39.

[42] Vos, *BTV*, 39.

[43] Vos, *BTV*, 140.

[44] Vos, *BTV*, 140. It is of interest to note that this statement comes in the context of Vos discussing the Sabbath. Cf. Dennison, Jr., "Vos on the Sabbath: A Close Reading," 68-70. Cf. also the discussion of "Federal Theology among the Reformed Orthodox" in Chapter Six. The primacy of eschatology is not a Vosian discovery.

[45] Vos, *BTV*, 140.

typified..."[46] In other words, protology is eschatological and eschatology precedes soteriology.[47]

## John Owen

- **Adam's Pre-Redemptive Theology: Natural and Supernatural Revelation**

As noted earlier, Owen says that Adam's theology was simple, pure, and undivided...."[48] In Chapter 4 of Book I, "The Natural Theology of the First Man," he discusses Adam's pre-fall theology.

Man "was created pure and placed with undefiled nature under the laws of creation."[49] In this state, "true theology was also natural and God-given."[50] In other words, it was revealed. But it was not "complete or fully in-born because it has always been subject to increase and clarification by revelation...,"[51] though Adam's theology was pure. He knew "God as Creator, Lawgiver, and Rewarder."[52] He was perfectly fit to render "obedience to God in accord with the covenant of works under which he had been placed."[53] Adam's theology was both natural and supernatural; some of it was revealed by creation, some of it "contained revealed elements not perceptible to nature."[54] Owen identifies the covenant of works as a revealed element not perceptible to nature.[55]

> The whole covenant relationship in which the first man then stood, God's requirement that mankind should obey Him (with promise of eternal felicity and reward), are matters which concern God's gracious will and which could only be known by His free choice to reveal them. Nevertheless, as this knowledge or relationship to God was born with humanity, we may denominate it "natural theology." That which

---

[46] Vos, *BTV*, 140. We will discuss Vos on the Sabbath briefly below.

[47] The primacy of eschatology is something found in Owen and many of his contemporaries through the doctrine of the covenant of works. This was amply displayed in Chapter Six and will be illustrated in Owen below.

[48] Owen, *BTO*, 17.

[49] Owen, *BTO*, 20.

[50] Owen, *BTO*, 20.

[51] Owen, *BTO*, 20. It will be noted below that the covenant of works was added revelation in Adam's pre-fall state.

[52] Owen, *BTO*, 20.

[53] Owen, *BTO*, 20.

[54] Owen, *BTO*, 21.

[55] Owen, *BTO*, 21.

derives its nature from first principles is not inaptly styled "necessary" or "natural." We might conclude that the light of the knowledge of God's will is *not* natural to mankind, for it is neither an attribute of human nature by necessity nor is it of such a quality that it cannot be separated from it. It cannot be derived from any inborn faculty of the soul by natural strength, yet it *is* natural to mankind in view of his historical status as having been created in rectitude of nature, and placed under God's law with ultimate regard to God's glory.[56]

Though Owen identifies the covenant of works as "natural theology," he still viewed it as a special revelation of God's gracious will. It *is not* natural in terms of being "derived from any inborn faculty" though it *is* natural "in view of his [i.e., mankind's] historical status as having been created in rectitude of nature and placed under God's law..."[57] Natural theology for Owen, it should be remembered, refers to all that Adam knew about God prior to the fall.[58]

- **Adam's Pre-Redemptive Theology: The Teleological Function of the Law**

Owen discusses God's Lordship in creation as it impinges upon man's status as creature and the goal or end for which God created man. He argues that

---

[56] Owen, *BTO*, 21.

[57] Owen, *BTO*, 21. Just how the covenant of works is revealed he does not say here.

[58] "Natural theology" for Owen is not some neutral, middle ground where believers engage in evidential apologetics with unbelievers. Instead, as Stephen P. Westcott says, "...he sees natural theology as a *phase* of theology, a true theology for Adam, fatally wounded by the fall, and lingering on until superseded by either revealed theology (for the elect) or superstitious apostasy (for the reprobate), in whose idolatrous worship the last remnants of natural theology died out." Cf. Owen, *BTO*, 705. Richard A. Muller defines natural theology among the Protestant orthodox a follows: "**theologia naturalis:** *natural theology;* viz., the knowledge of God that is available to reason through the light of nature. ...It is insufficient to save man but sufficient to leave him without excuse in his sins. The Protestant orthodox include virtually no natural theology in their systems and never view natural theology, human reason, or the light of nature as a foundation upon which revealed theology can build." Cf. Muller, *Dictionary*, 302. Carl R. Trueman adds, "Owen's rejection of natural theology after the Fall should not be seen in terms of the abolition of the objective revelation in itself; but of its subsequent insufficiency to lead sinful humanity to its appointed end in the eternal enjoyment of God." Cf. Trueman, *Claims of Truth*, 59.

as God arranges and brings about the appropriate and final end of each of His creatures in accordance with His own supreme and sovereign laws and His dominion over His creation, it is necessary to the creatures' dependence that there should be revealed laws and regulations from God, designed to bring about those ends. All creatures—because they are dependent upon their Creator—rejoice in the progress to fulfillment of His plans for them. Such laws apply to the whole spectrum of creation, rational as well as irrational.[59]

It is of interest for our purposes at this point to note that Owen acknowledges God's right to determine the end or goal for man and the means whereby that goal may be obtained. He is very clear as to the means, when he says, for instance:

> ...it is necessary to the creatures' dependence that there should be revealed laws and regulations from God, designed to bring about those ends [i.e., the ends of creation].[60]

> ...He [God the Creator] has a right to expect fear and worship from all beings since He alone is Almighty ("If I be a Master, where is my fear?" Malachi 1:6).[61]

> By these means [i.e., God's law] both the creature's continued obedience to God and its ultimate destiny are established.[62]

> The law's supreme requirement is that this excellent and great Benefactor, this supreme Ruler and Rewarder, be loved, worshipped, and feared.[63]

The *means* for man to obtain the *end* for which he was created was obedience to God's law.

---

[59] Owen, *BTO*, 23.
[60] Owen, *BTO*, 23.
[61] Owen, *BTO*, 23.
[62] Owen, *BTO*, 23.
[63] Owen, *BTO*, 23-24.

- **Adam's Pre-Redemptive Theology: Eschatology Prior to Soteriology**

The goal or end, however, was not the *created* status of Adam. Obedience to God's law could have brought man to his goal or final destination. Owen says:

> In this way [i.e., obedience to God's law] the moral order of creation, which embraces all justice and holiness–for it must, as God the Creator is just and holy–might continue upwards *until it reaches its final destination.*[64]

> This [i.e., the essential nature of the law] consisted of a health-giving light by which he could walk and demonstrate his obedience according to the law, and so *finally be rewarded eternally.*[65]

> Such, then, was the theology of Adam–formed in a state of innocence and moral dependence on God, and, in willing subjection to God's commands, he experienced the *potential* for eternal felicity in the enjoyment of the presence of his Creator.[66]

Adam was created with a *potential* for what he did not possess by creation. He could have been finally *rewarded eternally.* Obedience to God's law could have brought him (and the rest of creation) to a *final destination.* This is the covenant of works. This is the eschatology of Eden.

- **Adam's Pre-Redemptive Theology: *Imago Dei***

Owen argues that Adam was created in God's image and

> was fully furnished with the wisdom and moral light required to enter into this relationship. He was enabled to know God, he had the witness of the unspoiled creation about him, and he enjoyed the immediate and sacramental presence of the Lord. Equipped with such a theology, there was, clearly, nothing lacking for his acceptable and due worship of God, or to hinder his living and acceptable and happy life.[67]

---

[64] Owen, *BTO*, 24. Emphases added.
[65] Owen, *BTO*, 24. Emphases added.
[66] Owen, *BTO*, 24. Emphases added.
[67] Owen, *BTO*, 25.

"From these factors," Owen says, "we can make an estimate of the obedience required" of Adam, along with the promised reward and "gauge the true nature of the first sin and its threatened punishment."[68] As for the obedience, it must be willing, intelligent, and voluntary. Owen adds that "...voluntary obedience was a means of signing and sealing it [i.e., the covenant of works] on Adam's part."[69] The reward consisted in "the secure and eternal enjoyment of God."[70]

- **Adam's Pre-Redemptive Theology: Edenic Probation**

It is at this point that a clear doctrine of Edenic probation is stated by Owen. He says:

> Neither did God offer any other reward for obedience when the covenant was revealed to Adam. What would have occurred when the fixed period of time had elapsed, and it became Adam's reward to enjoy God uninterruptedly forever, has been the subject of much deep and dangerous dispute. Remember that God Himself knew full well that this would never be. We can go no further than what has been established; which is that the fountainhead of our race, *if* he had remained in his first state of sinlessness, would have, at length, obtained a reward for his fidelity, and that reward would have been undisturbed enjoyment of God as was revealed in the terms of the covenant.
>
> Here we must stop, for neither the sacred page nor the events themselves give any clue to the time-scale of the probation or the way in which Adam would have passed from the possibility of sin and entered into the joy of the Lord forever.[71]

Note that a reward was offered for obedience as revealed in the covenant of works. The covenant of works, then, is pre-redemptive, Special Revelation and not strictly co-equal with the act of creation. This reward would have been given to Adam after the fixed time [i.e., "the time-scale of the probation"] appointed by God had elapsed. The reward was something Adam did not enjoy by creation – namely, uninterrupted and undisturbed enjoyment of God forever. Adam's obedience would have

---

[68] Owen, *BTO*, 25.

[69] Owen, *BTO*, 25. Here Owen uses language functionally equivalent to dipleuric.

[70] Owen, *BTO*, 25. Elsewhere Owen says that the first theology had the possibility of establishing eternal well-being, but this was lost for man by the fall into sin. Cf. Owen, *BTO*, 28.

[71] Owen, *BTO*, 25.

brought him to that state of being which will be the lot of all those in Christ in the final, eschatological state – i.e., without the possibility of sin. The reward offered to Adam in the covenant of works (i.e., the undisturbed enjoyment of God), is the very same reward obtained by Christ in the New Covenant.[72]

- **EXCURSUS: The Temporal Revelation of the Covenant of Works in Owen – Absolutely or Relatively Coeval with Creation?**

Owen makes what may at first glance appear to be a perplexing statement. He says, "The covenant was coeval with mankind, but voluntary obedience was a means of signing and sealing it on Adam's part."[73] This appears to be saying that creation and covenant are strictly and absolutely temporally coextensive. In other words, it gives the appearance that the covenant of works is part of Natural Theology/General Revelation and not necessarily of pre-redemptive Supernatural Theology/Special Revelation. Rehnman sheds some light on this thorny issue. He argues that Owen teaches that divine covenants are unilateral in origin (i.e., monopleuric) and bi-lateral in execution (i.e., dipleuric).[74] In other words, God sovereignly imposes the covenant of works upon Adam and Adam takes upon himself its stipulations. But how did Adam come to know the stipulations? Rehnman argues that God revealed them to Adam. He says:

> Theology was then, as noted, primarily but not exclusively natural, because it was from the beginning subject to augmentation by further revelation. Special revelation was necessary in addition to obedience, and God revealed the promise of the reward supernaturally to man. Thus, according to Owen, the covenant of creation or of works necessarily belonged to supernatural theology, for the gift of eternal life could only be known through the will of God.[75]

In Owen's thought, the covenant of creation therefore belonged to supernatural theology, for the gift of eternal life could only be known through the will of God, namely through the sacramental precept concerning the tree of the knowledge of good and evil. This necessity

---

[72] Owen, *BTO*, 26.
[73] Owen, *BTO*, 25.
[74] Rehnman, *Divine Discourse*, 167.
[75] Rehnman, *Divine Discourse*, 167-68.

of supernatural theology has in all likelihood to do with the end of man, for, as Owen contends, man is created for a supernatural end and needs a revelation adapted to this end.[76]

Taken in the wider context of Owen and seventeenth-century Reformed orthodoxy, the perplexing statement above should be understood as follows. (1) As noted, Owen elsewhere says of the revelation Adam possessed via creation that it was not "complete or fully in-born because it has always been subject to increase and clarification by revelation…"[77] The covenant of works was just such an increase. (2) 'Coeval' can and ought to be understood in a relative sense. For, in fact, Genesis 2:16-17 was revealed, strictly speaking, immediately subsequent to man's creation. (3) Owen himself admits that "the covenant was revealed to Adam."[78] (4) Owen is utilizing the concepts of monopleurism and dipleurism in this context. When he says, "The covenant was coeval with mankind, but voluntary obedience was a means of signing and sealing it on Adam's part,"[79] he must mean relatively coeval because supernaturally revealed by God (i.e., monopleurically). The execution of the covenant by Adam in 'signing and sealing' it reveals the concept of dipleurism. (5) Owen's confessional theology embodied in the Savoy Declaration makes a distinction between the creation of man and the revelation of the covenant of works. Savoy VII:1 says:

> The distance between God and the creature is so great, that although reasonable creatures do owe obedience unto him as their Creator, yet they could never have attained the reward of life, but by some voluntary condescension on God's part, which he hath been pleased to express by way of covenant.

This condescension is a monopleuric covenantal act of God. Savoy VII:2 goes on, "The first covenant made with man, was a covenant of works, wherein life was promised to Adam, and in him to his posterity, upon condition of perfect and personal obedience." Genesis 2:17 is cited as Scripture proof. This paragraph reflects the Reformed orthodox understanding of both the monopleuric and dipleuric natures of the covenant of works. (6) The discussion in Chapter Six, "Federal Theology among the Reformed Orthodox and Beyond," showed that several

---

[76] Rehnman, *Divine Discourse*, 84.
[77] Owen, *BTO*, 20.
[78] Owen, *BTO*, 25.
[79] Owen, *BTO*, 25.

Reformed orthodox theologians (i.e., at least Cocceius, Coxe, and Witsius) viewed the covenant of creation or works as relatively coeval with creation and as an immediately subsequent form of Supernatural Theology.[80] In conclusion, Owen's position is carefully nuanced and is not, therefore, to be understood as teaching that the covenant of works is absolutely coeval with Adam's creation. The covenant of works in Owen, therefore, is a condescending act of God revealed to Adam immediately subsequent to his creation. Adam's created and covenantal states can be distinguished but not separated.[81]

- **Adam's Pre-Redemptive Theology: The Fall into Sin**

**1. The nature of the first sin and its punishment.** The first sin "was an attempt at total subversion of God's order and a striving to escape from moral dependence upon God."[82] The essence of sin, according to Owen at this point, is twofold: subversion of God's order and autonomy. God's judgment, therefore, consigns man to an eternity of separation from him in both body and soul.[83]

**2. The fall into sin is a historical event.** What he goes on to discuss is "the destruction of the natural theology of Adam, as a result of it."[84] Owen says, "The health-giving light of the first theology was extinguished through sin, and that creation-theology suffered annihilation."[85] What does Owen mean by this? He qualifies as follows:

> Remember that no teaching may truly be called theology which does not rely on, and trust in, a revelation from God by which the theologian may be pleasing to God and at last enjoy Him forever. Such a revealed pattern is necessary for all "way-farers"[86] in order for them to know God, and to demonstrate their obedience and their acceptance of the covenantal relationship into which God has been pleased to enter with

---

[80] Cf. also the discussion in Ward, *God & Adam*, Chapter 4, entitled "Emergence of a post-creation, pre-fall covenant," 59-66 and Chapter 11 entitled "Law and covenant: the two states of the pre-fall Adam," 99-103. Ward adds several more names to the brief list mentioned above (i.e., Cocceius, Coxe, and Witsius).

[81] Ward, *God & Adam*, 99.

[82] Owen, *BTO*, 26.

[83] Owen, *BTO*, 26.

[84] Owen, *BTO*, 27.

[85] Owen, *BTO*, 27.

[86] In the context of Owen's discussion, a "wayfarer" is any man after the fall into sin who has not yet died. Cf. Owen, *BTO*, 18-19.

them. But, as I have said, that first and foundational covenant and theology was done away with by the fall.[87]

**3. Sin makes obedience to the covenant of works impossible.** Due to the fall into sin, the covenant of works can no longer be a means through which man demonstrates his obedience to God and acceptance of the elements of the primeval covenant. Adam disobeyed and, hence, rejected the covenant and forfeited its promised reward. Sin makes obedience to this covenant impossible. "The first theology taught all things well and truly; its doctrine was all good but now no one could possibly conform to it!"[88] The principle of perfect obedience to God's law still stands, but the ability to obey accordingly was lost at the fall. Concerning the first theology (i.e., the covenant of works), Owen adds:

> Without any doubt, its cardinal teaching is now as true as ever, 'Those who keep the law shall live.' The covenant itself remained, but man had forfeited all ability to respond to it and to meet God in it.[89]

"The fall" says Owen, "made no changes in... man's obligations to God..."[90] It did alter man's relationship to God, but not his responsibilities. The fall also brings with it the necessity of new knowledge, if man is to be saved from the effects of sin. Natural theology is "no longer sufficient to direct sinners in the way of life."[91] The "knowledge of God as Creator, Ruler, and Recompenser..." (i.e., the covenant of works) cannot now direct man in right walking with God. A knowledge of God as gracious and compassionate is now needed. This knowledge comes "through Jesus Christ as Savior."[92]

---

[87] Owen, *BTO*, 27.
[88] Owen, *BTO*, 27.
[89] Owen, *BTO*, 27-28. Cf. Leviticus 18:5.
[90] Owen, *BTO*, 28.
[91] Owen, *BTO*, 28.
[92] Owen, *BTO*, 28.

# CHAPTER ELEVEN
# REDEMPTIVE, SPECIAL REVELATION
# AND THE GARDEN OF EDEN

## Geerhardus Vos

- **Introduction**

Vos sees in Genesis 3 "the characteristics of God's saving approach to, and dealing with, man..."[1] He sees both justice and grace "turned towards fallen man."[2] Justice is seen in the three curses; grace "lies implicitly in the curse upon the Tempter."[3] God is revealed as seeking and interrogating man after the fall. "[T]his breathes the spirit of One who prepared for the ultimate showing of grace."[4]

Man's shame from nakedness is a revelation of the loss of innocence.[5] Shame is because sin is. General Revelation coupled with man's sin produced shame and fear. God addresses this shame and fear with Special Revelation. Vos notes that man and woman do not hide themselves from each other, but from God. Shame and fear "operate with reference to God."[6] "The divine interrogation reduces the sense of shame and fear to its ultimate root in sin."[7]

- **Revelation through the Curse**

**1. The Serpent.** Vos discusses the curse upon the serpent first. It is here that grace is revealed. Four principal elements of ultimate victory are revealed "in the formulation given to this curse."[8] First, Vos sees "divine initiative in the work of deliverance."[9] He sees this in the words, "I will

---

[1] Vos, *BTV*, 41. Though Vos uses the term "redemptive" in the chapter title and the first sentence of the first paragraph, he does so, as he says, "by anticipation."
[2] Vos, *BTV*, 41.
[3] Vos, *BTV*, 41.
[4] Vos, *BTV*, 41.
[5] Vos, *BTV*, 41.
[6] Vos, *BTV*, 41.
[7] Vos, *BTV*, 41.
[8] Vos, *BTV*, 42.
[9] Vos, *BTV*, 42.

put enmity" (notice the first person singular pronoun). This is not an appeal to man but a divine promise.

Second, Vos sees the essence of deliverance revealed here. He says it "consists in a reversal of the attitude assumed by man towards the serpent and God respectively."[10] Man's sin illustrated that he had put himself in league with the serpent and in opposition to God. The curse upon the serpent is a promise that God has taken it upon himself to bring man back into league with him and in opposition to the serpent. "God being the mover in the warfare against Satan, man, joining in this, becomes plainly the ally of God."[11]

Third, Vos sees a declaration of the "continuity of the work of deliverance…"[12] "[E]nmity extends to the *seed* of the woman and of the serpent."[13] Here God promises that "he will keep up the enmity in the line of human descent and will not allow it to die out."[14] The seed of the woman refers to "the organism of the race" and, specifically, that part of the race that becomes the enemy of the serpent. These are those who will be brought into the orbit of redemption, and not "all individuals."[15] Vos holds that the seed of the serpent refers to the evil spirits who serve Satan outside of the human race.[16]

Fourth, "the issue of the enmity is foretold."[17] On the part of the serpent, he shall bruise the heel of the woman's seed. On the other hand, the woman's seed shall bruise the head of the serpent.

**2. The Seed.** Vos takes *seed* in the collective sense as it relates to both the serpent and the woman.[18] However, this does not mean it cannot refer ultimately to a future individual. "The promise is, that somehow out of the human race a fatal blow will come which shall crush the head of the serpent."[19]

Does the text indicate how this might take place? Vos thinks so.

---

[10] Vos, *BTV*, 42.
[11] Vos, *BTV*, 41.
[12] Vos, *BTV*, 42.
[13] Vos, *BTV*, 42.
[14] Vos, *BTV*, 42.
[15] Vos, *BTV*, 42.
[16] Vos, *BTV*, 42.
[17] Vos, *BTV*, 43.
[18] Vos, *BTV*, 43.
[19] Vos, *BTV*, 43.

...indirectly the possibility is hinted at that in striking this fatal blow the seed of the woman will be concentrated in one person, for it should be noticed that it is not the seed of the serpent but the serpent itself whose head will be bruised. In the former half of the curse the two seeds are contrasted; here the woman's seed and the serpent. This suggests that as at the climax of the struggle the serpent's seed will be represented by the serpent, in the same manner the woman's seed may find representation in s single person...[20]

Immediately after mentioning a Messianic reference in Genesis 3:15, Vos qualifies as follows:

...we are not warranted, however, in seeking an exclusively personal reference to the Messiah here, as though He alone were meant by 'the woman's seed'. Old Testament Revelation approaches the concept of a personal Messiah very gradually. It sufficed man to know that through His divine power and grace God would bring out of the human race victory over the serpent. In that faith could rest. The object of their faith was much less definite than that of ours, who know the personal Messiah. But none the less, the essence of this faith, subjectively considered, was the same, viz., trust in God's grace and power to bring deliverance from sin.[21]

Vos does not deny a Messianic reference altogether; he denies exclusivity to a Messianic reference.[22] The object of faith as the personal Messiah grows and develops over time in Old Testament revelation. The essence of faith remains the same.

**3. Human Suffering.** Here justice is revealed. As a result of sin, justice comes to the woman and the man in the form of a curse (i.e., the pain of labor).

---

[20] Vos, *BTV*, 43.

[21] Vos, *BTV*, 44.

[22] Vos is certainly more guarded with Genesis 3:15 than the Reformed orthodox theologians we surveyed in Chapter Six and Owen is below. This seems a bit out of balance with Vos' statements referenced above about the Christocentricity of Scripture. Cf. Robert L. Reymond, *A New Systematic Theology of the Christian Faith* (Nashville: Thomas Nelsen Publishers, 1998), 535-37, where he takes Vos to task for being, in the mind of Reymond, not explicitly Christocentric enough in his exegesis of Genesis 3:15 in his *Biblical Theology*.

## John Owen

* **Introduction: "The Renewal of Theology after the Fall"**

The title of Book II is "Theology from Adam to Noah." Chapter 1 is "The Renewal of Theology after the Fall."[23] Owen describes theology subsequent to the fall as "the phase of theological development which succeeded it [i.e., "innate or natural theology"] and took its place."[24] Owen qualifies by recognizing the fact that natural theology has not totally ceased. He says:

> Rather the strands of the two combine; remnants of the former surviving the inroads of corruption and combining with the latter and, so, *progressing* onwards through *several noteworthy stages* which must be examined in turn.[25]

Postlapsarian theology respects nature, is progressive, and delivered in stages. It "is at root of one and the same kind, complete in itself but with a completeness arrived at, strengthened, and illuminated by *successive stages* of divine illumination."[26] Owen says there are "various stages of supernatural revelation which made up this renewed theology."[27] These stages "are renumerated for us by the Apostle in Hebrews 1:1."[28]

* **Genesis 3:15: The *Protevangelium* and Covenant of Grace**

Owen argues that "the pre-diluvian Adamic theology ...took its ground on the first evangelical promise."[29] He calls this the *protevangelium*.[30] This comes out of God's infinite grace, wisdom, and love.[31] Since, for Owen, "all true theology is based on some form of divine covenant," the evangelical promise is a covenant of grace.[32] It has its own commands

---

[23] Owen, *BTO*, 169.
[24] Owen, *BTO* 169.
[25] Owen, *BTO*, 169. Emphases added.
[26] Owen, *BTO*, 169. Emphases added.
[27] Owen, *BTO*, 170.
[28] Owen, *BTO*, 170.
[29] Owen, *BTO*, 170, 185.
[30] Owen, *BTO*, 170. Cf. also Owen, *BTO*, 375.
[31] Owen, *BTO*, 170.
[32] Owen, *BTO*, 170. In Book 3, Chapter 1, 207, Owen says, "There is, therefore, no good reason to deny that God's promise [i.e. in Genesis 3:15] really had the true nature of a covenant..." Cf. the discussion below in the Chapter Thirteen, "Redemptive, Special

and requirements and is backed up by its own gracious promises.[33] It is graciously grounded in "the mediator of the covenant."[34]

> This covenant was then a matter of pure grace alone, and was founded upon one who bound himself to take on all its conditions. In a word, this new phase of theology consisted of the teachings and promises of the covenant.[35]

The basis of this covenant of grace is found in the words of Genesis 3:15, "I will put enmity between thee and the woman, and between thy seed and her seed: it shall bruise thy head, and thou shalt bruise his heel." This is none other than a prefigurement of Christ. This is "the very marrow and core of the new theology."[36]

> From this time onward, it was revealed that righteousness and, in righteousness, gracious acceptance with God could never be sought at home by acceptable performance or inborn strength, but must be received from another who alone could overcome the danger of eternal death.[37]

> ...the promise of a coming one, a Savior, who would enter this world by taking on Himself a human body, "the seed of the woman" (Genesis 3:15), "made of a woman" (Galatians 4:4), and through whom restoration might be obtained. This future incarnation the Apostle would call "bringing the first begotten into the world" (Hebrews 1:6), and, by it, Christ was to "come into the world" (Hebrews 10:5).[38]

Indeed, Owen claims that the essential elements of soteriology are contained in Genesis 3:15.

> ...our doctrine concerning the Savior and Mediator and His appointed work, along with justification by grace, evangelical repentance, eternal rewards, and the resurrection of the body is all embraced (however

---

Revelation from Noah to Abraham" and the discussion above in Chapter Six, "Federal Theology among the Reformed Orthodox and Beyond."

[33] Owen, *BTO*, 170.

[34] Owen, *BTO*, 170. Note how Owen is more explicitly federal in his terminology than Vos.

[35] Owen, *BTO*, 171.

[36] Owen, *BTO*, 171. Note how Owen is more explicitly Christocentric than Vos.

[37] Owen, *BTO*, 171.

[38] Owen, *BTO*, 172.

obscurely) in the heads which I have enumerated above out of this first promise.[39]

- **A New Phase of Theology and Its Two-Fold Ethic: Moral Law and Positive Law**

The revelation of God as Redeemer in Christ is a "new phase of theology..."[40] Though the "root purpose of theology–the eternal enjoyment of God–certainly remained the same...there now took place a forward movement not only of teaching, but also of means and principles."[41] Owen sees the commands of this new theology as twofold: (1) the perpetuity of all the moral commands of natural theology (which includes "all the commands of the Decalogue"[42]) and (2) "the institution of sacrifice–that cornerstone of Adamic, pre-diluvian theology."[43] In other words, the moral law and the positive law of sacrifice (i.e., acceptable worship) are the essential commands of the new theology.[44] God does not accept worship unless it is revealed worship. He rejects "all human innovation in His worship..."[45] The rite of sacrifice was calculated to typify the coming Messiah.[46] It was revealed by God and thus is an illustration of what we know as the regulative principle of worship.[47] All acceptable worship comes from "the personal revelation of God's own will."[48] Since Paul, in Hebrews 9:22, affirms that "forgiveness of sins...could not take place without the shedding of blood," even "those skins from which the Lord fashioned tunics for the first human pair may have come from the very first sacrifices."[49]

This, then, was the essence of the Adamic or post-lapsarian theology. Within it lay, as it were, in embryo the whole doctrine of salvation for

---

[39] Owen, *BTO*, 173.

[40] Owen, *BTO*, 175.

[41] Owen, *BTO*, 176.

[42] Owen, *BTO*, 177.

[43] Owen, *BTO*, 177 and 371. Cf. Reymond, *A New Systematic Theology*, 536, where he discusses Vos' refusal "to see the divine institution of expiatory sacrifice in Genesis 3:21." This refusal creates a wedge between Vos and Owen on this issue.

[44] At this juncture, Owen quotes Arminius and disagrees with his assertion that acceptable worship came as a result of man's religious feeling. Cf. Owen, *BTO*, 178ff.

[45] Owen, *BTO*, 179.

[46] Owen, *BTO*, 179.

[47] The worship God desires is the worship God requires in his word.

[48] Owen, *BTO*, 180.

[49] Owen, *BTO*, 180.

sinners. Subsequent clarification would all be matters of degree. The whole was founded on divine promise which, being clarified during the journey the Church, at length, was fully revealed in the gospel. The norm for obedience to God was explained, at the ordained time, in the Decalogue, and its inner nature and practice would be demonstrated by the prophets. The pattern for external or formal worship was instituted, according to the divine will, by the teaching medium of the sacrifices. In all of this, a truly prophetic utterance was given for all generations— No worship is accepted by God which has not been instituted by God Himself![50]

---

[50] Owen, *BTO*, 183.

# CHAPTER TWELVE

# REDEMPTIVE, SPECIAL REVELATION

# FROM ADAM TO NOAH

### Geerhardus Vos

Vos views the period from Adam to Noah as characterized by two features:

> In the first place, its significance lies not in the sphere of redemption, but in the sphere of the natural development of the race, although it has ultimately an important bearing on the subsequent progress of redemption. Secondly, revelation here bears on the whole a negative rather than positive character.[1]

These two features serve the purpose of this period or revelation. Vos says this period "was intended to bring out the consequences of sin when left so far as possible to itself."[2] God delays the progress of redemption to illustrate what happens to man when he is left to himself. But even this period serves the purpose of redemption.

> Hence, before the work of redemption is further carried out, the downward tendency of sin is clearly illustrated, in order that subsequently in the light of this downgrade movement the true divine cause of the upward course of redemption might be appreciated. This constitutes the indirect bearing of the period under review on redemption.[3]

Vos sees three stages at this point of redemptive history: (1) the rapid development of sin (i.e., degeneration); (2) common grace illustrated "in the gift of invention for the advance of civilization in the sphere of nature;" and (3) the abuse of these gifts serving "the progress of evil in the world."[4] All of this illustrates "the inherent tendency of sin to lead to ruin, and its power to corrupt and debase whatever of good might still

---

[1] Vos, *BTV*, 45.
[2] Vos, *BTV*, 45.
[3] Vos, *BTV*, 45.
[4] Vos, *BTV*, 45.

develop."[5] Cain's murder of Abel "illustrates a rapid development of sin... When this is compared with the act committed in paradise, it becomes evident that a rapid progress in corruption of the human heart had taken place."[6]

The degenerative power of sin in the sphere of nature is illustrated in the abuse of the gifts afforded by common grace. Natural progress is first seen in the fact of Enoch building a city. Soon after that "the inventions of cattle-raising, of music, of metal-working appear."[7] Lamech's song in Genesis 4:23-24 is viewed as "an expression of Titan arrogance. It makes its power its god, and carries its god, i.e. its sword, in its hand. ...the spirit of Lamech depends upon itself alone."[8] Lamech also introduces polygamy into the life of man.

Though Vos sees the narrative of Genesis 4-5 as negative, he also sees it as subservient to the purpose of redemption. Just as Cain and Able are seen as opposites, so are the Sethite Enoch and the Cainite Lamech. Enoch walked with God, while Lamech was full of pride and arrogance.[9] Enoch enjoyed "supernatural intercourse with God."[10] His translation is a proclamation "that where communion with God has been restored, there deliverance from death is bound to follow."[11] The narrative does have some rays of light. However, as Vos adds, "Even the good kept alive was not enabled to force back the evil."[12]

The power of sin and its tendency to degenerate is next illustrated in the intermarriages between the Cainites and the Sethites. This displays, once again, the active tendency of sin to corrupt. The godly line of men (i.e., "the sons of God") intermarries with "the daughters of men." This interpretation of "the sons of God" fits the overall purpose of this period of redemptive history.[13] It illustrates the corrupting power of sin among man unchecked by an influx of special grace.

In Genesis 6:3 and 5-7, "we have the divine summing up of the issue of the period, and the judgment pronounced upon the prediluvian race."[14] God states that the restraining influence of his Spirit shall soon be lifted

---

[5] Vos, *BTV*, 46.
[6] Vos, *BTV*, 46.
[7] Vos, *BTV*, 46.
[8] Vos, *BTV*, 46.
[9] Vos, *BTV*, 47.
[10] Vos, *BTV*, 47.
[11] Vos, *BTV*, 47.
[12] Vos, *BTV*, 48.
[13] Vos, *BTV*, 50.
[14] Vos, *BTV*, 49.

(Genesis 6:3). He assesses the moral state of man (Genesis 6:5), reveals his grief over the sinful race (Genesis 6:6), then pronounces a judgment of catastrophic destruction (Genesis 6:7). It is quite obvious that God's judicial recourse against man's sin and its fruit is a testimony to the fact that he must have placed man on the earth for other reasons.[15] Also, Genesis 6:8, "But Noah found grace in the eyes of the Lord," is illustrative of restorative grace in the midst of sin and misery.

### John Owen

Owen begins by discussing the first defection of the church "in the apostasy of Cain."[16] Cain sinned against all three elements of Adamic theology. Owen lists the three elements as follows: (1) the promise of the coming Mediator, (2) positively instituted worship, and (3) the Decalogue.[17] Cain became "the proto-hypocrite...the type and model of all such down to the end of the world (1 John 3:12)."[18] He was expelled from the church and cursed as a vagabond. Hence, Owen says, "...Cain was braded with a curse and solemnly banished from the bounds of the Church."[19] Owen asserts that "all the corrupters of the Adamic theology" at the time of Cain were banished from the Church which caused renewal "and flourishing down to the time of Enos."[20] This is the first ante-diluvian reformation of the church.[21]

Owen picks up on Genesis 4:26, where it says, "...men began to call on the name of the LORD." This calling on the name of the LORD occurred in the days of Enos. Owen interprets this as men invoking "the name of God in a special way."[22] He sees this as "a reformation of the

---

[15] Vos, *BTV*, 51.

[16] Owen, *BTO*, 184.

[17] Owen, *BTO*, 184. These three parts of Adamic theology become programmatic for Owen. Cf. Rehnman, *Divine Discourse*, 165, where he says, "Owen conceives of revelation as revolving around or consisting in three principles or parts. These three are faith in the Mediator, obedience to the moral law, and adherence to divinely appointed worship, and it is these three principles that are expanded during the history of supernatural revelation."

[18] Owen, *BTO*, 185.

[19] Owen, *BTO*, 188.

[20] Owen, *BTO*, 191.

[21] Owen, *BTO*, 192.

[22] Owen, *BTO*, 193.

Church indicated in the text."[23] "This constituted the second ante-diluvian reformation of the Church."[24]

Owen comments on this second ante-diluvian reformation of the church, concentrating on Enoch walking with God (Genesis 5:24), as follows:

> By virtue of this signal reformation, pure theology flourished and, with it, the true Church for a further period of a thousand years or thereabouts. During this period, God gave a most notable example of the reward of obedience in the translation of Enoch (Genesis 5:24), and thus set His seal on true theology and provided a pledge of life eternal.[25]

The second reformation of the Church is followed by degeneration through the influence of Cainites and Sethites "by links of marriage and other civil ties, into the company of the pious."[26] This period illustrates "the fatal outcome of readmitting corruption into the Church after any period of reformation."[27] The corruption was so widespread that "God intervened to put an end to that dispensation and, along with the post-lapsarian Adamic theology, by over-throwing the apostates in the waters of the great deluge."[28]

This widespread apostasy came as a result of the sons of God marrying the daughters of men (Genesis 6:1-2). "The sons of God were those who had, from the days of Enos, established distinct assemblies for the worship of God, professing their adoption by Him as his sons."[29] They "were the righteous, godly Church, adhering in faith to that degree of theology which they had been granted."[30] Church and world were now fused. There was no longer any distinction between the two. Owen draws this lesson: "In all ages, free association with the wicked leads inevitably to the downfall of the Church." Genesis 6:12 is the divine commentary on this period; "for all flesh had corrupted their way on the earth."

---

[23] Owen, *BTO*, 194.
[24] Owen, *BTO*, 195.
[25] Owen, *BTO*, 195.
[26] Owen, *BTO*, 195.
[27] Owen, *BTO*, 196.
[28] Owen, *BTO*, 196.
[29] Owen, *BTO*, 197. Owen discusses the angel view of the sons of God. He rejects it for at least two reasons: (1) because of the nature and state of angels and (2) because of the context and content of the wider Mosaic narrative. Cf. Owen, *BTO*, 196.ff.
[30] Owen, *BTO*, 226.

# CHAPTER THIRTEEN
# REDEMPTIVE, SPECIAL REVELATION
# FROM NOAH TO ABRAHAM

### Geerhardus Vos

### • Noachian Revelation and Its Stages

Commenting on Genesis 6:8, "But Noah found favor in the eyes of the LORD," Vos says, "The continuity of the race is preserved. God saves enough out of the wreck to enable Him to carry out His original purpose with the self-same humanity He had created."[1] God's purpose of redemption is in pursuit of God's original plan in the creation of man.

Vos then picks up revelation immediately after the flood.[2] He sees here "positive, constructive measures… taken for the further carrying out of the divine purpose."[3] He sees the covenant with Noah as a "*berith* of nature."[4] Its sign, the rainbow, is "absolutely universal in its reference"[5] and, being "a phenomenon of nature," proves that this covenant "is made with every living creature, nay, with the earth herself…"[6] Though this covenant serves the purposes of redemption, it does so only indirectly. Redemptive covenants have "bloody, sacramentally dividing signs."[7]

Vos sees the Noachian revelation unfolding in three stages: (1) Genesis 8:20-22 "recites the purpose of God, expressed in a monologue, to institute a new order of affairs."[8] (2) Genesis 9:1-7 "describes the measures taken that give content and security to this order."[9] And (3) Genesis 9:8-17 "relates how the new order was confirmed in the form of a *berith*."[10]

---

[1] Vos, *BTV*, 51.
[2] No explanation is given why Vos does not comment on Genesis 6:9-8:19.
[3] Vos, *BTV*, 51.
[4] Vos, *BTV*, 51.
[5] Vos, *BTV*, 51.
[6] Vos, *BTV*, 51.
[7] Vos, *BTV*, 51.
[8] Vos, *BTV*, 51.
[9] Vos, *BTV*, 51.
[10] Vos, *BTV*, 51.

**1. The institution of a new order of affairs.** The first stage of the Noachian revelation is comprised of the monologue of Genesis 8:20-22. It is the institution of a new order of affairs. "The regularity of nature in its great fundamental processes will henceforth continue."[11] No judgment like the diluvian judgment will ever come to the earth again.

**2. The means ordained to secure the new order.** The second stage reveals to us the measures taken to secure the new order (Genesis 9:1-7). Vos lists three "ordinances instituted to make possible and safeguard this programme of forbearance."[12] They are the propagation (Genesis 9:1), protection (Genesis 9:2, 5-7), and sustenance of life (Genesis 9:3-4).

**3. The covenant confirming the new order.** The third stage involves God giving "His promise in the form of a *berith* through adding a solemn sign to it."[13] This brings out the "sureness of the order instituted."[14] However, this order has its limits. "The promise to Noah has its limits in the eschatological crisis, which shall bring the earth to an end…"[15]

- **Revelation between Noah and the Patriarchs**

Vos breaks this era down into four headings: "[1] the prophetic deliverances of Noah with regard to his descendants; [2] the table of the nations; [3] the confusion of tongues; [4] the election of the Shemites."[16]

**1. The prophecies of Noah.** Genesis 9:20-27 (vv. 25-27) contain the prophecies of Noah. He curses Canaan (Ham) and blesses Japheth and Shem. Vos sees these prophecies as representing "the high-water mark of the advancing tide of revelation."[17] The curse on Canaan marks out the future Canaanites as a cursed people. This has affects upon the history of redemption.

The blessing upon Shem is next. "This is the first time in Scripture God is called the God of some particular group of mankind."[18] God is

---

[11] Vos, *BTV*, 52.
[12] Vos, *BTV*, 52.
[13] Vos, *BTV*, 54.
[14] Vos, *BTV*, 52.
[15] Vos, *BTV*, 55.
[16] Vos, *BTV*, 56.
[17] Vos, *BTV*, 56.
[18] Vos, *BTV*, 58.

revealed "in the capacity of Jehovah, the God of redemption..."[19] Vos says this is a *berith*-formula. God is blessed by Noah because "He is willing to be the God of Shem."[20]

Japheth's blessing comes next. Though Vos says it is "of more uncertain interpretation,"[21] he concludes as follows:

> The prophecy, both in its proximate political import and as to its ultimate spiritual consequences, was fulfilled through the subjugating of Shemitic territory by the Greeks and Romans. For this blessing became one of the most potent factors in the spread of the true religion over the earth. Delitzsch strikingly remarks: 'We are all Japhetites dwelling in the tents of Shem'.[22]

**2. The table of the nations.** Genesis 10 contains the table of the nations. Its purpose is proleptic and subservient to the purposes of redemption. Vos says:

> It is a chapter belonging to the genealogy of redemption. The idea embodied in the table is that, while for the proximate future the Shemites will constitute the race of redemption, yet the other nations are by no means permanently dismissed from the field of Sacred History. Their names are registered to express the principle that in the fullness of time the divine interposition meant to return to them again, and to re-enclose them in the sacred circle.[23]

**3. The confusion of tongues.** The confusion of tongues occurs in Genesis 11:1-9. The city built by man "was inspired first by the desire to obtain a centre of unity, such as would keep the human race together."[24] The goal was "a gigantic empire, glorifying man in his independence of God."[25] God's interference comes as a result of "His promise, that the sinful development of humanity will not again issue into a repeated catastrophe on the scale of the deluge."[26] A divided humanity dilutes the concentration of the power of sin. The sins of separate nations are not as

---

[19] Vos, *BTV*, 57.
[20] Vos, *BTV*, 58.
[21] Vos, *BTV*, 58.
[22] Vos, *BTV*, 58-59.
[23] Vos, *BTV*, 59.
[24] Vos, *BTV*, 59.
[25] Vos, *BTV*, 59.
[26] Vos, *BTV*, 59.

equally destructive as an undivided humanity.[27] Commenting on the division of languages, Vos concludes:

> Now it is through maintaining the national diversities, as these express themselves in the difference of language, and are in turn upheld by this difference, that God prevents realization of the attempted scheme. Besides this, however, a twofold positive divine purpose may be discerned in this occurrence. In the first place there was a positive intent that concerned the natural life of humanity. Under the providence of God each race or nation has a positive purpose to serve, fulfilment of which depends on relative seclusion from others. And secondly, *the events at this stage were closely interwoven with the carrying out of the plan of redemption.* They led to the election and separate training of one race and one people. Election from its very nature presupposes the existence of a larger number from among which the choice can be made.[28]

Finally, Vos discusses the "election of the Shemites to furnish the bearers of redemption and revelation."[29]

## John Owen

- **Introduction**

Owen announces his discussion of this period as follows: "We will now devote our attention to an examination of the restoration, spread, and development of theology in the period from the flood to the call of Abraham."[30] Owen recognizes this as a period of the divine economy.[31] Owen here and elsewhere acknowledges that the Bible's theology is developing – it is heading somewhere.

Noah was the sole exception to the corruption of all flesh mentioned in Genesis 6:11-12. He was "God's 'preacher of righteousness' (2 Peter 2:5), and by whose ministry Christ 'preached unto the spirits in prison' (1 Peter 3:19)."[32] Owen references 2 Peter 3:5-7 as Peter expressing "the

---

[27] Vos, *BTV*, 60. Vos quotes Delitzsch while making this point.

[28] Vos, *BTV*, 60. Emphases added.

[29] Vos, *BTV*, 60. As will be noted in the conclusion, Vos sees biblical history as redemptive history. At some level or another, revelation always serves the purposes of redemption.

[30] Owen, *BTO*, 199.

[31] Owen, *BTO*, 202.

[32] Owen, *BTO*, 199.

sweep of this period of the divine economy..."[33] He understands the world that was destroyed by water as "the people then inhabiting it..."[34] Noah was excepted because he was a righteous man. This righteousness, according to Owen (referencing Hebrews 11), was obtained by faith.[35] This faith was saving faith and had as its object "the promised seed..."[36] He adds:

> Now, all such saving faith looks upon the promised seed, and that Noah had this faith before the flood is proven by the fact that this was exactly when God distinguished him by this testimony to his righteousness. We can say, therefore, that Noah was righteous and pleasing to God, walking blamelessly in His sight, by virtue of that Adamic, pre-diluvian theology which we have explained in the previous book. Following the flood, this theology was, by God's grace, *enlarged and clarified by successive degrees* to the Church as it was re-organized in Noah's family, as we shall see.[37]

Owen follows these words with another very important paragraph in light of our purposes:

> Earlier, we had occasion to divide the theology of sinners who lived before the flood into three parts—the promise of grace, the law of nature, and divinely established worship. With the new revelations made to Noah, the first was enlarged, the second explained more fully, and the third stabilized.[38]

Owen's "three parts" of theology are clearly paradigmatic for his unfolding discussion of redemptive history.

- **The Nature and Essence of a Divine Covenant**

Owen acknowledges that "...the first *express* mention of a covenant"[39] occurs in this period of redemptive history. Oddly, Genesis 9:9 is

---

[33] Owen, *BTO*, 202.

[34] Owen, *BTO*, 203.

[35] Owen, *BTO*, 204.

[36] Owen, *BTO*, 204.

[37] Owen, *BTO*, 204. Emphases added. Owen is quick to acknowledge that the object of all saving faith to this point in redemptive history is the promised seed.

[38] Owen, *BTO*, 204.

[39] Owen, *BTO*, 205.

referenced as proof.[40] He next discusses what constitutes a divine covenant.

> God had already established with Adam, as we have seen, that famous promise of a coming seed to be sent forth by divine grace and spiritual blessing, to be a Mediator, which had all the needed factors for the establishment of a divine Covenant; that is, on the one hand both a promise and the provision of the means by which that promise might be obtained (i.e. by grace), and on the other hand the need for obedience and full commitment to the covenant terms. The promise always demands a requirement of obedience, for obedience is nothing but the due observance of the means instituted for obtaining of the thing promised—in this case, especially applicable when the required obedience is simply moral, and so is really external to the covenant itself, and is rendered pleasing and acceptable to God only because He has chosen to sovereignly institute the covenant in those terms; which, in turn, can only be a matter of pure revelation from Himself. So it is that in this passage the promise is referred to as a covenant. There are indeed, other reasons why this promise means the same as covenant, but this is not the place for expounding them at length. We will, therefore, satisfy ourselves with a few points about the Hebrew word for "covenant" itself.[41]

It appears that Owen is going back to Genesis 3:15 in the above comments. He finds there "all the needed factors of a divine Covenant."[42] The promise of the seed is the first revelation of the covenant grace.

He then has a brief lexical discussion concerning the meaning of the word 'covenant.' He references Grotius ("to cut" or "to cut out"), Cocceius ("to choose" or "to set in order"), Mercer, and Ball.[43] Owen says "...the Scriptures show it often to mean nothing else than God's own inalienable 'free gift' or 'promise' (2 Samuel 23:5; Jeremiah 31:31-32, and Numbers 18:9), all of which signify that which is established as a statute or decree from God (Jeremiah 33:21)..."[44] He then adds these interesting words, "...very often it is employed where no pact or

---

[40] Owen, *BTO*, 205. The first use of the word covenant in the Old Testament is Genesis 6:18.

[41] Owen, *BTO*, 205.

[42] Owen, *BTO*, 205.

[43] Owen, *BTO*, 205-06. He calls Cocceius "that worthy scholar" and disagrees with Ball on a minor issue.

[44] Owen, *BTO*, 205-06.

agreement of parties has taken place."[45] After a few brief comments about *suntheke* and *diatheke*, he concludes:

> So it is that God's covenants do not depend upon our will or on any condition which can be fulfilled by us. They have all their effect and virtue from the authority, the grace, and the faithfulness of God Himself. The promise of grace is absolute, and the covenant contains no conditions which are not included in the promise itself. Therefore, it is senseless and absurd for men to attempt to explain the nature and meaning of the divine Covenant from the circumstances of human covenants, which are mutually agreed between men. In the same way, *foedus*, among the Latins, does not always signify a solemn pact between parties...[46]

He draws this conclusion: "There is, therefore, no good reason to deny that God's promise [i.e. in Genesis 3:15] really had the true nature of a covenant."[47]

- **The Noahic Covenant: The First Stage of the Development of a Post-Diluvian Theology**

**1. Its function.** This discussion of the nature and essence of a divine covenant sets the stage for Owen's understanding of the function of the Noahic covenant. "[T]he covenant was *the first stage of the development of a post-diluvian theology*."[48] The covenant involves "*increased revelation* given to Noah...".[49] And this is the first time "the way of communication opened between sinners and God through the person of the Mediator is expressly called a covenant relationship."[50] This is also the first time God "established a visible sign of His covenant, His 'bow in the clouds' (Genesis 9:11, 13)."[51]

---

[45] Owen, *BTO*, 206.

[46] Owen, *BTO*, 206. It appears that Owen is here expressing a monopleuric view of God's covenants.

[47] Owen, *BTO*, 207. Owen is articulating the essence of monopleurism here. This is further evidence that the seventeenth-century Reformed orthodox definition of covenant is not to be reduced to a compact or agreement between equals. It is much more nuanced than that.

[48] Owen, *BTO*, 209. Emphases added.

[49] Owen, *BTO*, 209. Emphases added.

[50] Owen, *BTO*, 209.

[51] Owen, *BTO*, 209.

**2. Its promise.** The promise of the Noahic covenant refers to both the realm of "temporal blessing" and the realm of "spiritual grace."

> It is certainly true that in the Genesis passage the promise refers primarily to the things of this life, and the sign itself is the covenantal sign of a temporal blessing; but, nevertheless, spiritual grace, or the love of God freely given to the faithful, is chiefly intended; for such was the economy of that period until Christ was manifested in the flesh, that all these things should be "a shadow of good things to come" (Hebrews 10:1), of which Christ is the "high priest" (Hebrews 9:11). The eternal covenant subsists, as we have seen, only in Christ, and some temporal blessings emanated from it to all men. Yet the inner essence of the covenant is spiritual, and pertains only to Christ, and has reference through Him to his elect.
>
> In this manner, the pre-deluge Adamic theology was enlarged by new revelations, by the pronouncement of the covenant and by its visible token. By these things was the faith of the believers of those days confirmed. The allocation of the rainbow as the covenant sign emphasized the grace-promises, strengthened the evidence of God's sovereignty over nature, and was an encouragement to right and acceptable worship. So, thereby, all of the essential parts of true theology were strengthened by the covenant and its visible token.[52]

**3. Its contribution to the progress and development of redemptive history.** The progress of theological knowledge can be seen at this point by the fact that "divine commands were added to this theological basis; further revelation and requirement for faithful obedience, as theology regained itself after its terrible downfall."[53] The first added divine command was the prohibition of the shedding of blood (Genesis 9:5-6). Owen acknowledges that the crime of murder had already "been recognized by natural law, as the crime and punishment of Cain witness."[54] Now it gains positive law status. The second added commandment involved "forbidding the eating of meat along with its blood..." (Genesis 9:4).[55]

**4. Its redemptive-historical context.** Prior to discussing Canaan, Owen briefly traces the unfolding of theology up to the post-diluvian period:

---

[52] Owen, *BTO*, 210. Notice how Owen is utilizing his three parts of theology as a grid through which to interpret redemptive history.

[53] Owen, *BTO*, 210.

[54] Owen, *BTO*, 211.

[55] Owen, *BTO*, 212.

... we have seen the natural theology of Adam enriched by the promise of a Messiah, given new purposes, and established for new uses better suited to that new condition of sinfulness into which Satan had beguiled mankind by his wicked subtlety. And we have seen this further strengthened and enlarged by new revelations and the institution of a solemnly-established covenant with its visible sign and various commandments. By these the rule of faith, obedience, and due worship was established in the eight-person Church.[56]

Owen sees the natural theology of Adam added to because of the entrance of sin. The promise of a Messiah meets the conditions brought in by the fall into sin. Any new revelation is seen as building upon the basic structure. Revelation is organic. The rule of faith is the promised Messiah; the rule of obedience is the Decalogue; and due worship is whatever God has revealed for the particular era under consideration.

## • Canaan's Sin and Noah's Curse

Noah's curse upon Canaan (Genesis 9:25ff.) was due to his transgression of "the dictates of that inner reason through which...all mankind are prompted to honor and respect their parents"[57] (Genesis 9:22). Owen offers some reasons why the curse was uttered against Canaan:

> ...the curse is clearly uttered against Canaan, either because he was at that time his father's special favorite, being (as I suppose) his youngest son, because he stood with his father in this unspeakable sin and spectacle, because his family, among all the descendants of Ham, would be first to depart from the Church and the true worship of God, or perhaps to encourage the Israelites when about to depart for the promised land by the knowledge that the people with whom they were about to engage in warfare had been cursed of God, and long since devoted by Him to slavery and destruction. However this may be, it is quite certain that Ham himself, in the person of his son, was cursed and expelled from the family of God.[58]

---

[56] Owen, *BTO*, 217-18.

[57] Owen, *BTO*, 218.

[58] Owen, *BTO*, 220. Owen adds these comments immediately after the proposed reasons why Canaan was cursed: "Extraordinarily ludicrous are some of the nonsenses indulged in by early writers concerning a prefiguring of the passion of Christ in the drunkenness of Noah, and the way in which they see types of the cross, sacraments,

Though Owen does not take a position on this issue, it is of interest to note that he suggests that Moses included this curse to encourage the Israelites who were about to cross into the promised land.

Owen views Canaan's sin as "the occasion of Ham's long concealed hypocrisy breaking visibly forth and resulting in a great scandal in the Church..."[59] Noah's curse constitutes the expulsion of Ham "from the society of the pious..."[60] This, according to Owen, is "another example of ecclesiastical reform..."[61] He calls it "the reformation of the Noachian Church..."[62] The words of Noah in Genesis 9:26-27, "Blessed be the LORD, The God of Shem, And may Canaan be his servant" are viewed as words of consolation and encouragement to a more strict obedience and diligence in the service of God to the Church in its "pitifully reduced condition..."[63]

Though he was exiled from the Church because the human race had not been "scattered wide across the face of the earth, Ham's settlements would still be in the same tract of country as those of his brethren."[64] Owen sees this as the reasons for "a renewed outbreak of evil."[65] This lead to the building of the tower of Babel.

- **The Tower of Babel**

Owen viewed the tower as a means through which man sought to "gain a lasting reputation and glory"[66] for his own fame (Genesis 11:3-4).[67] He denies that the tower was built in order to ascend into heaven or to protect man from another universal flood. Owen gives the reason for the tower as follows:

---

gentiles, Jews, and ministers of the Word— all in the wine, in Ham, Japhet, and the cast-aside garments!" (Owen, *BTO*, 220).
[59] Owen, *BTO*, 220.
[60] Owen, *BTO*, 220.
[61] Owen, *BTO*, 220.
[62] Owen, *BTO*, 221.
[63] Owen, *BTO*, 221.
[64] Owen, *BTO*, 221.
[65] Owen, *BTO*, 221.
[66] Owen, *BTO*, 222.
[67] Owen, *BTO*, 225-26.

The true reason is that they were so full of pride and vainglory that they wished to establish a name and reputation for themselves by the monumental structure, as indeed Moses relates in Genesis 11:4.[68]

God's displeasure was clear and long-lasting. Owen says:

Now would fall upon them a dreadful punishment from God to whom their attempt was hateful. Their languages were confused and their mighty labor made abortive, while they themselves were scattered far and wide across the face of the whole earth. From that day down to the coming of the Messiah, God would permit the greater part of the human race to walk apart from Him and in their own paths![69]

Concerning the confusion of languages, Owen says:

There has been much controversy over the confusion of languages, but this is not the proper place to go deeply into that subject. I will just make a few points about the primal language and the reason for its later name.[70]

The "few points" takes us into Owen's view of and arguments for Hebrew as the primal language, "coeval with the world."[71] He saw the Church at the time of Babel as having "...no connection with the sin of the tower-builders"[72] and, hence, of the subsequent judgment of the confusion of languages. He firmly believed that "Hebrew was, indeed, the first language" and that "loss of that language served as a punishment."[73] Owen adds:

After being the common and only language of mankind for 1757 years down to the confusion of languages, it continued in use among those

---

[68] Owen, *BTO*, 226.

[69] Owen, *BTO*, 222.

[70] Owen, *BTO*, 226.

[71] Owen *BTO*, 235. Owen discusses Hebrew as the primal/primeval language here (226-41) and its antiquity in Book IV (395-431). I mention this only in passing because it is beyond the scope of our purposes.

[72] Owen, *BTO*, 226.

[73] Owen, *BTO*, 236.

Shemites who had not been involved in the insane attempt of the building of the tower.[74]

The confusion of languages caused the loss of revealed theology over time among all but the faithful Shemites. These were the reasons why mankind "gradually drifted into the practice of all kinds of idolatry."[75]

---

[74] Owen, *BTO*, 238-39.

[75] Owen, *BTO*, 240. The next twelve chapters (242-358) of Book 3 take up the issue of "The Origin and Progress of Idolatry." Though Owen's history of idolatry is fascinating and displays a wide range of reading, it is beyond the scope of our purposes so will only be mentioned in passing.

# CHAPTER FOURTEEN
# REDEMPTIVE, SPECIAL REVELATION
# FROM ABRAHAM TO MOSES

### Geerhardus Vos

- **Introduction: The Historicity of the Patriarchal Period**

Vos entitled the chapter where he discusses this period as "Revelation in the Patriarchal Period." In it he first discusses the historicity of the patriarchs. He says strongly "that the historicity of the patriarchs can never be, to us, a matter of small importance."[1] The reason why Vos says this is due to his view of Special Revelation as "the drama of redemption."[2] If the Bible existed to present moral examples, the historicity of the patriarchs would not be such an important issue. But, as Vos says, "The whole matter depends on how we conceive of man's need as a sinner."[3] In fact, if the patriarchs are not historical figures, they become useless from Vos' point of view. They serve no redemptive purpose. If they are myths, then so can Adam and Eve be and so can Jesus. However, Vos says:

> If there be no historicity before that [i.e., Moses], then the process of redemption loses itself in a prehistoric mist at its beginnings. The only logical position is that, *if* a history of redemption is needed, it should begin with Adam and Eve.[4]

Obviously, Vos holds that a history of redemption is needed and thus, the historicity of Adam and Eve, the Patriarchs, Moses, and Jesus.

---

[1] Vos, *BTV*, 67. Vos clearly and emphatically challenges the critical biblical theologians of his day.

[2] Vos, *BTV*, 67.

[3] Vos, *BTV*, 67.

[4] Vos, *BTV*, 68.

- **The Form and the Content of Revelation in the Patriarchal Period**

Vos sees a distinction "between the form and the content of revelation in the patriarchal period."[5] As to its form or mode, we are given "for the first time more or less circumstantial description..."[6] Revelation both increases in frequency and "becomes more restricted and guarded in its mode of communication."[7] Vos is referring, primarily, to the theophanies connected with this era of redemptive history. Theophanies were a visible manifestation of God.[8] Revelation also came through visions and dreams at this time.[9] But "the most important and characteristic form of revelation"[10] utilized by God during this period came through the Angel of the Lord. Vos lists the biblical references where the Angel of the Lord is discussed, then adds this commentary:

> The peculiarity in all these cases is that, on the one hand, the Angel distinguishes himself from Jehovah, speaking of Him in the third person, and that, on the other hand, in the same utterance he speaks of God in the first person.[11]

Vos holds that this can only be so if "behind the twofold representation there lies a real manifoldness in the inner life of the Deity."[12] The purpose for this mode of revelation was twofold: to reveal God's interest in drawing near to his people (the sacramental intent) and to anticipate the incarnation of Christ (the spiritualizing intent).[13]

- **The Distinctive Features of Revelation in the Patriarchal Period**

**1. Election.** Vos discusses the distinctive features of revelation during this period. The first principle is that of election. For the first time in history, one family of the earth is chosen out of all others to carry

---

[5] Vos, *BTV*, 69.
[6] Vos, *BTV*, 69.
[7] Vos, *BTV*, 69.
[8] Vos, *BTV*, 69.
[9] Vos, *BTV*, 69-72.
[10] Vos, *BTV*, 72.
[11] Vos, *BTV*, 72.
[12] Vos, *BTV*, 73. Vos does not believe that theophanies were, at this point, intended to reveal the doctrine of the Trinity.
[13] Vos, *BTV*, 76.

forward "the redemptive, revelatory work of God..."[14] For Vos, "This is the tremendous significance of the call of Abraham."[15] Now "...the whole course of the special work of God is confined within the narrow channel of one people."[16] However, this narrow channel is not an end, but a means. Vos views Abraham's election and further developments through Israel "as a particularistic means toward a universalizing end."[17]

> The very fact of Canaan being chosen for the abode of the sacred family was an indication of this kind. For although, compared with Mesopotamia, Canaan was a place of relative seclusion, and this entered as one motive for putting the patriarchs there, nevertheless archaeological research of recent times has shown that in itself Canaan was by no means a land lying isolated, aside from the great commerce and international life of the ancient world. It was actually a land where the lines of intercourse crossed. In the fulness of time its strategic position proved of supreme importance for the spreading abroad of the Gospel unto the whole earth.[18]

The most explicit evidence for the election of Abraham as a means to a universalizing end is found in Genesis 12:3, "...And in you all the families of the earth shall be blessed." However, this "universalistic design was forced somewhat into the background"[19] during the Mosaic period. Israel's organization as a nation and the Mosaic Law with its strict, seclusive rules served to hedge the people of God from the other nations.[20] This was not the case with the patriarchal period. Vos comments on this as follows:

> ...the principles on which God dealt with the patriarchs were of a highly spiritual nature, such as would make them universally applicable. Paul had a profound insight into this universalistic purport of patriarchal religion. The reasoning [*Gal.* 3.15ff.] is in substance as follows: through the *diatheke* with Abraham the relation between God and Israel was put on a foundation of promise and grace; this could not be subsequently changed, because the older arrangement remains regulative for later institutions [vs 15], and the law was by no less than

---

[14] Vos, *BTV*, 76.
[15] Vos, *BTV*, 76.
[16] Vos, *BTV*, 76.
[17] Vos, *BTV*, 77.
[18] Vos, *BTV*, 77.
[19] Vos, *BTV*, 78.
[20] Vos, *BTV*, 78.

430 years later than the Abrahamic *berith*. The revealed religion of the Old Testament in this respect resembles a tree whose root system and whose crown spread out widely, while the trunk of the tree confines the sap for a certain distance within a narrow channel. The patriarchal period corresponds to the root growth; the freely expanding crown to the revelation of the New Testament; and the relatively constricted form of the trunk to the period from Moses to Christ.[21]

The principle of election can be viewed on two fronts, according to Vos. One is individual, the other national. The individual always remains. The national element for Israel served its purpose and has been abolished.[22] However, Vos does believe in a future visitation of God's grace upon Israel in its *racial* capacity.[23]

**2. Biblical religion is based on historical divine interpositions.** "The second distinctive feature of God's revelation to the patriarchs concerns the objectivity of the gifts which it bestows."[24] Vos is referring to "the beginning of a factual religion, a religion attaching itself to objective divine interpositions on behalf of man."[25] He points out that objective, historical interposition by God produces subjective change in man – not the other way around. God gives promises to the patriarchs. It is not so much what they would do for God but what he will do for them. Biblical religion is based on the solid ground of historical divine interpositions. This causes the faithful to look back and look forward. They look back to what God says he will do and they look forward to its fulfillment. The force of religion is not human potencies but divine power exhibited through promises made and fulfilled. According to Vos, "Biblical religion is thoroughly eschatological in its outlook."[26] God promised three gifts to Abraham and the patriarchs: "first, the chosen family would be made into a great nation; secondly, that the land of Canaan would be their possession; thirdly, that they were to become a blessing for all people."[27]

---

[21] Vos, *BTV*, 78-79.
[22] Vos, *BTV*, 79.
[23] Vos, *BTV*, 79.
[24] Vos, *BTV*, 79.
[25] Vos, *BTV*, 79.
[26] Vos, *BTV*, 80.
[27] Vos, *BTV*, 80.

**3. Divine monergism.** The third distinctive feature of revelation at this juncture is

> that it emphasizes most strongly, both in word and act, the absolute monergism of the divine power in accomplishing the things promised; otherwise expressed, the strict supernaturalism of the procedure towards fulfilling the promises.[28]

Vos sees this principle illustrated in the life of Abraham, especially in the birth of Isaac.

While discussing the patriarch Isaac, Vos, in agreement with Delitzsch, seeks to interpret the fact that so much of Isaac's life is a repetition of Abraham's. Why is there so much striking similarity? Why the recapitulation? Vos says "the reason for this must lie in the need of thus expressing some important revelation principle."[29] The patriarchal revelation at this point is typical of the history of redemption as a whole. Here's how Vos explains himself:

> The redeeming work of God passes by its very nature through three stages. Its beginnings are marked by a high degree of energy and productivity; they are creative beginnings. The middle stage is a stage of suffering and self—surrender, and is therefore passive in its aspect. This in turn is followed by the resumed energy of the subjective transformation, characterizing the third stage. Now the middle one of these stages is represented by Isaac.[30]

### John Owen

- **The Patriarchal Period: A New Phase of Unfolding Theology**

Owen views the patriarchal period as "a new phase of Church history based upon a new unfolding of theology."[31] This new phase "was brought about in the call of Abraham..."[32] Abraham was called, renewed and justified by faith.[33] He "was handed on theology–the theology that is,

---

[28] Vos, *BTV*, 81.

[29] Vos, *BTV*, 91.

[30] Vos, *BTV*, 92.

[31] Owen, *BTO*, 360. Owen uses various terms to describe the nature of revelation at this period: "...a new unfolding of theology" (360), "...splendid advance in theology" (367), "...amplified and renewed theology..." (367).

[32] Owen, *BTO*, 360.

[33] Owen, *BTO*, 365.

of Noah, clarified and amplified by new revelations."[34] The rich quality of the revelation given to Abraham is seen in these words of Owen:

> So, clear manifestations of the divine will and of the mystery of grace would now be brought forward by the new light thrown upon post-fall theology, that hardly a richer harvest of truth would be granted within any revelationary [*sic*] period up to the advent of Him for whom all was preparing.[35]

Notice, first, how Owen views the revelation given to Abraham as *dependent upon* and *expansive of* previous revelation[36] and, second, that it is of such a nature that there is "hardly a richer harvest of truth" between it and the advent of Christ.

- **Evidences of Revelatory Advance in the Patriarchal Period**

Owen then lists various ways which indicate revelatory advance in this period.

**1. Further explanations of Messianic revelation.** "[T]here were now given far clearer and more complete explanations of the ancient promises which had been repeated on sundry occasions (Genesis 12:3, 7; 13:15-16; 15:1, 5, 6; 17:1, 2, 9; and 22:17-18)."[37] Owen is, of course, referring to Messianic revelation. "In this period, the promise of the conquering and joy-bringing seed is renewed at least seven times."[38]

**2. Richer demonstrations of covenant grace.** "[T]here was added to this unfolding of the promise a richer demonstration and clarification of covenant grace."[39] This is seen by God speaking in covenantal language to Abraham and attaching his name and attributes to the "undertaking of

---

[34] Owen, *BTO*, 365.

[35] Owen, *BTO*, 365.

[36] This sounds very similar to Vos, where he says, "[Each epoch] was prepared for by what preceded, and being in turn preparatory for what follows" and "So dispensation grows out of dispensation, and the newest is but the fully expanded flower of the oldest" (Vos, *RHBI*, 11; cf. Bernard, 44 for similar words).

[37] Owen, *BTO*, 365.

[38] Owen, *BTO*, 366.

[39] Owen, *BTO*, 366.

His covenant."[40] The seed *promises* all have the previous seed *promise* as their foundation and look forward to Christ.[41]

**3. Covenantal exclusiveness.** God restricts his covenant to Abraham and his family so "that no one could obtain eternal blessedness unless connected with that family (Genesis 12:3)."[42]

**4. The sign of the covenant.** "[C]ircumcision was now instituted as the specific 'sign of the covenant' (Genesis 17:11)."[43]

**5. Covenantal privileges and the infant seed of believers.** The privileges of covenant or "Church, are so communicated onwards through the infant seed of believers, who are the special concern of God's covenant grace, so that it would never be suffered to die out completely."[44]

**6. God's special friendship with Abraham.** "God took him [Abraham] into His special friendship and granted him repeated revelations over the years..."[45] Owen admits that many of these revelations were private and not intended for universal use and so does not see them as concerning his purposes.

---

[40] Owen, *BTO,* 366.
[41] Owen, *BTO,* 366.
[42] Owen, *BTO,* 366.
[43] Owen, *BTO,* 366.
[44] Owen, *BTO,* 366-67.
[45] Owen, *BTO,* 367.

# CHAPTER FIFTEEN

# REDEMPTIVE, SPECIAL REVELATION

# FROM MOSES TO CHRIST

### Geerhardus Vos

- **Introduction**

Vos covers this period under these three headings: (1) "The place of Moses in the organism of Old Testament revelation," (2) "The form of revelation in the Mosaic period," and (3) "The content of the Mosaic revelation."[1] Of these three headings, the third is given considerably more space.[2]

- **The Place of Moses in the Organism of Old Testament Revelation**

Moses, according to Vos, is the prominent figure of Israel's early post-patriarchal history. "The oldest writing prophets, Amos and Hosea" both testify to Moses' prominence (Hosea 12:13; Amos 3:1-2; cf. Isaiah 63:11; Jeremiah 15:1).[3] The "significance of Moses, when we place him within the unfolding scheme of revelation, can be made clear in several directions."[4] First, Moses was "instrumental in bringing the great patriarchal promises to an incipient fulfillment, at least in their external, provisional embodiment."[5] Second, "Moses also occupies a dominant place in the religious development of the Old Testament."[6] He takes prominence over all subsequent Old Testament prophets. He was set over all God's house (Numbers 12:7). Indeed, "He may be fitly called *the redeemer* of the Old Testament."[7] Moses' "figure acquires *typical*

---

[1] Vos, *BTV*, 100.
[2] The first two headings are discussed in eight pages; the last in 73.
[3] Vos, *BTV*, 103.
[4] Vos, *BTV*, 103.
[5] Vos, *BTV*, 103.
[6] Vos, *BTV*, 103.
[7] Vos, *BTV*, 104.

proportions to an unusual degree."[8] New Testament redemption terminology can be traced back to him. "There was in his work such a close connection between revealing words and redeeming acts as can be paralleled only from the life of Christ."[9] Many of the acts of Moses were supernatural. He was typological of Christ. "This typical relation of Moses to Christ can easily be traced in each of the three offices we are accustomed to distinguish in the soteric work of Christ."[10] Moses also retained a peculiar relation to the people of Israel as does Christ to Christians.

- **The Form of the Mosaic Revelation**

Moses, like no other prophet in the Old Testament, enjoyed direct communications of God. "In this respect also *Moses seems to have prefigured Christ*."[11] No one else in the Old Testament reflected the divine glory as did Moses because no one had the privileges of Moses. Four forms of revelation are connected to Moses: (1) the pillar and the cloud, (2) the Angel of Jehovah, (3) the Name of Jehovah, and (4) the Face of Jehovah.[12] These forms "express the permanence of the divine presence"[13] and are distinguished from the more fleeting forms of the patriarchal period. Due to the fall into sin, the abiding presence of God is not a universal reality among men. However, that is "the ultimate design of all God's converse with man."[14] Though Enoch walked with God, the flood brought about a shift in God's "sacramental revelation-presence."[15] Vos says, "God has, as it were, withdrawn this sacramental revelation-presence into heaven."[16] This was, however, an abnormal state.

> This, however, was an abnormal state of things, for the ultimate design of all God's converse with man is, that He may make His abode with His people. Consequently from now on all revelation tends towards the realization of this design. The theophanies of the patriarchal period

---

[8] Vos, *BTV*, 104. Emphasis added. Vos explicitly acknowledges typological functions of Moses.

[9] Vos, *BTV*, 104.

[10] Vos, *BTV*, 104. Prophet, Priest, and King.

[11] Vos, *BTV*, 105. Emphases added.

[12] Vos, *BTV*, 106.

[13] Vos, *BTV*, 106.

[14] Vos, *BTV*, 106. This makes all revelation eschatological in its thrust.

[15] Vos, *BTV*, 106.

[16] Vos, *BTV*, 106.

must be regarded as incipient fulfillments of it. But the fulfillment was only partial. The presence was there only at times; it was granted to a few select persons only; it was confined to the great turning-points in their history; it was veiled in deepest mystery. With the time of Moses there came the opposite to this in all respects.[17]

- ### The Content of the Mosaic Revelation

Vos discusses the Mosaic period of revelation under five headings: (1) the factual basis of the Mosaic organization given in the redemption from Egypt; (2) the making of the *Berith* with Israel with which the organization entered into being; (3) the general nature of the organization, the theocracy; (4) the Decalogue; and (5) the ritual law.[18]

**1. The factual basis of the Mosaic organization given in the redemption from Egypt.** Vos says, "The exodus from Egypt *is* the Old Testament redemption."[19] Vos bases this assertion on what he calls "the inner coherence of Old Testament and New Testament religion itself."[20] Though the forms of religion in Old and New Testament differ, they "are yet one in principle."[21] The common feature of the Old and New Testaments is *"the realism of redemption."*[22] The exodus, the greatest redemptive act of God in the Old Testament era, illustrates "how inseparably revelation through words is united to facts, nay how for whole stretches the demarcation line between acts and words may even seem to have been lost altogether."[23]

Vos discusses six "outstanding principles of the exodus-deliverance that were thus made regulative of all future salvation and bind things past and things to come indissolubly together."[24] These principles are: (1) deliverance from foreign bondage; (2) deliverance form sin; (3) a display of divine omnipotence; (4) a demonstration of sovereign grace; (5) the name Jehovah; and (6) the Passover .[25] He views the exodus as defining

---

[17] Vos, *BTV*, 106.

[18] Vos, *BTV*, 109.

[19] Vos, *BTV*, 109. Vos adds, "This is not an anachronistic, allegorizing manner of speaking."

[20] Vos, *BTV*, 109.

[21] Vos, *BTV*, 109.

[22] Vos, *BTV*, 109.

[23] Vos, *BTV*, 109.

[24] Vos, *BTV*, 110.

[25] Vos, *BTV*, 110-21.

redemption for us – "a deliverance from an objective realm of sin and evil."[26] This redemption is typological of Christ's redemption.[27] The exodus also rescued the people "from inward spiritual degradation and sin."[28] It delivered them from the idolatry of the Egyptians, yet they fell into idolatry relatively quickly. Why so? "The history of the wilderness journey with its repeated apostasies, such as the worship of the golden calf, becomes unintelligible, unless we may assume that the people had left Egypt in a corrupt state religiously."[29] The exodus displays God's power in two primary ways: the plagues and the dividing of the water.[30] The exodus is a display of sovereign grace in that "[t]he Egyptians were judged with respect to their idolatry, and the Israelites were rescued and spared, in spite of having become associated with their oppressors in idolatrous practices."[31] Sovereign grace is further displayed via the concept of sonship, since it is unmeritorious by nature.[32] Finally, the Passover shows that grace cannot "be exercised without an accompanying atonement."[33]

**2. The making of the *Berith* with Israel with which the organization entered into being.** Exodus 24 presents the ratification of the covenant. The nature and content of the covenant are sovereignly imposed. No co-operation between God and man is hinted at. However, the ratification of this covenant does take the consent of those covenanted with.[34] The Passover, according to Vos, "might properly be called an anticipation of the *berith*-making at Sinai."[35] Both have the same two elements – sacrificial expiation and a sacrificial meal.[36]

**3. The general nature of the organization, the theocracy.** The purpose of the theocracy (i.e., Jehovah being the supreme authority and power in Israel's national life) was "not to teach the world lessons in political

---

[26] Vos, *BTV*, 110.

[27] Vos, *BTV*, 111.

[28] Vos, *BTV*, 111.

[29] Vos, *BTV*, 112.

[30] "Nevertheless He saved them for His name's sake, That He might make His mighty power known" (Psalm 106:8; cf. vv. 21-22).

[31] Vos, *BTV*, 113.

[32] Vos, *BTV*, 114.

[33] Vos, *BTV*, 119.

[34] Vos, *BTV*, 121-22. Both the monopleuric and dipleuric aspects of the covenant are mentioned here.

[35] Vos, *BTV*, 123.

[36] Vos, *BTV*, 123.

economy, but in the midst of a world of paganism to teach true religion, even at the sacrifice of much secular propaganda and advantage."[37] Vos adds, "The significance of the unique organization of Israel can be rightly measured only by remembering that the theocracy typified nothing short of the perfected kingdom of God, the consummate state of heaven."[38]

**4. The Decalogue.** According to Vos, "The Decalogue strikingly illustrates the redemptive structure of the theocracy as a whole."[39] It opens by reminding the Israelites of God's deliverance. Its aim is the holiness of the covenant people. It is adjusted to the needs and weaknesses of the people yet remains an idealistic ethical norm.[40]

The Decalogue finds its primary application to Israel, yet has a world-wide ethical application as well. Though it has redemptive-historical "adjustments"[41] uniquely applicable to Israel, it still has "universal application…"[42] It applied to Israel under the Old Covenant, but has other uses as well (i.e., "all ethical relationships" and "the life of all believers"[43]).

"The most striking feature of the Decalogue is its specifically religious character."[44] The redeeming act of God is the motive behind the conduct demanded and the basis for such conduct. In other words, religion is the basis for ethics.

The fourth commandment gets much more comment from Vos than the others.[45] One of the reasons is due to its origin and modified applicability throughout redemptive history.

---

[37] Vos, *BTV*, 125.

[38] Vos, *BTV*, 126. Here we see Vos identify typology explicitly.

[39] Vos, *BTV*, 129.

[40] Vos, *BTV*, 130.

[41] Vos, *BTV*, 131. Cf. Appendix Two on "John Owen and Reformed Orthodoxy on the Functions of the Decalogue in Redemptive history" for similar language.

[42] Vos, *BTV*, 131. Cf. Appendix Two on "John Owen and Reformed Orthodoxy on the Functions of the Decalogue in Redemptive history" for similar language.

[43] Vos, *BTV*, 131.

[44] Vos, *BTV*, 132.

[45] Vos only discusses the first four commandments. He does so because the last six refer to man's relationship with man; the first four deal with man's relationship with God. The last six commandments, according to Vos, ought to be discussed in a course on Ethics. Cf. Vos, *BTV*, 134 and Dennison, "Vos on the Sabbath: A Close Reading," 61-70, esp. 61-62.

It must be remembered that the Sabbath, though a world-aged observance, has passed through the various phases of the development of redemption, remaining the same in essence but modified as to its form, as the new state of affairs at each point might require. The Sabbath is not only the most venerable, it is likewise the most living of all the sacramental realities of our religion. It has faithfully accompanied the people of God on their march though the ages.[46]

Another reason for the fourth commandment getting more discussion is due to the principle underlying it: "man must copy God in his course of life."[47] God's rest is prototypical of man's. "It stands for consummation of a work accomplished and the joy and satisfaction attendant upon it."[48] This is not only the duty of man individually but of that of the entire race throughout its history.

But probably the greatest reason why Vos gives so much attention to the fourth commandment is due to its eschatological function. Dennison comments, "...the fourth precept is an idealizing of a transhistorical and eschatological paradigm."[49] Vos says:

Before all other important things, therefore, the Sabbath is an expression of the eschatological principle on which the life of humanity has been constructed. There is to be to the world-process a finale, as there was an overture, and these two belong inseparably together. To give up the one means to give up the other, and to give up either means to abandon the fundamental scheme of Biblical history. Even among Jewish teachers this profound meaning of the Sabbath was not entirely unknown. One of them, being asked what the world to come would be like, answered that it would resemble the Sabbath. In the law, it is true, this thought is not developed further than is done in the primordial statement about God's resting on the seventh day and hallowing it. For the rest, the institution, after having been re-enforced in the Decalogue, is left to speak for itself, as is the case with most institutions of the law. The Epistle to the Hebrews has given us a philosophy of the Sabbath on the largest of scales, partly in dependence on Psa. 95 [*Heb.* 3, 4].[50]

---

[46] Vos, *BTV*, 139. Vos acknowledges emphatically that we have been released from any typical elements connected to the Sabbath in the Old Testament, "but not from the Sabbath as instituted at Creation. In light of this we must interpret certain New Testament statements such as Rom. 14.5, 6; Gal. 4.10, 11; Col. 2.16, 17." Cf. Vos, *BTV*, 143.

[47] Vos, *BTV*, 139.

[48] Vos, *BTV*, 140.

[49] Dennison, "Vos on the Sabbath," 62.

[50] Vos, *BTV*, 140.

The weekly Sabbath is symbolic and typical of "the eschatological structure of history."[51] Life is not aimless; it has a goal beyond it. The successful probation of the covenant of works would have brought the sacramental Sabbath "into the reality it typified, and the entire subsequent course of the history of the race would have been radically different."[52] The theocracy is a typical and "temporary 'mirror' of an eschatological and permanent state, i.e., holiness to the Lord in the arena of the perfect and eternal Sabbath."[53] "[T]he Sabbath principle and the theocratic era both contain and point to something beyond themselves—a heavenly theocracy and an everlasting Sabbath rest."[54] The theocracy functions as a recapitulation of the symbolic and typological pre-redemptive revelation and the covenant of works in the Garden of Eden. The Christian Lord's Day, the first day of the week,[55] is both a looking back to the resurrection as the accomplishment of redemption (i.e., "[t]he new exodus in the eschatological lamb of God"[56]) and "a sign looking forward to the final eschatological rest."[57] "Weekly sabbatizing is a mirror imaging of eschatological sabbatizing."[58] Though the theocracy was a temporary institution, its antitype being the church (ultimately in glory), the weekly Sabbath remains with the people of God until its antitype, the eternal state, comes in its fullness.[59] "Our weekly Sabbath now is a reflection of our resurrection union with him who has entered perfectly into his rest—and waits to welcome us to a consummate everlasting Sabbath."[60]

**5. The ritual (ceremonial) law.**[61] Vos sees in the ritual law "the gospel of Moses... enshrined."[62] The ritual law is both symbolic and typical. "A symbol is... something that profoundly portrays a certain fact or principle or relationship of a spiritual nature in a visible form."[63] A type

---

[51] Vos, *BTV*, 140.

[52] Vos, *BTV*, 140.

[53] Dennison, "Vos on the Sabbath," 62.

[54] Dennison, "Vos on the Sabbath," 62.

[55] Cf. Dennison, "Vos on the Sabbath," 67 for a discussion on the change of the day.

[56] Dennison, "Vos on the Sabbath," 62.

[57] Vos, *BTV*, 141.

[58] Dennison, "Vos on the Sabbath," 64.

[59] Dennison, "Vos on the Sabbath," 62-63, 66.

[60] Dennison, "Vos on the Sabbath," 68.

[61] In Vos, *BTV*, 143, Vos acknowledges that the ritual law "...is what by another name is called the ceremonial law."

[62] Vos, *BTV*, 143.

[63] Vos, *BTV*, 144.

points to something that "will become real or applicable in the future."[64] A type is prospective. Vos views the ritual law as both symbol and type. He says:

> ...the things symbolized and the things typified are not different sets of things. They are in reality the same things, only different in this respect that they come first on a lower stage of development in redemption, and then again, in a later period, on a higher stage. Thus what is symbolical with regard to the already existing edition of the fact or truth becomes typical, prophetic, of the later, final edition of that same fact or truth. From this it will be perceived that a type can never be a type independently of its being first a symbol. The gateway to the house of typology is at the farther end of the house of symbolism.[65]

Once what a thing symbolizes is discovered, then (and only then) can that which it typifies be discovered, "for the latter can never be aught else than the former lifted to a higher plane."[66] And "[t]he bond that holds type and anti-type together must be a bond of vital continuity in the progress of redemption."[67] Without this bond "all sorts of absurdities will result, such as must bring the whole subject of typology into disrepute."[68] The unique feature about typology in the Mosaic period of revelation is that "now...a system of types is established, so that the whole organism of the world of redemption, as it were, finds a typical embodiment on earth. The types are shadows of a body which is Christ."[69]

Vos gives careful qualification to his view on typology: "We must not infer from our comparatively easy reading of the types that Israelites of old felt the same ease in interpreting them. It is unhistorical to carry back into the Old Testament mind our developed doctrinal consciousness of these matters." [70]

The tabernacle is both a symbol of God's dwelling with his people[71] and type "as regards the final embodiment of salvation in the Christian state."[72] As far as its symbolic function goes, Vos calls it "a concentrated

---

[64] Vos, *BTV*, 144.

[65] Vos, *BTV*, 145.

[66] Vos, *BTV*, 146.

[67] Vos, *BTV*, 146.

[68] Vos, *BTV*, 146. Vos is seeking to guard typology from becoming allegorical.

[69] Vos, *BTV*, 147.

[70] Vos, *BTV*, 148.

[71] Vos cites Exodus 25:8 and 29:44-45.

[72] Vos, *BTV*, 148.

theocracy."[73] The need for the tabernacle is "created by His [God's] relation to Israel..."[74] God is not in need of comfort or shelter. His dwelling in the tabernacle symbolizes his "intimate association" with Israel.

> It means intimate association [*Gen.* 30.20; *Psa.* 5.4; *Prov.* 8.12]. The dwelling with His people is to satisfy God's desire to have a mutual identification of lot between Himself and them. Thus understood, the concept helps us to feel somewhat of the inner warmth and God-centered affection, and on the part of God, the man-seeking interest of Old Testament religion.[75]

God's presence in the tabernacle also brings to bear his majesty, holiness, immanence, and transcendence. The tabernacle is a holy place or sanctuary because God is there. The tabernacle displays God's condescending love for his people without eclipsing his majesty and the corresponding desired affects in the souls of the Israelites – awe and fear.[76]

The tabernacle is also the place where the Israelites offer their worship to God. "It is the palace of the King in which the people render Him homage."[77] And it is this because of God's special presence there. "The tabernacle, then, represented not merely symbolically the indwelling of God among Israel, but actually contained it."[78] It was Jehovah's house.

The tabernacle also symbolized God's heavenly habitation and the eschatological or ideal destiny of God's people. Vos says:

> If the tabernacle symbolized the heavenly habitation of God and the ideal destiny of God's people has always been to be received of Him to the most consummate fellowship there, then there must have been at least an ideal reflex and foreshadowing of this in the tabernacle. In

---

[73] Vos, *BTV*, 148.

[74] Vos, *BTV*, 149.

[75] Vos, *BTV*, 149.

[76] Vos, *BTV*, 150. "The coexistence of these two elements, that of trustful approach to God and that of reverence for the divine majesty, is characteristic of the Biblical religion throughout. Even the religious attitude exemplified by Jesus retains it, for if He teaches us to address God as Father, He immediately adds to this the qualification 'in heaven', lest the love and trust towards God should fall to the level of irreligious familiarity with God" (Vos, *BTV*, 151).

[77] Vos, *BTV*, 151.

[78] Vos, *BTV*, 154.

accordance with this principle the names given to God's celestial palace and to the earthly sanctuary are identical. *Ma'on, hekhal, zebhul* are used indiscriminately of both. The point raised is not without theological importance. It touches the question of the nature of religion, and the part played in it by God and man respectively. In the ideal covenant-fellowship, here portrayed, the divine factor is the all-controlling one. Man appears as admitted into, adjusted to, subordinated to, the life of God. Biblical piety is God-centred.[79]

The tabernacle typified both Christ and the Church. Vos asks this question: "where do these religious principles and realities, which the tabernacle served to teach and communicate, reappear in the subsequent history of redemption, lifted to their consummate stage?"[80] His answer is Christ and the Church. God tabernacled among men in the Word become flesh (John 1:14). The resurrection was the rebuilding of the Old Testament temple (John 2:19-22). "This affirms the continuity between the Old Testament sanctuary and His glorified Person."[81] All that the tabernacle and temple stood for pointed to Him. "He as the antitypical tabernacle is revelatory and sacramental in the highest degree."[82]

Vos goes further and argues that "what is true of the Christ is likewise true of the Church...because the Church is the body of the risen Christ."[83] The Church is called the house of God because it is now the dwelling of Jehovah.

The sacrificial system "forms the centre of the rights of the tabernacle."[84] Sacrifice is due to the presence of sin and resultant need of expiation. The altar is the place where sacrifice is offered and received by Jehovah. This reminds us that worship involves an act of man toward God and his corresponding response. Sacrifice is an act of worship, but worship is more than sacrifice.[85] Sacrifice is man's giving "the gift of life to God."[86] But worship includes God's response of receiving the sacrifice and "a sacramental transaction, something God does, and in regard to

[79] Vos, *BTV*, 154.
[80] Vos, *BTV*, 154.
[81] Vos, *BTV*, 154-55.
[82] Vos, *BTV*, 155.
[83] Vos, BTV, 155.
[84] Vos, *BTV*, 155.
[85] Vos, *BTV*, 158.
[86] Vos, *BTV*, 159.

which man is purely receptive, passive." Vos identifies God's response as "the divine answer to prayer."[87]

Vos sees the relationship between the offerer and the sacrifice as symbolico-vicarious. This theory "presupposes the recognition by ritual itself that nothing can be done in man himself with the proper effect, and that, therefore, a substitute must take his place."[88] The perfect animal is offered as a substitute for the imperfect offerer. Christ is the perfect anti-type in the ethical sphere.[89] The laying on of hands by the offerer also symbolized a transfer of the offerer's sin ("liability to death-punishment"[90]) to the anti-type of the animal.[91] Next comes the slaying of the animal which signifies that "death is the penalty for sin, vicariously inflicted in sacrifice."[92] Shed blood is the symbol of death,[93] which is the punishment for sin. All of this clearly points to the vicarious atonement of Christ. Not only does he offer himself as an ethically perfect substitute for sinners, he also takes their sin and guilt upon himself and satisfies the wrath of God. In other words, "Christ not merely in His positive service, but through His suffering and death made up for the abnormality of our sin. He satisfied the justice of God."[94] Atonement (or covering from *kapper*) is man's need due to sin. The ritual law is God's initiative to cover man due to his sin.[95] The burning of the animal upon the altar also had symbolic meaning. Vos argues against it symbolizing eternal punishment as an extension of the slaying of the animal. Instead, he argues from the use of the verb *hiqtir* (descriptive of burning) to "a process whereby something is changed into a finer substance."[96] Since "the law speaks of the altar-burning as yielding a sweet odour of delight to Jehovah"[97] and since Christ (John 17:19) and Paul (Ephesians 5:2) use ritual language while "speaking of Christ's active obedience"[98] in the language of consecration as it relates to the death on the cross, then the symbolism involved with the burning must

---

[87] Vos, *BTV*, 158.
[88] Vos, *BTV*, 160.
[89] Vos, *BTV*, 162.
[90] Vos, *BTV*, 163.
[91] Vos, *BTV*, 162-63.
[92] Vos, *BTV*, 163.
[93] Vos, *BTV*, 164.
[94] Vos, *BTV*, 166. This comes in a section where Vos is discussing Leviticus 17:11.
[95] Vos, *BTV*, 167-68.
[96] Vos, *BTV*, 169.
[97] Vos, *BTV*, 169.
[98] Vos, *BTV*, 169.

be typological of "an active consecratory obedience offered to God on behalf of sinners by Christ."[99] Finally, the sacrificial meal symbolized the absence of hostility and the presence of friendship.[100]

## John Owen

- ### Introduction: Special Revelation is now Inscripturated

Owen sees the Church[101] becoming "increasingly more brilliant, more visible, and more glorious than in any of her previous phases"[102] from Abraham onward. Abraham passed along what he had received in terms of knowledge of God and forms of worship.[103] But the time was approaching when new revelation would change things once again. Owen adds:

> ...all of these rules were observed to the best of his capacity by each individual until the time came when they were destined to be overtaken by a newer and more developed form of organized worship.[104]

The worship of the Church suffered greatly during Egyptian bondage but God raised up Moses as his mediator and go-between in order to reveal more of his will.[105] Owen sees this period as one of "immense amplification of theological light."[106] "In fact, at no period in her history has the Church advanced by so detailed instructions."[107] This is the first time God combines worship and ecclesiastical gatherings and inscripturates his will. Prior to this, revelation was given then passed on by oral transmission. The period of revelation with Moses is different.

> Heavenly teaching, the knowledge of God, had been gradually revealed and expanded on various occasions since the foundation of the universe, and now at length it was brought together and systematized

---

[99] Vos, *BTV*, 169.

[100] Vos, *BTV*, 169-70.

[101] Owen defines the Church of God as "the assembly of His [i.e., God's] people..." Cf. Owen, *BTO*, 370.

[102] Owen, *BTO*, 370.

[103] Owen, *BTO*, 371.

[104] Owen, *BTO*, 371.

[105] Owen, *BTO*, 372-73.

[106] Owen, *BTO*, 373.

[107] Owen, *BTO*, 373.

into one general and stable method of worship and obedience, and presented to the church as a body of unified truth. These truths, down to this period, had been mostly preserved by *oral* transmission, and had suffered by being totally lost in some parts of the world while, in others, they were rendered useless by the mixture of superstitious and heretical opinions. Now, by the wonderful love of God for His Church, and by His special provision, this was enshrined in written records. In this way theology was removed from the responsibility of mortal men and was protected from the results of human defilement or corruption, whatever be the spiritual state of the theologians themselves. To that early body of revelations and institutions, now collected into a compact body, were added new revelations, and thus arrived that complete rule of right worship of God, and of living to His glory, which would suffice the Church, with no need of further new teachings until the advent of Him in whom all the treasures of wisdom and knowledge were to dwell.[108]

Special revelation now becomes inscripturated revelation. Scripture is God speaking to man "...*no less directly than if he were hearing God speaking with His own voice to them,* exactly as did Adam when he heard the voice of the Lord in the garden."[109]

## • The Doctrinal Content of the Mosaic Period

Owen considers the Mosaic period in terms of its doctrinal content as suggesting "nothing else but a more clear annunciation of the first *evangelical* promise."[110] The institutions and sacrifices "confirm, prefigure, and expound the promised Mediator, His coming redemptive work, and the eternal salvation which would, in time, be won through His shed blood."[111] The rites and legal ceremonies were typological of and "summed up in eternal life through the Messiah yet to be revealed."[112] Christ and his Apostles affirmed this in the New Testament.

---

[108] Owen, *BTO,* 373-74.

[109] Owen, *BTO,* 375.

[110] Owen, *BTO,* 375. Here the concepts of the Christocentricity and organic development of redemptive history can be clearly seen in Owen's words.

[111] Owen, *BTO,* 376.

[112] Owen, *BTO,* 376.

- **The Sacred Principles of Mosaic Theology**

Owen taught that within the Mosaic theology there "are several heads or sacred principles of such heavenly teaching that they form the immovable foundations upon which all the institutions of divine worship rest."[113] All acceptable religious worship is grounded in divine revelation. "God has, in no way and at no time, from the foundation of the world, allowed human judgment to give His worship its limits or measure."[114] Owen sees three sub-points to this principle "of which frequent mention is made in the books of the Old Testament."[115]

**1. All true theology is revealed theology.** Owen says "that no teaching about God, or concerning His worship, can be considered as true theology *except those* which *He alone* has revealed, and so placed beyond all doubt."[116] All acceptable worship is revealed worship and written down in Scripture. The sovereign will of God is the determining factor concerning the elements of worship. Man's emotions are not the grounds upon which to build a theology of worship. Nothing can be added to God's will concerning his worship, except what he adds. This "is firmly grounded in the second commandment of the Decalogue."[117]

**2. Salvation comes through Christ by grace alone.** Owen says "that righteousness, acceptance before God, deliverance from sin, in short, eternal salvation, is to be obtained only through the promised seed, and that as a consequence of pure grace alone."[118] He continues:

> This is to say, the further revelation of a promised Mediator between God and man, who was to win redemption by the eternal sacrifice of Himself, to win sinners back to God. It taught that all grace was centered in this coming one, solely and eternally. Thus, that foundational principle of supernatural theology, of salvation and reconciliation of sinners to God, which had at first been obscurely revealed at the giving of the first promise, which had been renewed with the covenant in the

---

[113] Owen, *BTO*, 434.

[114] Owen, *BTO*, 434. This language is that of the regulative principle of worship as enshrined in the Westminster Confession of Faith XXI, Savoy Declaration XXII, and the Second London Confession of Faith – 1689 XXII.

[115] Owen, *BTO*, 434.

[116] Owen, *BTO*, 434.

[117] Owen, *BTO*, 435.

[118] Owen, *BTO*, 435.

days of Noah, expounded more clearly still to Abraham, was now at length openly and clearly displayed.[119]

Owen sees what he calls the "Mosaic development"[120] as including "the following surpassing dogmas"[121] – total depravity, regeneration, and reconciliation through blood sacrifices which "prefigured another and outstanding sacrifice."[122]

**3. Mosaic ordinances were temporary.** The ordinances of the Mosaic theology *"were designed to last only for a pre-determined period."*[123] "This is really but to say that in the fullness of time One would appear in whom all things were summated, One endowed with authority as lawgiver, who would declare the whole will of God in its perfection."[124]

> To His words all are required to be obedient under penalty of excommunication from the congregation of the Lord (Deuteronomy 18:16-19). It was in the light of these Mosaic principles that the mighty foundation, the headstone and corner, Jesus Christ—the seed promised to Adam and Abraham—came and took His place in the Israelite Church. In this way, arose the glory and honor of that Church, as God periodically enlarged it and heaped honors upon it by which it became an ever more radiant symbol of the more excellent glory of the spiritual government of the Church by Christ (2 Corinthians 3).[125]

Not all who lived under this phase of theology looked "ahead to the end and abolition of these things" but many did, who "burned with eager longing to enjoy the things prefigured by these presentations."[126] God raised up prophets to preserve the Word of God, acceptable worship, and to "sustain the Church in her height and bright expectation, and hope of spiritual glory to be revealed and purchased by the ministry of the Messiah."[127]

---

[119] Owen, *BTO*, 435-36. Here we see a clear example of the Christocentric, progressive, organic nature of redemptive history from the pen of Owen.
[120] Owen, *BTO*, 436.
[121] Owen, *BTO*, 436.
[122] Owen, *BTO*, 437. Here we see the intersection of *historia salutis* with *ordo salutis* categories.
[123] Owen, *BTO*, 437.
[124] Owen, *BTO*, 437.
[125] Owen, *BTO*, 437.
[126] Owen, *BTO*, 437-38. Here Owen is utilizing symbolism and typology.
[127] Owen, *BTO*, 438.

- **Defection and Apostasy**

Owen sees "a twofold defection of the Jewish Church from this new phase of theology..."[128] There was a partial apostasy spanning from the "establishment of Mosaic worship down to their captivity in Babylon."[129] This apostasy was a partial defection from the doctrine of "the universal plenitude and perfection of the Holy Scriptures..." and, resulting from that, "the infamous superstition and man-made worship which was, at length, to be so gravely rebuked by the Holy Spirit."[130] "[T]hey began to consider it right and lawful to think up for themselves what they chose to do in the worship of God, groundlessly and out of their own fancy, as if the glory of God depended upon their mere will and whim."[131] "God employed the extraordinary ministry of the prophets to sweep away this insanity."[132] The apostasy in worship occurred in two ways: (1) "in regard to the object of worship" and (2) "with regard to the means of worship."[133] "All worship is either human and natural, or else divine and instituted by God Himself at His own good pleasure. When apostasy occurs, this latter is usurped by an arbitrary worship system."[134] Owen traces the history of idolatry in the Old Testament in Chapters 3-10 of Book 5.[135]

The Mosaic theology which "taught a gratuitous justification and eternal salvation to be realized through the merits and mediation of Messiah...became obscured..."[136] It was replaced with "a soul-destroying error concerning justification through the works of the law and correct observance of ceremonies and rites."[137] Messianic expectation was obscured as follows:

> So also the essential teaching of Mosaic theology concerning the coming, earthly ministry of Messiah, who would change the Mosaic rites when they had fulfilled their predetermined purpose and run their

---

[128] Owen, *BTO*, 439.
[129] Owen, *BTO*, 440.
[130] Owen, *BTO*, 441.
[131] Owen, *BTO*, 441.
[132] Owen, *BTO*, 441.
[133] Owen, *BTO*, 441.
[134] Owen, *BTO*, 461.
[135] Cf. Owen, *BTO*, 446-86.
[136] Owen, *BTO*, 487.
[137] Owen, *BTO*, 487.

course, they turned away from and built instead a figment of the perpetuity of their rituals.[138]

Apostasy brought with it God's displeasure and eventual "chastisement of the 70 years captivity."[139]

"The exile was a deserved chastisement, but it came from a merciful Father, in view of national sins."[140] The exile is the way God purged the temple, the city, and the land of apostasy. It "would suffice for its [i.e., the Jewish Church's] thorough cleansing and ultimate restoration."[141] Once the duration of this purging had been completed, the return from captivity came about in order to "bring about a thorough reformation of the Church, along the lines of her revealed theology."[142] The books of Ezra, Nehemiah, Haggai, Zechariah, and Malachi "testify to this process."[143]

- **Ezra's Reformation**

Owen calls this reformation 'Ezra's reformation', having "five essential elements."[144] The elements are: (1) restoration of the temple; (2) institution of the great national synagogue; (3) a revision of the copies of the Scriptures; (4) preaching of the word of God; and (5) separation of the mixed peoples.

**1. The restoration of the temple.** Owen does not discuss the restoration of the temple because others have dealt with it and "it does not properly belong to our purpose."[145]

**2. The institution of the national synagogue.** Ezra instituted the synagogue, according to Owen, at this time.[146] He understands the terms 'synagogue' and 'council' as synonyms. It began in the desert, "when Moses instituted the council of seventy-one to assist him."[147] "[T]his

---

[138] Owen, *BTO,* 487.
[139] Owen, *BTO,* 488.
[140] Owen, *BTO,* 489.
[141] Owen, *BTO,* 489.
[142] Owen, *BTO,* 489.
[143] Owen, *BTO,* 490.
[144] Owen, *BTO,* 490.
[145] Owen, *BTO,* 490.
[146] Owen, *BTO,* 490.
[147] Owen, *BTO,* 490.

synagogue or council was speedily reconstituted on the peoples return from their captivity."[148] Its purpose was to maintain authority and order. Its membership was comprised of "inspired men, prophets and pen-men of the Holy Spirit."[149] "As this reform of the Church closely followed the first institution of Mosaic theology, so it was necessary that the reformers, prophets and God-chosen men, should be like that one man Moses."[150]

**3. The separation of the mixed peoples.** Owen discusses next the separation of the mixed peoples – i.e., "the putting away of strange wives..."[151] The intermingling of foreign wives with the people of God had increased "from the days of Solomon onward."[152] It was through this putting away that the Church was further purified.

**4. The revision of the Scriptures.** The revision of sacred Scripture is discussed next. He describes it as follows:

> No one will deny that Ezra and his colleagues and fellow prophets had before them ancient copies of the Scriptures, preserved down to their days with the greatest faithfulness. Still some scribal errors must have crept into copies made during the period of dispersion, and to these they now devoted their greatest efforts. In so detecting and removing all such blemishes from the sacred text they surely enjoyed the powerful guidance and inspiration of God. It is during this period of correction that some would place their fiction of a "change in the Hebrew script" but, as we have already seen, Ezra could not desire, nor was he at all able, to change the writing. In fact, he was in honor bound to keep that ancient script in which the sacred penmen and prophets has [*sic*] originally written, according to the pattern shown them by God Himself.[153]

Owen vehemently denies that the Scriptures were entirely lost and "now miraculously restored from memory, and reduced to writing by Ezra."[154]

---

[148] Owen, *BTO*, 490.
[149] Owen, *BTO*, 491.
[150] Owen, *BTO*, 491.
[151] Owen, *BTO*, 492.
[152] Owen, *BTO*, 492.
[153] Owen, *BTO*, 494.
[154] Owen, *BTO*, 494.

He also argues extensively for "a divine (inspired) origin"[155] of the Hebrew vowel-points, whether they were introduced by Ezra or coeval with the language. His point is that either way, the vowel-points are of divine origin.[156]

**5. The preaching of the word.** Owen finally discusses the preaching of the word of God at this time of Ezraitic reformation. He references Nehemiah 8:1-8. Public preaching had been neglected during the defection of the people. God had appointed that the priests and Levites should preach (Malachi 2:7; Deuteronomy 33:10) and the people should seek their "expositions of the mind and meaning of God, from their lips."[157] "A neglect of preaching is a most sure sign of defection in the Church, and carefulness in this matter is as sure a sign of reformation."[158] The Ezraitic reformers re-established preaching as soon as possible and "were blessed with wonderful success."[159]

- **Apostasy after Ezra's Reformation: The Abolition of the Theocracy and Prophetic Ministry**

Apostasy, however, was lurking around the corner. "In the passage of time, yet again a defection of ungrateful men followed this renewal of the Church and a dreadful and horrible ruin pursued hard on the heels of that defection."[160] The prophetic ministry continued and was the cause of maintaining some purity in the Jewish Church. But God withdrew the prophetic ministry in time and, as a result, "the foundations of the Jewish Church commenced to crumble and the structure tottered towards an inevitable overthrow."[161] The influx of Greek philosophy resulted "in the undermining of all true theology."[162] "[S]chools quite unlike those ancient 'schools of the prophets'" arose and became "centers for the production of endless disputes, convoluted intricacies, and the spawning of sects, just as the parent Greek philosophy had fragmented into so

---

[155] Owen, *BTO,* 495. Cf. "Digression on the Origin of the Hebrew Vowel-Points," Owen, *BTO,* 495-533.

[156] This was a typical view in Owen's day.

[157] Owen, *BTO,* 534.

[158] Owen, *BTO,* 535.

[159] Owen, *BTO,* 535.

[160] Owen, *BTO,* 537.

[161] Owen, *BTO,* 537.

[162] Owen, *BTO,* 538.

many warring schools of thought."[163] Out of such schools came the Pharisees, Sadducees, and Essenes. These Jewish schools of thought "proved far more damaging to the Jews than the Greeks, because their speculations...concerned religion and the due worship of God, the interpretation of the Scriptures–all that is sacred..."[164] Due to outside influences, the people became "greatly ignorant of the sacred language."[165] This was due to their mingling with the Gentiles. The common folk became ignorant of sacred things and their teachers were arrogant, blind, and vain, which were "prime causes of this defection."[166] "This is just to say that the people lacked the *letter*, and the leaders the *spirit* of the Scriptures. The result was a universal apostasy."[167] During this time the theocracy was abolished and "[t]he Church no longer enjoyed a prophetic ministry."[168] Owen adds these chilling words reminiscent of our own day:

> The people were daily exposed to the mingling of the gentiles; they had all but forgotten their primitive language, their doctors and teachers were consumed with internecine strife of opinion in the fashion of pagan philosophers keen to advance the standing of their own schools. Sects were everywhere being generated; no reformer stood out to oppose the crops of tares daily springing from such noxious fields; all, in short, was evidently and openly rushing onwards to final ruin.[169]

Owen sees the 400 years between Malachi and John the Baptist as a form of judgment due to apostasy. No prophet was raised up to confront the people. God "had added that final 'push of prophecy' at Malachi 4:4-6, after which there was to cease completely for some centuries that extraordinary and prophetic ministry...employed for the Church's reformation over so many ages."[170] "[T]he Jewish Church sank rapidly into final ruin."[171] Owen traces this final apostasy under three headings.

---

[163] Owen, *BTO*, 538.
[164] Owen, *BTO*, 538.
[165] Owen, *BTO*, 538.
[166] Owen, *BTO*, 539.
[167] Owen, *BTO*, 539.
[168] Owen, *BTO*, 539.
[169] Owen, *BTO*, 539. Owen then enters upon two digressions – the first on the origin and utility of the Septuagint and the second on the origin and utility of the Targums. Cf. Owen, *BTO*, 540-53.
[170] Owen, *BTO*, 554.
[171] Owen, *BTO*, 554.

**1. The first principle of Mosaic theology (i.e., the primacy of the Scriptures) was attacked and overthrown.** Owen argues that due to this, new schools of thought arose which gave birth to the traditions of men which our Lord condemned.[172]

**2. Justification by faith was attacked and overthrown.** The "second fundamental head of Mosaic theology, justification, or how a sinful man might regain the favor of the Almighty"[173] was also attacked and overthrown. Their pride motivated them and "they boasted 'Abraham was our father' (Matthew 3:9 Luke 3:8) with haughty face and hardened neck."[174] Their pride left no room for repentance. This is what John the Baptist "felt it necessary to attack... (Matthew 3:8)."[175] They felt themselves "a people who, therefore, must need no repentance and are well-pleasing to God."[176] "Nothing was more repugnant to them than the idea that God bestows benefits on mankind for no merits of their own."[177] They did not see themselves as sinners in need of divine grace and pardon. They viewed themselves as naturally able to offer God what he required for acceptance with him. They believed "that their worship and ceremonies are the basis for their acceptance, and that their works will save them and make them pure in God's sight."[178] They believed "that no man could be saved, except by the works of the Law."[179] "In this fashion, the final phase of the ancient Jewish Church apostatized from the second vital principle of Mosaic theology–the way of justification before God for sinful men."[180]

**3. Messianic hope was lost.** The third fundamental principle of Mosaic theology "concerns the advent, life, and ministry of Messiah."[181] Messiah was revealed in the Mosaic theology as "equipped and endowed with all authority by His Father... to institute new ways of worship and new

---

[172] Owen deals with Second Temple Judaism and the supposed use of Jewish traditions by the New Testament in a digression entitled, "Digression of Jewish Rites and Christianity," 560-82.

[173] Owen, *BTO*, 583.

[174] Owen, *BTO*, 583.

[175] Owen, *BTO*, 583.

[176] Owen, *BTO*, 583.

[177] Owen, *BTO*, 584.

[178] Owen, *BTO*, 584.

[179] Owen, *BTO*, 585.

[180] Owen, *BTO*, 585.

[181] Owen, *BTO*, 585.

ceremonies, since the old and typical legal ones were progressively fulfilled in Him."[182] The Messianic hope created by Mosaic theology had long been lost among the Jewish Church, so much so that they subjected him to "a cruel and tortuous death."[183] Owen says that "the prime basis and foundation of the apostate Jewish theology [became] the absolute unchangeableness of their ceremonial law."[184] This is what the Apostle Paul dealt with in the book of Hebrews (Hebrews 7:12-16).[185] Owen argues that "the whole ceremonial law, the entire solemn administration of the Mosaic institutions of worship, depended upon the high priesthood."[186] Since that priesthood was supplanted by Christ, the ceremonial law attached to that priesthood could be and was supplanted by Christ and his new forms of worship. Owen adds, "Christ was not just the new high priest, but the only true and real high priest, of whom all the previous priests had been but types, and it is of His priesthood that God swears there shall be no end."[187] When Christ came he also did away with Jerusalem as the "specific location for the performance of …solemn worship…"[188] Owen comments:

> Jerusalem had been chosen and set apart by God as the seat of His solemn worship. This the Apostles in no way deny. With the coming and ministry of Messiah, a sacrifice would be made there–at Jerusalem–which would, henceforward, allow acceptable worship to God to be raised anywhere and everywhere on earth. This the last of the prophets, Malachi had predicted (Malachi 1:11). And lest there should still lack anything for the establishing of this truth, God had declared in advance that, in the days of Messiah, He would raise up for Himself priests and Levites from among the gentiles themselves (Isaiah 66:21). And this was confirmed by the speedy destruction of Jerusalem.[189]

---

[182] Owen, *BTO*, 585.

[183] Owen, *BTO*, 585.

[184] Owen, *BTO*, 585.

[185] Owen, *BTO*, 586.

[186] Owen, *BTO*, 586. Cf. Appendix 2, "John Owen and Reformed Orthodoxy on the Functions of the Decalogue in Redemptive History" for crucial nuances used while describing the types and functions of law in Scripture.

[187] Owen, *BTO*, 587.

[188] Owen, *BTO*, 587.

[189] Owen, *BTO*, 588.

# CHAPTER SIXTEEN

# REDEMPTIVE, SPECIAL REVELATION
# AND THE NEW TESTAMENT: GEERHARDUS VOS

## Introduction: The Structure of New Testament Revelation

Vos observes that "[t]here are three ways in which the structure of New Testament Revelation can be determined from within Scripture itself."[1] This is vital for Vos "for we dare not impose upon the divine process and its product a scheme from any outside source."[2] Vos identifies three scriptural sources from which to identify the structure of New Testament revelation: (1) indications in the Old Testament; (2) the teachings of Jesus; and (3) the teachings of Paul and the other Apostles.

- **Indications in the Old Testament**

"The Old Testament is a forward-stretching and forward-looking dispensation."[3] Eschatological and Messianic prophecy point to "an absolutely perfect and enduring state to be contrasted with the present and its succession of developments."[4] "The Old Testament, through its prophetic attitude, postulates the New Testament."[5] The promise of the New Covenant in Jeremiah 31:31-34 is a crystallization of the Old Testament forward-looking prophetic element which brings with its fulfillment a "new order of affairs…"[6]

- **The teachings of Jesus**

Jesus picks up on Jeremiah's language ('new covenant') at the Last Supper. Vos says, "It is evident that our Lord here represents His blood (death) as the basis and inauguration of a new religious relationship of the disciples to God."[7] This "new order of affairs…is of final

---

[1] Vos, *BTV*, 299.
[2] Vos, *BTV*, 299.
[3] Vos, *BTV*, 299.
[4] Vos, *BTV*, 299.
[5] Vos, *BTV*, 299.
[6] Vos, *BTV*, 300.
[7] Vos, *BTV*, 300.

significance. It reaches over into the eschatological state, which of itself makes it eternal."[8] "What we call the 'New Covenant' here appears at the outset as an eternal covenant."[9]

The contrast between the old and the new "is not in the first place a contrast of revelation."[10] It refers to "a new era in religious access to God."[11] Vos adds, "Of a new period of divine self-disclosure they do not speak, although that, of course, is presupposed under the general law that progress in religion follows progress in revelation."[12]

- **The teachings of Paul and the other Apostles**

"Paul is in the New Testament the great exponent of the fundamental bisection in the history of redemption and of revelation."[13] Thus he speaks of law and faith and "we find the formal distinction between the 'New *Diatheke*' and the 'Old *Diatheke*' [2 *Cor.* 3.6, 14]."[14] There is in Paul "a contrast between two religious ministrations, that of the letter and that of the Spirit, that of condemnation and that of righteousness."[15]

The Epistle to the Hebrews functions as "the clearest information in regard to the structure of redemptive procedure, and that particularly, as based on and determined by the structure of revelation."[16] "How intimately to the writer the unfolding from the Old into the New is bound up with the unfolding of revelation, may be seen from the opening words of the Epistle."[17] Former revelation is preparatory to the latter.

The new dispensation is final. "It is not one new disclosure to be followed by others, but the consummate disclosure beyond which nothing is expected."[18] It is such because it is God speaking in his Son. "[T]he New Testament revelation is on organic, and in itself completed, whole."[19] Jesus not only reveals truth but is presented as "the great fact

---

[8] Vos, *BTV*, 300.
[9] Vos, *BTV*, 300.
[10] Vos, *BTV*, 300-01.
[11] Vos, *BTV*, 301.
[12] Vos, *BTV*, 301.
[13] Vos, *BTV*, 301.
[14] Vos, *BTV*, 301.
[15] Vos, *BTV*, 301.
[16] Vos, *BTV*, 301. Cf. Vos, *The Teaching of the Epistle to the Hebrews*.
[17] Vos, *BTV*, 301.
[18] Vos, *BTV*, 302.
[19] Vos, *BTV*, 302.

to be expounded."[20] This is exactly what the Apostles did and what the rest of the New Testament is about.

As Vos has noted before, redemptive acts precede and prepare for redemptive-revelatory words. As the Old Testament postulates the New Testament, so the coming, life, ministry, death, and resurrection of Christ postulate the apostolic writings. "The relation between Jesus and the Apostolate is in general that between the fact to be interpreted and the subsequent interpretation of this fact."[21] However, alongside of Jesus' acts were his teachings as well, "with a preliminary illumination of them", though "more sporadic and less comprehensive than that supplied by the Epistles."[22]

In terms of analyzing the revelation embodied in the New Testament, Vos says, "[t]he first and great division within our field, then, is that between revelation through Christ directly and revelation mediated by Christ through the Apostolate."[23] Vos sees the nativity, the preaching of John the Baptist, the baptism of Jesus, and the probation or temptation of Jesus as requiring "preliminary attention before entering upon a survey of the revelation-content of His work."[24]

While considering the question of the expectation of further revelation, Vos says:

> Unless we adopt the mystical standpoint, which cuts loose the subjective from the objective, the only proper answer to this question is, that new revelation can be added only, in case new objective events of a supernatural character take place, needing for their understanding a new body of interpretation supplied by God. This will actually be the case in the eschatological issue of things. What then occurs will constitute a new epoch in redemption worthy to be placed by the side of the great epochs in the Mosaic age and the age of the first Advent.[25]

Vos' ensuing discussion of New Testament theology is as follows: (1) revelation connected with the nativity; (2) revelation connected with

---

[20] Vos, *BTV*, 302.
[21] Vos, *BTV*, 303.
[22] Vos, *BTV*, 303.
[23] Vos, *BTV*, 303-04.
[24] Vos, *BTV*, 304.
[25] Vos, *BTV*, 304.

John the Baptist; (3) revelation in the probation of Jesus; and (4) the revelation of Jesus' public ministry.[26]

## Revelation Connected with the Nativity

The nativity is what theology calls the incarnation. The incarnation was "a vertical movement from heaven to earth, from the divine to the human, in which the pre-existent Messiah appears entering into human nature, the super-historical descends into the stream of history."[27] There are traces of this theology of the nativity in Jesus' teaching in the Synoptics and more so in John. But "with Paul the doctrine emerges in rounded-off explicit form…"[28] "But these all mark later stages in the progress of New Testament revelation."[29] Vos reminds us, however, "that the event precedes, the interpreting revelations follow."[30]

The event of the nativity is spoken of "in terms of prophecy and fulfillment, thus moving along the level pathway of history."[31] What Jehovah promised to the fathers had come to pass and "now assumed the concrete form of the actual."[32] The supernatural entered history "and so [became] a piece of the historical in its highest form."[33]

Vos discusses the characteristic features of the various aspects of the nativity under eight headings.

- **The Use of Old Testament Modes of Expression**

Vos says, "There is in them [i.e., aspects of the nativity] a close adjustment to the Old Testament as to the mode of expression used."[34] This displays continuity between the Old and New Testament revelations and was best suited to be understandable to the people who were initially

---

[26] Sadly, Vos did not complete the section on the New Testament. There is no discussion of revelation given by Jesus through his appointed revelatory organs – i.e., the Apostolate. He did, however, publish *Pauline Eschatology* and *The Teaching of the Epistle to the Hebrews* which, in part, fill the gap.
[27] Vos, *BTV*, 305.
[28] Vos, *BTV*, 305.
[29] Vos, *BTV*, 305.
[30] Vos, *BTV*, 305.
[31] Vos, *BTV*, 305.
[32] Vos, *BTV*, 305.
[33] Vos, *BTV*, 305.
[34] Vos, *BTV*, 306.

addressed by the Gospel writers – those "nurtured on the Old Testament."[35]

- ## Relation to the Organism of the Old Testament History of Redemption

The second characteristic feature is "a perceptible intent to fit the new things into the organism of the Old Testament History of Redemption."[36]

> The nativity is connected with the house of God's servant David, as was spoken by the holy prophets, [*Lk.* 1.69, 70]; it is the fulfilment of the oath sworn to Abraham, [vs. 73]; the prophecy of which it is the culmination extends from the beginning of the world, [vs. 70]. In David, Abraham, the Creation, the dominating epochs of the Old Testament are seized upon; the chronological nexus is, as it were, the exponent of the oneness of the divine work through the ages and of the divine purpose from the outset to lead up to the Messiah.[37]

- ## Redemptive Character

The third feature is "[t]he new procedure to be ushered in is throughout described as bearing a redemptive character."[38] This comes about by the fact that the narrative assumes a state of sin and unworthiness in those addressed "and the corresponding signature of grace and salvation."[39] The tone of sovereign mercy is seen in the words of Mary (Luke 1:46, 51-53). God is fulfilling his promise to the patriarchs (Luke 1:54, 55, 72, 73).

- ## Absence of the Political Element

The fourth feature "is the absence of the political element from these pieces."[40] This is unlike revelation connected to the Old Covenant.

---

[35] Vos, *BTV*, 306.
[36] Vos, *BTV*, 306.
[37] Vos, *BTV*, 306.
[38] Vos, *BTV*, 306.
[39] Vos, *BTV*, 306.
[40] Vos, *BTV*, 307.

- **Absence of a Legalistic Judaic Element**

The fifth is "[t]he legalism of Judaism is nowhere in evidence."[41] This turns the Jewish expectation on its head. The legalistic Judaism of the day expected Israel to obey the law then Messiah would come. The Lucan narrative turns this around. Two examples are given. "Of John the Baptist, Gabriel predicts that he shall turn many of the children of Israel to Jehovah their God [*Lk.* 1.16]." "To Joseph it is predicted that Jesus' chief work will consist in saving His people from their sins [*Matt.* 1.21]."[42]

- **The Bond between the Testaments: Messianic Fulfillment of Ancient Eschatological Prophecy**

The sixth characteristic feature is "[t]he closeness of the bond with the Old Testament [that] is shown through the proclamation into these early revelations of the two lines of ancient eschatological prophecy."[43] These two lines were the coming of Jehovah in a supreme theophany and the coming of Messiah. Vos says, "The full development of New Testament revelation has first fully disclosed their convergence through its teaching that in the divine Messiah Jehovah has come to His people."[44]

- **Intimations of Soteric Universalism**

The seventh feature is "[t]here are certain intimations of the universalism (destiny to include other nations) of the Gospel in these disclosures."[45] Simeon says that that God's salvation will "lighten the Gentiles, side by side with its being a glory for the people of Israel [*Lk.* 2.32]."[46]

- **The Virgin Birth**

The last feature is stated as follows: "As a last element lending distinctive character to these revelations, we must mention the supernatural birth of the Messiah to be brought about without human

---

[41] Vos, *BTV*, 307.
[42] Vos, *BTV*, 307.
[43] Vos, *BTV*, 307.
[44] Vos, *BTV*, 308.
[45] Vos, *BTV*, 308.
[46] Vos, *BTV*, 308.

paternity."[47] The virgin birth of our Lord reminds us that a unique person was born, a person with no human paternity, called both the son of Mary (Mathew 1:21, 23) and the Son of the Highest, the Son of God (Luke 1:32, 35).

## Revelation Connected with John the Baptist

John the Baptist is seen by Vos as "a way-preparing messenger sent before the face of the Lord..."[48] He "belongs half-way to the fulfilment-era" because the "culmination of Old Testament prophecy is in him..."[49] John was the fore-runner to the Messiah and Kingdom of God. "As a messenger he comes immediately before the reality..."[50] Through John the Kingdom moves "out of the sphere of pure futurity belonging to it under the Old Testament...which made him 'more than a prophet'" and "'greatest of them born of women'."[51] John was yet less than the least in the kingdom of heaven (Matthew 11:11). Vos explains:

> The true interpretation is that the Baptist would not partake of the privileges of the already coming Kingdom of which others partook through their association with Jesus. He continued to lead his life apart, on the basis of the Old Testament.[52]

John expected judgment to come with Messiah's first advent. This produced in him a "somewhat impatient enquiry in regard to the Messianic authentification of Jesus."[53] Vos says:

> In it the Old Testament once more, as it were, voices its impatience about the tarrying of the Messiah. But as there, so here, the impatience centred on one particular point, the slowness of God's procedure in destroying the wicked. John had been specifically appointed to proclaim the judgment-aspect of the coming crisis. Hence a certain disappointment at the procedure of Jesus. ...It was not Jesus' task for the present to judge, at least not in that way. The judgment would come at a subsequent stage. After all, Jesus had not lost sight of John's question. He answered it in the most delicate, yet forceful way. As the

---

[47] Vos, *BTV*, 309.
[48] Vos, *BTV*, 313.
[49] Vos, *BTV*, 313.
[50] Vos, *BTV*, 313.
[51] Vos, *BTV*, 313.
[52] Vos, *BTV*, 313.
[53] Vos, *BTV*, 313.

subsequent discourse reveals, His heart was full of appreciation of the greatness of John, and, as the Fourth Gospel proves, full of love for his person on account of the generosity of John's self-effacement in the service of the Messiah [3.30; 5.35].[54]

Vos discusses revelation connected with John the Baptist under these headings: (1) John the Baptist and Elijah; (2) John the Baptist's testimony to Jesus; (3) John's baptism; (4) the baptism of Jesus by John; (5) the descent of the Spirit on Jesus; and (6) the post-baptismal testimony of the Baptist to Jesus.

- **John the Baptist and Elijah**

John was "a reproduction of Elijah, that great prophet of repentance [*Matt.* 11.14; 17.10-13]."[55] He was the fore-runner Elijah. The Jews appeared to have expected "a literal resurrection of Elijah."[56] Thus John denied he was Elijah in the realistic Jewish sense (John 1:21). He "would not have denied being so in the symbolic sense affirmed by Jesus, as little as he would have disclaimed that the prophecies of Isaiah and Malachi were being fulfilled in him."[57]

- **John the Baptist's Testimony to Jesus**

"John's fore-running of Jesus was to all intents a fore-running of the entire Old Testament with reference to the Christ."[58] Vos says that "the real substance of the Old Testament was recapitulated in John."[59] The two Old Testament elements of law and prophecy "were plainly summed up in the message: 'Repent, for the Kingdom of Heaven is at hand.'"[60]

- **John's Baptism**

The baptism of John finds its

---

[54] Vos, *BTV*, 313-14.
[55] Vos, *BTV*, 314.
[56] Vos, *BTV*, 314.
[57] Vos, *BTV*, 314.
[58] Vos, *BTV*, 315.
[59] Vos, *BTV*, 315.
[60] Vos, *BTV*, 315.

precedents and analogies...in the Old Testament...on the one hand in the washings preparatory to the making of the Old Covenant [*Ex.* 19.10, 14] and on the other in the great outpouring of water which the prophets announce will precede the eschatological era [*Isa.* 1.16; 4.4; *Mic.* 7.19; *Ezek.* 36.25-33; *Zech.* 13.1].[61]

John's baptism was more than a symbol. It was a baptism "intended to produce repentance."[62] It "must have constituted a true sacrament, intended to convey some form of grace."[63]

Vos does not think John's baptism belonged to the Old Dispensation, as the Romanists at the time of the Reformation, or as identical with Christian baptism, as most of the Protestants did. He says:

> Both positions are untenable: we shall have to say that John's baptism, together with all the Old Testament rites, had real grace connected with it, but only the Old Testament measure and quality of grace. What it had not was the Spirit in the specific Christian conception; for the bestowal of that, and its connection with baptism, are dependent on the Pentecostal outpouring of the Spirit. Consequently the baptism administered in the time between by the disciples of Jesus must be classified with the baptism of John, as a continuation thereof, and not as an anticipation of Christian baptism.[64]

John's baptism symbolized cleansing and a "reference to the quickening by the Spirit."[65] It was also "prospective to the fast-coming judgment and a seal of preparation for acquittal in this."[66]

- **John's Baptism of Jesus**

John's baptism of Jesus was unique in that Jesus was sinless and in no need of repentance, though it "fit into the general scheme of John's ministry."[67] Seeking to prove this, Vos makes six observations on Matthew 3:13-15. The last observation is that Jesus' baptism is testimony to "the vicarious relation of Jesus to the people of God."[68] Vos continues:

---

[61] Vos, *BTV*, 316.
[62] Vos, *BTV*, 317.
[63] Vos, *BTV*, 317.
[64] Vos, *BTV*, 317-18.
[65] Vos, *BTV*, 318.
[66] Vos, *BTV*, 318.
[67] Vos, *BTV*, 319.
[68] Vos, *BTV*, 319.

...Jesus' identification with the people in their baptism had the proximate end of securing for them vicariously what the sacrament aimed at, the forgiveness of sin. Even with regard to repentance we may reason analogously; for if Jesus bore sin vicariously, and received forgiveness vicariously, then there can be no objection on principle to saying that He repented for the people vicariously.[69]

- **The Descent of the Spirit on Jesus**

Vos is quick to assert that "[t]he baptism of Jesus was accompanied by two events of supreme importance – the descent of the Spirit and the announcement from heaven concerning Jesus' Sonship and Messiahship."[70] Vos states clearly that "the record does not lend itself to the theory of the baptism having been the occasion for the awakening of Jesus' Messianic consciousness."[71] He adds that "the assurance in the voice was not for Jesus alone."[72] Jesus received "the Spirit as a pledge of the Father's approval of His mind and purpose expressed in submitting to the baptism..."[73] "[O]ur Lord needed the Spirit as a real equipment of His human nature for the execution of His Messianic task."[74] The prophets of old enjoyed "visitations of the Spirit..." but "in the case of Jesus His entire life was equably in every word and act directed by the Spirit."[75] Though the Old Testament does not represent the Spirit as a dove, it "does represent the Spirit as hovering, brooding over the waters of chaos, in order to produce life out of the primeval matter."[76] Vos suggests that "[t]his might be suggestive of the thought, that the work of the Messiah constituted a second creation, bound together with the first through this function of the Spirit in connection with it."[77]

---

[69] Vos, *BTV*, 320.
[70] Vos, *BTV*, 320.
[71] Vos, *BTV*, 320.
[72] Vos, *BTV*, 320.
[73] Vos, *BTV*, 321.
[74] Vos, *BTV*, 321.
[75] Vos, *BTV*, 322.
[76] Vos, *BTV*, 322.
[77] Vos, *BTV*, 322.

## • The Post-Baptismal Testimony of John the Baptist to Jesus

Vos discusses a triad of declarations by John (John 1:15, 30; 1:29, 36; and John 1:34) and adds comment upon John 3:27-36. Because it is difficult to determine if John is the speaker throughout this latter passage (some think the Evangelist is the speaker beginning in verse 31) Vos treats this separately.

John 1:15 says, "John testified about Him and cried out, saying, "This was He of whom I said, 'He who comes after me has a higher rank than I, for He existed before me.'"" John 1:30 says, "This is He on behalf of whom I said, 'After me comes a Man who has a higher rank than I, for He existed before me.'" Vos says that this declaration

> distinguishes in the Messiah's career two stages: the stage in which He comes after the Baptist, that is to say, succeeds the latter in public ministry; the stage in which He nevertheless preceded John in the latter's appearance upon the scene; this can refer only to the Messiah's activity under the Old Testament.[78]

Vos views the existence of Christ predicated here as relating "to the eternal existence of our Lord, usually called his pre-existence [cp. *John* 1.1, 18]."[79] His existence and activity under the Old Testament finds its basis in his eternal or pre-existence. This marks the farthest advance in John's Christology, but in complete accord with Old Testament roots (Malachi 3:1).[80]

John 1:29 says, "The next day he saw Jesus coming to him and said, 'Behold, the Lamb of God who takes away the sin of the world!'" John 1:36 says, "and he looked at Jesus as He walked, and said, 'Behold, the Lamb of God!'" This announces "the vicarious sin-bearing of Christ" just after the vicarious baptism of Christ.[81] This statement also has Old Testament roots. John must have had Isaiah 53 in his mind. There Isaiah depicts the Servant of Jehovah as possessing "innocence, meekness, and willingness to render vicarious service of the people through suffering and death."[82] The Lamb was of the same flock as the people. At his baptism he identified with the people. This phrase – the Lamb of God –

---

[78] Vos, *BTV*, 322.
[79] Vos, *BTV*, 323.
[80] Vos, *BTV*, 323.
[81] Vos, *BTV*, 324.
[82] Vos, *BTV*, 324.

"means the lamb performing this task of sin-bearing as belonging to and in the service of Jehovah."[83]

John 1:34 says, "I myself have seen, and have testified that this is the Son of God." This statement reflects upon John's "fidelity in observing and answering by witness the signal set for him by God in the descent of the Spirit upon Jesus."[84]

Finally, Vos discusses John 3:27-36. The point of the pericope is John's response to his disciples' concern over Jesus' greater popularity. John quickly exalts the Messiah and effaces himself. Vos takes the position that verses 31-36 are the Evangelist's, though a bit tentatively. Verses 31-36 further exalt the Messiah as John fades in the background.

## Revelation in the Probation of Jesus

Vos discusses this period under these headings: (1) the temptation in the wilderness; (2) the Lord's temptation and our own; (3) the specific form assumed by our Lord's temptation; (4) the Lord's temptation interpreted; and (5) temptability and peccability.

### • The Temptation in the Wilderness

Vos sees the temptation as a historical event. He references Matthew 12:29, "Or how can anyone enter the strong man's house and carry off his property, unless he first binds the strong *man*? And then he will plunder his house" as presupposing the binding of the strong man – Satan. Christ bound the strong man first and afterward cast out demons. The Holy Spirit led him into the temptation, functioning in the capacity of "His Messianic aspect."[85] Behind this stood God himself. From the point of view of Satan's activity this is a temptation, "from the point of view of the higher purpose of God a 'probation' of Jesus."[86] There is recapitulation involved here, which Vos notes below.

### • The Lord's Temptation and Our Own

Vos refuses to view the temptation simply as we might view our own. He explains:

---

[83] Vos, *BTV*, 326.
[84] Vos, *BTV*, 326.
[85] Vos, *BTV*, 332.
[86] Vos, *BTV*, 332.

In our case temptation chiefly raises the question of how we shall pass through it and issue from it without loss. In Jesus' case, while this consideration was not, of course, absent, the higher concern was not avoidance of loss, but the procuring of positive gain. And in order to see this we must compare it to the one previous occasion in Biblical history, when a procedure with an equally double-sided purpose had taken place, namely, the temptation of Adam related in Genesis, chapter 3.[87]

Christ is seen here as the Second Adam. Vos argues that Luke hints at this by "first carrying back the genealogy (in distinction from Matthew) to Adam, and then immediately subjoining to it this account of the probation of the Second Adam."[88] The parallel between Adam and Christ is antithetical from one point of view:

Adam began with a clean slate, as it were; nothing had to be undone, whilst in the case of Jesus all the record of intervening sin had to be wiped out, before the positive action for the procuring of eternal life could set in.[89]

## • The Specific Form Assumed by Our Lord's Temptation

Vos sees the temptations as Messianic temptations and, therefore, unique to the Messiah. But why does the Messiah undergo and endure such temptations? Why does he submit himself to temptations common to any man under ethical law? Why did he not assume his sovereign prerogatives over nature? Or, as Vos puts it, "[H]ow can Messiahship and submission to the ethical obligations of common human conduct go together?"[90] Vos' answer is that "his Messiahship…is…passing through a certain phase to which these creaturely limitations, attended by suffering, inseparably belong."[91] He continues:

He existed as Messiah in a state of humiliation. After that had been passed through, a state of exaltation would follow, in which these various things now offered to Him as temptations would become perfectly normal and allowable. What was not inherently sinful became so in His case, because of the law of humiliation and service under

---

[87] Vos, *BTV*, 333.
[88] Vos, *BTV*, 333.
[89] Vos, *BTV*, 333.
[90] Vos, *BTV*, 335.
[91] Vos, *BTV*, 335.

which His life had for the present been put. The animus of the temptation, from Satan's point of view, consisted in the attempt to move Him out of this spirit and attitude of service and humiliation, so as to yield to the natural desire for His Messianic glory without an interval of suffering. And this preliminary phase of Messiahship, which Satan suggests He should overleap, coincided in general with the condition and experience of a suffering man under God. Hence while Satan counsels Him to act like a super-man, in principle like God, our Saviour, with His repeated stress on what a man is obligated to, repudiates such self-exaltation. It is highly significant in this connection, that the words wherewith Jesus repels the tempter are taken from the Torah, the Book of the Law (Deuteronomy), as though by thus placing Himself under the Law Jesus wished to remind Satan of the real matter at issue, the question of humiliation versus the assertion of the prerogatives belonging to a state of glory.[92]

- ## The Lord's Temptation Interpreted

Vos' method of interpreting the temptations depends first on Jesus' response to them. He moves from Jesus' responses in the form of Old Testament quotations, to their contextual meaning, back to the intent of Jesus answer, then to Satan's point in the temptation.[93]

Matthew 4:3 says, "And the tempter came and said to Him, "If You are the Son of God, command that these stones become bread." The first temptation was answered with a reference to Deuteronomy 8:3, "…man does not live by bread alone, but man lives by everything that proceeds out of the mouth of the LORD." Vos says that the context of this Old Testament reference "reminds the Israelites that, through feeding them supernaturally on manna, He meant to teach them the lesson of the ability of God to supply nourishment without the natural processes."[94] Jesus applies this principle to himself. "[T]he probation consisted in placing before Him the necessity of exercising implicit trust in God as the One able to sustain His life notwithstanding the protracted fast."[95] Vos identifies this 'implicit trust' as "faith."[96] He adds:

> The temptation-suffering had to be borne with full appreciation, with full positive responsiveness to the plan of God. When Satan suggested

[92] Vos, *BTV*, 335.

[93] Vos follows the order found in the Gospel of Matthew.

[94] Vos, *BTV*, 336.

[95] Vos, *BTV*, 337.

[96] Vos, *BTV*, 337.

that He should turn the stones into bread, he was endeavouring to move Jesus out of this faith with reference to His humiliation into an attitude of independent sovereignty, such as properly belonged to the His exalted state only.[97]

The second temptation, found in Matthew 4:5-6, was as follows:

Then the devil took Him into the holy city and had Him stand on the pinnacle of the temple, [6] and said to Him, "If You are the Son of God, throw Yourself down; for it is written, 'HE WILL COMMAND HIS ANGELS CONCERNING YOU'; and 'ON *their* HANDS THEY WILL BEAR YOU UP, SO THAT YOU WILL NOT STRIKE YOUR FOOT AGAINST A STONE.'"

Jesus responded with a reference to Deuteronomy 6:16, "Jesus said to him, "On the other hand, it is written, 'YOU SHALL NOT PUT THE LORD YOUR GOD TO THE TEST'" (Matthew 4:7). In the historical context behind Deuteronomy 6 (Exodus 17 and Deuteronomy 9:22; and 33:8), "[t]o tempt Jehovah has the meaning of 'proving God', that is, of seeking to ascertain by experiment whether His power to lead them to Canaan could be relied upon."[98] This testing sprang "from doubt or outright unbelief."[99] If Jesus did as Satan suggested, he would have been "involved with an impious experimenting with the dependability of God."[100] That was the heart of the temptation.

The third temptation, Matthew 4:8-9, reads:

Again, the devil took Him to a very high mountain and showed Him all the kingdoms of the world and their glory; [9] and he said to Him, "All these things I will give You, if You fall down and worship me."

Vos says, "Here the act counseled is an act of Satan-worship, sinful *per se*."[101] The third temptation-suggestion is sinful in itself, unlike the former. "The question at stake was, whether God should be God, or Satan should be God, and correspondingly, whether the Messiah should be God's or Satan's Messiah."[102] Jesus answered, "Go, Satan! For it is

---

[97] Vos, *BTV*, 337.
[98] Vos, *BTV*, 338.
[99] Vos, *BTV*, 338.
[100] Vos, *BTV*, 338.
[101] Vos, *BTV*, 338.
[102] Vos, *BTV*, 339.

written, 'YOU SHALL WORSHIP THE LORD YOUR GOD, AND
SERVE HIM ONLY'" (Matthew 4:10). "The appeal is made to Deut.
6.13 where all idolatry is on principle forbidden."[103]

- **Temptability and Peccability**

How can a sinless being be tempted? And can a sinless being sin? "If a
person is liable to being tempted by something, this would seem to
involve an imperfection."[104] Yet "temptation has found entrance both in
the First and in the Second Adam…[and] its entrance alone did not imply
the presence of sin."[105] But, as Vos says, "Jesus was not only innocent
like Adam, He was possessed of and guided by the Spirit in all its
fullness, and still further…His human nature was owned by the Person of
the Son of God."[106] Basing the temptability and peccability of Christ
upon the presence of human nature does not solve the problem for "Jesus
in His exalted state, and also the saints in heaven, possess a human
nature, and yet are not thereby made capable of sinning."[107] Vos finally
gives these humble words of concession, "The double mystery, therefore,
that as to the temptability, and that as to the peccability of the Saviour,
here appears as one in its root, and we simply must confess our inability
to throw light upon it."[108]

## The Revelation of Jesus' Public Ministry

The last section of Vos' *Biblical Theology* is given over to the revelation
of Jesus' public ministry. He discusses this subject under six headings:
(1) the various aspects of Christ's revealing function; (2) the question of
development; (3) the method of Jesus' teaching; (4) Jesus' attitude
toward the Scriptures of the Old Testament; (5) Jesus' doctrine of God;
and (6) Jesus' teaching on the Kingdom of God.

---

[103] Vos, *BTV*, 339.
[104] Vos, *BTV*, 340.
[105] Vos, *BTV*, 340.
[106] Vos, *BTV*, 340.
[107] Vos, *BTV*, 341.
[108] Vos, *BTV*, 341.

- **Various Aspects of Christ's Revealing Function**

Vos identifies four divisions of revelation by Christ: Natural (or General Revelation), "extending from the creation of the world forward indefinitely,"[109] revelation "under the economy of the Old Testament, extending from the entrance of sin and redemption till the incarnation,"[110] revelation "during His public ministry on earth, extending from the nativity until His resurrection and ascension,"[111] and "revelation mediated by Him through His chosen servants, extending from the ascension until the death of the last inspired witness, speaking under the infallible guidance of the Holy Spirit."[112]

- **The Question of Development and the Method of Jesus' Teaching**

Vos makes a distinction between subjective and objective development. Since Jesus had a human nature, subjective development, in principle, cannot be objected to, though "not actually proven."[113] Objective development is clearly observable. It rose "from the capability of apprehension in the disciples" and "from the unfolding of the situation of the public ministry of our Lord…"[114]

- **Jesus' Attitude toward the Scriptures of the Old Testament**

Jesus attitude toward the Old Testament was, on the one hand, like "[e]very orthodox person, Jewish or Christian…"[115] On the other hand, he "held a conviction that went far beyond this, and in regard to which it would be preposterous for any Christian to say that he could apply the same thing to himself."[116] Vos continues:

> What we mean is this, that Jesus regarded the whole Old Testament movement as a divinely directed and inspired movement, as having *arrived at its goal in Himself*, so that He Himself in His historic

---

[109] Vos, *BTV*, 344.
[110] Vos, *BTV*, 344.
[111] Vos, *BTV*, 344.
[112] Vos, *BTV*, 344.
[113] Vos, *BTV*, 348.
[114] Vos, *BTV*, 348.
[115] Vos, *BTV*, 358.
[116] Vos, *BTV*, 358.

appearance and work being taken away, the Old Testament would lose its purpose and significance. This none other could say. He was the *confirmation and consummation* of the Old Testament in His own Person...[117]

Jesus' "discourse is full of words, phrases, forms of expression, derived from the Scriptures."[118] He quoted Scripture "in the supreme crises of His life."[119] He treated the Scriptures as a rule of faith and practice, while dealing with the Pharisees and Sadducees. He referenced Hosea in the Sabbath controversy. He bases the indissolubleness of marriage on the Genesis account.[120] He knew that the Scriptures must be fulfilled. "[T]he Old Testament was to him an organic expression of the truth and will of God."[121] Vos did not view the Old Testament as antithetical to the New. "The idea is that the old had the seeds of the new in itself."[122] Jesus did not utterly discard the Old Testament. Vos says:

> For this reason also a revolutionary discarding of the Old Testament is out of the question. The clearest proof for the maintenance of this identity between the two dispensations is in John 2.19-21. Here Jesus declares that the temple to be destroyed by the Jews will be raised up again in His raised body. As the former was a symbol of the Old, so the latter is the vital centre of the New, but the identity persists.[123]

That which was symbolic and typical gives was to its anti-type.

Vos discusses the Sermon on the Mount and the nature of fulfillment of the Law and the Prophets. He says that it "must...be interpreted on the principle of continuity."[124] Jesus did not come to improve the Law and the Prophets. He came to put them into practice. "[T]he whole idea of improving the Prophets lies wholly outside the mind of Jesus."[125] Jesus brings the Law and the Prophets with him into the eschatological state which he ushered in. He uses the Law and the Prophets in his reorganizing ministry, though they are applied in light of the conditions brought in by him.

---

[117] Vos, *BTV*, 358. Here the Christocentric nature of biblical revelation is patent.

[118] Vos, *BTV*, 358.

[119] Vos, *BTV*, 359.

[120] Vos, *BTV*, 359.

[121] Vos, *BTV*, 359.

[122] Vos, *BTV*, 362. This echoes the ancient words of Augustine referenced above.

[123] Vos, *BTV*, 362.

[124] Vos, *BTV*, 362.

[125] Vos, *BTV*, 362.

- ### Jesus' Teaching on the Kingdom of God[126]

"[T]he first message of Jesus at the opening of His public ministry concerned 'the Kingdom of God'."[127] "[T]he message is to all intents an eschatological message, and the Kingdom of which it speaks an eschatological state of affairs."[128] The phrase 'Kingdom of God' is not found in the Old Testament, while the idea is. The concept of the Kingdom of God in the Old Testament had two distinct conceptions. "It designates the rule of God established through creation and extending through providence over the universe."[129] This rule of God is not redemptive. It also refers to "a specifically redemptive Kingdom, usually called 'the theocracy'."[130] This is introduced in Exodus 19:6. This aspect of the Old Testament's teaching on the Kingdom was not alone, however, for

> ...the Old Testament likewise speaks of the Kingdom as a futurity. It may seem strange that what one has, one should still look forward to, and that not as a matter of relative improvement, but as a matter of absolutely new creation.[131]

Vos sees the Old Testament's view of the Kingdom as pointing forward to "[a] new Kingdom-appearance...of the great self-assertion of Jehovah..." which "amounted practically to a new Kingdom." [132] The theocracy was eclipsed at times so much so that "a bringing in of the Kingdom of God *de novo* could properly be spoken of."[133] Messianic prophesies unfolded in such a way as to lead to the expectation of the "realization of the entire eschatological hope..."[134] These phenomena explain the strangeness of 'what one has, one should still look forward to...' when it comes to the Kingdom.

The inauguration of the Kingdom of God, however, comes in two phases. "[I]n the unfolding of His [Christ's] ministry, the Old Testament

---

[126] Cf. Vos, *The Teaching of Jesus Concerning the Kingdom of God and the Church.*
[127] Vos, *BTV*, 372.
[128] Vos, *BTV*, 372. Cf. Semel, "Geerhardus Vos and Eschatology" in *Kerux* 10.2 (Sept. 1995): 35ff.
[129] Vos, *BTV*, 372.
[130] Vos, *BTV*, 373.
[131] Vos, *BTV*, 373.
[132] Vos, *BTV*, 373.
[133] Vos, *BTV*, 373.
[134] Vos, *BTV*, 373.

future thing resolves itself into two distinct phases or stages."[135] Jesus brings the Old Testament future thing present yet "it still remains future..."[136]

> Consequently the phenomenon of the Old Testament repeats itself: there are two Kingdoms, the one present, the other future, but both these have been obtained through the redivision of the one as yet undivided Old Testament eschatological Kingdom.[137]

Jesus' view of the Old Testament's concept of the Kingdom did not resemble that of first century Judaism. The Kingdom introduced by Jesus was a gracious Kingdom and "its tendency was in the direction of universalism [i.e., internationalism]."[138]

Vos understands the Kingdom in a concrete sense – the embodiment of the sway of God with its resulting realities[139] or "...the actual realization of His sway."[140] The phrase 'Kingdom of Heaven' is functionally synonymous with 'Kingdom of God.' This view "attaches itself to the Jewish custom of using the word Heaven'...in place of the name of God..."[141] "'Heaven' thus simply meant 'God' by a roundabout manner of speaking."[142]

Vos held to a two-sided conception of the Kingdom. It consists of "first the idea of a present, inwardly-spiritual development, and secondly, that of a catastrophic ending-up."[143] This is otherwise termed as the already/not-yet of the presence and future of the Kingdom. Jesus taught both the presence of the Kingdom and its future, eschatological-fulfillment phase. Luke 17:21, "...For indeed, the kingdom of God is within you," refers to the presence and spirituality or inwardness of the Kingdom.[144] The Parables describe "...both the present reality and the spiritual nature of the Kingdom..."[145] Vos adds this three-fold formula to show the clear distinctions between the two aspects of the Kingdom:

---

[135] Vos, *BTV*, 374.
[136] Vos, *BTV*, 374.
[137] Vos, *BTV*, 374.
[138] Vos, *BTV*, 374.
[139] Vos, *BTV*, 375.
[140] Vos, *BTV*, 385.
[141] Vos, *BTV*, 377.
[142] Vos, *BTV*, 377.
[143] Vos, *BTV*, 381.
[144] Vos, *BTV*, 382.
[145] Vos, *BTV*, 383.

(a) The present Kingdom comes gradually, the final Kingdom catastrophically;

(b) The present Kingdom comes largely in the internal, invisible sphere, the final Kingdom in the form of a world-wide visible manifestation;

(c) The present Kingdom up to the eschatological point remains subject to imperfections; the final Kingdom will be without all imperfections, and this applies as well to what had remained imperfect in the spiritual process of which the present Kingdom consisted, as to the new elements which the final Kingdom adds.[146]

Vos holds that the phrase 'the Kingdom of God' "means the actual exercise of the divine supremacy in the interest of the divine glory."[147] He sees the divine supremacy working in three spheres: "the sphere of power, the sphere of righteousness and the sphere of blessedness."[148]

Divine supremacy in the sphere of power is met at the close of the Lord's Prayer – "Thine is the Kingdom, and the power..." The casting out of demons is a display of divine Kingdom-power and an assertion of Messianic sovereignty.[149] The miracles as 'signs of the times' announce "the arrival or nearness of the Kingdom..." and "...are both symbolic of spiritual transactions and prophetic of things pertaining to the eschatological Kingdom."[150] The ministries of the Spirit with reference to Jesus, Pentecost, and indwelling believers are also 'signs of the times.' With reference to Jesus, he received the fullness of it and dispenses it to his followers.[151] This creates an organic mystical union between Christ and his people.[152] His people taste of the eschatological by the presence and ministry of the Spirit, the first fruits of more to come.

Vos next discusses divine supremacy in the sphere of righteousness. He defines righteousness as

that which agrees with and pleases God, and exists for His sake, and can only be adjudicated by Him. He is first of all, and above all, the interested Person. Without reckoning with Him in the three relations named there can be no actual existence of righteousness. There might

---

[146] Vos, *BTV*, 384.
[147] Vos, *BTV*, 386.
[148] Vos, *BTV*, 386.
[149] Vos, *BTV*, 386.
[150] Vos, *BTV*, 386.
[151] Vos, *BTV*, 387.
[152] Vos, *BTV*, 387.

be good or evil intrinsically considered as to results, but to speak of righteousness would under such circumstances have no meaning. And this God-referred righteousness is by no means a small department of religious life. Ethically considered, it covers all converse with God; to be righteous acquires the meaning of possessing and practising [*sic*] the true religion: righteousness is equivalent to piety. Our Lord's teaching on righteousness partakes throughout of this general character. Righteousness is from God as its source, it exists for God as its end, and it is subject to God as the ultimate Justifier.[153]

In our Lord's teaching there is a close connection between righteousness and the kingdom of God. In fact, Vos says, "the Kingdom (Kingship) of God is identified with righteousness."[154] When Jesus said, "They Kingdom come, Thy will be done" "...in all probability both 'coming' and 'being done' are, in harmony with Western exegesis, to be understood eschatologically."[155] Yet "righteousness appears as a consequent to the Kingdom, one of the many gifts which the new reign of God freely bestows upon its members."[156] This is in fulfillment of Jeremiah and Ezekiel. Jesus treats righteousness as an "entire gift as an undifferentiated unit."[157] "Paul has learned to distinguish between objective righteousness which becomes ours through imputation and the subjective kind which becomes ours through the inworking of the Spirit."[158] But Jesus also taught an objective righteousness as the ground of justification in the parable of the Pharisee and the publican:

> ...the publican went home justified and not the Pharisee, because the former professed not to possess any subjective righteousness, and the Pharisee was rejected because of his consciousness of possessing much.[159]

"Righteousness is with Paul largely objective status, with Jesus largely subjective condition."[160]

Vos discusses the principle of reward in Jesus teaching as it relates to the eschatological Kingdom. It is not that what man does he gets back in

---

[153] Vos, *BTV*, 392-93.
[154] Vos, *BTV*, 393.
[155] Vos, *BTV*, 393.
[156] Vos, *BTV*, 393.
[157] Vos, *BTV*, 394.
[158] Vos, *BTV*, 394.
[159] Vos, *BTV*, 394.
[160] Vos, *BTV*, 394.

the form of a proper equivalent.[161] Instead, as Vos says, "[t]his principle... is destructive of the religious relation."[162] Servants "are not inherently entitled to any reward; and, because the reward is not of necessity, neither can it be of exact equivalence..."[163]

Finally, Vos says, "the Kingdom of God is the supremacy of God in the sphere of blessedness."[164] Blessedness conferred in the Kingdom is three-fold: salvation, sonship, and life.[165]

Vos' final section is entitled "Kingdom and Church." He says, "The one clear case of development in our Lord's objective teaching on the Kingdom subject is to be found here."[166] He is referencing Jesus' words to Peter in Matthew 16:18ff. The Church and Kingdom "do not appear here as separate institutions."[167] The Church he is to build also has keys of administration, and these keys are the keys of the Kingdom. "Undoubtedly then, the Church and the Kingdom are in principle one..."[168]

The Church Jesus speaks of is his. This in no way means no Church existed prior to this statement. "His Church' should be understood in contrast to the Old Testament Church organization which had now come to an end to make place for the Messiah's Church."[169] "The future is spoken of, because the new dynamic could not enter into the Church until after His exaltation."[170]

---

[161] Vos, *BTV*, 395.

[162] Vos, *BTV*, 395.

[163] Vos, *BTV*, 395.

[164] Vos, *BTV*, 398.

[165] Vos, *BTV*, 399.

[166] Vos, *BTV*, 399.

[167] Vos, *BTV*, 400.

[168] Vos, *BTV*, 400.

[169] Vos, *BTV*, 400.

[170] Vos, *BTV*, 400.

# CHAPTER SEVENTEEN

# REDEMPTIVE, SPECIAL REVELATION

# AND THE NEW TESTAMENT: JOHN OWEN

## Introduction: The Final and Perfect Revelation from God – Evangelical Theology

Owen begins his exposition of Evangelical Theology with this astounding and far-reaching statement:

> We have not yet attained our objective, although we are hastening towards the end of our task. It has been my professed intent and stated purpose–almost my one and only purpose in this work–*to set forward the theology of Christ*. This is not just the teaching of the gospel but the disposition of mind which alone can embrace it, and that goal has been ever present before my eyes from the start of this volume. I have, therefore, held back until this final book matters directly concerning Christ (although Christ is the proper object of all theology), without obscuring the fact that Christ has always been vital to the whole theology of our fallen race.[1]

Here Owen's Christocentricity is obvious and central to all he has said and will say.

The task of adding "the final capstone of …revelation"[2] is given to the only-begotten Son of God. "With the utter overthrow of the Jewish Church, and with it the Mosaic theology on which it had been based," the Church was to be "transformed into her eternal state, perfect in its nature and thenceforward immutable."[3] The various stages of revelation and the primacy of the Son of God as the capstone of all revelation and the bearer of evangelical theology "is notably explained by the Apostle in his letter to the Hebrews [i.e., Hebrews 1:1-2]."[4] Owen adds, "My point here is that the immediate author of evangelical theology or gospel theology is Jesus Christ Himself, the only-begotten Son of God."[5] This is not to say that gospel theology does not predate the incarnation for, as Owen says,

---

[1] Owen, *BTO*, 591. Emphases added.
[2] Owen, *BTO*, 593.
[3] Owen, *BTO*, 592-93.
[4] Owen, *BTO*, 593.
[5] Owen, *BTO*, 593.

"...all true theology is, in a sense, gospel theology, for, in whatever stage it existed, its object and prime mover was God the Son."[6] First Peter 1:11 and 2 Peter 1:21 attest to this. The holy men of old preached Christ.[7] "It was He who, in times past, showed Himself in human form to the fathers, and He was that 'Angel of the Lord' with the Church in the wilderness (Acts 7:38)."[8] Owen continues:

> But, in regard to its specific administration, that only may be said to be evangelical theology which the Son of God brought in and taught in His own person when He came forth from the bosom of the Father. He alone was the true and unique Author of this theology, and He made it what it is–the final and perfect revelation from God.[9]

The Son brings with him the final revelation of God. No more revelation is needed, nor should be looked for.

### The Messiah's Coming

Owen considers "the timing of this coming of our Lord Jesus Christ, and the bringing in of this new revelation."[10] He came in 'the fullness of the time' (Galatians 4:4) and 'in the last days' (Hebrews 1:2). Owen first considers Galatians 4:4. Christ came "when divine long-suffering could wait no longer."[11] He came when idolatry and superstition was at its height.[12] The time in which he came was a time when "the finite limits of the human intellect and the created world had brought a halt to any further attempts to restore natural theology by means of philosophy."[13] The high-water of the intellectual pursuits of the Greeks and Romans had come. The supremacy of human and secular power had now reached its apex in the Roman Empire.[14] "The Jews longed for and looked for the manifestation of king Messiah, and the gentiles were no less eagerly looking for the return of the fabled golden age."[15] Owen adds:

---

[6] Owen, *BTO*, 593.
[7] Owen, *BTO*, 593.
[8] Owen, *BTO*, 593.
[9] Owen, *BTO*, 593.
[10] Owen, *BTO*, 594.
[11] Owen, *BTO*, 594.
[12] Owen, *BTO*, 595.
[13] Owen, *BTO*, 595.
[14] Owen, *BTO*, 596.
[15] Owen, *BTO*, 596.

To recapitulate, then, the human race was now employing itself to the ultimate of its power, in superstition as in wisdom, in domination as in indulgence, in vice as in virtue, clearly demonstrating the arrival of the "fullness of time." Then God graciously sent His Son to proclaim the gospel of peace to those near at hand and those far off.[16]

Christ came as a result of the foreordination of God (1 Peter 1:20). He came in accordance with that which was spoken by the mouth of his prophets since the world began (Luke 1:70). He came, having "been looked and sought for from the days of Adam..."[17] He came in fulfillment of Haggai 2:7 as "the desire of all nations."

Owen says that "the fullness of time and the end of days denote one and the same period."[18] Christ came "in the last days" as the Apostle affirms in Hebrews 1:1-3. The last days were those of the Jewish Church. The phrase "last days" is not to be understood in an absolute sense, but relatively as related to the Jewish Church. According to Owen, this phrase "also distinctly recalls the Old Testament prophecies which foretell of that terminal stage of the Hebrew Church"[19] (cf. Genesis 49:1 and Numbers 24:14). Owen closes this discussion as follows:

Christ, therefore, the Author of gospel theology, came in the fullness of time, and He came in the last days since, in God's plan, the last days of the Hebrew Church were the fullness in which he would send Messiah.[20]

## The Principles of Evangelical (Gospel) Theology

In Book VI, Chapter 2, Owen discusses the governing principles of evangelical theology.[21] He opens his discussion with introductory premises relating to Christ as the mediatorial revealer of God's will. He is uniquely suited for such a task for he is omniscient and possesses infinite knowledge according to his divine nature.[22] As the incarnate mediator, though, he knew only those things revealed to him by his Father, "...that is, [knew] them in the human nature which He

---

[16] Owen, *BTO*, 597.
[17] Owen, *BTO*, 597.
[18] Owen, *BTO*, 598.
[19] Owen, *BTO*, 599.
[20] Owen, *BTO*, 599.
[21] Owen, *BTO*, 604.
[22] Owen, *BTO*, 600.

condescended to take on Him in order to perform His work of mediation."[23] He was endowed with the Spirit without measure in order to carry out the work of revealing the will of God to men in its final form. Owen says:

> In all of this Christ appeared as God's intermediary with men. He was perfectly endued with knowledge of all that pertains to the obedience required by God for men, and, by His presence, He brought to light those things hidden in the Divine mind from eternity concerning the revelation of the glory of God, the setting up of the kingdom, the institutions of worship, the gathering of the Church, the calling, training and the consolation of the elect. In all this, He was the medium for the revelation of God's will to mankind.[24]

> This revelation of God's will, gifted to Christ by the Father, communicated by Christ through the Holy Spirit to the Apostles and others for the benefit of the entire Church, taken at its greatest extent, is the divine teaching or *theology of the gospel*...[25]

Owen then sets out to "overview the principle heads of this theology" and "identify its particular features and principal foundations"[26] – in other words, its governing principles. He briefly lists and discusses six principles:

> ...no one can grasp or rightly understand evangelical theology by human power or reliance on intellect, apply what outside assistance he will, for none of these things will bring him to experience the salvation to which this theology points the human mind. In this, its nature is distinct from all human sciences. ...(John 6:44).[27]

> ...it teaches that a man who wishes to learn the teachings which it sets forth in a saving and beneficial way (the end for which it was intended by its heavenly Author) must first be born again, that is, reborn spiritually. ...(John 3:3).[28]

---

[23] Owen, *BTO*, 600.
[24] Owen, *BTO*, 601-02.
[25] Owen, *BTO*, 602.
[26] Owen, *BTO*, 602.
[27] Owen, *BTO*, 603.
[28] Owen, *BTO*, 603.

...no one is reborn except through the power of the Holy Spirit, by whose almighty action they are bought from life to death [*sic*–'death to life'], as many as have been ordained of God (John 3:5-6, John 1:13, Titus 3:5).[29]

...the Holy Spirit alone can introduce anyone into a saving understanding of theology, and can alone bestow upon anyone the perception whereby the doctrines of the gospel may be understood unto salvation (John 16:13, 1 John 2:20, 1 Corinthians 2:10-16, 2 Corinthians 4:6).[30]

...the worship of God which this theology institutes is spiritual worship. The glory of it is not visible to men, nor is it open to the carnal intellect (2 Corinthians 3:6-10, John 4:21-24).[31]

...last, all worshippers of God in Christ, according to this evangelical theology, are by its nature separated from this world and are therefore, for that reason, and by virtue of having received the Spirit (which the world cannot receive) by the world hated, and always have been and will be so hated (2 Corinthians 6:14-18, John 15:18-19, John 14:16, Galatians 1:4).[32]

## Classifying Evangelical Theology

Owen readily acknowledges that "the division of its [i.e., evangelical theology] doctrines and the varieties of means by which it is communicated may allow for classification into various heads or stages..."[33] He adds:

that the principle divisions of this gospel teaching of theology, those things which concern the right worship of God, the obedience which is His due, are capable of being classified and arranged in order, sequence and method, according to the usual rules of philosophical arts and sciences. The subject matter handed down in the gospel has a certain development and dependency, so there is nothing to prevent the interrelationships being analyzed and set out in order and, as it were, scientifically. Creeds, Confessions of faith, catechisms and common-places [i.e., Dogmatics/Systematic Theology], along with all similar

---

[29] Owen, *BTO*, 603.
[30] Owen, *BTO*, 603.
[31] Owen, *BTO*, 604.
[32] Owen, *BTO*, 604.
[33] Owen, *BTO*, 605.

methodical arrangements of Biblical truths, seek to serve just that end.[34]

In principle, then, Owen is not utterly against Dogmatics/Systematic Theology. He continues:

> Thus, to sum the matter up, the entirety of divine truth has been revealed in Scripture by our Lord Jesus Christ, and such is theology, if we take the term in its very widest signification. It contains propositions which are capable of systematic arrangement, and its content is open to human intellects. These revealed propositions, along with such conclusions as may legitimately be drawn from them, may be reduced to a written system and made the source material for a discipline of study.[35]

But Owen is not content to leave it at that. Assuming the governing principles of evangelical theology laid down in Book VI, Chapter 2, Owen makes a distinction between theology 'in its very widest signification' and 'theology in its narrower and inner signification.' He says, "But all of this [i.e., systematic arrangement per above] is Christian philosophy, and still lacks the hallmarks of theology in its narrower and inner signification."[36] He elaborates:

> My point is that teaching, arranged and systemized in this manner, has nothing at all in it which exceeds the purely intellectual capability of natural man. In all of this, I stress we are by no means talking of realities themselves, but rather of methods and propositions by which it is attempted to describe those realities.[37]

Here Owen makes a distinction between theology objectively 'arranged and systemized,' and theology subjectively appropriated – theology 'in its widest signification' and 'theology in its narrower and inner signification.' Owen is focusing on theological knowledge which produces communion with God[38] and personal holiness.[39]

---

[34] Owen, *BTO*, 606.
[35] Owen, *BTO*, 607.
[36] Owen, *BTO*, 607.
[37] Owen, *BTO*, 607.
[38] Owen, *BTO*, 618.
[39] Owen, *BTO*, 610.

## Philosophy and Theology[40]

"[T]he deliberate intermingling of secular, philosophical ideas with evangelical doctrine"[41] was a great contributor to the declension and apostasy of the early Church. Owen is concerned here not with the *use* of philosophy, but its *abuse*.[42] He is clearly speaking about secular philosophy, along with its anti-theistic presuppositions and methodology. He loathes theology that is recast by the mold of secular philosophy's methodology.[43] The subject matter of much of medieval scholastic theology became "the bolings-down of Aristotelian metaphysics applied to the discussion of supernatural affairs."[44] Owen asserts emphatically that "[*a*] *philosophical method of teaching spiritual matters is alien to the gospel!*"[45] The gospel is eclipsed when it is reshaped by a "methodical-*philosophical* form!"[46] Due to this influence,

> theology has become a thorny and confused subject of study which men think to pursue exactly as they would any other art or science; that is, without any spiritual light or the assistance of the Holy Spirit.[47]

Rehnman admits that "*Theologoumena…*has exceedingly negative statements…"[48] when it comes to the use of philosophy in theology. He even says, "Aristotle, philosophy, and scholasticism are attacked in turn in *Theologoumena*, and this raises a difficulty in regard to our understanding of Owens's thought."[49]

---

[40] Cf. Rehnman, *Divine Discourse* 109ff. for an excellent discussion of this somewhat perplexing issue for Owen. It is while discussing the use of philosophy in theology that Owen makes statements which demean an element of the scholastic method. To be fair to Owen, he was most concerned about the abuse of philosophy not its use. In Rehnman, *Divine Discourse*, 119, Rehnman says, "…it is clear that Owen was opposed both to an excessive and a defective application of philosophy to theology."

[41] Owen, *BTO*, 667. Owen is so convinced of this that he devotes a 17 page (Owen, *BTO*, 668-84) digression entitled, "Digression on the Mingling of Philosophy with Theology".

[42] Owen, *BTO*, 668.

[43] Owen, *BTO*, 671.

[44] Owen, *BTO*, 676.

[45] Owen, *BTO*, 679.

[46] Owen, *BTO*, 680.

[47] Owen, *BTO*, 683-84.

[48] Rehnman, *Divine Discourse*, 120.

[49] Rehnman, *Divine Discourse*, 124-25. Cf. Rehnman, *Divine Discourse*, 123-28 for Rehnman's highly nuanced explanation of Owen's disparaging thoughts on philosophy in theology.

## Evangelical Ecclesiology

Owen prefaces his discussion of the state and condition of the church with these words:

> I have demonstrated already that in *each developing phase of theology* the revealed Word of God has been the source and pattern for the instruction of the Church in the right celebration of God's worship, as it has, at the same time, contained *the various stages of divine revelation*. We have seen how in the latter days, through the only-begotten Son who was ever in the bosom of the Father, all the deep mysteries of that *unfolding plan* have been made clear, demonstrating Christ's glory in the salvation of sinners and in His enabling them to acceptably bring worship to the Father. I have pointed out the general nature of this *now completed and perfect revelation*, and how, on the pattern of it, Christ founded His new Church, which is destined to last until the consummation of the ages. The plan of my work demands a brief account of the Church's state and condition, as this is imperatively required by what has gone before.[50]

The elements of evangelical ecclesiology are then stated and discussed. First, "Evangelical theology requires that the true Church consists of none but the regenerate."[51] John the Baptist prepared the way for this by proclaiming that repentance "was absolutely necessary for entrance into the kingdom of God; or, to put it a little differently, into the evangelical phase of the Church..."[52] Christ "received none into His fold who had not experienced genuine repentance."[53] Once Christ's preparatory ministry was complete, he entrusted his disciples with the calling and visible organization of the church upon the same terms of admission.[54]

Second, concerning its external form, Owen says:

> ...this evangelical theology required that the Church now be truly catholic—no longer confined to a single region of the earth or to any distinct tribe, family, race or nation, but instead to all conditions and kinds of men, throughout the entire globe.[55]

---

[50] Owen, *BTO*, 651. Emphases added.

[51] Owen, *BTO*, 651.

[52] Owen, *BTO*, 652.

[53] Owen, *BTO*, 652.

[54] Owen, *BTO*, 653.

[55] Owen, *BTO*, 654.

Owen goes so far as to say, "There is no trace of any teaching in the Old Testament, nor the slightest hint in the New Testament, of any permanent preference of a single location or city in God's plan."[56]

Third, concerning the worship of the evangelical church, the Lord Jesus

> gave instructions to His disciples, as subjects of His kingdom, by which evangelical worship was to be regularly and visibly carried out in this world to the glory of God and the consolation and edification of the faithful.[57]

Christ instituted spiritual worship, abolishing "all external magnificence, all carnal decoration…, and replaced all with a few and simple ceremonies of worship."[58]

---

[56] Owen, *BTO*, 654.
[57] Owen, *BTO*, 655.
[58] Owen, *BTO*, 656.

# CHAPTER EIGHTEEN
# COMPARATIVE ANALYSIS, UNIQUE CONTRIBUTIONS,
# AND CONCLUDING ASSERTIONS

## Introduction

We have attempted to place Geerhardus Vos and John Owen in their historical-theological contexts. We analyzed their respective works on Biblical/Federal Theology. There are various strands of similarities in their methodology and theology; but there are also some important dissimilarities worth noting. In this closing chapter, a brief (suggestive and certainly not exhaustive) comparative analysis will be conducted of their methodologies and theologies, a look at their unique contributions, then three final, concluding assertions will be made in light of our study.

## Comparative Analysis

- ## Similarities between Vos and Owen

**1. Similar methodologies.** Both works of Vos and Owen follow a very similar linear approach to the articulation of the history of redemption. Both went from the Old Testament to the New Testament; from the Garden to the cross and kingdom of Christ; from Adam, to Noah, to Abraham, to Moses, to the Prophets, to John the Baptist, to Christ, and to the Apostles.[1] They allowed the prominent themes of redemptive revelation to emerge as that revelation unfolded. They applied a historical-linear approach and articulated their respective works in that light.

Both works were covenantally conditioned. Vos and Owen started with the covenant of works and then articulated an organic, progressively unfolding covenant of grace. Of Owen, Rehnman says:

---

[1] It is of interest to note that neither Vos nor Owen finished the New Testament. Though Owen's purpose may have precluded him from doing so, Vos' purpose (i.e., a history of special revelation; cf. Vos *BTV*, v) did not. It is a sad fact that he does not deal with the complete revelation of the Gospels, revelation in the Book of Acts, the Epistles, and the Book of Revelation.

Owen follows the historical-economical method of federal theology in the prolegomenous *Theologoumena.*[2]

Owen follows an organization that may be called "history of supernatural revelation."[3]

Owen develops this distinctly historical organization or method of theology in connection with the federal theology developed by late sixteenth-century Reformed thinkers. Owen reflects the development and orientation of federal thought, for the order of supernatural revelation and the method of theology is based on divine covenants.[4]

**2. Similar views on the nature of revelation as organic and progressive.** Both Vos and Owen saw redemptive revelation as both organic and progressive. We saw these points made clearly and amply by Vos above. The same concepts, though less explicit, were in Owen as well. Rehnman even says of Owen:

Owen's unique development within or contribution to this tradition of federal thought consists then in his concept of the nature of revelation, for he extends federal theology to a view of the nature of revelation. This development can be expressed by two words, "organic" and "progressive."[5]

**3. Similar views on the distinction between General Revelation (or Natural Theology) and Special Revelation (or Supernatural Theology).** Both Vos and Owen carefully distinguished between General Revelation (Vos)/Natural Theology (Owen) and Special Revelation (Vos)/Supernatural Theology (Owen). Both viewed General Revelation/Natural Theology as insufficient for a proper theology.

**4. Similar views on pre-redemptive, Special Revelation/Supernatural Theology.** Vos held that the disclosure of the covenant of works can be categorized as pre-redemptive, Special Revelation. Owen held that Natural Theology needed supplementation – i.e., the covenant of works.

---

[2] Rehnman, *Divine Discourse*, 156.
[3] Rehnman, *Divine Discourse*, 157.
[4] Rehnman, *Divine Discourse*, 162.
[5] Rehnman, *Divine Discourse*, 165.

**5. Similar views on the covenant of works.** Both Vos and Owen adhered to an Edenic covenant of works. The covenant of works for both was not only important for Edenic anthropology and eschatology, it was vital for the proper understanding and articulation of subsequent, post-lapsarian soteriology.

**6. Similar views on the primacy of eschatology to soteriology.** For both Vos and Owen (and Reformed orthodoxy), eschatology precedes soteriology in the revelational scheme of Scripture. Eden was infused with eschatological potential. The probationary element of the covenant of works was a mechanism designed to translate Adam and those he represented to a higher, confirmed state of righteousness and immutable communion with God. The eschatology offered to Adam is what Christ, the last Adam, brings elect sinners to by his gracious work and power. God's eschatological 'plan A' is what Christ confers upon those he came to represent. Soteriology, then, became the exclusive means to the same end originally offered to Adam in the Garden.

**7. Similar views on Christ-centeredness.** Both Vos and Owen share a Christocentric and Christoclimactic hermeneutic. Though as will be discussed below, Owen was more explicit, we have seen that they both viewed Scripture as Christocentric and climactic. The Old Testament was preparatory of the Messiah, the Gospels present the historical facts of the Messiah, and the rest of the New Testament draws out the implications of Messianic fulfillment. If there was a 'central-dogma' in either of these men, it was the glory of God revealed in the face of Christ.

• **Dissimilarities between Vos and Owen**

**1. Owen interacted with more secondary sources than Vos did.** Owen was more conversant with the Western Christian tradition than Vos was and much more conversant with non-Christian thought. This is due, however, in large part to Vos' limited scope in his *Biblical Theology*. His stated purpose, as we have noted, was a history of redemption. This limits Vos' discussion to the Bible and his interpretation of it along with his (though relatively scant) interaction with secondary sources. Owen's scope was much, much broader and can be seen in his original title; *Theological Affirmations of All Sorts, Or, Of the Nature, Rise, Progress, and Study, of True Theology...with Digressions on Universal Grace, the Rise of the Sciences, Marks of the Roman Church, the Origin of Writing, Ancient Hebrew Script, Hebrew Punctuation, Jewish Versions and*

*Forms of Worship, and Other Things.*[6] As noted, Owen interacted with Christian as well as non-Christian authors. He interacted with philosophers and theologians – patristic, medieval, Reformation, and contemporary. Rehnman states the scope of Owen's work as follows:

> The object of *Theologoumena* is the discipline of theology, and it consists of dissertations on the origin, nature, and progress of the knowledge of God, and although it probably contains his introductory lectures to students of theology at the University of Oxford, it is perhaps one of Owen's more technical works. Its style is succinct and concise, but the width of learning it reveals is remarkable, as the treatise compasses nearly all the learning of that time, and digresses into numerous disputed points of doctrine.[7]

**2. Owen was more explicitly Christocentric than Vos.** This is certainly not to say that Vos was not Christocentric. However, Owen's Christocentricity was, simply, more explicit. This was seen in Owen's exposition and paradigmatic utilization of Genesis 3:15, which were more in line with Reformed orthodoxy than Vos', and Vos' reluctance to interpret and apply Genesis 3:15 in a primarily messianic manner.[8] Owen's Christocentricity has been noted by others. For instance, Kelly M. Kapic sees Owen's Christology shaping his anthropology[9] and view of the Sabbath. He says of Owen's view of the Sabbath:

> Although Owen views the Sabbath as a creation ordinance and not just as a shadow realized and done away with in Christ, his Christology shapes his doctrine of the Lord's day, *as it does with all his doctrine*, and he argues that any theology of the Sabbath not centered on its Lord effectively denies the risen Christ.[10]

Richard Daniels adds that Owen's "exegesis of the Old Testament demonstrates…that it is a Christ-centered book…"[11] He adds later that Owen

> …relates the Christian system of doctrine to the person of Christ. That is, it is one thing to say Christian theology ought to be Christocentric, it

---

[6] Owen, *BTO*, xii. This is J. I. Packer's translation of the full title.

[7] Rehnman, *Divine Discourse*, 17-18.

[8] Cf. Chapter Eleven, n. 22, above.

[9] Kapic, *Communion with God*, 43, 65.

[10] Kapic, *Communion with God*, 212-13. Emphases added.

[11] Daniels, *Christology of John Owen*, 517-18.

is quite another to actually understand the entire spectrum of theological *loci* Christocentrically, or to articulate one's theology in a way that manifests this Christocentricity. Owen does this, as we have observed with regard to the knowledge of God, creation, providence, the redemption of man, the mediatorial kingdom, the church, and the Christian life.[12]

Owen himself says, "He is the centre and circumference of all the lines of truth–that is, which is divine, spiritual, and supernatural."[13]

**3. Owen was quick to identify the object of saving faith as the Messiah in all eras of redemptive history.** Due to Owen's view of Genesis 3:15, he was quick to identify the Messiah as the object of saving faith from Adam onward. Vos, as we have seen, refused to be as explicit and was not as Christocentric in his view of the object of saving faith in the earlier eras of redemptive history.

### The Unique Contributions of Vos and Owen

- **Vos' unique contribution**

With the data presented in this dissertation, we are now able to interact with the four suggested unique contributions of Vos stated in Chapter Four, which are: (1) The Methodological Unification of the Princeton Old Testament tradition with the Federal Theology of Reformed Orthodoxy (Wallace); (2) The Unprecedented Development of the Organic Nature of Revelation as an Unfolding, Historical Process (Gaffin); (3) The Primacy of Eschatology or Vos' Intersecting-Plane Hermeneutic: The Intersection of the Protological and the Eschatological[14] (J. Dennison and Olinger); and (4) The Consistent Outworking of the Reformed Hermeneutical Principle that Scripture interprets Scripture (W. Dennison). All four have elements of truth to them, but only when sufficiently qualified. Vos did not invent or discover; he developed strands of doctrinal formulations already present in Owen and many of his Reformed orthodox contemporaries. Vos'

---

[12] Daniels, *Christology of John Owen*, 519.

[13] Owen, *Works*, I:79-80.

[14] Danny Olinger, "Vos's Verticalist Eschatology: A Response to Michael Williams," *Kerux* 7.2 (Sept. 1992): 30-38.

unique contribution is the post-Enlightenment development of *various strands* of Reformed orthodox federal theology under the rubric of biblical theology.

- **Owen's unique contribution**

As far as Owen's unique contribution, it seems safe at this juncture to agree with Rehnman:

> Owen's unique development within or contribution to this tradition of federal thought consists then in his concept of the nature of revelation, for he extends federal theology to a view of the nature of revelation. This development can be expressed by two words, "organic" and "progressive."[15]

In Chapter One it was noted that Richard B. Gaffin, Jr. labeled Geerhardus Vos as "the father of a Reformed biblical theology."[16] In terms of the post-Enlightenment genesis and subsequent development of biblical theology as a distinct discipline within the theological encyclopedia in Reformed theology there is no compelling reason to question such a title. Though there are traces of an undeveloped or proto-biblical theology at Princeton prior to his professorship, Vos still deserves the title 'father of a Reformed biblical theology' because he, like no other Reformed theologian to date, developed biblical theology and explored its implications, especially in the field of Pauline eschatology.[17]

Chapter One also gave the title 'grandfather of Biblical theology in the Reformed tradition' to the federal theology of the Reformed orthodox. The validity of this title deserves serious consideration due to the various strands of continuity both in methodology and theology we have noted between Vos and Owen. Since Owen is representative of the Reformed orthodox of the era of High Orthodoxy and because of the

---

[15] Rehnman, *Divine Discourse*, 165.

[16] Vos, *RHBI*, xiv.

[17] Cf. esp. Geerhardus Vos, *Pauline Eschatology* (Phillipsburg, NJ: P&R Publishing, 1930, re. 1991).

lines of affinity with Vos stated above, he could even be labeled as 'a grandfather (among many others) of a Reformed biblical theology.'

## Three Concluding Assertions

This brings us back to three points asserted in the 'Introduction.'

- **Our study has confirmed the assertion that Geerhardus Vos resuscitated federal theology under the rubric of biblical theology as a self-conscious Reformed and confessional theologian.**

Though with Vos' own nuances and terminology, there is enough methodological and theological continuity to confirm this (see above). The need for such resuscitation is most likely due to the poisoning and diversionary affects of the Enlightenment. The Enlightenment derailed the further development of seventeenth-century federal theology. The early Princeton theologians were dependant enough upon seventeenth-century Reformed orthodoxy that their theology and methodology was somewhat proto-typical for them. Vos developed what was handed down to him from the Old Testament department during his student days at Princeton. His knowledge of seventeenth-century federalism is obvious and was somewhat influential in his method and overall thought.

- **Our study has confirmed that the negative claims aimed at Reformed orthodox methodology and theology are empty and void of historical and theological adhesiveness.**

Both the Reformed orthodox and Vos were committed to the authority and infallibility of Scripture. They were Christ-centered in their approach to the history of redemption and both viewed Christ as the center of redemptive revelation. If such negative claims cannot be hurled at Vos, then they cannot be hurled at the federal theology of Reformed orthodoxy.

- **Our study has confirmed that both Vosian biblical theology and Owenian federal theology are compatible with Reformed confessional theology.**

Both men upheld their confessional commitments to the end. It is not possible to find an antithetical relationship between Vos' biblical theology and Owen's federal theology and their respective confessions of faith. Both men went from exegesis to theological synthesis and both found their theological synthesis and formulations faithfully articulated in the body of doctrine contained in the Westminster Confession and Savoy Declaration.

# APPENDIX ONE – ANALYTICAL OUTLINE

## The Family Tree of Reformed Biblical Theology:
## Geerhardus Vos and John Owen –
## Their Methods of and Contributions to
## the Articulation of Redemptive History

### PART I: PROLEGOMENA

I. **INTRODUCTION: JOHN OWEN AND GEERHARDUS VOS – REFORMED FEDERAL/BIBLICAL THEOLOGIANS?**
  A. Introduction
  B. The Grandfather of Biblical Theology in the Reformed Tradition: The Federal Theology of the Reformed Orthodox
  C. What is biblical theology and how does it relate to Federal Theology?
  D. The Methodological Approach of the Dissertation

II. **A BRIEF HISTORY OF BIBLICAL THEOLOGY**
  A. Introduction
  B. Reformation and Post-Reformation Protestant Scholastic era
  C. German Pietism
  D. The Enlightenment
  E. Nineteenth-Century Germany (the salvation-historical school)
  F. Nineteenth-Century Germany (the history of religions school)
  G. Twentieth Century (the "Biblical Theology Movement" and the conservative testimony)
  H. Late Twentieth Century to the Present
  I. Conclusion

**PART II: BIOGRAPHICAL, HISTORICAL, AND THEOLOGICAL**

III. **THE LIFE, MINISTRY, AND IMPACT OF GEERHARDUS VOS**
   A. The Life of Geerhardus Vos
   B. The Ministry of Geerhardus Vos
   C. The Impact of Geerhardus Vos

IV. **GEERHARDUS VOS, OLD PRINCETON, AND REFORMED BIBLICAL THEOLOGY IN HISTORICAL-THEOLOGICAL CONTEXT**
   A. Introduction
   B. Old Princeton and Biblical Theology prior to Vos
      1. Archibald Alexander
      2. Charles Hodge
      3. J. A. Alexander
      4. William Henry Green
   C. Influences upon Vos outside of Princeton
      1. Introduction
      2. Thomas Dehaney Bernard
      3. The Federal Theology of Reformed Orthodoxy
   D. Vos' Unique Contribution in Historical-Theological Perspective
      1. The Methodological Unification of the Princeton Old Testament tradition with the Federal Theology of Reformed Orthodoxy
      2. The Unprecedented Development of the Organic Nature of Revelation as an Unfolding, Historical Process
      3. The Primacy of Eschatology or Vos' Intersecting-Plane Hermeneutic: The Intersection of the Protological and the Eschatological
      4. The Consistent Outworking of the Reformed Hermeneutical Principle that Scripture interprets Scripture
   E. Conclusion

V. **THE LIFE, MINISTRY, AND LEGACY OF JOHN OWEN**
   A. The Life and Ministry of John Owen
   B. The Legacy of John Owen

     6.  Jonathan Edwards
  G.  John Owen: Reformed Orthodox Federal Theologian?

## PART III: ANALYSIS

**VII.** **ANALYSIS OF GEERHARDUS VOS' NATURE AND METHOD OF BIBLICAL THEOLOGY**
  A.  Introduction
  B.  "The Idea of Biblical Theology as a Science and as a Theological Discipline"
     1.  Introduction
        a.  Reasons for the lecture
        b.  Definition of theology
        c.  Supernatural revelation in light of the presence of sin in man
     2.  Definition of Biblical Theology
        a.  Its basic elements
        b.  Its detailed elaboration: The Characteristic Features of Supernatural Revelation
           (1)  Historical Progress
           (2)  Organic Development
           (3)  Covenantal-Expansiveness
           (4)  Christ-Centeredness
           (5)  Multiformity of Teaching
  C.  "The Nature and Aims of Biblical Theology"
     1.  Introduction
     2.  The General Features of God's Revealing Work
        a.  Historic progress
        b.  Organic development
        c.  Ever-increasing multiformity
     3.  Conclusion
        a.  Definition of Biblical Theology
        b.  Suspicion surrounding Biblical Theology
        c.  Practical value of Biblical Theology
        d.  Biblical Theology as the History of Special Revelation
  D.  "The Nature and Method of Biblical Theology"
     1.  Introduction
     2.  Working Definition of Biblical Theology and Its Implications

       a. Biblical Theology deals with the Bible from the historical standpoint

       b. Biblical Theology seeks to exhibit the organic growth and development of the truths of Special Revelation

       c. Biblical Theology begins in the Garden of Eden and ends with the closed canon of the New Testament

    3. The Use of the Phrase Biblical Theology

    4. Theology and the Necessity of Revelation

    5. Main Features of the Divine Activity of Revelation

       a. The historic progressiveness of the revelation-process

       b. The embodiment of divine revelation in history

       c. The organic nature of the historic process of divine revelation

       d. The practical adaptability of divine revelation

    6. Guiding Principles in Opposition to Critical/Rationalistic Biblical Theology

       a. The recognition of the infallible character of revelation is essential to every legitimate theological use made of this term

       b. Biblical Theology must likewise recognize the objectivity of the groundwork of revelation

       c. Biblical Theology is deeply concerned with the question of inspiration

    7. Methodological Approach

  E. Conclusion

## VIII. JOHN OWEN'S *BIBLICAL THEOLOGY*: PURPOSE AND DEFINITION OF THEOLOGY

  A. Purpose of Owen's *Biblical Theology*

  B. Owen's Definition of Theology

## IX. GENERAL AND SPECIAL REVELATION

  A. Geerhardus Vos

    1. Introduction

    2. The Relationship between General and Special Revelation apart from Sin

    3. The Relationship between General and Special Revelation under the Regime of Sin

        a.    The *form* of Special Revelation is changed under the regime of sin
        b.    The *content* of revelation is changed
        c.    The "*mood* of man in which he receives the supernatural approach of God" has fundamentally changed as well

B.  John Owen
    1.    Introduction
    2.    General Revelation
    3.    Special Revelation

## X.      PRE-REDEMPTIVE, SPECIAL REVELATION

A.  Geerhardus Vos
    1.    Introduction
    2.    The Principle of Life and what is Taught concerning it by the Tree of Life
    3.    Probation and what is Taught concerning it in the Symbolism of the Tree of Knowledge of Good and Evil
    4.    The Principle of Temptation and Sin Symbolized in the Serpent
    5.    The Principle of Death Symbolized by the Dissolution of the Body
    6.    EXCURSUS: The Covenant of Works and the Embodiment of the Sabbath Principle

B.  John Owen
    1.    Adam's Pre-Redemptive Theology: Natural and Supernatural Revelation
    2.    Adam's Pre-Redemptive Theology: The Teleological Function of the Law
    3.    Adam's Pre-Redemptive Theology: Eschatology Prior to Soteriology
    4.    Adam's Pre-Redemptive Theology: *Imago Dei*
    5.    Adam's Pre-Redemptive Theology: Edenic Probation
    6.    EXCURSUS: The Temporal Revelation of the Covenant of Works in Owen – Absolutely or Relatively Coeval with Creation?
    7.    Adam's Pre-Redemptive Theology: The Fall into Sin
        a.    The nature of the first sin and its punishment
        b.    The fall into sin is a historical event
        c.    Sin makes obedience to the covenant of works impossible

XI. **REDEMPTIVE, SPECIAL REVELATION AND THE GARDEN OF EDEN**
   A. Geerhardus Vos
      1. Introduction
      2. Revelation through the Curse
         a. The Serpent
         b. The Seed
         c. Human Suffering
   B. John Owen
      1. Introduction: "The Renewal of Theology after the Fall"
      2. Genesis 3:15: The *Protevangelium* and Covenant of Grace
      3. A New Phase of Theology and Its Two-Fold Ethic: Moral Law and Positive Law

XII. **REDEMPTIVE, SPECIAL REVELATION FROM ADAM TO NOAH**
   A. Geerhardus Vos
   B. John Owen

XIII. **REDEMPTIVE, SPECIAL REVELATION FROM NOAH TO ABRAHAM**
   A. Geerhardus Vos
      1. Noachian Revelation and Its Stages
         a. The institution of a new order of affairs
         b. The means ordained to secure the new order
         c. The covenant confirming the new order
      2. Revelation between Noah and the Patriarchs
         a. The prophecies of Noah
         b. The table of the nations
         c. The confusion of tongues
   B. John Owen
      1. Introduction
      2. The Nature and Essence of a Divine Covenant
      3. The Noahic Covenant: The First Stage of the Development of a Post-Diluvian Theology
         a. Its function
         b. Its promise
         c. Its contribution to the progress and development of redemptive history
         d. Its redemptive-historical context

4. Canaan's Sin and Noah's Curse
5. The Tower of Babel

## XIV. REDEMPTIVE, SPECIAL REVELATION FROM ABRAHAM TO MOSES

A. Geerhardus Vos
   1. Introduction: The Historicity of the Patriarchal Period
   2. The Form and the Content of Revelation in the Patriarchal Period
   3. The Distinctive Features of Revelation in the Patriarchal Period
      a. Election
      b. Biblical religion is based on historical divine interpositions
      c. Divine monergism
B. John Owen
   1. The Patriarchal Period: A New Phase of Unfolding Theology
   2. Evidences of Revelatory Advance in the Patriarchal Period
      a. Further explanations of Messianic revelation
      b. Richer demonstrations of covenant grace
      c. Covenantal exclusiveness
      d. The sign of the covenant
      e. Covenantal privileges and the infant seed of believers
      f. God's special friendship with Abraham

## XV. REDEMPTIVE, SPECIAL REVELATION FROM MOSES TO CHRIST

A. Geerhardus Vos
   1. Introduction
   2. The Place of Moses in the Organism of Old Testament Revelation
   3. The Form of the Mosaic Revelation
   4. The Content of the Mosaic Revelation
      a. The factual basis of the Mosaic organization given in the redemption from Egypt
      b. The making of the *Berith* with Israel with which the organization entered into being
      c. The general nature of the organization, the theocracy

C.  Revelation Connected with John the Baptist
1.  John the Baptist and Elijah
2.  John the Baptist's Testimony to Jesus
3.  John's Baptism
4.  John's Baptism of Jesus
5.  The Descent of the Spirit on Jesus
6.  The Post-Baptismal Testimony of John the Baptist to Jesus
D.  Revelation in the Probation of Jesus
1.  The Temptation in the Wilderness
2.  The Lord's Temptation and Our Own
3.  The Specific Form Assumed by Our Lord's Temptation
4.  The Lord's Temptation Interpreted
5.  Temptability and Peccability
E.  The Revelation of Jesus' Public Ministry
1.  Various Aspects of Christ's Revealing Function
2.  The Question of Development and the Method of Jesus' Teaching
3.  Jesus' Attitude toward the Scriptures of the Old Testament
4.  Jesus' Teaching on the Kingdom of God

XVII.  **REDEMPTIVE, SPECIAL REVELATION AND THE NEW TESTAMENT: JOHN OWEN**
A.  Introduction: The Final and Perfect Revelation from God – Evangelical Theology
B.  The Messiah's Coming
C.  The Principles of Evangelical (Gospel) Theology
D.  Classifying Evangelical Theology
E.  Philosophy and Theology
F.  Evangelical Ecclesiology


**PART IV: CONCLUSION**


XVIII.  **COMPARATIVE   ANALYSIS   AND   CONCLUDING WORDS**
A.  Introduction
B.  Comparative Analysis
1.  Similarities between Vos and Owen
    a.  Similar methodologies

        b.   Similar views on the nature of revelation as organic and progressive

        c.   Similar views on the distinction between General Revelation (or Natural Theology) and Special Revelation (or Supernatural Theology)

        d.   Similar views on pre-redemptive, Special Revelation/Supernatural Theology

        e.   Similar views on the covenant of works

        f.   Similar views on the primacy of eschatology to soteriology

        g.   Similar views on Christ-centeredness

    2.   Dissimilarities between Vos and Owen

        a.   Owen interacted with more secondary sources than Vos

        b.   Owen was more explicitly Christocentric than Vos

        c.   Owen was quick to identify the object of saving faith as the Messiah in all eras of redemptive history

C.   The Unique Contributions of Vos and Owen

    1.   Vos' unique contribution: the post-Enlightenment development of various strands of Reformed orthodox federal theology under the rubric of biblical theology

    2.   Owen's unique contribution: the development of the nature of redemptive revelation as organic and progressive within the Reformed orthodox model of federal theology

D.   Three concluding assertions

    1.   Our study has confirmed the assertion that Geerhardus Vos resuscitated federal theology under the rubric of biblical theology as a self-conscious Reformed and confessional theologian

    2.   Our study has confirmed that the negative claims aimed at Reformed orthodox methodology and theology are empty and void of historical and theological adhesiveness

    3.   Our study has confirmed that both Vosian biblical theology and Owenian federal theology are compatible with Reformed confessional theology

# APPENDIX TWO – THE DECALOGUE IN THE THOUGHT OF KEY REFORMED THEOLOGIANS WITH SPECIAL REFERENCE TO JOHN OWEN

## Introduction

In this Appendix, we will explore the thought of John Owen, as well as several other Reformed theologians from the 16th-18th centuries, on the functions of the Decalogue. We will note the various nuances of terminology and theological formulation among Reformed theologians of the past. But we will also see basic methodological and theological continuity from John Calvin to Thomas Boston. This, once again, displays Owen's continuity with the Reformed tradition and the continuity among the Reformed orthodox on this subject. As will be seen, the Reformed orthodox approached this subject utilizing a redemptive-historical hermeneutic, something we noted in Chapter Six.

Our focus will be upon John Owen. He is not always easy to understand and has been misused on the issue of the functions of the Decalogue. We will seek to allow him to speak for himself, offer some observations, and compare Owen's statements with those of others before and after him. This will display, among other things, the fact that Owen fits within the broader theological tradition of Reformed thought on the functions of the Decalogue in redemptive history.

## John Owen and other Key Reformed Theologians from the 16th-18th Centuries on the Functions of the Decalogue

- ### The Perpetuity of the Decalogue under the New Covenant in Owen and Others

**1. John Owen.** In his Hebrews commentary, Owen teaches that Jeremiah 31:33 and 2 Corinthians 3:3 refer to the Decalogue being written on the heart of New Covenant saints. Commenting on Hebrews 9:5, he says:

> This law, as unto the substance of it, was the only law of creation, the rule of the first covenant of works; for it contained the sum and substance of that obedience which is due unto God from all rational creatures made in his image, and nothing else. It was the whole of what God designed in our creation unto his own glory and our everlasting blessedness. What was in the tables of stone was nothing but a

transcript of what was written in the heart of man originally; and which is returned thither again by the grace of the new covenant, Jeremiah 31:33; 2 Corinthians 3:3.[1]

Consider these observations relevant to our subject. *First*, the law, in the context of Owen's discussion, refers to the law contained on the tables of stone (i.e., the Decalogue). *Second*, Owen is considering the Decalogue "as unto the substance of it" and not necessarily as to the form and/or function of it under the Old Covenant.[2] *Third*, he claims that the Decalogue "was the only law of creation, the rule of the first covenant of works." *Fourth*, he claims that the Decalogue, as to the substance of it, "contained the sum and substance of that obedience which is due unto God from all rational creatures made in his image." *Fifth*, he claims that "what was in the tables of stone was nothing but a transcript of what was written in the heart of man originally." *Sixth*, he claims that "what was in the tables of stone" (and written on the heart of man at creation) is that "which is returned thither again by the grace of the new covenant." And *finally*, he references Jeremiah 31:33 and 2 Corinthians 3:3. Owen, on this exegetical basis, clearly believed in the perpetuity (as to its substance) of the entire Decalogue under the New Covenant.

Owen continues:

Although this law as a covenant was broken and disannulled by the entrance of sin, and became insufficient as unto its first ends, of the justification and salvation of the church thereby, Rom viii. 3; yet as a law and rule of obedience it was never disannulled, nor would God suffer it to be. Yea, one principal design of God in Christ was, that it might be fulfilled and established, Matt. v. 17, 18; Rom iii. 31. For to reject this law, or to abrogate it, had been for God to have laid aside that glory of his holiness and righteousness which in his infinite

---

[1] Owen, *Works of John Owen*, XXII:215.

[2] Protestant Scholasticism taught that the Decalogue summarily contains the moral law and is the inscripturated form of the natural law, as to its *substance*. A distinction was made between *substance* and *form*. *Substance* is one; *form* may vary. Hence, when the Westminster Larger Catechism Q. 98 says, "The moral law is summarily comprehended in the ten commandments," it refers to the fact that the *substance* (i.e., the underlying essence) of the Moral Law is assumed and articulated in the propositions of the Decalogue as contained in Exodus 20 and Deuteronomy 5. The *form* fits the redemptive-historical circumstances in which it was given. The *substance* or underlying principles are always relevant and applicable to man. The application may shift based on redemptive-historical changes, such as the inauguration of the New Covenant, but its *substance* and utility never changes.

wisdom he designed therein. Hence, after it was again broken by the people as a covenant, he wrote it a second time himself in tables of stone, and caused it to be safely kept in the ark, as his perpetual testimony. That, therefore, which he taught the church by and in all this, in the first place, was, that this law was to be fulfilled and accomplished, or they could have no advantage of or benefit by the covenant.[3]

From this statement, the following observations also are relevant. *First,* Owen distinguishes between how the Decalogue functioned in the covenant of works and how it functions "as a law and rule of obedience." *Second,* he connects this law with God's holiness and righteousness. In other words, Owen views the Decalogue as a perpetual "law and rule of obedience" because it is related to God's holiness and righteousness (i.e., his unchangeable nature).

Continuing, and concentrating on how Christ is the true ark (the antitype of the Old Covenant's Ark of the Covenant), he says:

In his *obedience unto God* according unto the law he is the true *ark,* wherein the law was kept inviolate; that is, was fulfilled, answered, and accomplished, Matt. v. 17; Rom. viii. 3, x. 4. Hence by God's gracious dealing with sinners, pardoning and justifying them freely, the law [i.e., Decalogue] is not disannulled, but established, Rom. iii. 31. That this was to be done, that without it no covenant between God and man could be firm and stable, was the principal design of God to declare in all this service; without the consideration thereof it was wholly insignificant. This was the original mystery of all these institutions, that in and by the obedience of the promised seed, the everlasting, unalterable law should be fulfilled.[4]

Several observations are worthy of note. *First,* in the context of Owen's discussion, the law is that which was placed in the ark (i.e., the Decalogue as written by God on stone tablets). *Second,* he says that this law was fulfilled, answered, and accomplished by Christ. *Third,* he says that the obedience of Christ to this law effects our justification. *Fourth,* he says that the law is not disannulled but established. *Fifth,* he teaches that all of this was typified in the Ark of the Covenant. And *finally,* he

---

[3] Owen, *Works,* XXII:215, 16.
[4] Owen, *Works,* XXII:217, 18.

says that the law is *everlasting* and *unalterable*, probably due to its reflection of God's holiness and righteousness.[5]

Owen's use of Jeremiah 31:33 and 2 Corinthians 3:3 was not novel. Others who held to his basic understanding argued for the perpetuity of the Decalogue under the New Covenant on the same exegetical grounds.[6]

**2. Herman Witsius.** In his *The Economy of the Covenants Between God and Man*, while discussing the reason that God "engraved them [Ten Commandments] with his own finger,"[7] Herman Witsius says:

> Both because they contained the declaration or testimony of the divine will, and because the preservation of them by the Israelites, was a testimony of the law given to, and received by them at Sinai. This writing also signified the purpose of God, to write the law on the hearts of his elect, according to the promise of the covenant of grace, Jer. xxxi. 33.

> Nor is it for nothing that God himself would be the author of this writing, without making use of any man or angel. For this is the meaning of the Holy Spirit, when he says, that the tablets were written with the finger of God, Exod. xxxi. 18. and that the writing was the writing of God, Exod. xxxii. 16. The reasons were, 1st. To set forth the pre-eminence of this law, which he permitted to be written by Moses. 2dly. To intimate, that it is the work of God alone, to write the law on the heart, which is what neither man himself, nor the ministers of God can do, but the Spirit of God alone. And thus believers are "the epistle of Christ, written not with ink, but with the Spirit of the living God," 2 Cor. iii. 3.[8]

Witsius goes on to discuss the effects of God's grace, saying, "But the grace of God will cancel that writing of sin, and in the room of it, will the

---

[5] Owen, *Works*, XXII:215.

[6] In my book *In Defense of the Decalogue* (*IDOTD*), I provided exegetical evidence that Jer. 31:33 and 2 Cor. 3:3 speak directly to the issue of the perpetuity of the Decalogue under the New Covenant. I provided references to Old Testament and New Testament scholars to this end. The scholars I referenced are not all Reformed confessionalists. I did this on purpose to show that one's confessional commitments do not necessarily cloud one's exegetical lenses. See Richard C. Barcellos, *In Defense of the Decalogue: A Critique of New Covenant Theology* (Enumclaw, WA: WinePress Publishing, 2001), 16-24 and 34-38.

[7] Witsius, *Economy of the Covenants*, II:170.

[8] Witsius, *Economy of the Covenants*, II:170, 171.

graver of his most Holy Spirit, engrave on the same table of our heart the characters of his law."[9]

The context is clear. Witsius sees Jeremiah 31:33 and 2 Corinthians 3:3 as testimonies to the perpetuity of the Decalogue under the New Covenant. As shown above, Owen used these texts in a very similar context and with the same practical result.

**3. Francis Turretin.** Turretin also references both Jeremiah 31:33 and 2 Corinthians 3:3. His use of these texts corresponds with Owen's and Witsius' use, at least to a degree. While discussing how the abrogation of the Moral Law (the Decalogue) is not to be considered absolutely, but relatively, he says,

> It is one thing to be under the law as a covenant to acquire life by it (as Adam was) or as a schoolmaster and a prison to guard men until the advent of Christ; another to be under the law as a rule of life to regulate our morals piously and holily. [10]

> The law is compared by Paul to "a dead husband" (Rom. 7:2, 3), not simply, but relatively with regard to the sway and rigorous dominion it obtained over us and the curse to which it subjected sinners; but not with regard to liberation from the duty to be performed to it. Thus the law threatening, compelling, condemning, is not "made for a righteous man" (1 Tim. 1:9) because he is impelled of his own accord to duty and is no longer influenced by the spirit of bondage and the fear of punishment (Rom. 8:15; Ps. 110:3), but the law directive and regulative of morals is always laid down for him and he ought to be under it. [11]

> What was given to the Jews as Jews can be for the use of the Jews alone; but what is given to the Jews as covenanted (or as the people of God simply) does not refer to them alone, but to all those who hold the same relation of people of God.[12]

Turretin says many more similar things. Suffice to say that he makes distinctions in the way the law is viewed. This is done to protect the Moral Law from an absolutist view of abrogation (see below) and to promote its perpetual utility. It is in this context that Turretin says, "'If

---

[9] Witsius, *Economy of the Covenants*, II:171.

[10] Francis Turretin, *Institutes of Elenctic Theology* (Phillipsburg, NJ: P&R Publishing, 1994), II:143.

[11] Turretin, *Institutes*, II:143.

[12] Turretin, *Institutes*, II:145.

ye be led of the Spirit, ye are not under the law' (Gal. 5:18, viz., compelling and cursing), but under it directing, inasmuch as the Spirit works that law upon our hearts (2 Cor. 3:2; Jer. 31:33)."[13] In this context, the law which directs is the Moral Law (Decalogue). Hence, it is the Decalogue which "the Spirit works upon our hearts."

**4. Thomas Boston.** Thomas Boston's notes to *The Marrow of Modern Divinity* reveal that at least one 18th century Reformed theologian held that Jeremiah 31:33 referred to the writing of the Decalogue on the heart under the New Covenant. Boston says:

> One will not think it strange to hear, that the ten commandments were, as it were, razed out of man's heart by the fall, if one considers the spirituality and vast extent of them, and that they were, in their perfection engraven on the heart of man, in his creation, and doth withal take notice of the ruin brought on man by the fall. Hereby he indeed lost the very knowledge of the law of nature, if the ten commandments are to be reckoned, as certainly they are, the substance and matter of that law; although he lost it not totally, but some remains thereof were left with him. Concerning these the apostle speaks, Rom. i. 19, 20; and ii. 14, 15. And our author teaches expressly, that the law is partly known by nature, that is, in its corrupt state, See page 181. And here he says, not simply, that the ten commandments were razed, though in another case (page 44), he speaks after that manner, where yet it is evident he means not a razing quite; but he says, "They were, as it were, razed." But what are these remains of them in comparison with that body of natural laws, fairly written, and deeply engraven, on the heart of innocent Adam? If they were not, as it were, razed, what need is there of writing a new copy of them in the hearts of the elect, according to the promise of the new covenant? "I will put my laws into their hearts, and in their minds I will write them," Heb. x. 16, and viii. 10; Jer. xxxi. 33.[14]

Like Witsius and Turretin before him, Boston proves that there were some in the 17th and 18th centuries who argued for the perpetuity of the Decalogue from Jeremiah 31:33 (and 2 Corinthians 3:3), i.e., on the same exegetical ground as Owen.

Though Owen's statements concerning Jeremiah 31:33 are not all equally clear, those provided above are clear enough to conclude that he

---

[13] Turretin, *Institutes*, II:143, 144.

[14] Edward Fisher, *The Marrow of Modern Divinity* (Edmonton, AB, Canada: Still Waters Revival Books, re. 1991), 177.

used it and 2 Corinthians 3:3 in a context which argues for the perpetuity of the Decalogue under the New Covenant. He does this in similar fashion as Witsius, Turretin, and Boston.

- **Matthew 5:17 and the Perpetuity of the Decalogue under the New Covenant in Owen and Others**

**1. John Owen.** In his Hebrews commentary, Owen argues for the perpetuity of the Decalogue under the New Covenant from Matthew 5:17. While discussing the foundations of the Sabbath, he says:

> From these particular instances we may return to the consideration of the law of the decalogue in general, and the perpetual power of exacting obedience wherewith it is accompanied. That in the Old Testament it is frequently declared to be universally obligatory, and has the same efficacy ascribed unto it, without putting in any exceptions to any of its commands or limitations of its number, I suppose will be granted. The authority of it is no less fully asserted in the New Testament, and that also absolutely without distinction, or the least intimation of excepting the fourth command from what is affirmed concerning the whole. It is of the law of the decalogue that our Savior treats, Matt. v. 17-19. This he affirms that he came not to dissolve, as he did the ceremonial law, but to fulfill it; and then affirms that not one jot or tittle of it shall pass away. And making thereon a distribution of the whole into its several commands, he declares his disapprobation of them who shall break, or teach men to break, any one of them. And men make bold with him, when they so confidently assert that they may break one of them, and teach others so to do, without offense. That this reaches not to the confirmation of the seventh day precisely, we shall after-wards abundantly demonstrate.[15]

Commenting on Hebrews 9:3-5, Owen says:

> Although this law as a covenant was broken and disannulled *by the entrance of sin,* and became insufficient as unto its first ends, of the justification and salvation of the church thereby, Rom. viii. 3; yet as a *law and rule of obedience* it was never disannulled, nor would God suffer it to be. Yea, one principal design of God in Christ was, that it might be fulfilled and established, Matt. v. 17, 18; Rom. iii. 31. For to

---

[15] Owen, *Works*, XXIII:372.

reject this law, or to abrogate it, had been for God to have laid aside that glory of his holiness and righteousness which in his infinite wisdom he designed therein. Hence, after it was again broken by the people as a covenant, he wrote it a second time himself in tables of stone, and caused it to be safely kept in the ark, as his perpetual testimony. That, therefore, which he taught the church by and in all this, in the first place, was, that this law was to be fulfilled and accomplished, or they could have no advantage of or benefit by the covenant.[16]

Owen used Jeremiah 31:33 and 2 Corinthians 3:3 as proof of the perpetuity of the Decalogue. His use of Matthew 5:17 is to the same end.[17]

**2. Zacharias Ursinus.** While discussing how abrogation affects the Moral Law, Ursinus makes the point that "the moral law, or Decalogue, has not been abrogated in as far as obedience to it is concerned."[18] He then argues, "God continually, no less now than formerly, requires both the regenerate and the unregenerate to render obedience to his law."[19] As one of the reasons that he offers in proof of this proposition, he says:

From the testimony of Scripture: "Think not that I am come to destroy the law, or the prophets; I am not come to destroy, but to fulfill." (Matt. 5:17.) This is spoken, indeed, of the whole law, but with a special reference to the moral law, which Christ has fulfilled in four respects[20] ...

---

[16] Owen, *Works*, XXII:215, 216.

[17] In *IDOTD*, I argued that Mt. 5:17 can be understood in such a way as not to eliminate the Decalogue from the New Covenant. As a matter of fact, I argued that it could be understood in such a way as not to eliminate the Old Testament from the New Covenant. For instance, after providing exegetical observations and conclusions and then testing my interpretation with the rest of the New Testament, I said: "The law of God, even the whole Old Testament, has its place under Christ, finding its realization in Him and its modified application in His kingdom. If the whole of the Old Testament is still binding, then certainly all its parts are as well." See Barcellos, *IDOTD*, 65. I realize my explanation has nuances Owen's may not.

[18] Zacharias Ursinus, *The Commentary of Dr. Zacharias Ursinus on the Heidelberg Catechism* (Edmonton, AB, Canada: Still Waters Revival Books, re. n.d.), 496.

[19] Ursinus, *Commentary*, 496.

[20] Ursinus, *Commentary*, 496.

Ursinus understands Matthew 5:17 in such a way as to demand the perpetuity of the Decalogue under the New Covenant, as did Owen.

**3. Francis Turretin.** While offering "Proof that the law is not abrogated as to direction,"[21] Turretin says, "Christ 'did not come to destroy but to fulfill the law' (Mt. 5:17). Therefore as it was not abolished but fulfilled by Christ, neither is its use among us to be abolished."[22]

It is now clear that Owen's view of Matthew 5:17 (shared by Ursinus and Turretin) does not require the elimination of the Decalogue in all senses under the New Covenant.

- **The Multi-functional Utility of the Decalogue in Owen and Others**

**1. John Owen.** Owen viewed the Decalogue as having more than one function. He did not view it as Old Covenant law alone. His understanding of the multi-functional utility of the Decalogue can be seen clearly in several places of his Hebrews commentary. For instance, commenting on Hebrews 9:5 (referenced above), he says, "The law [the Decalogue], as unto the substance of it, was the only law of creation, the rule of the first covenant of works."[23] Later he claims that "what was in the tables of stone was nothing but a transcript of what was written in the heart of man originally; and which is returned thither again by the grace of the new covenant."[24] Notice that he views the Decalogue as functioning several ways; *first*, "as unto the substance of it, ...the only law of creation"; *second*, "the rule of the first covenant of works"; *third*, that which "was in the tables of stone"; *fourth*, "a transcript of what was written in the heart of man originally"; and *fifth*, that "which is returned [to the heart of man] again by the grace of the new covenant."

Commenting on Hebrews 7:18, 19 (also referenced previously), he says:

> Nor is it the whole *ceremonial law* only that is intended by "the command" in this place, but the *moral law* also [emphasis his], *so far as it was compacted with the other into one body of precepts for the*

---

[21] Turretin, *Institutes*, II:142.
[22] Turretin, *Institutes*, II:142.
[23] Owen, *Works*, XXII:215.
[24] Owen, *Works*, XXII:215.

*same end* [emphasis added]; for with respect unto the efficacy of the whole law of Moses, as unto our drawing nigh unto God, it is here considered.[25]

Here he views the Decalogue as a unit "so far as it was compacted with the other [ceremonial law] into one body of precepts for the same end." In other words, he is considering the Decalogue not absolutely or in itself (see below), but relatively or as it was 'compacted' with the ceremonial law under the Old Covenant.

While discussing the causes of the Sabbath and arguing for the morality and immutability of the essence of the fourth commandment, he makes this statement concerning the nature and function of the Decalogue under the Old Covenant:

> The nature of the decalogue, and the distinction of its precepts from all commands, ceremonial or political, comes now under consideration. The whole decalogue, I acknowledge, as given on mount Sinai to the Israelites, had a political use, as being made the principal instrument or rule of the polity and government of their nation, as peculiarly under the rule of God. It had a place also in that economy or dispensation of the covenant which that church was then brought under; wherein, by God's dealing with them and instructing of them, they were taught to look out after a further and greater good in the promise than they were yet come to the enjoyment of. Hence the Decalogue itself, in that dispensation of it, was a schoolmaster unto Christ.[26]

*First*, Owen views the Decalogue as the core of the law of the Old Covenant. He says, "The whole decalogue, …as given on mount Sinai to the Israelites, had a political use, as being made the principal instrument or rule of the polity and government of their nation." *Second*, he makes the point that the Decalogue was "made the principal instrument or rule of the polity and government" of Israel under the Old Covenant. This is something that it was not until that time. He viewed it as already in existence, though in a different form and revealed in a different manner, but now being "made" something it was not. It was now "made" to fit the redemptive-historical conditions of the Old Covenant. This seems even more likely, since he goes on to say, "Some, indeed, of the precepts of it, as the first, fourth, and fifth, have either prefaces, enlargements, or additions, which belonged peculiarly to the then present and future state

---

[25] Owen, *Works*,XXI:458.
[26] Owen, *Works*, XVIII:365, 66.

of that church in the land of Canaan."[27] *Third,* he also viewed it as "a schoolmaster unto Christ."

Next, speaking of the Decalogue "in itself, and materially," he says:

> But in itself, and materially considered, it was wholly, and in all the preceptive parts of it, absolutely moral. Some, indeed, of the precepts of it, as the first, fourth, and fifth, have either prefaces, enlargements, or additions, which belonged peculiarly to the then present and future state of that church in the land of Canaan; but these especial applications of it unto them change not the nature of its commands or precepts, which are all moral, and, as far as they are esteemed to belong to the Decalogue, are unquestionably acknowledged so to be.[28]

Notice that he has transitioned from viewing the Decalogue in its Old Covenant functions to viewing the Decalogue in itself. We might say that he was considering it relatively speaking, as it functioned under the Old Covenant, but now he is considering it absolutely (or "in itself"), as it functions transcovenantally. *First,* he distinguishes between the Decalogue "as being made the principal instrument or rule of the polity and government of their [Old Covenant Israel's] nation" and "in itself." Hence, "in itself" and "in all the preceptive parts of it," the Decalogue is "absolutely moral." *Second,* he says that the Decalogue under the Old Covenant had redemptive-historical "prefaces, enlargements, or additions" peculiar to the conditions in which they [the church in the land of Canaan] lived. These are positive, covenantal appendages added to the Decalogue and applicable to Old Covenant Israel in the land of Canaan.

From these statements, the following observations are relevant to our purpose. *First,* Owen viewed the Decalogue both relatively and absolutely, depending on its function in redemptive history. *Second,* he viewed the Decalogue (i.e., that which "was in tables of stone... as unto the substance of it") functioning various ways and in all of the epochs of redemptive history. He saw it functioning in the Garden of Eden. He regarded it as the law of creation, the rule of the Adamic covenant of works, and the law that was written on Adam's heart. He then saw it functioning in a special manner under the Old Covenant. He also saw it functioning under the New Covenant. He taught that it was this same law, as unto its substance, "which is returned thither [to the heart of man]

---

[27] Owen, *Works,* XVIII:366.
[28] Owen, *Works,* XVIII:366.

again by the grace of the new covenant."[29] He viewed it as the rule of life for all men,[30] because "in all the preceptive parts of it" it is "absolutely moral." And as stated earlier, he viewed it as related to the active and passive obedience of Christ and hence, connected and essential to the doctrine of justification.[31]

**2. John Calvin.** In many places Calvin clearly identified the Decalogue as a special form of the Natural Law.[32] For instance, Calvin said, "Now that inward law, which we have above described as written, even engraved, upon the hearts of all, in a sense asserts the very same things that are to be learned from the two Tables."[33] Calvin "saw the revealed law as given in the ten commandments as a specially accommodated restatement of the law of nature for the Jews."[34] He clearly held that by nature Gentiles without special revelation possessed the general knowledge of the Decalogue, though that knowledge is obscured by sin.[35] Hesselink says, "There is no denying that for Calvin the content of the moral law is essentially the same as that inscribed on the hearts of humans 'by nature'."[36] Wendel says, "One can even say that, for Calvin, the Decalogue is only a special application of the natural law which God came to attest and confirm."[37]

Calvin's view of the multi-functional utility of the Decalogue is no secret. It is also evidenced by the fact that he clearly upheld the perpetuity of both tables of the law for New Covenant believers.[38] For instance, he says:

---

[29] Owen, *Works*, XXII:215.

[30] Owen, *Works*, XXII:215.

[31] Owen, *Works*, XXII:89, 90. "But in the new covenant, the very first thing that is proposed, is the accomplishment and establishment of the covenant of works, both as to its commands and sanction, in the obedience and suffering of the mediator."

[32] Some of the following material comes from Barcellos, *IDOTD*, 92, 93, and is used with permission from Founders Press.

[33] John Calvin, *Institutes of the Christian Religion* (Philadelphia: The Westminster Press, 1960), II.viii.1.

[34] I. John Hesselink, *Calvin's Concept of the Law* (Allison Park, PA: Pickwick Publications, 1992), 51.

[35] Calvin, *Institutes*, II.viii.1.

[36] Hesselink, *Calvin's Concept*, 10.

[37] Francois Wendel, *Calvin, Origins and Developments of His Religious Thought* (Grand Rapids: Baker Book House, re. 1997), 206.

[38] Calvin, *Institutes*, II.vii.13.

The whole law is contained under two heads. Yet our God, to remove all possibility of excuse, willed to set forth more fully and clearly by the Ten Commandments everything connected with the honor, fear, and love of him, and everything pertaining to the love toward men, which he for his own sake enjoins upon us.[39]

Calvin clearly held that the Decalogue, all Ten Commandments, functioned as the basic, fundamental law of the Bible and as a universal ethical canon for all men based on creation. He also believed in the basic centrality of the entire Decalogue under the New Covenant. Similar to Owen, Calvin holds to the multi-functional utility of the Decalogue.

**3. Zacharias Ursinus.** As stated above, in his *Commentary on the Heidelberg Catechism*, while discussing the question "To What Extent Has Christ Abrogated The Law, And To What Extent Is It Still In Force," Ursinus says, "The moral law has, as it respects one part, been abrogated by Christ; and as it respects another, it has not."[40] He continues, "But the moral law, or Decalogue, has not been abrogated in as far as obedience to it is concerned."[41] Ursinus, like Owen and Calvin, holds to a multi-functional utility of the Decalogue.

**4. Francis Turretin.** While discussing the use of the Moral Law, Turretin says:

A twofold use of the law may be laid down—absolute and relative. The former regards the law in itself; the latter regards the law in relation to the various states of man. The absolute (which obtains in every state of man) is that it may be a unique, full and certain rule of things to be done and avoided by each of us as well towards God as his neighbor. Thus there is no work truly and properly good and acceptable to God which does not agree with the law and is not prescribed by it; and whatsoever is not commanded nor forbidden by it is to be considered in its own nature indifferent and left to the freedom of man, unless this freedom has been restricted by some positive law.[42]

---

[39] Calvin, *Institutes*, II.viii.12.
[40] Ursinus, *Commentary*, 495.
[41] Ursinus, *Commentary*, 496.
[42] Turretin, *Institutes*, II:137.

In Turretin, the Moral Law or Decalogue is the inscripturated form of the Natural Law.[43] Notice that Turretin views the Moral Law absolutely and relatively. Viewing it absolutely, it is applicable "in every state of man." How does he view the Moral Law relatively? He continues:

> The relative use is manifold according to the different states of man. (1) In the instituted state of innocence, it was a contract of a covenant of works entered into with man and the means of obtaining life and happiness according to the promise added to the law...
>
> (2) In the destitute state of sin, the use of the law cannot be "justification" because it was weak in the flesh. ...Still there is a threefold use of the law [in man's destitute state of sin]. (a) For conviction... (b) For restraint... (c) For condemnation...
>
> (3) In the restored state of grace, it has a varied use with respect to the elect, both before and after their conversions. Antecedently, it serves (a) to convince and humble man... (b) To lead men to Christ...
>
> It not only antecedently prepares the elect man for Christ, but consequently also directs him already renewed through Christ in the ways of the Lord; serving him as a standard and rule of the most perfect life...[44]

Relatively, or considering the law in its relation 'to the different states of man,' the law has various functions as it pertains to the lost and the saved throughout all ages. In other words, there is a multi-functional utility to the law. Its utility transcends covenantal bounds. Due to the nature of the Decalogue, it cannot be eliminated from any era of redemptive history, which includes the New Covenant era. Turretin's view is that of Owen, Calvin, and Ursinus.

**5. Protestant Scholasticism.** Richard Muller defines Moral Law in Protestant scholastic thought as follows:

> [S]pecifically and predominantly, the *Decalogus*, or Ten Commandments; also called the *lex Mosaica* ..., as distinct from the *lex ceremonialis* ...and the *lex civilis*, or civil law. The *lex moralis*, which is primarily intended to regulate morals, is known to the *synderesis* [the innate habit of understanding basic principles of moral law] and is the basis of the acts of *conscientia* [conscience–the application of the innate habit above]. In substance, the *lex moralis* is identical with the *lex naturalis* ...but, unlike the natural law, it is given by revelation in a

---

[43] Turretin, *Institutes*, II:6, 7.
[44] Turretin, *Institutes*, II:138-140.

form which is clearer and fuller than that otherwise known to the reason.[45]

While defining the Mosaic Law, he says:

...the moral law or *lex moralis* (q.v.) given to Israel by God in a special revelation to Moses on Mount Sinai. In contrast to the moral law known in an obscure way to all rational creatures, the *lex Mosaica* is the clear, complete, and perfect rule of human conduct. The Protestant scholastics argue its completeness and perfection from its fulfillment, without addition, by Christ. Since the law does promise life in return for obedience, the Reformed argue that in one sense it holds forth the abrogated *foedus operum* (q.v.), or covenant of works, if only as the unattainable promise of the righteous God and the now humanly unattainable requirement for salvation apart from grace. In addition, the Reformed can argue that Christ's perfect obedience did fulfill the covenant of works and render Christ capable of replacing Adam as federal head of humanity. Primarily, however, the Reformed view the law as belonging to the Old Testament *dispensatio* (q.v.) of the *foedus gratiae* (q.v.), or covenant of grace. It is the norm of obedience given to God's faithful people to be followed by them with the help of grace. As a norm of obedience belonging to the *foedus gratiae*, the law remains in force under the economy of the New Testament. Lutheran orthodoxy, which does not follow the covenant schema typical of the Reformed, also views the law as the perfect standard of righteousness and the absolute norm of morals, which requires conformity both in outward conduct and inward obedience of mind, will, and affections.[46]

These definitions of key theological terms and concepts used by Protestant Scholasticism amply display that it held to the multi-functional utility of the Decalogue.

Owen's view of the multi-functional utility of the Decalogue comports with his view of abrogation (see below), Jeremiah 31:33, 2 Corinthians 3:3, and Matthew 5:17, and also with many of his theological contemporaries. There is a way to understand Owen on abrogation which both eliminates the Decalogue from the New Covenant and preserves it (see below). Relatively speaking, as the Decalogue functioned under the Old Covenant, it has been abrogated. Absolutely speaking, as the Decalogue represents and summarily comprehends the

---

[45] Muller, *Dictionary*, 173-74.
[46] Muller, *Dictionary*, 174.

Moral Law as to its substance, it has not and cannot be abrogated. It has more than one function.

- ### The Concept of Abrogation in Owen and Others

**1. John Owen.** Owen teaches that the whole law of Moses (even the moral element) has been abrogated. Commenting on Hebrews 7:18, 19, Owen says:

> I have proved before that "the commandment" in this verse [Heb. 7:18] is of equal extent and signification with "the law" in the next. And "the law" there doth evidently intend the whole law, in both the parts of it, moral and ceremonial, *as it was given by Moses unto the church of Israel* [emphasis added].[47]

Commenting on Hebrews 7:12, Owen says:

> It was the whole "law of commandments contained in ordinances," or the whole law of Moses, *so far as it was the rule of worship and obedience unto the church*; for that law it is that followeth the fates of the priesthood [emphasis added].[48]

> Wherefore the whole law of Moses, *as given unto the Jews*, whether as used or abused by them, was repugnant unto and inconsistent with the gospel, and the mediation of Christ, especially his priestly office, therein declared; neither did God either design, appoint, or direct that they should be co-existent [emphasis added].[49]

Owen, of course, carefully qualifies what he means by the whole law and its abrogation. Commenting again on Hebrews 7:18, 19, he says:

> Nor is it the whole *ceremonial law* only that is intended by "the command" in this place, but the *moral law* also [emphasis his], *so far as it was compacted with the other into one body of precepts for the same end* [emphasis added]; for with respect unto the efficacy of the whole law of Moses, as unto our drawing nigh unto God, it is here considered.[50]

Again, Owen says:

---

[47] Owen, *Works*, XXI:464.
[48] Owen, *Works*, XXI:428.
[49] Owen, *Works*, XXI:429.
[50] Owen, *Works*, XXI:458.

By all these ways was the church of the Hebrews forewarned that the time would come when the whole Mosaical law, *as to its legal or covenant efficacy*, should be disannulled, unto the unspeakable advantage of the church [emphasis added].[51]

This comes in a section in which Owen is showing how "the whole law may be considered ...absolutely in itself" or "with respect ...unto the end for which it was given" or "unto the persons unto whom it was given."[52] He calls the law "the whole system of Mosaical ordinances, as it was the covenant which God made with the people of Horeb. For the apostle takes 'the commandment,' and 'the law' for the same in this chapter; and 'the covenant,' in the next, for the same in them both."[53] Owen is concentrating on the whole Mosaic law, i.e., it is the law in its totality as it related to God's Old Covenant people that has been abrogated. Thus the abrogation of the law in Owen refers to the whole law as it functioned in Old Covenant Israel.[54]

**2. John Calvin.** This understanding of abrogation is found in Calvin also. Calvin taught that the abrogation of the law under the New Covenant in no way abrogates the Decalogue in every sense of the word. Commenting on Romans 7:2, Calvin says:

...but we must remember, that Paul refers here *only to that office of the law which was peculiar to Moses*; for as far as God has in the ten commandments taught what is just and right, and given directions for guiding our life, no abrogation of the law is to be dreamt of; for the will of God must stand the same forever. We ought carefully to remember that *this is not a release from the righteousness which is taught in the*

---

[51] Owen, *Works*, XXI:469.

[52] Owen, *Works*, XXI:466.

[53] Owen, *Works*, XXI:471.

[54] I defended this view of abrogation in my *IDOTD*. "Hearty agreement must be given when New Covenant theologians argue for the abolition of the Old Covenant. This is clearly the teaching of the Old and New Testaments (see Jeremiah 31:31-32; Second Corinthians 3; Galatians 3, 4; Ephesians 2:14-15; Hebrews 8-10). The whole law of Moses, *as it functioned under the Old Covenant*, has been abolished, including the Ten Commandments. Not one jot or tittle of the law of Moses functions *as Old Covenant law* anymore and to act as if it does constitutes redemptive-historical retreat and neo-Judaizing. However, to acknowledge that the law of Moses no longer functions *as Old Covenant law* is not to accept that it no longer functions; it simply no longer functions *as Old Covenant law*. This can be seen by the fact that the New Testament teaches *both* the abrogation of the law of the Old Covenant *and* its abiding moral validity under the New Covenant." See Barcellos, *IDOTD*, 61.

> *law, but from its rigid requirements, and from the curse which thence*
> *follows.* The law, then, as a rule of life, is not abrogated; but what
> belongs to it as opposed to the liberty obtained through Christ, that is,
> as it requires absolute perfection [emphasis added].[55]

It is important to note that "the term 'law' for Calvin may mean (1) the
whole religion of Moses...; (2) the special revelation of the moral law to
the chosen people, i.e., chiefly the Decalogue and Jesus' summary...; or
(3) various bodies of civil, judicial, and ceremonial statutes."[56] Calvin
says, "I understand by the word 'law' not only the Ten Commandments,
which set forth a godly and righteous rule of living, but the form of
religion handed down by God through Moses."[57] Calvin views the law in
various ways. So when he speaks of abrogation, he does not intend
absolute abrogation, but relative abrogation in terms of the law
considered not in itself, but in its redemptive-historically conditioned
use. Commenting on the concept of abrogation in Calvin, one Calvin
scholar said, "the Law was not in itself abrogated by the Christ, but only
the slavery and malediction attaching to it under the ancient Covenant."[58]
According to Calvin, therefore, the Moral Law has not been abrogated,
as such. What has been abrogated or fulfilled in Christ for believers is its
function as a curse. "The law itself is not abolished for the believer, but
only the *maledictio legis*... [F]or Calvin the law is related above all to
believers for whom, however, the *maledictio* is removed."[59]

**3. Zacharias Ursinus.** In his commentary on the Heidelberg Catechism,
while discussing the extent that Christ abrogated the law and the extent
that it is still in force, Zacharias Ursinus says:

> The ordinary and correct answer to this question is, that the ceremonial
> and judicial law, as given by Moses, has been abrogated in as far as it
> relates to obedience; and that the moral law has also been abrogated *as*
> *it respects the curse*, but not as it respects obedience [emphasis
> added].[60]

---

[55] John Calvin, *Calvin's Commentaries* (Grand Rapids: Baker Book House, re.
1984), IXX:246.

[56] Calvin, *Institutes*, II.vii, n. 1.

[57] Calvin, *Institutes*, II.vii.1.

[58] Hesselink, *Calvin's Concept*, 203.

[59] Hesselink, *Calvin's Concept*, 256.

[60] Ursinus, *Commentary*, 492.

The moral law has, *as it respects one part*, been abrogated by Christ; *and as it respects another*, it has not [emphasis added].[61]

But the moral law, or Decalogue, has not been abrogated *in as far as obedience to it is concerned.* God continually, no less now than formerly, requires both the regenerate and the unregenerate to render obedience to his law [emphasis added].[62]

**4. Francis Turretin.** A similar understanding of abrogation is found in Francis Turretin. In volume 2 of his *Institutes of Elenctic Theology,* Turretin entitles chapter XXIII as follows:

THE ABROGATION OF THE MORAL LAW
XXIII. Whether the moral law is abrogated entirely under the New Testament. Or whether in a certain respect it still pertains to Christians. The former we deny; the latter we affirm against the Antinomians.[63]

Notice Turretin's careful qualifications (i.e., "entirely" and "in a certain respect"). While discussing the abrogation of the moral law, he says, "In order to apprehend properly the state of the question, we must ascertain in what sense the law may be said to have been abrogated and in what sense not."[64] Then, after listing three senses in which the law has been abrogated, he says, "But the question only concerns its directive use—whether we are now freed from the direction and observance of the law. This the adversaries maintain; we deny."[65]

Turretin does what we have seen in others. He has a view of abrogation which both includes the Decalogue and does not include the Decalogue. This is because the law can be viewed from different theological and redemptive-historical vantage points.

**5. Protestant Scholasticism.** Finally, concerning the lex Mosaica [law of Moses], which, representing the view of Protestant Scholasticism, he defines as the moral law as given to Israel by God in a special revelation to Moses on Mount Sinai, Richard Muller says, "As a norm of obedience

---

[61] Ursinus, *Commentary*, 495.
[62] Ursinus, *Commentary*, 496.
[63] Turretin, *Institutes*, II:ix.
[64] Turretin, *Institutes*, II:141.
[65] Turretin, *Institutes*, II:141, 42.

belonging to the [covenant of grace], the law remains in force under the economy of the New Testament."[66] Muller recognizes the fact that Protestant Scholastics considered the law in different ways. Therefore, when we examine their statements about abrogation, we must take this into consideration. If we do not, we may take their statements on the abrogation of the law in an absolute manner and make them mean something they did not.

We have seen that Owen's view of abrogation was similar to Calvin's, Ursinus', Turretin's, and Protestant Scholasticism's. With them, he carefully and repeatedly qualifies what he means by abrogation. He stands clearly within Reformed orthodoxy at this point. His view of abrogation neither necessarily demands the elimination of the Decalogue as a unit in all senses under the New Covenant, nor is it contradicted by the inclusion of the Decalogue as a unit under the New Covenant. Though with his own nuances and emphases, Owen's view is substantially that of others in his day. It was Calvin's, Ursinus's, Turretin's, Protestant Scholasticism's, as well as that of the Westminster Confession of Faith, the Savoy Declaration, and the 2nd LCF.[67]

From the evidence presented, Owen must be understood to view abrogation as both including and not including the Decalogue, depending on how it is viewed. If this is the case, his understanding of abrogation, though with its own nuances and emphases, has clear and ample precedent in Calvin, Ursinus, Turretin, and Protestant Scholasticism.

## Conclusion

What can we conclude in light of the evidence presented?

- **Owen in the context of his own writings**

Primary source documentation of Owen has been presented on (1) the perpetuity of the entire Decalogue from Jeremiah 31:33 and 2 Corinthians 3:3, (2) Matthew 5:17 as it relates to the perpetuity of the Decalogue under the New Covenant, (3) the multi-functional utility of the Decalogue and (4) abrogation. Examining Owen on these subjects

---

[66] Muller, *Dictionary*, 174.
[67] See chapters 4 and 19 of these Confessions.

put us both into the primary documents themselves and within Owen's systematic thought on relevant theological issues. This was necessary in order to understand him on the primary issue under investigation.

Owen's view of abrogation must be carefully qualified, especially as it relates to the Decalogue and the New Covenant. On the one hand, he viewed the Decalogue as abrogated under the New Covenant. But he viewed it abrogated in terms of its function under the Old Covenant and along with the rest of the Old Covenant's law. His view of the abrogation of the Decalogue was not absolute, but relative. It concerned a specific redemptive-historical function of the Decalogue and not all redemptive-historical functions.

On the other hand, Owen did not view the Decalogue as abrogated under the New Covenant. He viewed it as perpetual because it contains "the sum and substance of that obedience which is due unto God from all rational creatures made in his image."[68]

These distinctions in his views on abrogation and the various redemptive-historical functions of the Decalogue are in his early and later statements in the Hebrews commentary. It may be difficult for us to understand them, taking them at face value, but once his careful qualifications are taken into account, along with his clear assertions concerning the perpetuity of the Decalogue under the New Covenant and the grounds for it, his meaning comes clearly into focus. But if we import into Owen our understanding of what certain statements mean or fail to understand his systematic thought, we are apt to misread him and either force on him something he never intended or force him to contradict himself.

- **The historical/theological context in which Owen wrote**

Primary source documentation has been presented from Calvin, Ursinus, Witsius, Turretin, Protestant Scholastic thought, and Boston. In doing so, the attempt was made to put Owen in historical and theological context. We found that his views on the matters examined were not novel and fit within the theological nomenclature of his contemporaries. Though what he said may be hard to understand and even appear novel to us, it was not so in his day.

---

[68] Owen, *Works*, XXII:215.

# BIBLIOGRAPHY

## General Discussion of the History of Biblical Theology

### 1. Books

Alexander, T. Desmond and Rosner, Brian S., editors. *New Dictionary of Biblical Theology*. Downers Grove, IL: InterVarsity, 2000, Reprinted 2003, 2006.

Austen, Simon *A Better Way: Jesus and Old Testament Fulfillment*. Fearn, Tain, Ross-shire, Great Britain: Christian Focus Publications, Ltd., 2003.

Calvin, John. *Institutes of the Christian Religion,* edited by McNeill, John T. and translated by Battles, Ford Lewis. *Library of Christian Classics*, volumes 20-21. Philadelphia: The Westminster Press, 1960.

Elwell, Walter A., ed. *Evangelical Dictionary of Biblical Theology*. Grand Rapids: Baker, 1996.

Goldsworthy, Graeme. *According to Plan: The Unfolding Revelation of God in the Bible–An Introductory Biblical Theology*. Downers Grove, IL: InterVarsity Press, 1991.

Hafemann, Scott J., ed. *Biblical Theology: Retrospect & Prospect*. Downers Grove, IL: InterVarsity Press, 2002.

Hasel, Gerhard F. *New Testament Theology: Basic Issues in the Current Debate*. Grand Rapids: William B. Eerdmans Publishing Company, 1978, reprinted 1993.

_____. *Old Testament Theology: Basic Issues in the Current Debate*. Grand Rapids: William B. Eerdmans Publishing Company, 1991, revised, updated, and enlarged fourth edition.

Ladd, George Eldon. *A Theology of the New Testament*, edited by Hagner, Donald A. Grand Rapids: William B. Eerdmans Publishing Company, 1974, Revised edition, 1993.

McKim, Donald K., editor. *Encyclopedia of the Reformed Faith*. Louisville and Edinburgh: Westminster/John Knox, 1992.

Oehler, Gustave Friedrich. *Theology of the Old Testament*, editor George E. Day. Grand Rapids: Zondervan Publishing House, n.d.

Strom, Mark. *The Symphony of Scripture: Making Sense of the Bible's Many Themes*. Phillipsburg, NJ: P&R Publishing, 2001.

Taylor, Marion Ann. *The Old Testament in the Old Princeton School (1812-1929)*. San Francisco: Mellen Research University Press, 1992.

Tenney, Merrill C. *Zondervan Pictorial Encyclopedia of the Bible, Volume One*. Grand Rapids: Zondervan Publishing House, 1975, 1976.

VanGemeren, Willem A. *The Progress of Redemption: The Story of Salvation from Creation to the New Jerusalem*. Grand Rapids: Zondervan Publishing House, 1988.

Ward, Rowland S. *God & Adam: Reformed Theology and the Creation Covenant*. Wantirna, Australia, New Melbourne Press, 2003.

## 2. Articles

Carson, D.A. "Current Issues in Biblical Theology: A New Testament Perspective," Bulletin for Biblical Research 5 (1995): 17-41.

Dennison, William D. "Reason, History and Revelation: Biblical Theology and the Enlightenment," *Kerux*, 18. 1 (May 2003): 3-25.

Gaffin, Richard B. "Systematic Theology and Biblical Theology," *Westminster Theological Journal*, 38 (1976): 281-99.

Gilbert, George H. "Biblical Theology: Its History and Its Mission," *The Biblical World* 6 (July-December 1895): 358-66.

Hasel, Gerhard F. "Biblical Theology Movement" in Walter A. Elwell, editor, *Evangelical Dictionary of Theology* (Grand Rapids: Baker Book House, 1984, Fourth Printing, July 1886), 149-52.

Klempa, William. "Cocceius, Johannes (1603-1669)" in Donald K. McKim, editor, *Encyclopedia of the Reformed Faith* (Louisville and Edinburgh: Westminster/John Knox Press, 1992), 73.

Payne, J. Barton. "Biblical Theology, OT, The Discipline of" in Merrill C. Tenney, editor, *Zondervan Pictorial Encyclopedia of the Bible, Volume One* (Grand Rapids: Zondervan Publishing House, 1975, 1976), 605-10.

Sandys-Wunsch, John and Eldridge, Laurence. "J.P. Gabler and the Distinction between Biblical and Dogmatic Theology: Translation Commentary, and Discussion of His Originality," *Scottish Journal of Theology* 33 (1980): 133-44.

Scobie, Charles H. H. "New Directions in Biblical Theology," *Themelios* 17.2 (January/February 1992): 4-7.

Taylor, William H. "Biblical Theology" in Merrill C. Tenney, editor, *Zondervan Pictorial Encyclopedia of the Bible, Volume One* (Grand Rapids: Zondervan Publishing House, 1975, 1976), 593-94.

Verhoef, Pieter A. "Some Thoughts on the Present-day situation in Biblical Theology," *Westminster Theological Journal*, 33 (1970): 1-19.

Wallace, Peter J. "The Foundations of Reformed Biblical Theology: The Development of Old Testament Theology at Old Princeton, 1812-1932," *Westminster Theological Journal* 59:1 (1997): 41-69.

### Geerhardus Vos: Life, Ministry, and Impact

#### 1. Books

Dennison, James T., Jr., editor. *The Letters of Geerhardus Vos*. Phillipsburg, NJ: P&R Publishing, 2005.
Olinger, Danny E. *A Geerhardus Vos Anthology: Biblical and Theological Insights Alphabetically Arranged*. Phillipsburg, NJ: P&R Publishing, 2005.
Taylor, Marion Ann. *The Old Testament in the Old Princeton School (1812-1929)*. San Francisco: Mellen Research University Press, 1992.
Vos, Geerhardus. *Grace and Glory*. Edinburgh: The Banner of Truth Trust, 1994.

#### 2. Articles

Dennison, James T., Jr. "What is Biblical Theology? Reflections on the Inaugural Address of Geerhardus Vos" in *Kerux*, 2.1 (May 1987): 33-41.
Jansen, J. "The Biblical Theology of Geerhardus Vos," *The Princeton Seminary Bulletin* 66:2 (1974): 23-34.
Olinger, Danny. "Vos's Verticalist Eschatology: A Response to Michael Williams" in *Kerux*, 7.2 (Sept. 1992): 30-38.

### Geerhardus Vos: Historical-Theological Context

#### 1. Primary Sources

Vos, Geerhardus. *Biblical Theology: Old and New Testaments*. Grand Rapids: Wm. B. Eerdmans Publishing Company, 1948, Reprinted June 1988.
_____. *Redemptive History and Biblical Interpretation: The Shorter Writings of Geerhardus Vos*, edited by Richard B. Gaffin, Jr. Phillipsburg, NJ: P&R Publishing, 1980.

_____. *The Pauline Eschatology*. Phillipsburg, NJ: Presbyterian and Reformed Publishing Company, 1930, reprinted 1991.

_____. *The Teaching of Jesus Concerning the Kingdom of God and the Church*. Eugene, OR: Wipf and Stock Publishers, 1903, reprinted 1998.

_____. *The Teaching of the Epistle to the Hebrews*. Eugene, OR: Wipf and Stock Publishers, 1956, reprinted 2001.

**2. Books**

Bernard, Thomas Dehany. *The Progress of Doctrine in the New Testament*. New York: American Tract Society, n.d.

Oehler, Gustave Friedrich. *Theology of the Old Testament*. Grand Rapids: Zondervan Publishing House, n.d.

Reymond, Robert L. *A New Systematic Theology of the Christian Faith*. Nashville, TN: Thomas Nelson Publishers, 1998.

**3. Articles**

Barcellos, Richard C. "*The Progress of Doctrine in the New Testament*, by T. D. Bernard – A Review Article (Part I)," *RBTR* IV:1 (January 2007): 7-26.

_____. "*The Progress of Doctrine in the New Testament*, by T. D. Bernard – A Review Article (Part II)," *RBTR* IV:2 (July 2007): 33-60.

Baugh, Steven M. "Hermeneutics & Biblical Theology," *Modern Reformation Magazine* 2.2 (November/December1993).

Dennison, James T. "What is Biblical Theology? Reflections on the Inaugural Address of Geerhardus Vos," *Kerux* 2.1 (May 1987): 33-41.

_____. "Vos on the Sabbath: A Close Reading," *Kerux* 16.1 (May 2001): 61-70.

Dennison, William D. "Reason, History and Revelation: Biblical Theology and the Enlightenment," *Kerux*, 18. 1 (May 2003): 3-25.

Gaffin, Richard B., Jr. "Biblical Theology and The Westminster Standards," *Westminster Theological Journal* 65 (2003): 165-79.

_____. "Geerhardus Vos and the Interpretation of Paul" in E. R. Geehan, editor, *Jerusalem and Athens: Critical Discussion on the Philosophy and Apologetics of Cornelius Van Til* (Phillipsburg, NJ: Presbyterian and Reformed Publishing Co., 1971), 228-43.

_____. "Systematic Theology and Biblical Theology," *Westminster Theological Journal*, 38 (1976): 281-99.

_____. "Vos, Geerhardus (*1862-1949*)" in Donald K. McKim, editor, *Dictionary of Major Biblical Interpreters* (Downer Grove, IL: InterVarsity Press, 2007), 1016-19.

Jansen, J. "The Biblical Theology of Geerhardus Vos," *The Princeton Seminary Bulletin* 66:2 (1974): 23-34.

McKim, Donald K. "Alexander, Archibald (1772-1851)" in Donald K. McKim, editor, *Encyclopedia of the Reformed Faith* (Louisville and Edinburgh: Westminster/John Knox Press, 1992), 5.

Olinger, Danny. "Vos's Verticalist Eschatology: A Response to Michael Williams," *Kerux* 7.2 (Sept 1992): 30-38.

Semel, Lawrence. "Geerhardus Vos and Eschatology," *Kerux* 10.1 (Sept 1995): 25-40.

Wallace, Peter J. "The Foundations of Reformed Biblical Theology: The Development of Old Testament Theology at Old Princeton, 1812-1932," *Westminster Theological Journal* 59:1 (1997): 41-69.

## 4. Dissertation

Taylor, Marion Ann. *The Old Testament in the Old Princeton School (1812-1929)*. San Francisco: Mellen Research University Press, 1992.

## 5. Internet Links

Dennison, James T., Jr. "Geerhardus Vos: Life Between Two Worlds." Accessed 26 May 2006. Available from http://www.kerux.com/documents/keruxv14n2a3.htm.

Harms, Richard H. "Flashback: Geerhardus Vos, Calvin's first Ph.D. Alum returned to teach in English at alma mater." Accessed 26 May 2006. Available from http://www.calvin.edu/publications/spark/2003/fall/flashback.htm.

## John Owen: Life, Ministry, and Legacy

## 1. Books

Barker, William. *Puritan Profiles: 54 Contemporaries of the Westminster Assembly*. Fearn, Ross-shire, Scotland: Christian Focus Publications, 1996.

Ferguson, Sinclair B. *John Owen on the Christian Life*. Edinburgh: The
    Banner of Truth Trust, 1987.
Kapic, Kelly M. *Communion with God: The Divine and the Human in
    the Theology of John Owen*. Grand Rapids: Baker Academic, 2007.
Oliver, Robert W. "John Owen – his life and times" in Robert W. Oliver,
    editor, *John Owen: The Man and his Theology* (Darlington, England:
    Evangelical Press, 2002), 11-39.
Orme, William. *The Life of John Owen*. Choteau, MT: Gospel Mission
    Press, re. 1981, first published in 1826.
Packer, J. I. *A Quest for Godliness: The Puritan Vision of the Christian
    Life*. Wheaton, IL: Crossway Books, 1990.
Rehnman Sebastian. *Divine Discourse: The Theological Methodology of
    John Owen*. Grand Rapids: Baker Academic, 2002.
Thomson, Andrew. *John Owen: Prince of Puritans*. Ross-shire, Great
    Britain: Christian Focus Publications, 1996, re. 2004.
Trueman, Carl R. *John Owen: Reformed Catholic, Renaissance Man*.
    Aldershot, Hampshire, UK: Ashgate Publishing, 2007.
Toon, Peter. *God's Statesman: The Life and Work of John Owen–Pastor,
    Educator, Theologian*. Grand Rapids: Zondervan Publishing House,
    First Zondervan printing 1973, 1971, The Paternoster Press.

## 2. Articles

Howson, Barry H. "The Puritan Hermeneutics of John Owen: A
    Recommendation" in *Westminster Theological Journal*  63 (2001):
    351-54.
Kapic, Kelly M. "Owen, John (*1616-1683*)" in Donald K. McKim,
    editor, *Dictionary of Major Biblical Interpreters* (Downers Grove,
    IL: IVP Academic, 2007), 795-99.
Toon, Peter. "Owen, John (1616-1683)," in Donald K. McKim, editor,
    *Encyclopedia of the Reformed Faith* (Louisville and Edinburgh:
    Westminster/John Knox Press, 1992), 269-70.

### John Owen: Historical-Theological Context

### 1. Primary Sources

*A Confession of Faith Put Forth by the Elders and Brethren of many
    Congregations of Christians (baptized upon Profession of their
    Faith) in London and the Country, Printed in the Year, 1677*.
    Auburn, MA: B&R Press, Facsimile edition, 2000.

Ames, Williams. *The Marrow of Theology*. Durham, NC: The Labyrinth Press, 1983.

Bolton, Samuel. *The True Bounds of Christian Freedom*. Edinburgh: The Banner of Truth Trust, Reprint edition, 1978.

Calvin, John. *Institutes of the Christian Religion*. Ed. John T. McNeill and trans. Ford Lewis Battles, *Library of Christian Classics*, vols. 20-21. Philadelphia: The Westminster Press, 1960.

Coxe, Nehemiah and Owen, John, edited by Miller, Ronald D., Renihan, James M., and Orozco, Francisco. *Covenant Theology From Adam to Christ*. Palmdale, CA: Reformed Baptist Academic Press, 2005.

Dickson, David. *Truth's Victory Over Error*. Edmonton, AB, Canada: Still Water Revival Books, re. nd.

Edwards, Jonathan. "A History of the Work of Redemption, containing the outlines of a Body of Divinity, including a view of Church History, in a method entirely new" in *The Works of Jonathan Edwards, Volume One*. Edinburgh: The Banner of Truth Trust, reprinted 1990.

Fisher, Edward. *The Marrow of Modern Divinity: In Two Parts – Part I. the Covenant of Works and the Covenant of Grace; Part II. An Exposition of the Ten Commandments*. Edmonton, AB, Canada: Still Water Revival Books, Reprint edition, 1991.

Owen, John. *Biblical Theology*. Transl. Stephen Wescott. Soli Deo Gloria, 1997.

_____. *The Works of John Owen*, 23 vols., ed. William H. Goold. Edinburgh: The Banner of Truth Trust, 1987 edition.

Turretin, Francis. *Institutes of Elenctic Theology, Volume Two*. Phillipsburg, NJ: P&R Publishing, 1994.

Ursinus, Zacharias. *The Commentary of Dr. Zacharias Usinus on the Heidelberg Catechism*. Edmonton, AB, Canada: Still Water Revival Books, re. n.d.

Watson, Thomas. *A Body of Divinity*. Carlisle, PA: The Banner of Truth Trust, re. 1986.

*Westminster Confession of Faith*. Glasgow: Free Presbyterian Publications.

Witsius, Herman. *The Economy of the Covenants Between God and Man: Comprehending A Complete Body of Divinity, Two Volumes*. Escondido, CA: The den Dulk Christian Foundation, re. 1990.

## 2. Books

Bierma, Lyle D. *German Calvinism in the Confessional Age: The Covenant Theology of Caspar Olevianus*. Grand Rapids: Baker Books, 1996.

Clark, Gordon H. *What Do Presbyterians Believe?* Philipsburg, NJ: Presbyterian and Reformed Publishing Company, 1956.

Crampton, W. Gary, *What Calvin Says*, Jefferson, Maryland: The Trinity Foundation, 1992.

Daniels, Richard. *The Christology of John Owen*. Grand Rapids: Reformed Heritage Books, 2004.

De Greff, Wulfert, *The Writings of John Calvin*, Grand Rapids: Baker Book House, 1993.

Evans, G. R., McGrath, A.E., Galloway, A.D., editors. *The History of Christian Theology 1: The Science of Theology*. Grand Rapids: Eerdmans, 1986.

Ferguson, Sinclair B. *John Owen on the Christian Life*. Edinburgh: Banner of Truth, 1987.

Girardeau, John L. *The Federal Theology: Its Import and Its Regulative Influence*. Greenville, SC: Reformed Academic Press, 1994.

Golding, Peter. *Covenant Theology: The Key of Theology in Reformed Thought and Tradition*. Ross-shire, Scotland: Mentor, 2004.

Haykin, Michael A. G. *Kiffin, Knollys and Keach*. Leeds, England: Reformation Today Trust, 1996.

Helm, Paul. *Calvin and the Calvinists*. Edinburgh: Banner of Truth, 1982.

Heppe, Heinrich. *Reformed Dogmatics*. London: The Wakeman Trust, n.d.

Hodge, A.A. *Confession of Faith*. Edinburgh: The Banner of Truth Trust, re. 1983.

Kapic, Kelly M. *Communion with God: Relations Between the Divine and the Human in the Theology of John Owen*. Grand Rapids: Baker Academic, 2007.

Karlberg, Mark W. *Covenant Theology in Reformed Perspective: Collected Essays and Book Reviews in Historical, Biblical, and Systematic Theology*. Eugene, OR: Wipf and Stock Publishers, 2000.

Ladd, George Eldon. *A Theology of the New Testament*. Grand Rapids: William B. Eerdmans Publishing Company, 1993.

Lewis, Peter. *The Genius of Puritanism*. Haywards Heath Sussex, England: Carey Publications, 1977, Second edition 1979.

Lillback, Peter A. *The Binding of God: Calvin's Roll in the Development of Covenant Theology*. Grand Rapids: Baker Academic, 2001.

McCoy, Charles S. and Baker, J. Wayne. *Fountainhead of Federalism: Heinrich Bullinger and the Covenantal Tradition*. Louisville: Westminster/John Know Press, 1991.

McGowan, A. T. B. *The Federal Theology of Thomas Boston*. Edinburgh: Rutherford House, 1997.

McGrath, Alister E. *A Life of John Calvin*. Grand Rapids: Baker Book House, 1990.

_____. *Reformation Thought: An Introduction*. Grand Rapids: Baker, Second edition, 1993.

_____. *The Intellectual Origins of the European Reformation*, Grand Rapids: Baker Book House, 1993 paperback reprint.

McNeill, John T., *The History and Character of Calvinism*, London, Oxford, New York: Oxford University Press, 1954, 1967 paperback.

Merle d' Aubigne, J.H., *History of the Reformation of the Sixteenth Century*, Grand Rapids: Baker Book House, reprinted from the edition issued in London in 1846.

Muller, Richard A. *Christ and the Decree: Christology and Predestination in Reformed Theology from Calvin to Perkins*. Grand Rapids: Baker Book House, 1986, Second printing, November 1988.

_____. *Dictionary of Latin and Greek Theological Terms*. Grand Rapids: Baker Book House, 1985.

_____. *Post-Reformation Reformed Dogmatics*, 4 volumes. Grand Rapids: Baker Academic, 2003.

Murray, John. *The Covenant of Grace*. Phillipsburg, NJ: Presbyterian and Reformed Publishing Company, Reprinted 1988.

Niesel, Wilhelm, *The Theology of John Calvin*, London: Lutterworth Press, 1956.

Oliver, Robert W., ed. *John Owen: The Man and His Theology*. Phillipsburg, N.J.: P&R / Darlington: Evangelical Press, 2002.

Packer, J. I. *A Quest for Godliness: The Puritan Vision of the Christian Life*. Wheaton, IL: Crossway Books, 1990.

Pelikan, Jaroslav, *Reformation of Church and Dogma*, Chicago and London: University of Chicago Press, 1985.

Ramsey, D. Patrick and Beeke, Joel R. "Introduction: The Life and Theology of Herman Witsius (1636-1706)" in *An Analysis of Herman Witsius's The Economy of the Covenants*. Grand Rapids: Reformation Heritage Books and Fearn, Ross-shire, Scotland: Christian Focus Publications, 2002.

Rehnman, Sebastian. *Divine Discourse: The Theological Methodology of John Owen*. Grand Rapids: Baker Academic, 2002.

Renihan, James M. *True Confessions: Baptist Documents in the Reformed Family*. Owensboro, KY: Reformed Baptist Academic Press, 2004.

Ryken, Leland. *Worldly Saints: The Puritans as they Really Were*. Grand Rapids: Zondervan Publishing House, 1986.

Schaff, Philip. *The Creeds of Christendom, Volume III: The Evangelical Protestant Creeds*. Grand Rapids: Baker Books, Reprinted 1996.

Shaw, Robert. *An Exposition of the Westminster Confession of Faith*. Fearn Ross-shire, Scotland: Christian Focus Publications, re. 1998.

Shedd, William G. T. *History of Christian Doctrine*, I. Minneapolis: Klock & Klock, 1889, re. 1978.

Steinmetz, David C., *Calvin in Context*, New York: Oxford University Press, 1995.

_____. *Luther in Context*, Grand Rapids: Baker Book House, 1995.

Trueman, Carl R. *John Owen: Reformed Catholic, Renaissance Man*. Aldershot, Hampshire, England: Ashgate Publishing Company, 2008.

_____. *The Claims of Truth: John Owen's Trinitarian Theology*. Carlisle: Paternoster, 1998.

Trueman Carl R. and Clark, R. Scott, editors. *Protestant Scholasticism: Essays in Reassessment*. Carlisle, Cumbria, UK: Paternoster Press, 1999.

van Asselt, Willem J. *The Federal Theology of Johannes Cocceius (1603-1669)*. Leiden, The Netherlands: Brill, 2001.

van Asselt, Willem J. and Dekker, Eef, editors. *Reformation and Scholasticism: An Ecumenical Enterprise*. Grand Rapids: Baker Academic, 2001.

von Rohr, John. *The Covenant of Grace in Puritan Thought*. Atlanta: Scholars Press, 1986.

Waldron, Samuel E. *A Modern Exposition of the 1689 Baptist Confession of Faith*. Darlington, Co. Durham, England: Evangelical Press, Second edition, 1995.

Warfield, Benjamin B. *The Westminster Assembly and Its Work*. Grand Rapids, MI: Baker Book House Company, re. 1991.

Ward, Rowland S. *God & Adam: Reformed Theology and The Creation Covenant – An Introduction to the Biblical Covenants – A Close Examination of the Covenant of Works*. Wantirna, Australia: New Melbourne Press, 2003.

## 3. Articles

Barcellos, Richard. "Appendix One: Outline of Coxe" in Nehemiah Coxe and John Owen, edited by Ronald D. Miller, James M. Renihan, and Francisco Orozco, *Covenant Theology From Adam to Christ* (Palmdale, CA: Reformed Baptist Academic Press, 2005), 313-15.

_____. "John Owen and New Covenant Theology: Owen on the Old and New Covenants and the Functions of the Decalogue in Redemptive History in Historical and Contemporary Perspective," *Reformed Baptist Theological Review* I:2 (July 2004): 12-46.

Bierma, Lyle D. "Federal Theology in the Sixteenth Century: Two Traditions?," *Westminster Theological Journal* (1983): 304-21.

_____. "The Role of Covenant Theology in Early Reformed Orthodoxy," *Sixteenth Century Journal* (1990): 453-62.

Howson, Barry H. "The Puritan Hermeneutics of John Owen: A Recommendation," *Westminster Theological Journal* 63 (2001): 351-76.

Kapic, Kelly M. "Owen, John (*1616-1683*)" in Donald K. McKim, editor, *Dictionary of Major Biblical Interpreters* (Downer Grove, IL: InterVarsity Press, 2007), 797-98.

Klauber, Martin I. "Continuity and Discontinuity in Post-Reformation Reformed Theology: An Evaluation of the Muller Thesis," *Journal of the Evangelical Theological Society* 33-34 (1990): 467-75.

_____. "Hermeneutics and the Doctrine of Scripture in Post-Reformation Reformed Thought," *Premise* Volume II, Number 9 (1995): 8ff.

Klempa, William. "Cocceius, Johannes (1603-1669)" in Donald K. McKim, editor, *Encyclopedia of the Reformed Faith* (Louisville and Edinburgh: Westminster/John Knox Press 1992), 73-74.

Lea, Thomas D. "The Hermeneutics of the Puritans," *Journal of the Evangelical Theological Society*, 39 (1996): 271-84.

Letham, Robert. "The Foedus Operum: Some Factors Accounting for Its Development," *Sixteenth Century Journal* 16 (1983): 457-68.

McCoy, Charles S. "Johannes Coccieus: Federal Theologian," *Scottish Journal of Theology*, XVI (1963): 352-70.

McKim, Donald. "Ames, William (1576-1633)" in Donald K. McKim, editor, *Encyclopedia of the Reformed Faith* (Louisville and Edinburgh: Westminster/John Knox Press, 1992), 6.

_____. "Ramus, Peter (1515-1572)" in Donald K. McKim, editor, *Encyclopedia of the Reformed Faith* (Louisville and Edinburgh: Westminster/John Knox Press, 1992), 314

_____. "Perkins, Williams (1558-1602)" in Donald K. McKim, editor, *Dictionary of Major Biblical Interpreters* (Downers Grove, IL: InterVarsity Press, 2007), 815.

_____. "Perkins, William (1558-1602)" in Donald K. McKim, editor, *Encyclopedia of the Reformed Faith* (Louisville and Edinburgh: Westminster/John Knox Press, 1992), 274-75.

Muller, Richard A. "Calvin and the Calvinists: Assessing Continuities and Discontinuities between Reformation and Orthodoxy: parts 1 and 2," *Calvin Theological Journal* 30 (1995): 345-75; 31 (1996): 125-60.

_____. "Orthodoxy, Reformed" in Donald K. McKim, editor, *Encyclopedia of the Reformed Faith* (Louisville and Edinburgh: Westminster/John Knox Press, 1992), 265-69.

_____. "Sources of Reformed Orthodoxy: The Symmetrical Unity of Exegesis and Synthesis" in Michael S. Horton, editor, *A Confessing Theology for Postmodern Times* (Wheaton, IL: Crossway Books, 2000), 43-62.

_____. "The Covenant of Works and the Stability of Divine Law in Seventeenth Century Reformed Orthodoxy: A Study in the Theology of Herman Witsius and Wilhemus A` Brakel," *Calvin Theological Journal* 29 (1994): 75-101.

_____. "The Myth of Decretal Theology," *Calvin Theological Journal* 30 (1995): 159-67.

_____. "The Use and Abuse of a Document: Beza's *Tabula praedestinationis*, the Bolsec Controversy, and the Origins of Reformed Scholasticism" in Carl R. Trueman and R. Scott Clark, editors, *Protestant Scholasticism: Essays in Reassessment* (Carlisle, Cumbria, UK: Paternoster Press, 1999), 33-61.

Murray, John. "Covenant Theology" in *Collected Writings of John Murray, Volume Four* (Edinburgh: The Banner of Truth Trust, 1982), 216-40.

_____. "The Adamic Administration" in *Collected Writings of John Murray, Volume Two* (Edinburgh: The Banner of Truth Trust, 1977), 47-59.

Osterhaven, M. Eugene. "Covenant" in Donald K. McKim, editor, *Encyclopedia of the Reformed Faith* (Louisville and Edinburgh: Westminster/John Knox Press, 1992), 84-87.

Renihan, James M. "An Excellent and Judicious Divine: Nehemiah Coxe" in Nehemiah Coxe and John Owen, edited by Ronald D. Miller, James M. Renihan, and Francisco Orozco, *Covenant*

*Theology From Adam to Christ* (Palmdale, CA: Reformed Baptist Academic Press, 2005), 7-24.

_____. "Confessing the Faith in 1644 and 1689," *Reformed Baptist Theological Review* III:1 (July 2006): 33-47.

_____. "Theology on Target: The Scope of the Whole," *Reformed Baptist Theological Review* II:2 (July 2005): 36-53.

Trueman, Carl R. "John Owen's *Dissertation on Divine Justice*: An Exercise in Christocentric Scholasticism," *Calvin Theological Journal* 33 (1998): 87-103.

Steinmetz, David C. "The Superiority of Pre-Critical Exegesis," *Theology Today* (April 1980): 27-38.

Sweeney, D. A. "Edwards, Jonathan *(1703-1758)*" in Donald K. McKim, editor, *Dictionary of Major Biblical Interpreters* (Downers Grove, IL: InterVarsity Press, 2007), 397.

van Asselt, Willem J. "Cocceius, Johannes" in Donald K. McKim, editor, *Dictionary of Major Biblical Interpreters* (Downers Grove, IL: InterVarsity Press, 2007), 316-7.

_____. "Structural Elements in the Eschatology of Johannes Cocceius," *Calvin Theological Journal* 35 (2000): 76-104.

_____. "The Doctrine of the Abrogations in the Federal Theology of Johannes Coccejus (1603-1669)," *Calvin Theological Journal* 29 (1994): 101-16.

_____. "The Fundamental Meaning of Theology: Archetypal and Ectypal Theology in Seventeenth-Century Reformed Thought," *Westminster Theological Journal* 64 (2002): 319-35.

van Vliet, Jan. "Decretal Theology and the Development of Covenant Thought: An Assessment of Cornelis Graafland's Thesis with a Particular View to Federal Architects William Ames and Johannes Cocceius," *Westminster Theological Journal* 63 (2001): 393-420.

Vos, Arvin. "Scholasticism" in Donald K. McKim, editor, *Encyclopedia of the Reformed Faith* (Louisville and Edinburgh: Westminster/John Knox Press, 1992), 342.

Vos, Geerhardus. "The Doctrine of the Covenant in Reformed Theology" in *Redemptive History and Biblical Interpretation* (Phillipsburg, NJ: P&R Publishing, 1980), 234-67.

Wallace, Dewey D., Jr. "Federal Theology" in Donald K. McKim, editor, *Encyclopedia of the Reformed Faith* (Louisville and Edinburgh: Westminster/John Knox Press, 1992), 136-37.

## John Owen

### 1. Primary Sources

Owen, John. *Biblical Theology*. Transl. Stephen Wescott. Soli Deo Gloria, 1994.

_____. *The Works of John Owen*, 23 vols., ed. William H. Goold. Edinburgh: The Banner of Truth Trust, 1987 edition.

### 2. Books

Daniels, Richard. *The Christology of John Owen*. Grand Rapids, MI.: Reformed Heritage Books, 2004.

Ferguson, Sinclair B. *John Owen on the Christian Life*. Edinburgh: Banner of Truth, 1987.

Kapic, Kelly M. *Communion with God: Relations Between the Divine and the Human in the Theology of John Owen*. Grand Rapids.: Baker Academic, 2007.

Oliver, Robert W., ed. *John Owen: The Man and His Theology*. Phillipsburg, N.J.: P&R / Darlington: Evangelical Press, 2002.

Rehnman, Sebastian. *Divine Discourse: The Theological Methodology of John Owen*. Grand Rapids: Baker Academic, 2002.

Toon, Peter. *God's Statesman: The Life and Work of John Owen–Pastor, Educator, Theologian*. Grand Rapids: Zondervan Publishing House, First Zondervan printing 1973, 1971, The Paternoster Press.

Trueman, Carl R. *John Owen: Reformed Catholic, Renaissance Man*. Aldershot, Hampshire, England: Ashgate Publishing Company, 2008.

Trueman, Carl R. *The Claims of Truth: John Owen's Trinitarian Theology*. Carlisle: Paternoster, 1998.

### 3. Articles

Barcellos, Richard. "John Owen and New Covenant Theology." *Reformed Baptist Theological Review* I:2 (July 2004): 12-46.

Howson, Barry H. "The Puritan Hermeneutics of John Owen: A Recommendation." *Westminster Theological Journal* 63 (2001): 351-76.

Rehnman, Sebastian. "John Owen: A Reformed Scholastic at Oxford" in *Reformation and Scholasticism*. ed. Willem van Asselt and Eef Dekker, 181-203. Grand Rapids: Baker Academic, 2001.

Toon, Peter. "Owen, John (1616-1683)," in Donald K. McKim (ed.) *Encyclopedia of the Reformed Faith* (Louisville and Edinburgh, 1992), 269-70.

Trueman, Carl R. "John Owen's Dissertation on Divine Justice: An Exercise in Christocentric Scholasticism," *Calvin Theological Journal* 33 (1998), 87-103.

## 4. Reviews

Boersma, Hans. "Review of *The Claims of Truth: John Owen's Trinitarian Theology*, by Carl R. Trueman." *Evangelical Quarterly* 73 (2001): 267-69.

Holmes, Stephen. "Review of *Divine Discourse: The Theological Methodology of John Owen* by Sebastian Rehnman." *Journal of Theological Studies* 56 (2005): 836-37.

Kapic, Kelly M. "Review of *Divine Discourse: The Theological Methodology of John Owen*, by Sebastian Rehnman." *Westminster Theological Journal* 65 (Spring 2003): 154-57.

Klauber, Martin I. "Review of *Divine Discourse: The Theological Methodology of John Owen*, by Sebastian Rehnman." Journal *of the Evangelical Theological Society* (June 2004): 364-66.

Knapp, Henry M. "Review of *Divine Discourse*, by Sebastian Rehnman." *Calvin Theological Journal* 38 (2003): 186-88.

Knapp, Henry M. "Review of *John Owen: The Man and His Theology*, edited by Robert W. Oliver." *Calvin Theological Journal* 39 (2004): 444-46.

Muller, Richard A. "Review of *Claims of Truth: John Owen's Trinitarian Theology*, by Carl Trueman." *Calvin Theological Seminary* 32 (Nov. 1998): 522-24.

# SCRIPTURE INDEX

# NAME AND SUBJECT INDEX

CPSIA information can be obtained at www.ICGtesting.com
Printed in the USA
LVOW01s1432100715

445774LV00002B/299/P